LOSING THE CENTER

LOSING THE CENTER

The Decline of American Liberalism, 1968–1992

JEFFREY BLOODWORTH

UNIVERSITY PRESS OF KENTUCKY

Scholarly publisher for the Commonwealth, serving Bellarmine University, Berea College, Centre College of Kentucky, Eastern Kentucky University, The Filson Historical Society, Georgetown College, Kentucky Historical Society, Kentucky State University, Morehead State University, Murray State University, Northern Kentucky University, Transylvania University, University of Kentucky, University of Louisville, and Western Kentucky University.

Editorial and Sales Offices: The University Press of Kentucky
663 South Limestone Street, Lexington, Kentucky 40508-4008
www.kentuckypress.com

17 16 15 14 13   5 4 3 2 1

Library of Congress Cataloging-in-Publication Data

Bloodworth, Jeffrey.
  Losing the center : the decline of American liberalism, 1968-1992 / Jeffrey Bloodworth.
      pages cm
  Includes bibliographical references and index.
  ISBN 978-0-8131-4229-6 (hardcover : alk. paper) — ISBN 978-0-8131-4230-2 (epub) — ISBN 978-0-8131-4231-9 (pdf)
  1. Liberalism—United States—History—20th century. 2. United States—Politics and government—20th century. I. Title.
  JC574.2.U6B57 2013
  320.51'3097309045—dc23   2013015478

This book is printed on acid-free paper meeting the requirements of the American National Standard for Permanence in Paper for Printed Library Materials.

Manufactured in the United States of America.

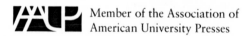 Member of the Association of
American University Presses

Contents

Introduction

Liberalism

Gone with the Wind

This time, Atlanta did not burn. One hundred thirty years after Union forces torched the city, it was ground zero for a decidedly different watershed event: the 1994 "Republican revolution." Hardly a native southerner, the revolution's architect, Newt Gingrich, nevertheless felt the weight of history. Instead of bearing the inherited stigma of disunion and defeat, the Republican had stomached Democratic dominion over the Congress and the old Confederacy. Frustrated, he fought to reverse the Democrats' institutional and regional power. With Democrats controlling the House since Eisenhower and the South since Reconstruction, Gingrich battled deep historical attachments in his drive for a Republican majority.

On November 8, 1994, those efforts came to fruition, and Gingrich's victory celebration became the center of the political world. As reports of the liberal body count trickled in, Atlantans—at least those at Gingrich's festivities—cheered and jeered. Highlighted by the losses of two high-profile governors, Mario Cuomo and Ann Richards, and House Speaker Tom Foley, election night proved both dramatic and historic. In addition to those luminaries, dozens of Democrats lost their seats and with them their congressional majority. In the process, Gingrich became the first southern GOP speaker since 1874.[1]

Sifting through the ashes of defeat, many liberals blamed themselves and the voters. George McGovern believed that "Democrats quit fighting," while Congresswoman Cynthia McKinney faulted the "nativists and the racists."[2] Small children, however, knew differently. Waving signs proclaiming "Liberals, your time is up!" kids at the Gingrich celebration apparently understood something most Democratic grown-ups ignored: liberalism, like Atlanta in 1864, lay in ruins.[3]

While Bill Clinton would earn reelection in 1996, *winning* is not synonymous with *governing*. Indeed, in 1994, McGovern (almost) grasped the gist of the Democrats' dilemma. Befuddled, the senator explained: "It's almost as though people don't want to say 'liberal.'"[4] A political scarlet letter, the dreaded L-word had cost Clinton his congressional majority and imperiled his young presidency. To save his political skin, he soon declared: "The era of big government is over."[5] In contrast, Republicans fought among themselves to prove who was "conservative before conservative was cool."[6]

While Clinton's "big government" pronouncement secured his reelection, it was no bold gambit. Rather, the president simply recognized political reality: liberalism was moribund. Liberalism's demise was not the work of a Republican revolution or Clinton's haphazard first years in office but instead resulted from decades of ideological incoherence and political ineptitude. In the years between the 1968 Chicago Democratic convention and Bill Clinton's election, liberals, like the ancient Israelites, wandered the political wilderness. This book depicts that era and attempts to explain what happened to American liberalism during the wilderness years.

The L-Word

American liberalism is the most slippery of creeds. While their dogma was scarcely the antistatist doctrine of the eighteenth century, twentieth-century liberals maintained its fundamental principles yet pursued them in innovative ways. Emphasizing freedom, progress, and rationality, liberals, of the eighteenth or the twenty-first century, remain, ideologically speaking, remarkably similar.[7] For Thomas Jefferson, for instance, liberal goals were achievable once "unnatural" (feudal) institutions and oppressive (monarchical government) restraints were removed. By the late nineteenth century, liberals encountered a world free of these bugaboos. Monopolies, Jim Crow, and urban strife revealed that merely unleashing human freedom scarcely achieved all liberal goals.

As a result of these realities, twentieth-century liberals looked to the state as an instrument to attain their long-cherished aims. With the *New Republic*'s Herbert Croly calling for Progressives to pursue Jeffersonian ends via Hamiltonian means, latter-day liberals founded a new course. Through this "surrogate socialism," Progressives sought to tame the excesses of the urban, industrial world via the state. Unlike their West European, socialist brethren, Progressives remained true to much of their classic liberal dogma.

Eschewing "equality of result" for a liberal "equality of opportunity," they maintained their creed's conventional values and goals but fit them for the exigencies of a new age.

Not surprisingly, as liberalism evolved, so did its adherents. Consequently, William Jennings Bryan, an agrarian reformer and Christian fundamentalist, embraced the Progressive standard. A generation hence, the New Deal attracted urban, white ethnics rather than evangelical farmers. Both a central strength and an Achilles heel, liberalism's mutable character enabled intellectuals to refashion it for new challenges and times. In this way, liberal policies and political coalitions shifted and changed according to the era.

Politically irrelevant during the early interwar era, liberals found that the Great Depression offered them political opportunity. Bemoaning capitalism's lopsided distribution of power and wealth throughout the 1920s, liberal intellectuals thought they understood the global crisis. Armed with a coherent understanding of events and a charismatic leader, liberals dominated the 1930s. In the process, they institutionalized New Deal–style statism into the fabric of American life. Moreover, with FDR at the center and New Deal liberalism as a governing philosophy, liberals built a durable and lasting political coalition.

The Vital Center

Though Democrats maintained the Roosevelt coalition for decades, their ideology scarcely remained static. Indeed, the postwar and post-FDR era presented new challenges. Ever nimble, intellectuals and activists refashioned their creed. In his 1949 *The Vital Center: The Politics of Freedom,* the historian and political activist Arthur Schlesinger Jr. offered his vision. Synthesizing the historical lessons of the New Deal, the Holocaust, and Stalinism with Reinhold Niebuhr's theology, he created a blueprint for postwar liberalism—the Vital Center.[8]

Imbued with FDR's optimism, and tempered by Niebuhr's pessimism, Vital Center liberals conceived their creed as an antiutopian fighting faith committed to national greatness at home and human freedom abroad.[9] In opposing ideological extremism on the Left and the Right, Vital Center liberals were anti-Communist by definition.[10] To rally the Left to the anti-Communist (and anti-Soviet) banner, Schlesinger helped found Americans for Democratic Action. This turn against America's wartime ally and organizational push prompted Popular Front liberals to counterattack. Led by former vice president Henry Wallace, they sought to maintain cordial relations with the Kremlin.

In this way, the 1948 election offered Democrats a choice between a Vital Center and a Popular Front path for postwar liberalism. Once Truman won the White House and easily disposed of Wallace's Progressive Party challenge, he enabled Vital Center liberals to define Democratic policy well into the postwar era.

Following the Eisenhower interregnum, activists looked for a leader to enact their Vital Center liberal vision for an era of affluence and a changing Cold War. Always a proponent of a strong executive, Schlesinger found a Vital Center vessel in the junior senator from Massachusetts—John Kennedy. Unlike most intellectuals who enter the political fray, Schlesinger, and other Vital Center liberals, made their mark on the Kennedy campaign and presidency.[11]

Though historians have debated the legacy of Kennedy's truncated administration, its Vital Center agenda offered substantial possibilities. Specifically, Kennedy's domestic policy, which married qualitative and quantitative liberalism, could have kept educated middle- and working-class Democrats together. In a similar balancing act, a Vital Center foreign policy recognized the necessity of promoting human freedom abroad while accepting the limits of American power.

Whether Kennedy could have kept liberals on a decidedly Vital Center path is unknown. What is certain is that Lyndon Johnson was unable to do so. Indeed, by 1968, liberals were divided into two hostile camps—New Politics versus Vital Center liberals. As did the Great Depression and the postwar world, events of the late 1960s required liberals to, yet again, reexamine and refashion their creed for a changing world. Pushed by Vietnam and the civil rights movement, middle-class and educated liberals gravitated toward the New Politics. This time their novel liberalism undermined, rather than attracted, a governing coalition.

The New Politics

Energized by their opposition to the Vietnam War, New Politics liberals gained control of the Democratic Party during the 1970s. In the process of dominating state parties and local machineries, activists redefined liberalism. New Politics liberals believed that the war in Vietnam was inherently evil. No amount of tinkering with policy or troop numbers would satisfy them, short of complete and immediate withdrawal. Moreover, these predominately young, educated, and middle-class activists reasoned that the liberalism of Hubert Humphrey and Lyndon Johnson was wholly corrupted by interest group politics and foreign interventionism. In sum, they sought to replace the New Deal coalition with an electoral alliance that could enact their "authentic" liberal vision.

Ironically, in spite of the name, there was little that was novel about the New Politics. New Politics liberalism harkened back to the Mugwumps of the nineteenth century, the Progressives of the early twentieth century, and the Stevensonians of the 1950s.[12] Their siren, Eugene McCarthy, epitomizes this political tradition. Framing all issues in terms of high principle, McCarthy, and his followers, eschewed economic concerns that had been the basis of New Deal liberalism's success in favor of moral piety. Indeed, to McCarthy and New Politics liberals, politics was more about moral rectitude than electoral success.

Mindful of Vietnam, as opposed to Stalinism, and drawing on a middle-class reformist tradition, New Politics liberals differed from their New Deal or Vital Center brethren. Predominately young, educated, and middle-class, activists were largely indifferent to the issues of working-class Democrats. Instead, they exhibited a "moralistic dedication to principle" that held the New Deal's interest group liberalism in disdain.[13]

In 1972, New Politics activists flexed their organizational and electoral muscle and took the Democratic nomination for George McGovern. The senator's consequent landslide defeat has obscured this campaign's legacy. More than a political fiasco, the McGovern insurgency also revealed a Democratic Party in transition. Gone were the New Deal's labor-liberal coalition and the Vital Center's anticommunism.[14] The 1972 campaign signaled New Politics liberalism's ascendance and concomitant changes in the party's composition, issues, and electoral fortunes. In this light, George McGovern is as significant in understanding contemporary American liberalism as FDR was in deciphering its midcentury equivalent.[15]

The McGovern insurgency hardly ended with Nixon's victory. A generational and ideological watershed, the 1972 election also ushered in a new liberal age. During this epoch, New Politics liberals slowly captured Democratic Party machinery.[16] In positions of influence, they shaped and altered party policy. From anti-anticommunism and abortion rights to a newfangled populism, activists proffered an innovative liberalism for a new era. Unfortunately for them, voters rejected it.

By any metric, New Politics stances on defense and social issues proved unpopular. From landslide defeats in national elections—1972, 1980, 1984, and 1988—to losing entire regions—the South and the West—Democrats hemorrhaged votes for a generation. Indeed, the New Politics enabled conservatives to characterize political races as competitions between "insurgent values of a liberal elite" and Middle American ideals.[17] As a result, Republicans came to dominate American politics.

To remain competitive, Democrats were forced to soft-pedal the New Politics and emphasize competence (Michael Dukakis) or personality (Jimmy Carter). Consequently, liberals relied less on ideological appeals in an era in which dogma had become increasingly important. Terming this reality *the Democrats' dilemma,* Steve Gillon has depicted contemporary liberalism's political cul-de-sac; unable to navigate an "ideological obstacle course" and attract a coalition of the have-nots, liberals no longer champion the "common man." Without a consistent creed, and lacking their historic populist appeal, Democrats simply drift from one election to the next.[18]

Gillon is partially correct. Contemporary liberals do confront a quandary. It is, however, one of their own making. And its sources are found in the 1970s.

The 1970s and Malaise

In terms of popular sentiment, bad hair, Evel Knievel, pet rocks, and *Star Wars* represent the 1970s. The decade was not merely significant in terms of disco and kitschy fads, however; it was also decisive in the demise of American liberalism. In the interval between Senator Eugene McCarthy's quixotic quest for the presidency in 1968 and Ronald Reagan's election in 1980, liberals lost control of the American political agenda. Though it took decades for conservatives to capture the Congress, it was during the 1970s when liberals cemented their embrace of the New Politics and sealed their political demise.

During the 1970s, liberals faced choppy electoral waters and profound policy challenges. Indeed, Republicans hardly fared much better in their attempts to stymie inflation and unemployment and produce stability in a restive world. Despite the common challenges, it was liberals who created a lasting impression of ineptitude. In the words of one pollster, voters came to believe that, "if the Democratic Party took your dog for a walk around the block, they wouldn't come back with the same animal."[19] Emblematic of this was President Carter's infamous "Malaise" speech.

Without a doubt, Jimmy Carter encountered a myriad of complex policy challenges. From the energy crisis and inflation to the American hostages in Iran and the Soviet invasion of Afghanistan, it seemed the entire world had colluded to implode his presidency. During the 1979 Fourth of July weekend, the energy crisis and the Carter administration both reached their nadir.

In the midst of this annual vacation weekend, gasoline shortages forced thousands of service stations to close across the Northeast.[20] Meanwhile, Carter was traveling to Tokyo for an economic summit. Saddled with a 26 percent approval rating and tens of thousands of angry would-be travelers, he was urged by his pollster, Pat Caddell, to come home. On his abrupt return, the president prepared a speech on the energy crisis. Caddell, however, had second thoughts. Downplaying gas shortages, inflation, and unemployment, the pollster convinced Carter that a "broader crisis of confidence," not short-term economic shocks, had pushed his presidency to the brink.[21] According to him, Vietnam, Watergate, and inflation had so undermined Americans' faith in themselves that a major presidential address was required.

After canceling the energy crisis speech, Carter spent eight secluded days at Camp David. Conferring with ordinary citizens and religious, political, and business leaders, the president devoted serious time and thought to the sorry state of America's soul. Like Moses descending from Mount Sinai, he returned to Washington to deliver the results. In a nationally televised address from the Oval Office, Carter claimed: "The erosion of our confidence in the future is threatening to destroy the social and political fabric of America."[22] While the president's talk temporarily raised his approval ratings, sincerity is not inspirational leadership.

The so-called Malaise speech not only marked the beginning of the end of Carter's presidency; it revealed the pitiful condition of American liberalism. In his address, the president recounted the ways in which Americans had lost faith in liberal internationalism, quantitative progress, and basic institutions. Ironically, Carter was talking not so much about the American people as about liberals.

The 1980s: Reagan and the Social Issues

The 1980s cemented liberalism's demise. Aided by events, policy successes, and his rare charisma, Ronald Reagan dominated and defined his era. Solely crediting the Great Communicator with the GOP's ascendancy, however, oversimplifies the Democrats' woes. Indeed, throughout the 1980s, liberals remained their own worst enemy. By constantly ignoring the social issues and refusing to reconfigure their dogma, Democrats consigned themselves to the minority. In fairness, liberals proffered their own set of social issues, which included abortion rights, gun control, and busing. These concerns, however, ran counter to the positions a clear majority of voters held.[23] Conservatives might have ridden a poor economy into power, but they used the social issues to govern and build a majority coalition.

Starting with the 1968 election, the social issues emerged as decisive electoral matters. Rising crime rates, busing, urban riots, drug use, out-of-wedlock pregnancies, and the youth rebellion became central to voters.[24] By promising "law and order" and a return to old-fashioned morality, the GOP was able to eclipse the salience of economic issues. And, despite successive electoral routs in 1972, 1978, 1980, 1984, and 1988, New Politics liberals stubbornly refused to address the social issues. Emblematic of this was the 1988 presidential election, when Democrats nominated Michael Dukakis to run against Reagan's legacy and his vice president, George H. W. Bush.

An admirable and capable public servant, the long-serving Massachusetts governor was a prototypical New Politics liberal. The technocratic and good government reformer opposed the death penalty and strict sentencing, supported abortion rights, backed gun control, and hailed from the liberal Northeast. With Reagan personally popular and his domestic and foreign policies viewed favorably, the governor hardly seemed a good political fit for 1980s America.

Despite all these liabilities, the GOP's nominee, George H. W. Bush, remained vulnerable. Distrusted by conservatives, and hampered by Reagan's immense shadow, the vice president was trailing Dukakis by seventeen points in the polls in early August 1988. Making political hay with an "I'm-on-your-side" theme, the nominee exposed the traditional Republican weakness on economic issues. After a largely harmonious Democratic convention, the governor, instead of pressing his advantage, toured western Massachusetts.[25] In the interim, Lee Atwater, Bush's campaign manager, redeemed his promise to turn a convicted rapist and murderer into "Dukakis's running mate."[26]

Intending to take away the governor's "I'm-on-your-side" mantra, Atwater made Willie Horton synonymous with Dukakis. Convicted of a 1974 murder, and sentenced to life in a Massachusetts state prison, Horton earned a weekend furlough as part of a Dukakis-backed rehabilitation program. While on furlough in 1987, Horton kidnapped a couple and repeatedly raped the woman and beat her boyfriend. Stealing their car, he fled before police finally captured him.

Seizing political opportunity, Atwater created the infamous Willie Horton campaign commercial. As the African American inmate's mug shot flashed across the screen, the narrator detailed the Massachusetts "weekend pass" program and Horton's subsequent crimes. Undoubtedly and intentionally pushing voters' racial buttons, the ad was also brutally effective. Suddenly, the governor's once formidable lead dissolved into a deficit. Fair or not, Willie Horton and the governor's stance on violent crime became the "social issue" of the 1988 election.

Unfortunately for the Democrats, their candidate only made matters worse. After refusing to attack in kind, Dukakis entered the second presidential debate desperate to prove his crime-fighting bona fides. During the contest, the moderator, Bernard Shaw, gave the governor an opportunity for political redemption. Asked whether, if his wife were "raped and murdered," he would "favor an irrevocable death penalty for the killer," Dukakis turned the opening into kryptonite.[27] Stiff and wooden, the governor reaffirmed his anti–death penalty stance before pivoting to banal campaign talking points. Voters, however, did not care about anticrime programs. They gauged the candidate's visceral reaction. If Dukakis failed to passionately react to an attack on his wife, then "I'm on your side" rang hollow.

Taken together, Willie Horton and the second debate reconfirmed what Middle Americans thought they knew about Democrats: they were not on their side. Malaise and Dukakis did not emerge overnight. The evolution from John Kennedy's quest for national greatness to Carter's apprehension and Dukakis's trepidation occurred through a series of fits and starts. As the majority party and the primary liberal vehicle, Democrats held their unwieldy coalition together from 1932 through the late 1960s. After 1968, New Politics liberals sealed their own demise by pursuing an unpopular agenda. From 1968 through the early 1990s, pieces and parts of the coalition came unglued, and liberalism became the ideology of a distinct minority.

The conventional narrative of liberalism's demise begins with Lyndon Johnson's domestic overreach and escalation in Vietnam; it ends with the riots and protests of the late 1960s. According to this version of events, 1968 signaled the beginning of liberalism's decline. Yet, in spite of Vietnam and campus unrest, Hubert Humphrey nearly won the White House, and, throughout the early 1970s, Democrats scored impressive, if uneven, gains in elections at all levels. Thus, it was not merely 1968 but during the 1970s and 1980s when the liberal coalition was finally torn asunder.

Despite its domestic and international achievements, liberalism suffered a slow death by a thousand cuts throughout the 1970s and 1980s. Unlike the 1960s, when powerful liberals such as Carl Albert (Oklahoma), Sam Rayburn (Texas), Frank Church (Idaho), and Mike Mansfield (Montana) hailed from what we today call *red states*, liberalism has today become the reserve of coastal elites, urbanites, intellectuals, minorities, and the young.

The story behind the demise of liberalism is as multifaceted and complex as the Roosevelt coalition itself. To effectively tell this story in all its diversity and intricacy, this work employs biographies of representative figures. In this way, the narrative mirrors the New Deal coalition's diversity and variety and the multiplicity of policy failures leading to its decline. A study of key liberal politicians, activists, and policy intellectuals reveals the history of liberalism during the 1970s and 1980s. Donald Peterson, Charles Stenvig, Fred Harris, Harold Ford, Henry Jackson, Jimmy Carter, Morris Udall, Ben Wattenberg, Bella Abzug, Lindy Boggs, and Dave McCurdy are representative of the New Deal coalition's disparate nature and the story of its ultimate demise.

The chapter devoted to Donald Peterson depicts the rise of the New Politics. Once New Politics liberals, like Peterson, controlled the Democratic Party, the New Deal coalition was undone. They did so through subtraction and addition. First on their list was the white working class. To their minds, the white working class was not so much a political ally as an obstacle to reform. In Minneapolis, New Politics liberals had so marginalized the white working class that Charlie Stenvig led a political revolt against the new Democratic establishment. This phenomenon was repeated in cities across the nation as working-class Democrats opted for tough guy mayors and politicians.

Some New Politics liberals understood the implications of losing a linchpin of the New Deal coalition. As the son of an Oklahoma sharecropper, Fred Harris thought he understood working-class voters; he did not. Ignoring the social issues entirely, he introduced a neopopulist economic program to attract working-class Democrats. A convoluted mixture of economic radicalism and political pandering, the program appealed to wealthy elites and college students instead.

Adding to the defection of working-class Democrats was the loss of southern whites from the New Deal coalition. With conservatives capitalizing on racial divisions within the New Deal coalition, the onus was put on liberals to bridge their rifts and build a genuinely biracial Democratic Party. Entrenched white racism posed a genuine obstacle to a biracial political coalition. Indeed, a generation after the Voting Rights Act's passage the South (minus Texas) boasted one African American congressman, Harold Ford. Ford, however, came to Congress from a majority-white district. His career reveals that biracial coalitions were possible and that the current state of southern politics—conservative Republican whites versus liberal Democratic blacks—was not inevitable.

Adding to this complicated stew was the 1982 Voting Rights Act. Mandating majority-minority districts offered mixed blessings. Though the numbers of elected southern black officials expanded exponentially, the change proved decisive in the South's realignment. With white moderates deprived of black voters, the region swung hard to the right. Moreover, with black and white districts no longer competitive, southern (white) Republicans and (black) Democrats moved to the political extremes.

In conjunction with losing southern whites, liberals lost their competitive edge in the American West. While the West was never the Solid South, hydroelectric dams and other federally financed internal improvements had made Democrats into the champions of western economic development. New Politics liberals, however, turned against this model. Moreover, as Morris Udall realized, environmentalism was not necessarily anathema to westerners. It was their obtuse manner that ignited the 1979–1980 Sagebrush Rebellion. As a result, liberals lost the West.

Liberals were not merely obtuse when it came to the West. They also ignored the welfare issue. Conservatives claimed that welfare soaked the working and middle classes for the benefit of the nonworking poor. Prior to the 1970s, many, if not most, Americans believed that liberal programs benefited them. During the 1970s, however, New Politics advocates championed the guaranteed-income plan aimed at the nonworking poor. This turnabout allowed conservatives to claim, with some credibility, that Democratic programs were no longer benefiting the working and middle classes.

In the midst of spiraling inflation and shrinking real income, *welfare* became a pejorative used to denigrate liberalism. Indeed, Jimmy Carter's promise of welfare reform was central in bringing working-class and southern Democrats back into the fold. While the Iranian hostage crisis and the economy undermined Carter, his failure to enact welfare reform signaled liberals' inability to reform their creed.

Domestic issues were not the only realm where Carter created conflicted policy. His administration's foreign policy zigged toward a hard-line Soviet stance and then zagged back to détente. The president's confused foreign policy reflected how fractured liberals had become in terms of foreign policy. Regarded as an unrepentant Cold Warrior, Henry Jackson tried to bridge this divide by popularizing international human rights as a cornerstone of a new liberal consensus on foreign policy.

Through promoting a policy that attracted Vital Center and New Politics liberals, Jackson smoothed over liberal divides while he also promoted his presidential hopes. The popularity of international human rights notwithstanding, the political wounds and hard feelings associated with the Vietnam War were just too pronounced for Jackson to win over New Politics liberals. It was a political unknown, Jimmy Carter, who took Jackson's issue and made human rights the cornerstone of his foreign policy.

In conjunction with Jackson, Ben Wattenberg tried to revive Vital Center liberalism. Modeled after Americans for Democratic Action, the Coalition for a Democratic Majority (CDM) was designed to unite trade unionists, policy intellectuals, and grassroots activists. Despite the CDM's early organizational successes, the New Politics establishment was too entrenched. As a result, the CDM abandoned Jimmy Carter for Ronald Reagan. Forfeiting these neoconservatives to the GOP left a significant intellectual void within a party that sorely needed its shibboleths challenged.

New Politics liberals not only transformed the Democratic Party; they also significantly influenced the women's movement. While they did not spark the women's movement, their moralism and activism helped shape it. The three-term congresswoman, activist, and feminist leader Bella Abzug embodies the intersection of the New Politics and the women's movement.

Combining the moralism, activism, and issues of the New Politics, with second wave feminism's aims and sensibilities, Bella Abzug's New Politics feminism promised to advance both agendas by forging a broad political alliance. Unfortunately for them, New Politics feminism ran afoul of Middle American sensibilities and gender norms. Abzug helped alter the Congress for the better, but, in the process, she, and other New Politics feminists, turned *feminism* into a pejorative and associated the movement with the Democrats.

New Politics feminists were prescient in, at least, one regard. Women did become a significant bloc of Democratic voters. Starting with the 1980 election, the "gender gap" emerged. Shorthand for Ronald Reagan's lagging popularity with women, the gender gap eventually spelled trouble for all Republicans. However, it hardly heralded a feminist voting bloc. Rather, a majority of women voters differed from men on two key and specific public policies: defense and social welfare. Significantly, men and women did not substantially vary on supposed "women's issues": abortion, the Equal Rights Amendment, and female candidates.

Misunderstanding the gender gap, Walter Mondale named Geraldine Ferraro as his running mate. Instead of spawning a women's voting bloc, the prochoice Catholic initiated a backlash. With Ferraro, Democrats learned the perils of exploiting the gender gap while ignoring divisive cultural issues. Lindy Boggs, by contrast, represented the future of successful gender gap politicking. Soft-pedaling divisive social issues, Democrats learned during the 1990s how to cultivate the women's vote without prompting a backlash.

Faced with the problem presented by the gender gap, a grouping of moderate Democrats finally pushed back. Founding the Democratic Leadership Council, moderates established an organizational foothold. Led by Richard Gephardt, Bill Clinton, and Dave McCurdy, these Democrats slowly altered party orthodoxy. By no means a majority in their own party, moderates proffered a centrist liberal agenda that returned Democrats to the White House.

Choosing to tell the story of liberalism through the use of representative figures and biography has limitations. In the estimation of many academic historians, biography, as a tool of historical inquiry, is positively unfashionable. Despite the fact that the educated public devours biography, the discipline has become outmoded in the eyes of the academy. Critics rightly argue that biography and the use of representative figures fail to fully convey the nuances and complexities of a given historical moment or situation. While this criticism contains much accuracy and truth, writing and research always entail value judgments and choices that privilege one set of facts and individuals over others.

Despite the shortcomings of the method, the use of representative individuals enables historians to tell a complicated story in a concise manner for a wide audience. In his seminal *The New Radicalism in America*, Christopher Lasch claimed that the use of representative figures allowed historians who "listen[ed] carefully" to articulate and exceptional people to "learn more about a given society than by more formal sociological anal-

ysis."[28] Lasch's social history of American intellectuals, and Richard Hofstadter and Alonzo Hamby's use of representative figures in their political
histories *The American Political Tradition* and *Liberalism and Its Challengers* inspired the structure and biographical nature of this work.[29] Through
the biographies of liberal activists, politicians, and policy intellectuals, this
book attempts to offer a coherent and readable narrative of liberalism's wilderness years.

A narrative detailing political ineptitude and loss could potentially bore.
Fortunately, these liberals and the Democrats' wilderness years are anything
but dull. Indeed, after a generation of historical writing that blames liberalism's demise on conservatives, pseudoprogressives, and the stupidity of the
American voter, it is time that liberals are invested with agency. While events
ostensibly collaborated to demolish the New Deal coalition, in actuality liberals were primarily responsible for their doctrine's downfall. This book is
written so that liberals, armed with a sound understanding of the past, can
resurrect their creed.

1

Latte Liberals

Donald Peterson and the
Birth of the New Politics

Lyndon Johnson never saw it coming. With party regulars, senate barons, and big city mayors in his back pocket, the president might have dealt with the nervous nellies in the antiwar movement, but his renomination seemed secure. Sure, Gene McCarthy was challenging him, but the Minnesotan lacked credibility. Long seen as a liberal up-and-comer, by 1967 McCarthy had so soured on Senate life that colleagues regularly mocked his commitment. A decade prior, he had so burned with ambition that he forsook a safe House seat, the Americans for Democratic Action (ADA) chairmanship, and the Ways and Means Committee for a long-shot senate bid; ten years later, when he challenged LBJ, few took the bid seriously.[1]

Among those who intimated the run was less than serious was McCarthy himself. Indeed, in his statement proclaiming his entry into the 1968 primaries, the senator never declared himself a candidate for either the presidency or the Democratic nomination.[2] Instead of aiming for the White House, McCarthy claimed, he merely wanted to change Johnson's Vietnam policy. Though the Minnesotan never admitted his real goal, Donald Peterson surely did. Working behind the scenes, Peterson had convinced McCarthy to enter the Wisconsin primary, challenge the president, and, in the process, transform American liberalism.[3]

Peterson saw McCarthy's challenge, not as just another campaign, but as signaling a fundamental break with the "old politics" and the birth of a "new politics." Declaring that McCarthy had "sav[ed] my political soul," he knew that the ensuing political struggle was no workaday campaign. To his mind, they had embarked on "a crusade."[4] As a key figure in the senator's decision to run, the state chairman of McCarthy's Wisconsin campaign, and the leader of the Badger state's Democratic delegation to Chicago, Pe-

Donald Peterson (courtesy personal collection of Donald Peterson)

terson played an outsized role in the 1968 presidential election. More important than that, however, the Wisconsinite also became a national leader in the nascent New Politics movement.

Though political lore credits New Leftists, who got "clean for Gene," McCarthy attracted a traditional and clean-cut demographic: educated, middle-class whites. From Al Gore Jr. and his professor Martin Peretz to the student activist David Mixner and the businessman Donald Peterson, McCarthy supporters, young and old, shared similar straitlaced traits. Though their siren lost the nomination fight, these New Politics liberals moved from the McCarthy campaign to control the Democratic Party during the 1970s.

In the process of dominating state parties and local machineries, activists redefined liberalism. Gone was Vital Center liberalism, which was born from the triple crisis of depression, world war, and the Cold War. Owing to this strife-laden milieu, the Vital Center emphasized working-class politics, collective security, and liberal internationalism. Mindful of Vietnam, rather than Stalinism, and drawing on a Progressive middle-class reformist tradition, activists created a new liberal style and Democratic Party.

The Peace Progressives

Just as the New Politics harked back to the Progressive era, so, too, did its foreign policy borrow from the past. Many of these anti-Vietnam liberals, like Peterson and McCarthy, were the intellectual descendants of the peace progressives. Highlighted by an influential cadre of U.S. senators—Robert La Follette, George Norris, and Burton K. Wheeler—peace progressives challenged the prevailing norms of liberal internationalism.[5] From World War I through the early 1940s, these midwestern and western senators led a bloc of foreign policy dissent. In this way, New Politics activists were part and parcel of a vital political tradition within twentieth-century liberalism.

Thus, the LBJ-McCarthy spat over Vietnam was merely a continuation of an ongoing battle within the ranks of liberalism that had been raging for decades. This contest over foreign policy had originally pitted Woodrow Wilson against the peace progressives. Wilson promoted liberal internationalism, an activist foreign policy that advanced American-style democracy abroad through a mixture of diplomacy and force.[6] In contrast, peace progressives believed that interventionist foreign policies were inevitably rooted in economic self-interest and sacrificed domestic reform.[7]

Never resolving their fundamental differences, the peace progressives saw themselves largely undermined by the Second World War. In addition, the New Deal–inspired political realignment left old Progressive insurgents, of either party, without a political base. Indeed, by 1946, leading peace progressives such as Burton Wheeler, Robert La Follette Jr., and Henrik Shipstead left the Senate in defeat, while liberal internationalism crested.

Owing to the triple crisis of depression, world war, and the Cold War, Wilsonian internationalism became triumphant among self-identified liberals. However, even in the midst of this consensus, there remained a scattering of old peace progressives in the Congress—all nominally Republican and hailing from the Upper Midwest. From Senator William Langer of North Dakota to Congressmen Merlin Hull and Gardner Winthrow of Wisconsin, these insurgents opposed virtually every aspect of President Harry Truman's diplomatic package.[8]

Virtually channeling the late Progressive-era champion from Wisconsin

Robert La Follette, these latter-day peace progressives accused bankers and oil barons of making U.S. foreign policy.[9] Predictably and prophetically, this bloc, led by Langer, also opposed American policy in Indochina. Thus, even as liberal internationalism appeared victorious, peace progressivism remained (barely) alive. Owing to the Vietnam War, the liberal internationalist–peace progressive conflict reemerged with renewed vigor. And this time, the peace progressives won.

More than New Hampshire, it was McCarthy's sweeping victory in the Wisconsin primary that revealed the creed's return. Wisconsin was fertile ground for the peace progressive message. Indeed, the doctrine's most solid political base had always been the Upper Midwest. Encompassing the Dakotas, Minnesota, Wisconsin, and Nebraska, the Upper Midwest has often been characterized as an isolationist rather than a peace progressive stronghold. Some claim that the Midwest's geographic insularity has rendered the region hostile to outside influences. According to this view, midwesterners have sought to retain their isolation by opposing an activist foreign policy.

Foreign policy and regional specialists have speculated that anything from agrarian radicalism to ethnocultural factors explain the region's isolationism. Adding to the midwestern isolationism trope is the tendency of observers to freely ascribe to the region both the best and the worst attributes of national life. Indeed, with politicians extolling the heartland's "family values" and cultural critics terming the region "the nesting place [for] the benign and banal," the Midwest regularly serves as a national Rorschach test.[10] This outcome should hardly surprise. Decades ago, Richard Leopold presciently warned his fellow diplomatic historians that, if "the international aspects" of the Midwest were "ignor[ed]," "glib generalizations" would eventually replace well-researched understandings of the region.[11]

The Midwest is no more and no less isolationist than any other American region. Instead, midwesterners boast a variety of internationalist traditions deeply rooted in the nation's impulse to redeem the world. While distinctly American, the Upper Midwest's peace progressive tradition is also rooted in the ethnic composition and religious traditions of its European settlers.[12] By 1900, nearly 80 percent of the populations of Wisconsin, Minnesota, and North Dakota were composed of Northern European immigrants. They brought with them religious traditions that were either avowedly pacifistic or cynical about the Old World's constant wars.[13] By custom, they were wary of liberal internationalism's global commitments.

In addition to Wisconsin's immigrant stock, the University of Wisconsin's intellectual community boasted influential neo-Beardians, like William Appleman Williams. In turn, these intellectual heavyweights influenced the state's political Left. Thus, it is hardly an accident that latter-day peace progressives—New Politics liberals—took root so strongly in Wisconsin. The state and the region were a long-standing bastion of the creed and served as the launching pad for its renaissance in 1968.

Like the Badger state, Donald Peterson came to peace progressivism by birth and temperament. In 1927, when he was two years old, his family left their small farming community of Renville, Minnesota, for Minneapolis.[14] A tall, sober, serious, and bespectacled redhead, Peterson lived most of his adult life in the upper midwestern states of Minnesota, South Dakota, and Wisconsin. A salesman and business executive, he became increasingly politically active in the late 1960s. Indeed, in 1967 and 1968, he led the fight in Wisconsin and at the Chicago Democratic Convention for Senator Eugene McCarthy. Thereafter, from 1969 through 1971, Peterson and his New Politics liberal allies took control of the state Democratic Party of Wisconsin.

Like so many of his generation, Peterson was a veteran of the Second World War. A first lieutenant and aerial navigator for the Fifth Air Force, he flew thirty-nine combat missions in the South Pacific. As a twenty-year-old, he saw the devastated city of Hiroshima from his plane and later recalled: "It was a brown spot—just a brown spot. . . . It seems inconceivable that we ever even considered using this thing—the Bomb."[15]

After the war, Peterson married and attended college part-time. After studying economics and political science for three years at the University of Minnesota and Macalester College in St. Paul, he quit and devoted himself to business full-time.[16] From 1945 through 1954, he helped his father operate an independent trucking firm that hauled petroleum products throughout the Minneapolis–St. Paul region. After they lost their largest contract, he took a sales job with the Standard Oil Company. While working for Standard Oil, Peterson became involved with the Democratic Farmer-Labor Party (DFL). With Peterson serving as precinct captain and his wife, Roberta, working as the DFL county chairwoman of Wright County, Minnesota, the two became party activists.

In 1956, at the age of thirty-one, Peterson declared his candidacy to represent the Twenty-seventh Legislative District in the Minnesota state legislature. Running as a self-identified liberal in a conservative district resulted in a poor showing at the polls. Years later Peterson recalled: "I got my just reward."[17] Professionally, he was chafing for more opportunity as well. Complaining that Standard Oil offered slow advancement and low pay, he left for a sales job in South Dakota.[18]

In 1957, Peterson moved his wife and four children to Aberdeen, South Dakota, where he sold heavy-duty road construction machinery for the Foster-Bell Company.[19] It was there that he gained his first exposure to national politics. In 1962, Peterson quit his job to manage George McGovern's bid for a Senate seat. As McGovern's campaign manager, he exhibited considerable skill in building a formidable organization. While the five-hundred-vote margin of victory was bare, McGovern became South Dakota's first freshman Democratic senator since 1930.

Though McGovern won the election, Peterson did not follow him to Washington as a member of his staff. Engaged in a running dispute over control of the campaign, Peterson and McGovern clashed so intensely that the senator-elect fired him. Starting in early September 1962, Peterson complained that the candidate's personal secretary and scheduler, Pat Donovan, continually overstepped the bounds of her job. Concerned that Donovan curtailed his campaign management, he issued a terse ultimatum: "Either I'm the campaign manager, or I'm not. Miss Donovan must return to Washington."[20] McGovern ignored the ultimatum, but one month after his election he summarily dismissed Peterson.

Peterson's stint as McGovern's campaign manager reveals his political and organizational talents as well as his moralistic worldview. Moreover, the episode shows his strong personality and unwillingness to compromise his principles. These traits served him well when he worked for Gene McCarthy's campaign and later as a New Politics insurgent. Indeed, his rendering of political topics into moral issues is a hallmark of both his career and New Politics liberalism.

With four children to feed, Peterson had little time to brood and ruminate over lost opportunities. After landing a position as a law book salesman, he moved his family to Eau Claire, Wisconsin. Selling law books entailed travel to every courthouse and law office throughout the state. For Peterson, this job was ideal, and within two years he became a veritable expert on Wisconsin politics and possessed contacts from Green Bay to Eau Claire.

By the mid-1960s, Peterson plunged back into politics, first as a county officer, then as district chairman, and later as chairman of the Wisconsin chapter of ADA. In 1967, he quit sales to serve as vice president of Black River Dairy Products. As did his career advances, Peterson's political activities also mushroomed.[21]

In 1967, events and casualties were rapidly escalating in Southeast Asia. Outraged at this turn of events, Peterson worked with Allard Lowenstein in the "dump Johnson" movement.[22] In the late summer of that year, Lowenstein and Peterson hatched a plan to defeat LBJ in the Wisconsin primary. Since they lacked a candidate, the pair wanted Wisconsin Democrats to vote "no" in the state's upcoming presidential primary. In pursuit of this goal, Peterson established Concerned Wisconsin Democrats (CWD), which sought to rally the "no" vote.[23]

The CWD opposed Johnson on the basis of one issue—Vietnam. Though Peterson had supported Johnson through 1966, he abandoned the president because, as he saw it, the war in Vietnam was "senseless and futile, and . . . a waste of resources urgently needed at home."[24] Indeed, Peterson, through the CWD, alleged that Americans had "inherited the foreign policy of Goldwater while voting for Johnson."[25] There were, however, larger overriding principles that separated the organization from the president.

In the early post-1945 era, most liberals had not only rejected peace progressivism but also rebuked its foundational assumptions. In the shadow of the Holocaust and Soviet domination of Eastern Europe, notions of the inevitability of progress and the innate goodness of humanity surely seemed naive. However, as the memory of Hitler and of Stalin's crimes receded and the bloody reality of Vietnam emerged, New Politics activists challenged Cold War tenets.

Vital Center liberals predicated their reformist doctrine on the fundamental justness of American society, the Soviet Union's inherent aggression, and the inevitability of interest group politics. As far as New Politics activists were concerned, however, the basic fairness of American society was shrouded in the smoke and fires of the Watts and Detroit riots; interest group politics amounted to sleazy backroom deals; and a commitment to anticommunism had led to a meaningless and immoral war in Vietnam.

In Wisconsin, Vital Center liberalism meant the Milwaukee congressman Clement Zablocki. The son of a Polish immigrant grocer, "Clem" worked his way through college before being swept into Congress on Harry Truman's 1948 coattails.

A product of Milwaukee's Southside, Zablocki shared a visceral anticommunism with millions of Americans who had relatives living in Soviet-dominated Eastern Europe; their anticommunism was as personal as their allegiance to Franklin Roosevelt's Democratic Party.[26]

Known for his bushy moustache, South Milwaukee accent, and short stature, Zablocki, not surprisingly, staunchly supported the Vietnam War.[27] Hardly a conservative, he also backed civil rights and denounced George Wallace, who fared quite well in working-class Milwaukee.[28] The longtime incumbent might have wielded significant power, but he remained remarkably normal. A member of Milwaukee's Blessed Sacrament Parish, the congressman mowed his own lawn and even stuffed his own sausages.[29]

Despite Zablocki's considerable political heft, 1967's stormy political atmosphere was conducive to Peterson's insurgent "no" campaign. At first, leading Wisconsin Democrats rejected the scheme. Calling for an affirmative protest against LBJ, Pat Lucey, a longtime leader of the Badger state Democrats, termed a rumored Eugene McCarthy bid preferable to the "no" campaign.[30] In spite of this dynamic, McCarthy's early intimations of a challenge failed to entice Peterson.

In the winter of 1967, Peterson traveled to St. Paul to meet McCarthy; after this meeting, he pronounced himself "converted." There, in the senator's living room, Peterson and McCarthy hatched the scheme that ignited a presidential campaign and brought down LBJ. According to the plan, Peterson and the CWD would "invite" McCarthy to enter the Wisconsin primary. From there, the senator's candidacy would provoke a wider "dump Johnson" movement.[31]

In November 1967, Peterson, through the CWD, drafted a letter urging McCarthy to enter Wisconsin's primary.[32] In response to the request, the senator entered the contest and declared his candidacy. Serving as the state chairman of the senator's campaign in Wisconsin, Peterson used the CWD to form the nucleus of the McCarthy organization. By January 1968, he had the McCarthy campaign up and running.

Using every available resource, Peterson built a cooperative relationship with the Madison-based magazine *The Progressive* (formerly *La Follette's Weekly*). This partnership quite literally symbolized peace progressivism's reemergence in the McCarthy campaign. More tangibly, the publication's national mailing list reaped $50,000 in campaign donations. In addition, when McCarthy forces lacked campaign literature, *The Progressive* simply printed off thousands of its March 1968 editorial endorsing the senator's presidential run. The journal also loaned the campaign its associate editor, Arnold Serwer, who coordinated the thousands of student volunteers who flooded into Wisconsin.[33] With Peterson managing the chaos, by February the McCarthy campaign had active organizations in all twenty-two of Wisconsin's most populated counties and counted at least thirteen hundred volunteers around the state.[34]

Despite these extraordinary efforts, Peterson still dealt with a mercurial candidate. In the days leading up to the New Hampshire primary, McCarthy canceled four long-standing commitments in Wisconsin. In reaction, Peterson thrashed, fumed, and threatened—all to no avail.[35] When McCarthy finally showed, he and his organization distinguished themselves as the "most difficult to arrange of any of the [candidates]" with their "rude and officious" behavior.[36] McCarthy hardly limited these manners to Wisconsin; four days after telling George McGovern that he "definitely had decided not to enter [the South Dakota] primary," the senator did just that.[37]

Despite these rocky moments, in early March McCarthy very nearly upset LBJ in New Hampshire. This outcome prompted Bobby Kennedy's entry into the scrum. Two weeks later, LBJ announced his withdrawal from the race, which meant that the vice president, Hubert Humphrey, also became a candidate. Despite the now crowded field, McCarthy scored an impressive victory in Wisconsin and showed well in the other fourteen primaries across the nation. Owing to the vagaries of Democratic nominating procedures, Robert Kennedy's truncated candidacy, Hubert Humphrey's late entry, and the paucity of state primaries, no candidate possessed the necessary delegates for the nomination.

In 1968, however, nearly all primaries amounted to a beauty contest; most delegates were not necessarily bound to cast their votes in accordance with the results. The seeming oddity of this rule emerged for good reason: the fifteen state primaries lacked uniform rules and procedures. Thus, in some states, the incumbent's name never appeared on the ballot. For those endorsing LBJ, for instance, they would vote for a favorite son, a state official who served as a stand-in for the incumbent. Moreover, Humphrey barely participated in the primaries. Thus, while McCarthy and RFK received nearly two-thirds of all primary votes, these totals reflected just fifteen states where the names of LBJ and Humphrey sometimes never appeared on the ballot.

In the absence of a definitive front-runner, and armed with the party establishment's backing, Humphrey remained the presumptive nominee. In the months between the Wisconsin primary and the August national convention, McCarthy refused to concede. Instead, his campaign called for what they considered a "fair share" of national convention delegates as they prepared for battle for the Democratic nomination.

The fight to retain pro-McCarthy delegations for the national convention revealed New Politics liberals' skills at organizing and bureaucratic infighting. In states where McCarthy scored a primary victory, activists pushed for winner-take-all. Conversely, in states where McCarthy lost, his forces pressed for a fair "minority share" of delegates. In Minnesota, where Humphrey defeated McCarthy, the senator's forces filed a lawsuit over the delegate selection process. Accusing Humphrey of "undemocratic" practices, the McCarthy campaign overlooked its own habits; it had removed the democratically elected mayors of Minneapolis and St. Paul and Humphrey supporters, Arthur Naftalin and Thomas Byrne, from its list of Minnesota delegates.[38]

In a similar hard-nosed spirit, Peterson worked to secure a pro-McCarthy Wisconsin delegation. Armed with these supporters, Peterson intended to fight for his candidate's nomination. Failing that, he planned to disrupt the convention and expose party leaders' "unfair politics." Meanwhile, Wisconsin's Democratic regulars worked on a pro-Humphrey Badger state delegation. From their perspective, since the vice president was destined to take the nomination, his backers should constitute the delegation. Indeed, state law required the Wisconsin delegation to vote for the state primary's victor, McCarthy, until that candidate received less than one-third of the convention's total ballots. Thus, the senator would receive his votes no matter the delegate.

Peterson, loudly and publicly, objected to the state party's machinations. Calling the delegates "Trojan horses," Peterson wanted delegates who were "morally committed" to McCarthy.[39] In pursuit of this goal, he fought the party establishment in the courts and newspapers. To avoid just such intraparty squabbles, Wisconsin Democrats proffered an existing rule. Under the plan, district-level Democratic organizations would choose the delegates, while each candidate reserved the right to veto the roster.[40]

Despite the squabbling, by virtue of his Wisconsin primary victory, McCarthy ultimately controlled the state delegation's composition. Even state party officials conceded this point.[41] Rejecting the state party's slate, he handpicked a delegation of McCarthy loyalists. To his mind, the fight against the Vietnam War and the struggle for a pro-McCarthy delegation were one and the same. Only by defeating Humphrey could activists end the war, purify the party, and replace it with a New Politics.

McCarthy had not only salvaged Peterson's "political soul"; to Peterson their political "crusade" signaled the demise of the "old politics" and the birth of a "new politics."[42] Eschewing the Vital Center's emphasis on the working class and messy great power internationalism, the New Politics pushed for fundamental change. Shocked by the civil rights backlash, urban riots, and Vietnam, New Politics liberals brooked no compromise when it came to these core issues. Believing that Democrats fell short on these counts because of the party's establishment, Peterson sought to purge the party of "unprincipled leaders."[43] Put more colorfully, one highly placed McCarthy supporter said of the Democratic leadership: "You don't compromise with a rattlesnake."[44]

Stomping on the snake's head, Peterson threatened to boot Democratic regulars from the party if they failed to fall in line.[45] In the midst of this fuss, one McCarthy activist and delegate, Roy Traynor, removed himself from Peterson's delegation. Terming the leader's heavy-handed ways "foreign to the tradition of the Wisconsin Democratic Party," Traynor left just before the fun began at the Wisconsin Democratic Party's state convention.[46] Convened in July, and controlled by Peterson and the McCarthyites, the convention saw the insurgents flex their newfound political muscle. As a result, the new party platform opposed the Vietnam War and supported abortion rights. With Democratic officeholders calling these new planks "junk," the Milwaukee County Democratic Council and a state party spokesman threatened to write their own platform.[47]

Fearing that the state convention merely foreshadowed the antics to come on the national stage in Chicago, Democratic regulars challenged the validity of Peterson's delegation. In questioning the delegates' party bona fides and commitment to the eventual nominee, the establishment raised valid issues. For instance, Peterson had summarily removed the McCarthy supporter and congressman Henry Reuss from the delegation.[48] In lieu of Reuss and other party regulars, he added David Fries, chairman of the Wisconsin Socialist Party, and Sandra Utech, who joined the Democratic Party only on her selection as a delegate.[49] Additionally, any number of Wisconsin's delegates publicly claimed that they would support only McCarthy as the party's nominee. Despite these complaints, the convention's credentials committee tossed aside the establishment's challenges. As a result, Peterson prepared for battle.

Dispensing with tradition, the delegation ignored the state party chair, Richard Cudahy, and tapped Peterson to lead it.[50] Claiming the delegation finally represented "the people," Peterson made an estimation of "the masses" that foreshadowed a common New Politics assumption: white educated professionals were the new proletariat. Of the nine delegates nominated for leadership positions, six were academics, two were lawyers, and one was a professional activist.[51]

Noting this, San Francisco mayor Joseph Alioto said that, out of all the delegations he addressed, he had not seen "as much intellectual activity" as there was in the Badger state group.[52] Unquestionably smart, Peterson tapped a professor of political science, Karl Andresen, to sit on the important Democratic convention platform committee. Summarily replacing Congressman Henry Reuss with a novice was merely the first of many unorthodox moves on Peterson's part.

Decidedly unconventional, Peterson's Wisconsin delegation made its mark in Chicago. In front of a national television audience, the group distinguished itself. From nominating a surprise vice presidential nominee and forcing the convention's temporary adjournment to proposing that the entire convention reconvene in another city, these New Politics activists made their presence known.[53] Indeed, many Americans, along with NBC's Chet Huntley, noted that Don Peterson was "a man to watch."[54]

In the days prior to the convention, delegates prepared for several major floor fights over Vietnam, the unit rule, and the seating of delegates.[55] Peterson looked to the Vietnam "peace plank" vote with particular interest. McCarthyites sought a Democratic platform plank calling for a bombing halt in North Vietnam.[56] Widely recognized as McCarthy's most loyal and dedicated force, Peterson, along with the Badger state delegation, led the fight for the peace plank.[57] To suppress media attention to the Democrats' schism over Vietnam, party leaders scheduled the peace plank debate for midnight.[58] Thus, it was not until twelve o'clock that Hale Boggs began reading a summary of the party's fifteen-thousand-word platform. At 1:00 A.M., he finally arrived at the section on Vietnam.

On cue, the Badger state delegate frantically waved the Wisconsin standard while delegates rhythmically clapped and shouted "No!" Amid the uproar, Peterson stood at the Wisconsin microphone and pled: "It's now 1:10 in the morning and I think every delegate in the hall wants to go home and go to bed."[59] With Richard J. Daley turning shades of pink and red, the convention chairman, Carl Albert, tried to gavel the delegates back into order. Finally relenting to the chaos, Albert adjourned the convention until noon.

In addition to the peace plank fight, the Wisconsin delegation raged at the heavy-handed security on the convention floor and top-down management of the entire proceedings. Blaming LBJ, Peterson moaned: "The presence of Lyndon Johnson at this convention is overwhelming."[60] Another Wisconsin delegate, Milwaukee's activist attorney Ted Warshafsky, equated the convention floor to "a concentration camp atmosphere."[61] Concentration camp or not, after losing the peace plank debate Peterson led a "spontaneous" demonstration. Calling the display "thrilling," delegates paraded around the hall weeping, singing, and wearing black armbands of protest.[62] Not to be outdone, Daley ordered the convention band to play military songs throughout the demonstration.[63]

While McCarthyites marched inside the convention hall, the Chicago police pounded protesters outside. In reaction to the police riot, Peterson led a two-thousand-person march in protest of Mayor Daley and his police department's brutality. Earlier in the day, Peterson had announced the protest by telling a cheering crowd that he was taking a "walk" at 4:00 P.M., explaining: "I'm just tired of being told what to do and how to do it. I'm tired of being herded aboard a bus and whisked to the convention hall. This walk will be the first free thing I've done since I've been here."[64]

As they walked from their hotels toward the downtown convention site, marchers chanted "Join us," to the young protesters camped out in the city parks.[65] With the hippies and yippies joining the ranks, Peterson's "walk" swelled into a five-block-long queue. When the Chicago police finally stopped Peterson for his "illegal march," he feared a violent clash and ordered the demonstrators to disperse.[66] His combined activism inside and outside the convention hall brought Peterson considerable media attention. After one interview, NBC's Chet Huntley called him the convention's unknown hero because he "says what he thinks and doesn't care what anybody thinks about him."[67]

Not all Wisconsin Democrats shared Huntley's assessment. Of the state's fifty-nine delegates, ten were committed to Humphrey. Led by Milwaukee congressman Clem Zablocki, these Democrats seethed with anger. Richard Steinberg, a Milwaukee County councilman, termed the delegation "a disgrace to the state."[68] One Humphrey delegate walked out of the convention, accusing McCarthy supporters of using "the blood of kids . . . for cheap political purposes."[69] Zablocki called Peterson's decision to disperse his march "the smartest thing he's done since he's come to the convention."[70]

Even after losing the vote on the peace plank and with Humphrey sweeping toward the nomination, Peterson refused to relent. Meanwhile, downtown Chicago's streets were teeming with police and protesters and tear gas so thick that Hubert Humphrey could smell it from his twenty-fifth-floor hotel window. Outraged that Democrats ignored the anarchy by commencing with the presidential nomination roll call, Peterson demanded that the convention move to another city since "thousands of young people are being beaten in the streets of Chicago."[71] Gaveling him out of order, Carl Albert hoarsely thundered: "Wisconsin is not recognized for that purpose."[72] Perplexed, mesmerized, and befuddled, Peterson yelled at Albert: "What kind of convention is this?"[73] Millions of Americans watching the proceedings from their living room couches surely agreed.

Though his antics hurt Democrats in 1968, Peterson and his New Politics acolytes felt that was exactly the point. Once McCarthy lost the nomination, they worked to undermine Humphrey. One McCarthy delegate admitted as much. The cartoonist for the *Village Voice* and playwright Jules Feiffer summed up this collective attitude by declaring: "It was Nixon who got elected tonight, and I don't give a damn."[74] Peterson worked to turn Feiffer's avowal into prophecy.

After Humphrey secured the presidential nod, Peterson and the Wisconsin delegation sabotaged the vice presidential nomination process. Claiming that the convention was "rigged," forty-two of Wisconsin's delegates abstained from voting for Maine's Senator Edmund S. Muskie. The remaining seventeen split their ballots every which way, voting for twenty-eight-year-old Julian Bond (who was constitutionally too young to serve), Allard Lowenstein, and the incarcerated chairman of the New Hampshire delegation, David Hoeth.[75]

Predictably, Peterson was met with a barrage of criticism and praise for his work at the convention. Wisconsin's First Congressional District chair called for his removal from the party, while other dignitaries termed his shenanigans "shameful."[76] One less eloquent critic compared Peterson to a wet chicken that "didn't know whether to go back to the coop or just stand there and squawk."[77]

In contrast to the critics, one sympathetic correspondent complimented Peterson's demonstration of "patience and humanitarianism."[78] Echoing this sentiment, the television host and sportswriter Dick Schaap praised Peterson for the "impressive and heartening stand of the Wisconsin delegation" and invited him to be a guest on his show.[79]

Though some activists began efforts to establish a fourth party, the "New Party," Peterson refused this course. Instead, he called for New Politics liberals to reform the Democrats from within.[80] Writing to his fellow activists in the fall of 1968, Peterson urged: "Don't let the rascals grind you down! Stay with the party and change it." In pursuit of this goal, he helped form the New Democratic Coalition (NDC).[81] Believing that the Roosevelt coalition teetered on the edge of collapse, the NDC aimed to revive it through the New Politics while reversing racial discrimination, the Cold War, and the "monolithic conformism of 'the great consensus.'"[82]

While Nixon squeaked to victory in 1968, Peterson and other New Politics liberals foresaw the coming of a new and motley Democratic coalition. Composed of McCarthy, Robert Kennedy, and George Wallace supporters, the coalition would be joined by dispossessed "Negros and Mexican-Americans."[83] According to Peterson, this disparate coalition shared one common goal—a desire for enhanced living and working conditions.[84] Though Peterson's reasoning seemed perfectly logical on paper, a christening party for the Rhode Island NDC reveals the kinks in it.

Of the more than one thousand attendees, few, if any, dispossessed minorities or George Wallace supporters made an appearance. Instead, upper-middle-class whites and college students constituted the vast majority.[85] In addition to the Rhode Island soiree, a May 1969 NDC fund-raiser further illustrates the decidedly upper-class flavor of the New Politics. With Lauren Bacall, Harry Belafonte, George Plimpton, Tony Randall, Jules Feiffer, and Norman Mailer in attendance, the New Politics proved it could attract celebrities.[86] Unfortunately, it did not do as well with Clem Zablocki's constituents.

Though New Politics adherents are easily categorized by their income group (middle class) and racial homogeneity (white), a definition is more slippery. Peterson defined the "New Politics" as "the young confronting the old": "New politics is based on issues—crucial issues such as the war, poverty . . . and participatory democracy."[87] More specifically, New Politics liberals bandied an educated, white, and middle-class agenda. Whatever their exact agenda, Peterson possessed clear aims and an organization dedicated to achieving them.

While Humphrey battled Nixon, in October 1968 the NDC held its first national meeting. Elected national cochair, Peterson declared his intent to forge a new coalition and take over the Democratic Party.[88] To his mind, since New Politics liberalism's issues were popular with a younger and more urban electorate, success lay within their grasp. Despite these buoyant assertions, the tenor and tone of the October conference lacked optimism.[89]

Though New Politics liberals believed that George Wallace's supporters were potentially theirs, one speaker termed them "culturally underdeveloped." Another delegate warned that Wallace's popularity could translate into "genocidal repression and fascism."[90] With or without the Alabaman's voters, Peterson and other New Politics liberals believed that their brand of liberalism represented a majority viewpoint. According to this calculus, the combined McCarthy-RFK primary vote totals revealed that a majority of Democrats preferred the New Politics.[91] Thus, Humphrey represented a minority rump of the Democratic Party.

Lacking prominent Democrats in the movement, Peterson cautioned against waiting for a "political prince charming to . . . solve all your political troubles."[92] His admonition made sense because Gene McCarthy conspicuously avoided the group and, seemingly, politics. Though Minneapolis hosted the NDC conference, McCarthy refused to attend. Instead, he opted to write about the World Series for *Life* magazine. When NDC cochairs Peterson and Paul Schrade tried to pay a courtesy call, he skipped out citing "other commitments."[93] As Peterson planned for the future and Humphrey fought for his political life, McCarthy observed: "There's some kind of redundancy in baseball socks these days."[94]

Adding to this curious behavior, McCarthy abandoned his Senate Foreign Relations Committee seat, which went to a Vietnam War supporter. After this curious move, he backed a southern conservative, Russell Long, over Edward Kennedy for Senate majority whip. Griping about McCarthy's recent actions, Peterson lamented: "Nobody knows what he's been up to."[95] Undeterred, Peterson and his NDC colleagues continued their work. In Wisconsin and states across the country, they gained effective control over state parties and reshaped liberalism in the process.

By the summer of 1969, Peterson and his allies controlled the Wisconsin Democratic Party. During June's state party convention, New Politics liberals flexed their organizational muscle and newfound strength. Terming pro-Johnson Democrats "dissidents," Peterson turned the tables on his opponents; soon, his agenda became the state party's program as well.[96] In a battle played out in the party's Resolutions Committee, New Politics liberals "proclaimed we have no damn business in Vietnam" and passed a motion calling for an immediate troop withdrawal.[97] After the vote on withdrawal, many Democrats, especially those from Milwaukee County, left the hall while the insurgents gave themselves a standing ovation.

Proclaiming that "the NDC is the party now," Peterson and his New Politics liberal followers passed their entire agenda. Offering diplomatic recognition to China and Cuba, the Wisconsin state Democratic Party also promised to curb the "unwholesome influences of the military establishment."[98] One of the few failed NDC proposals called for tripling the beer tax. Using the organization's own philosophy against this proposal, a delegate pleaded: "Why tax the workingman's champagne?"[99] Beer tax or no, two NDC members, Donald Peterson and Pat Lucey, emerged from the convention as the front-runners for the 1970 Democratic nomination for governor.[100]

Not all Democrats were pleased with this situation. Among them was Clem Zablocki. Representing the heavily unionized and Polish Fourth District of Milwaukee, the congressman—and his constituents—typified the old New Deal coalition. To his mind, Peterson "substituted a warped sense of values for the traditional principles for which the party has always stood."[101] He grew so incensed by the new platform he threatened to refuse party funds.[102]

Despite Zablocki's protests, by the early 1970s New Politics liberals "dominate[d] the party from Milwaukee to Eau Claire, from Mellen to Madison."[103] For years, Dane County (Madison) Democrats had battled and lost to their Milwaukee counterparts. Indeed, in 1966, the former only barely defeated a resolution by the latter that praised LBJ's Vietnam policy. By contrast, at the 1971 convention New Politics liberals thunderously approved a resolution denouncing the Johnson administration for "deceiving the American public."[104] In that same year, Wisconsin Democrats elected Peterson to serve as a Democratic National Committee committeeman. Voted on by party delegates, Peterson carried eight of the state's ten congressional districts.[105]

Not satisfied with a dominant voice in the party, Peterson and his allies recruited their own slate of candidates against Democrats they deemed "worthless."[106] High on their list of political rubbish was Zablocki. Liberal in domestic issues but a foreign policy hawk, the congressman ran afoul of the New Politics owing to the Vietnam War. Hardly a doctrinaire foreign policy conservative, Zablocki later authored the 1973 War Powers Act and cowrote the 1982 Boland-Zablocki Amendment, which ended funding to the Nicaraguan Contras.[107]

Intent on instituting New Politics reform across the state, Peterson ran for governor. Starting a year before the 1970 election, he traveled the state to deliver his message. Oddly, his campaign for state government centered on Vietnam: "If we don't solve this war, then we won't have the resources for the other things which may eventually wipe us off this planet."[108] Calling himself the "people's advocate," he pledged to return political power to ordinary people, end the Vietnam War, and safeguard the environment.

The 1970 gubernatorial campaign amounted to a political laboratory. New Politics activists had proved they could capture party machinery. This race tested whether they could win an election. Unfortunately for Peterson, he was not the only New Politics liberal in the race. The former lieutenant governor and 1966 Democratic nominee for governor Pat Lucey also jumped in the contest. While Lucey enjoyed the front-runner status, he and Peterson shared nearly identical traits.[109]

Members of the New Democratic Coalition, Peterson and Lucey also looked eerily alike. Both in their midforties, they sported black horn-rimmed glasses and parted their short, well-kempt hair to the side. As a result of their remarkable similarities, when Eugene McCarthy endorsed Peterson, he, nonetheless, promised to campaign for Lucey if he won the primary.[110] Moreover, when George McGovern promised to campaign for Peterson, Lucey cried foul. Echoing McCarthy and McGovern, John Kenneth Galbraith said that the race between Lucey and Peterson amounted to a "choice between two good men."[111]

Unlike the insurgents who constituted the New Politics movement, Lucey was a longtime party insider. As party chair in the late 1950s, he helped revive Wisconsin's long-moribund Democratic Party.[112] Though his 1966 race for governor led many to doubt his political acumen, activists feared a Lucey-Peterson primary fight would throw the nomination to Milwaukee mayor Henry Maier.[113] Consequently, party members begged Peterson not to run.[114]

Rather than drop out of the race, Peterson spent the summer of 1970 crisscrossing Wisconsin in his camper trailer "Bandwagon."[115] Supported by scads of volunteers and a full-time staff of eleven, he campaigned six days a week.[116] With a straightforward style and analytic tone, Peterson appealed to other educated professionals. Turning his back on Milwaukee's working-class wards, he hit Madison's tony Blackhawk Country Club and the city's swanky Shorewood Hills.[117]

Emphasizing issues and leadership rather than partisan appeals, Peterson believed that "people want leaders who demonstrate an independent stature."[118] To his mind, inducing political agnostics back into the electoral process would provide his margin of victory. Moving beyond the narrow confines of traditional interest group politicking, he called for a Department of Consumer Protection.[119] Unlike labor issues, which pitted one interest group against another, consumer protection theoretically allowed the candidate to transcend petty politics for society's general welfare.

At the height of the summer primary campaign, Peterson grasped onto a consumer protection issue to highlight his core themes: the miniskirt. Campaigning as a champion of the women's movement and consumer protection, he made the miniskirt shorthand for both issues. In the summer of 1970, fashion designers had capitalized on the fad by unveiling the midiskirt, a slightly less revealing garment than its iconic cousin; Peterson, however, cried foul. Accusing the garment industry of "creating an artificial market" for the product, he made the midiskirt a consumer protection issue.[120] While a *Green Bay Press Gazette* poll revealed that readers also preferred the miniskirt to the midiskirt, they were hardly clamoring for consumer protection.[121]

Much to Peterson's chagrin, it was not the candidates' vision of the New Politics that decided the primary. Ironically, it was Lucey's appeal to law-and-order voters and prolife Catholics that spelled the difference. In the midst of the hotly contested Democratic primary, a bombing rocked the University of Wisconsin. Intended to destroy the Army Mathematics Research Center, located inside Sterling Hall, the bomb failed to damage its target but succeeded in gutting much of the building.

In the wee morning hours of August 24, four university students parked a van filled with one hundred gallons of fuel oil and seventeen hundred pounds of nitrogen fertilizer outside Sterling Hall.[122] The subsequent blast ripped through the six-story building, killing a physicist, wounding four graduate students, and causing over $6 million in damages.[123] In addition to killing or wounding five, the bombing fundamentally changed the political environment.

The handiwork of student radicals, the bombing represented the culmination of years of campus riots and unrest. In the eighteen months prior to the attack, the Wisconsin governor used the national guard twice to restore order to the Madison campus. During one campus rampage, just months before the bombing, protesters smashed the windows of the very building the radicals later bombed.[124] Indeed, in the past year, protesters had directed four bombs at Madison-area military facilities. Ranging from firebombs aimed at ROTC offices to explosives dropped from a stolen plane onto an ammunition plant, the political violence had been germinating and escalating for some time.[125]

With campus protests turning increasingly violent, the issue became a top-shelf concern for nearly all statewide candidates. For example, Lloyd Bentsen defeated incumbent Senator Ralph Yarborough in the Texas Democratic primary by painting him as an ally of student radicals. In Wisconsin, Pat Lucey used the Madison bombing in a similar fashion. With the primary scheduled in the weeks just after the attack, Lucey traveled the state calling for a crackdown on violent protesters. In one day of campaigning, he held press conferences in Green Bay, Madison, LaCrosse, and Wausau demanding that student radicals be prosecuted as criminals.[126]

Caught off guard by Lucey's offensive, Peterson stumbled. When asked whether he thought the Madison bombing would undermine his campaign, he managed a meek: "Gee, I hope not."[127] The bombing could not have occurred at a more inopportune time for Peterson. For months, he had railed against the use of the national guard to quell campus unrest, urging instead communication to defuse the violence. As governor, he promised to reduce campus protests by sharing a beer with students at university bars.[128] His lone law-and-order initiative entailed decentralizing police departments into a "federation of neighborhood police forces" run by a locally elected commissioner.[129]

In addition to his cagey offensive against campus violence, Lucey made common cause with Clem Zablocki on abortion. Months before the primary, Zablocki had threatened to vote for a write-in candidate rather than choose between the two New Politics liberals.[130] That summer, however, a federal district court struck down Wisconsin's restrictive abortion laws. While New Politics liberals were delighted, Milwaukee's working-class and Catholic Democrats scarcely shared their sentiment. Breaking from Peterson and staying with his coreligionists, Lucey announced his opposition to abortion.[131] Capitalizing on their shared issue, Lucey finagled a well-publicized "private" meeting with Zablocki.[132] Armed with this "unofficial" endorsement, Lucey toured Milwaukee's Polish festivals with America's former ambassador to Poland, John Gronouski.[133]

The combination of law and order, abortion, and ethnic politics proved the difference. With Milwaukee County Democrats voting for Lucey, the former lieutenant governor took nearly 60 percent of the vote.[134] More than a simple loss in his maiden electoral campaign, Peterson's travails represented a microcosm of the problems the New Politics confronted. In Wisconsin, for example, Democrats were competitive if and only if they captured two-thirds of the Milwaukee County vote.[135] In much the same way, liberals across the nation still required the votes of urban, working-class Democrats.

While New Politics liberals had wrested control of the Wisconsin Democratic Party away from Clem Zablocki and his constituents, these voters remained central to winning an election. Peterson and his New Politics allies found that it was one thing to gain control of a party's apparatus but quite another to win a general election or to govern.

2

Revolt of the Joe Six-Packs

Charles Stenvig and the White Ethnic Revolt

In 1970, Milwaukee's white ethnics ended Donald Peterson's electoral career. Ironically, ten years prior, these very same Beertown southsiders proved crucial in another hotly contested campaign with national implications. In 1960, JFK and Hubert Humphrey squared off in the Wisconsin primary. Unlike 1970, when Peterson ignored working-class Poles, Kennedy and Humphrey vied for these voters.[1] With little policy differences separating the two, Catholic Democrats opted for their coreligionist. As in 1968, Humphrey also came up short in 1960. Proving their significance, white ethnics made the difference in all three elections, 1960, 1968, and 1970. New Politics liberals, nevertheless, simply discarded them.

For decades, the North's white working class served as the New Deal coalition's linchpin. Dominating organized labor and nonunion blue-collar jobs, white ethnics brought their unions' heft and manpower to the Democratic Party. Hailing from Eastern and Southern Europe, by 1970 upward of forty million white ethnic Americans lived in fifty-eight scattered industrial cities across the Northeast and the industrial Midwest.[2] Alternately called *blue-collar* or the overly generic *working-class,* by the late 1960s white ethnics suffered from an identity crisis.[3]

Spawned from economic threats, burgeoning crime, and an indifferent Democratic Party, this group's existential predicament helped produce a conservative political realignment. One leading Italian-American activist captured his community's popular sentiment toward the major political parties: "Nobody has done anything for ethnics since Social Security."[4] When liberals offered an ally, Hubert Humphrey, unions rallied to the party of FDR. In the months prior to the 1968 election, unions registered 4.6 million voters, delivered 115 million pamphlets, founded 638 phone banks, and dispatched 72,000 canvassers and 94,000 Election Day volunteers.[5]

Charles Stenvig (courtesy Minnesota Historical Society)

Though organized labor possessed proven clout, liberals deemed it re-
dundant. As far as New Politics activists were concerned, a new coalition of
the educated middle class, intellectuals, minorities, youth activists, and the
elderly promised to free Democrats from a reactionary working class. The
economist and political gadfly John Kenneth Galbraith termed the group
a "sociological artifact" of the past. Claiming that "intellectual" laborers
already outnumbered the working class by nearly eight million, Galbraith
predicted that middle-class professionals would soon dominate the American workforce and electorate. Meanwhile, according to him: "Trade unions
[would] retreat, more or less permanently, into the shadows."[6]

It was not just Galbraith proffering these opinions. In one of the best-
selling books of 1970, *Future Shock,* Alvin Toffler declared that Americans had managed "to throw off the yoke of manual labor" and reduce the
working class to a relic of the past.[7] Certain intellectuals not only convinced
themselves that white-collar workers outnumbered blue-collar laborers;
they routinely pronounced the entire white working class racist. Following
this meme to its logical extreme, many liberals equated working-class issues,
such as law and order, with pure and simple bigotry. The New Politics activist Adam Walinsky put it bluntly: "There are now only two identifiable
ethnic groups—blacks and those who hate them."[8] In the late 1960s and
early 1970s, New Politics liberals made it clear which category they placed
white ethnics in.

The Law-and-Order Issue

By the 1960s, African American males had become the face of violent urban crime.[9] In this way, racism and bigotry surely constituted a significant
part of the gumbo that was the law-and-order issue. Fear of crime and lawlessness, however, scarcely emanated from bigotry alone. After all, between
1960 and 1980, violent crime jumped by 367 percent.[10] More specifically,
from 1965 to 1970 crimes against property increased by 147 percent, violent felonies jumped by 126 percent, while the numbers of murder, rape,
and assault doubled.[11] Adding to the problem of spiraling crime rates, the
white working class could not afford to flee crime-ridden neighborhoods for
the suburbs. Thus, not only did crime rise precipitously, but working-class
neighborhoods were also far more likely to be at the wave's epicenter than
were middle-class suburbs.

While New Politics activists pursued their issues, they ignored working-class concerns about escalating lawlessness. Indeed, even establishment liberals remained remarkably obtuse. Until the later 1960s, Democrats, generally, rejected crime statistics as false. Even when they finally admitted the reality of spiraling criminality, they did so in a patronizing fashion. Attorney General Nicholas Katzenbach told women who were "terrified by the possibility of being raped by a stranger" that they should hardly be concerned since "the odd[s] of that happening may be about the same as those of being hit by lightning."[12]

Frustrated by liberals' casual attitude toward crime, riots, and student protests, working-class voters looked for alternatives. In 1969, the white working class staged a political revolt, making it the Year of the Cop. Responding to rising crime rates and a groundswell of disaffected voters, Charles Stenvig, Sam Yorty, and Frank Rizzo left the police force and won the mayor's offices in Minneapolis, Los Angeles, and Philadelphia. Key to the Year of the Cop were working-class whites who turned out in droves for these law-and-order political novices. After decades of loyalty to the Roosevelt coalition, they opted for backlash politics.

No one event encapsulates this phenomenon more than the 1969 Minneapolis mayoral race. In a city noted for its progressive impulses and activist mayors, police detective Charlie Stenvig's successful mayoral campaign signaled the extent of the blue-collar backlash against liberalism. Through making liberal permissiveness on crime and protests a signature issue, Stenvig defeated two liberal opponents. Scarcely a flash in the pan, the cop-cum-mayor ruled the local political scene for nearly a decade.

It is hardly an accident that Stenvig emerged in the very state and region that also produced Eugene McCarthy. The senator's political life encapsulates the middle-class and educated ethos of the New Politics and helps explain the white working-class revolt. Born in rural Minnesota and educated by Catholic monks, McCarthy entered the Benedictine order. Following his expulsion owing to "intellectual pride," he married and founded a utopian commune. After a brief stint as a sociology professor at the College of St. Thomas, McCarthy entered electoral politics.[13]

In 1964, LBJ effectively blocked the rising star's path to national office by choosing a Minnesotan, Hubert Humphrey, as vice president. After this disappointing turnabout, the senator did what came naturally: moralizing. In a fashion similar to the opposition of his hero, Thomas More, to the power-hungry and corrupt King Henry VIII, McCarthy challenged Johnson. Inspired by his example, New Politics activists organized and took control of

Minnesota's Democratic Farmer-Labor Party (DFL) and state and local parties nationally. With the DFL in middle-class liberal hands, soon the white working class looked for alternatives.

During the 1970s, Minnesota's vehicle for blue-collar liberalism, the DFL, lost touch with its working-class base, a development that reveals the extent of a larger and national trend. In 1969, New Politics liberals captured precinct caucuses in Minneapolis and denied old-line DFL'ers their customary places at nominating conventions.[14] Thus, the party's backbone, organized labor, was no longer the dominant voice. As a result, working-class issues such as crime, student protesters, and race riots were further consigned to the margins, which reduced the DFL's hold over its blue-collar constituency.

In this milieu, Stenvig's career neatly encapsulates how and why liberals lost the white working class. During the 1970s, liberals forsook working-class whites. In turn, working-class whites slowly abandoned the Democratic Party. As a nonaligned bloc of voters, they searched for a political movement that responded to their issues and concerns. Until Ronald Reagan appeared on the national scene, the movements they drifted toward self-destructed: an assassin's bullet paralyzed George Wallace, a jury indicted Spiro Agnew, and Congress forced Richard Nixon's resignation.

Minnesota's Political Culture

Though the mere mention of Minnesota and the DFL conjures images of crusading liberals, the state's political character is best described as egalitarian, cussedly independent, and culturally traditional. Directly descended from the avowedly antiestablishment Non-Partisan League, the DFL used Minnesota's egalitarian political culture to attract blue-collar support for its activist agenda.

In 1922, for example, the DFL's gubernatorial candidate, Magnus Johnson, was derided by elites as a dumb and ignorant "dirt farmer." Just as Stenvig used rhetoric fifty years later, Johnson used elite derision to his political advantage. Standing in a pile of manure as he spoke to farmers, he owned elite ridicule and turned it back on his opponents.[15] Through such cleverness, DFL'ers used the state's egalitarian and populist political culture to attract the white working class.

Though working-class Minnesotans supported the DFL's social welfare, education, and labor legislation, they remained culturally traditional. A

1969 poll revealed that 88 percent of all Minnesotans expressed a "strong" belief in God, while 70 percent attended at least one church service within the last month.[16] The DFL might have dominated Minnesota politics for nearly two decades, but the party owed its success to its appeal to working-class sentiment. Once crime, riots, and the counterculture became a focal point of concern, it became the victim of these very same forces.

During the strife-ridden summer of 1967, in which race riots erupted across the country, Minneapolitans experienced the largest racial disturbance in their history. In the 1960s, the city's African American population had grown by 38 percent. Blacks, however, still constituted only 4.5 percent of the entire Twin City population.[17] On a warm July night, north Minneapolis, home to most of the region's twelve thousand black residents, exploded in violence. Over the course of two nights, black youths rioted and even controlled the area's main commercial thoroughfare, the ten-block Plymouth Avenue district.[18]

Sparked by two separate and unrelated incidents, the riot mirrored similar urban unrest in Detroit and Los Angeles. A white policeman's interference in a fight between two African American women (who were brawling over a wig) produced an angry crowd. The nascent disturbance metastasized when news that a white tavern owner had shot a black patron reached the mob.[19] With these events in mind, crowds of angry rioters roamed the Plymouth Avenue district, chucking rocks at police cars and setting fire to area businesses.[20] Unlike past race-related disturbances, "this time," police officials remarked, the rioters "stood up to us."[21] When firemen arrived to battle the blazes, rioters pelted them with rocks and bricks. As an eight-block stretch of Plymouth Avenue businesses burned, firemen refused to return.[22]

In response to the melee, Minnesota's governor, Harold LeVander, sent six hundred national guardsmen to the area with orders to "shoot looters on sight."[23] Tiny in comparison to Detroit or Watts, this race riot rocked white Minnesotans' belief that they were immune to racial violence. Indeed, for years Walter Mondale told his Senate colleagues: "No such thing could happen in Minnesota."[24] Shocked and humbled, Mondale, along with the rest of white Minnesota, realized that race relations were not as convivial as they imagined.

Throughout the 1960s the quintessential liberal, Arthur Naftalin, presided over Minneapolis. Popular and affable, the former college professor governed Minneapolis in the activist tradition of Hubert Humphrey. In 1969, after four consecutive two-year terms, he left office.[25] Though Naftalin ruled during an era of general prosperity, intermittent racial violence, spiraling crime rates, and student unrest had increasingly interrupted civic life. For instance, Betty Wood, a middle-aged housewife and working-class Minneapolitan, claimed that her family had resorted to "carr[ying] guns" from fear of crime.[26]

In the midst of this environment, and in the throes of a series of much-publicized demonstrations across the nation, the contest to replace Mayor Naftalin commenced. In a normal cycle, Naftalin's anointed successor would have been formidable. The year 1969, however, was anything but ordinary. In control of the DFL's nominating caucuses, New Politics activists tapped one of their own, Gerard Hegstrom.[27] A newcomer to politics, he lacked ties to organized labor and received no union endorsements.

Meanwhile, the Republican Party endorsed the Harvard-educated city council president, Dan Cohen. A thirty-two-year-old self-described liberal, Cohen practiced a brand of hardball politics that belied his young age. During his time as president of the Minneapolis City Council, that body had enjoyed its most productive years in recent history. Famous for his temper, Cohen routinely tongue-lashed reporters and nearly came to blows with city councilman Arne Carlson. Accusing his fellow Republican of "los[ing] his belly" for failing to support a strong open housing ordinance, Cohen ran the city council with a stern, yet decidedly liberal, hand.[28]

Despite his strong advocacy for civil rights, Cohen still locked horns with the city's black leadership. In 1967, Arthur Naftalin, Dan Cohen, and the president of the Minneapolis NAACP, Harry Davis, established a human rights commission. Because the body possessed broad enforcement and appointment powers, the NAACP scored a significant victory with its creation. The appointment process to fill the fifteen-member commission, however, resulted in a bruising public struggle pitting Davis against Cohen.

The controversy centered on Davis's appointment of Ronald Edwards to the commission. Popular with black youths, the young African American activist had developed a reputation as a radical. The combination of his radicalism and four misdemeanor convictions caused Cohen to balk at this appointment. Defiant, Davis called a news conference at which he boldly declared: "Dan Cohen, you are not the master, and we are not your niggers. . . . [*Pause.*] Dan, we're not your niggers."[29] Shaken by this turn of events, Cohen burst into tears during negotiations with black leaders. Despite the drama, Cohen won, and Edwards lost his commission seat.

In addition to Hegstrom and Cohen, the mayoral field featured eight other hopefuls. The most colorful contenders included Albert Falk, a homeless man who ran on a platform of panhandling rights.[30] In addition to Falk, the forty-one-year-old police detective Charlie Stenvig also announced his candidacy. With the slogan "Take the Handcuffs off the Police," Stenvig promised to stop the "hoodlums" by employing active policing that "doesn't wait for burning and looting": "[We'll] stop it before it starts."[31]

Tapping into popular sentiment, Stenvig, and millions of other Americans, had tired of race riots, student protesters, and their hyperbolic rhetoric. This anger was not merely confined to Spiro Agnew, George Wallace, and Ronald Reagan. None other than Groucho Marx captured the frustration that most Americans over thirty held toward the anarchic political scene: "I never thought the time would come when I'd be rooting for Nixon . . . [but] kids today are detestable."[32] With or without the Marx Brothers, as the only major candidate who staked his mayoral race on law and order Stenvig owned the major campaign issue.

Adding to the fire, in April 1969, the month of the mayoral primary, students in Minnesota, New York, California, South Carolina, and Massachusetts made headlines by capturing campus halls and instigating confrontations. At the University of Minnesota, students staged a protest to show support for an earlier demonstration.[33] Contemporaneous with events in Minneapolis, at Cornell University forty armed African American students seized a university hall to protest "racist attitudes."[34] And at the Atlanta University Center students held the board of trustees hostage to publicize their demands.[35]

With the student revolt nearing its apex, working-class whites expressed their resentments at the ballot box. Indeed, David Roe, state president of the Minnesota AFL-CIO, said there was "no question about it" that organized labor supported Stenvig because of university demonstrations.[36] Stenvig came honestly to his working-class resentment of student protesters, rioters, and liberal elites. Products of a cloistered world of weekly bridge games, Bible fellowship, and bowling leagues, Stenvig and his wife, Audrey, were prototypical Middle American squares.[37]

Reminiscent of a movie, the two met in high school on a double date (Charlie was with Audrey's friend). Audrey later explained that, when they married after Stenvig returned from a stint in the service, in their world she "was an old lady of 20."[38] Like their neighbors, the Stenvigs had tastes that were modest and confined to what they knew. Because Charlie hated "anything fancy," a typical Stenvig dinner consisted of hamburgers and French fries.[39] After earning a college degree from Augsburg College under the GI Bill, Stenvig took a job as a policeman for the University of Minnesota; one year later he joined the Minneapolis police force.[40]

Fit and trim at the age of forty-one, Stenvig had a full head of snow-white hair that testified to his years as a police detective and labor leader. Head of the 770-member Police Officers Federation of Minneapolis, he was already a well-known union activist.[41] As a labor leader, he perfected his populist brand of political leadership. Claiming to speak for the average policeman against a "clique" of elites leading the force, he infused the union with greater militancy. For instance, in the winter of 1967, he led a march on City Hall to present a list of wage demands. When those grievances were not met, off-duty policemen and firemen formed an "informational-bannering line" effectively sealing off City Hall.

Though, by law, policemen and firefighters were forbidden to strike, the Stenvig-led protest had all the trappings of a traditional labor dispute. For instance, the Teamsters refused to cross the bannering line, which effectively blocked the delivery of fuel oil to City Hall. From the very start, Stenvig had intended to use the Teamsters to "freeze out" the city and gain wage concessions.[42] After weeks of this standoff, the sheriff's department forcibly moved the bannering line so drivers could deliver fuel to City Hall. As the driver prepared his delivery, Stenvig threatened: "I don't know who you are but you are going to get your head knocked."[43] A union tough guy, Stenvig brought his brand of rough-and-tumble politics from the labor hall to a face-off against the liberal establishment.

In the midst of a season filled with campus unrest and violence, Stenvig's law-and-order message resonated. Most observers, however, gave him no chance of even finishing second in the open primary. Surprising everyone, Stenvig captured nearly 50 percent of the vote and carried nine of the city's thirteen wards, including former DFL strongholds.[44] Indeed, the only real contest was over second place. With Cohen narrowly capturing second on the strength of traditionally Republican areas, Hegstrom finished third. Adding to the ignominy, the Democrat failed to carry his own neighborhood ward. The two wards he did carry were, in predictable New Politics fashion, almost exclusively composed of university students and professors.[45]

Buoyed by favorable political conditions and strong working-class support, Stenvig faced a liberal, Dan Cohen, in June's general election. "Charlie" or "Chuck"—never Charles—hit the campaign trail. Punctuating the end of a sentence with the aphorism "isn't that right," as in, "The mayor

is the Police Commissioner of Minneapolis, isn't that right?" Stenvig promised: "The mayor's main job is being the head of the police department."[46]
Rather than copy George Wallace, Stenvig consciously avoided bigoted
appeals.[47] He said of minorities and public disturbances: "I've seen those
demonstrators and I've sometimes had to look awfully hard for a black
American among them. . . . There are very few black Americans doing it and
I don't think the ones that are are a fair representation of the black Americans of Minneapolis."[48]

In Minneapolis, Wallace-style racial appeals amounted to a political li-
ability. During the 1968 presidential race, area unions had waged such a
massive negative campaign against the Alabaman that they had created a
lasting negative impression.[49] Moreover, according to polls, 90 percent of
Minnesotans believed that African Americans favored nonviolent protest,
while a large plurality, 44 percent, preferred total racial integration.[50] Realizing Wallace's negative appeal in Minnesota, Cohen called Stenvig "nothing more than George Wallace in Minneapolis clothes."[51] Stenvig, however,
disassociated himself from the governor. He not only refused Wallace's offer
to campaign on his behalf; he also said of Alabama's most renowned citizen:
"Both George Wallace and I believe in strict law enforcement . . . but after
that our views separate."[52]

In addition to his antipathy for Wallace, Stenvig also cultivated black
support. For example, Richard Parker, an African American, was an early backer who became a member of the mayor's inner circle.[53] Moreover,
Stenvig had forged personal relationships with minorities prior to his political career. In 1963, he saved an African American infant's life with mouth-
to-mouth resuscitation. The child's mother, who campaigned for Stenvig,
regularly told the media: "He wasn't a racist when he put his lips to my
baby's!"[54] When a constituent asked him about accepting a black neighbor,
Stenvig claimed he would welcome one because "we're all brothers and sis-
ters under the skin."[55] Owing to his moderate rhetoric, Stenvig polled well
in African American wards.

Rather than blaming African Americans for crime and student protests,
Stenvig assailed suburban, liberal elites, whom he claimed controlled City
Hall and ignored "the good, honest, law-abiding citizens."[56] Promising to
undermine "the power structure from Wayzata" (a wealthy western Minneapolis suburb), Stenvig's populist appeals were class based rather than racial.[57] In this vein, he directed his complaints at City Hall's urban renewal
projects, which transformed working-class neighborhoods.[58] As Stenvig saw

it, suburban liberals levied taxes they did not pay to alter neighborhoods they did not live in.[59]

Using populist class resentments to his advantage, Stenvig railed against unelected elites. He accused the heads of the Dayton department stores, the *Minneapolis Star* and *Tribune,* and the city's leading law firms of badmouthing his candidacy because they were "afraid they'll have a working man as mayor."[60] These ad hoc allegations merely reinforced the notion that a Stenvig candidacy threatened an established order his working-class backers had grown to disdain. On the eve of the election, one Minneapolitan correctly predicted: "Stenvig will be elected, certainly not because he is a better candidate with better qualifications, but because voters are sick and tired of endless endorsements and other tactics used by the Establishment."[61]

Tapping into this sentiment, Stenvig claimed: "People are sick and tired of politicians and intellectuals. . . . They [the people] want an average workingman from the community to represent them—and that's me."[62] In this way, he fomented populist sentiment. Consequently, in a debate staged before the Teamsters, which refused to endorse a candidate, one observer claimed: "[The] labor union made it clear . . . that Charles Stenvig is its choice."[63] Cohen might have earned organized labor's *official* endorsement, but the rank and file wanted Stenvig, a sentiment that he transformed into a foot-powered organization of nearly one thousand volunteers.[64]

Despite Stenvig's overwhelming primary victory, Cohen believed that the combination of Republican and DFL votes could carry him to victory. Reaching out to any potential allies, he sought and received the DFL's endorsement. Moreover, in a highly unusual move, President Nixon invited him to the White House, endorsed his candidacy, and termed Stenvig a force of "reaction and extremism."[65] Armed with the GOP, the DFL, and the president's endorsement, Cohen possessed everything except passion and followers. In contrast, Stenvig's campaign coordinator, a homemaker, Marion Olson, said of the organization she built: "It wasn't the money, it was something money couldn't buy . . . dedicated manpower . . . from people who wanted good government so bad they gave up television, their bedroom slippers, and everything else and went out day after day knocking on doors."[66]

The national attention and local scrutiny produced the biggest voter turnout for a mayoral election since 1949. In spite of Cohen's superior financing and endorsements, he got steamrolled. With no professional staff and virtually no paid media, Stenvig won 60 percent of the vote. Running strongest in precincts won by Barry Goldwater in 1964, the mayor-elect also polled well in working-class and DFL strongholds; Stenvig won 68 percent of the vote in wards with average or below incomes and nearly 70 percent of all union ballots. While city elites staggered in disbelief, one Stenvig supporter understood the victory: "There are few times when the average guy can kick the Establishment in the teeth. . . . Chuck gave us a chance."[67]

On the night of his election, Stenvig established his administration's populist tone. In what he described as his first official act as mayor, Stenvig named his chief adviser: "God, and don't you forget it."[68] Though God's appointment to the Stenvig administration probably struck many as cornpone, the sentiment resounded with Minnesotans. According to one pollster: "Minnesotans [were] almost of one voice in declaring their belief in God and in Jesus Christ."[69] More important than God, however, was voters' desire for law and order. One machinist expressed this common sentiment by asking the newly elected mayor to "start jailing some of them guys who are breaking the law, regardless of race, creed, or color."[70] An African American watchman echoed this refrain, claiming: "All should be treated equally with no distinction. Anyone who breaks the law should be prosecuted."[71]

Though Stenvig rolled to victory, the city's political powers hardly welcomed him to the office. Denied the mayorship since 1959, Republicans hungered for power. With or without that office, since the GOP controlled ten of the council's thirteen seats it intended to run the city.[72] Eager to disprove his critics and actually govern, Stenvig told a gathering of reporters: "I'm not stupid, I'm not irrational, and I'm not goofy. . . . I'm going to think about a lot of things before I make any statements. And then you can see how goofy I am."[73] In pursuit of this, Stenvig reached out to Arthur Naftalin, and the outgoing mayor defied tradition by extensively cooperating with the mayor-elect.[74]

Though Stenvig consorted with Naftalin, he was in no mood to jettison his populist and antiestablishment ways. During the transition period, for example, he refused a luncheon invitation from the Minnesota Executive Organization, a forum composed of influential business elites. Instead, he attended a Police Federation meeting.[75] Skipping over the tried and true, he staffed his administration with campaign aides, Richard Parker and Thomas Ogdahl, who boasted criminal records.[76] Predictably, he ignored the ensuing criticism. The episode revealed a tendency to disregard those who assailed his judgment while listening only to his populist supporters.

Stenvig scarcely needed to cultivate his populist image. Living in a neat, three-bedroom ranch house, similar to everyone else's in his south Minneapolis neighborhood, the mayor remained a regular Joe. At his inaugural ball, he broke out his drum set, played with the band, and reveled in the attention.[77] In his inaugural address, the newly minted mayor promised "action." Decrying the "theory, flowery speeches, and news releases" of former administrations, he eschewed public relations and promised to solve problems without the adornments.[78]

In contrast to what his detractors claimed, Stenvig offered an affirmative agenda. Focused on the needs of working-class constituents, he also confronted a burgeoning fiscal crisis and sought to reduce taxes. In pursuit of this, he traveled to Washington, DC, and various national venues to lobby for his program. Within weeks of assuming office, he met with high-level Washington officials and Vice President Spiro Agnew.[79] At the National Congress of Cities, he lobbied for the federal funding of local police departments. During one debate, he connected union wages for police with proper law enforcement.[80]

Moving beyond his pleas for federal funding of local police, Stenvig urged Minnesota's governor, Harold LeVander, to call a special legislative session to address an urban fiscal crisis. Working with the AFL-CIO's state chief, David Roe, he backed a letter-writing campaign to convince the governor of the special session's necessity. Maintaining, as did the leaders of St. Paul and Duluth, that urban Minnesota failed to receive a fair share of the state's sales tax receipts, Stenvig urged a revised funding formula.[81] Under Stenvig's leadership, Minnesota's mayors and city councils made a united plea for a special session to redress the issue.[82]

Ignoring Stenvig's substantive activities, city council leaders accused the mayor of "hollow political rhetoric" that spawned "negative reaction[s]" against progressive ideas.[83] Angry, Stenvig claimed that he intended to revive the city and attract working- and middle-class families to live in Minneapolis so the metropolis was not reduced to "a core city with insurmountable problems."[84] Within seven months of assuming office, Stenvig and the city council were reduced to little more than finger-pointing and shouting at one another through the press.[85]

Despite, or perhaps because of, this gridlock, Stenvig commanded much popular support. One poll taken six months into his term revealed that 65 percent of Minneapolitans thought Stenvig was doing either a "fair, good, or outstanding" job.[86] More significantly, when the mayor and the city's establishment locked horns, the public usually sided with Stenvig. One official complained that, in comparison to Naftalin, who "you could say anything you wanted about," "if you utter one unkind word about Stenvig, our phone will ring its head off."[87]

Not confined to Minneapolis, Stenvig's popularity reached to Hollywood. The Academy Award–winning screenwriter Stirling Silliphant became so fascinated with the story that he started production on a movie based on Stenvig's life. Producers planned to cast the tough guy Lee Marvin in the role of Stenvig. Owing to Marvin's initial curiosity, several major studios expressed "deep interest" in the project.[88] Though the biopic fell through, Stenvig, obviously, had captured the public's fancy.

Owing to his ongoing fracas with the council members, Stenvig turned to acts of symbolic governance. Issuing proclamations declaring "Day of Prayer," "Bible Week," and "United States Day," he also supervised the policing of antiwar demonstrations.[89] During the October 1969 Moratorium Day demonstration against the Vietnam War, Stenvig personally managed police patrols and even arrested several protesters, a scene captured by television cameras and replayed on the nightly news.[90]

In the same vein, he vetoed a resolution declaring "Peace Action Day," explaining it was backed by socialists.[91] As if socialists were not enough, Stenvig refused to join thirty-seven other Minnesota mayors in signing a "Declaration of World Citizenship" because, as he said, "I'm a U.S. citizen not a world citizen."[92] Though the *Minneapolis Tribune* castigated Stenvig for his "negative influence," these shenanigans undoubtedly delighted his working-class constituents.[93]

In the winter of 1971, Stenvig prepared for what observers predicted would be a tough reelection campaign. Armed with 85 percent approval ratings and a loyal cadre of supporters, he appeared formidable.[94] Despite his stratospheric approval ratings, the DFL remained confident that its candidate, Harry Davis, could unseat the mayor. A school board member, son of a Teamster, and director of the Golden Gloves boxing program, Davis seemed, in many ways, an ideal choice.

Told by Hubert Humphrey, "Someday you may be mayor of Minneapolis," Davis plunged into politics.[95] In addition to this august beginning, prominent businessmen so disliked Stenvig they gave the challenger sizable campaign contributions. Smart, talented, and blessed by the Minneapolis establishment, Davis faced one significant hurdle—he was black.[96]

Regardless of Minnesota's reputation for racial comity, the race's signature issue, busing, kept Davis from running a color-blind campaign. As in every other major American city of the early 1970s, busing and school desegregation emerged as hot-button issues in Minneapolis. Months before the mayoral election, in November 1970, Davis, along with a unanimous school board, designed and presented their desegregation plan. Integrating students through "pairing" economically similar and contiguous neighborhood schools, the "school-pairing" plan was intended to minimize fears.

Instead of quelling anger, the school-pairing plan outraged the white working class. Partially motivated by racial bias, parents also rebelled because their neighborhoods, not middle- and upper-class areas, were the first scheduled for integration. Called "Pearl Harbor for the Minneapolis School Board" by the *Minneapolis Star,* the plan sparked immense discord.[97] One school board meeting, which allowed parents to query board members, lasted from 5:00 P.M. to 5:00 A.M.—despite a three-minute limit per questioner.[98]

Although his popularity emanated from a perception that his populist views came from the heart, Stenvig remained keenly attuned to public opinion. His critics claimed, with validity, that the mayor formed many opinions almost entirely in response to popular opinion. Even Stenvig admitted: "If I get enough pressure, I bend."[99] Sensing the political winds, he seized on the school-pairing controversy as his ticket to reelection. That the school-pairing plan was a modest proposal to avoid court-ordered desegregation was irrelevant; Stenvig knew his base and used the issue to bludgeon Harry Davis.

Realizing that Davis faced an uphill struggle, the Minneapolis business community and high-profile DFL leaders ardently supported his election. As a result, Davis outspent both Stenvig and his Republican opponent, Bruce Rasmussen. In raising $52,000, Davis nearly tripled the Stenvig campaign's spending from 1969. In addition, when Davis campaigned in white working-class neighborhoods, Congressman Don Fraser and Hubert Humphrey walked the wards with him to personally introduce the newcomer to wary constituents.

Despite Humphrey's personal backing for his opponent, Stenvig earned organized labor's wholehearted support. For the first time in the party's history, labor officially backed a non-DFL nominee for mayor. Owing to "pressure from the rank and file," the Teamsters announced its endorsement four months before the primary.[100] Following the Teamsters, the Building and Construction Trade Council, the United Labor Committee, the Central Labor Union, and the Local, State, County, and Municipal Employees Federation also endorsed the mayor.[101] Of all the large and significant unions, only the staunchly pro-DFL United Auto Workers (UAW) refused to back Stenvig. Rather than endorse Davis, the UAW remained neutral.

Though Stenvig's job performance accounted for some of labor's resounding support, one labor leader privately admitted: "Let's face it. The color thing had a lot to do with it."[102] Adding to Davis's racial barrier was the school-pairing issue. Though the mayor's opposition to desegregation surely emanated from racial bigotry, it also stemmed from antiestablishment populism.

One leading labor leader captured the essence of this populist reaction to school pairing: "The guy next door [who] works like a dog all day . . . comes home and worries all night—taxes, mortgages, wages, the whole bit. So he picks up a paper or he watches TV and there's some big shot telling him what to do. Quite frankly he resents it."[103] Put simply, Stenvig and his working-class constituents resented suburban elites gentrifying neighborhoods they did not live in and desegregating schools their children did not attend. The fact that school pairing called for racial integration merely fueled the populist revolt.

Despite stratospheric poll numbers and organized labor's endorsements, Stenvig remained "scared to death of getting eliminated in the primary."[104] He need not have been. The Republican nominee, Bruce Rasmussen, was a candidate in name only. Davis outspent Rasmussen by nearly ten to one, while Stenvig outpaced the GOP nominee by a twelve-to-one margin.[105] While Rasmussen penned lengthy press releases replete with footnotes, Davis pounded the pavement, shook hands at factory gates, and hosted coffee parties. Unlike his Republican rival, the polished DFL nominee ran a professional and organized campaign that all but guaranteed a Stenvig-Davis general election face-off.[106]

In contrast to Davis, Stenvig did not even campaign until the week before the April primary and, except for one speech, never responded to his opponents' criticisms. While the mayor was relatively quiet, his organization was busy pounding over 8,000 yard signs into the ground, in comparison to Davis's 3,000 and Rasmussen's 150.[107] In the weeks prior to the general election, Stenvig's army of volunteers coalesced and formed the T-Party, which fielded candidates for various city offices. Led by Stenvig, who captured 63 percent of the vote and won all the city's thirteen wards, ten T-Party candidates also advanced to the general election.[108]

Stenvig's overwhelming showing in the primary devastated any hopes Davis had of recapturing the DFL's working-class vote. In the aftermath, the only reply a humbled and confused Davis could manage was a meek: "We thought we were a lot closer."[109] New Politics liberals, who still controlled the DFL, were mesmerized and confused by Stenvig's popularity. Indeed, the DFL nominee complained that, though he met "people all over the city who think the way I do," the mayor's popularity left him "more and more confused."[110] In the weeks leading to the general election, polls showed the mayor's support at 75 percent, while Davis struggled to reach 25 percent.

In the face of such dismal prospects, and against an opponent who refused to campaign, Davis goaded the mayor. At a Citizen's League breakfast meeting, the challenger said of his opponent: "I wonder if anyone in this room will admit that the man who sits in the mayor's chair is totally incompetent."[111] Unfortunately for him, Stenvig's competence was never a campaign issue.

Rather than the mayor's competence, desegregation and other assorted racial issues dominated the five-week general election campaign. Eventually, Stenvig agreed to five debates. In these venues, the mayor relied on bombast and evasion, which foreshadowed his increasingly erratic behavior. Equating the pairing plan and desegregation with mandatory busing, which was not an apt comparison, Stenvig played to his constituency's fears. In fact, during one debate he claimed that, if the judiciary ordered busing, "[he] would override the court's order," a power clearly beyond the bounds of a mayor.[112] Reminiscent of George Wallace, Stenvig played to racial fears and electrified his supporters, who at the conclusion of one debate spit on Davis.

Stenvig, however, was not the only candidate employing racial politics. Davis realized that, barring any surprises, his campaign was a lost cause. Though both major newspapers endorsed him, a *Minneapolis Star* poll predicted a Stenvig victory by a three-to-one margin. Aside from the debates, Stenvig employed a "Rose Garden" strategy wherein he campaigned by vetoing city council expenditures and largely remained silent. Frustrated by the mayor's refusal to engage him in a war of words, Davis asked a reporter: "What can we do to spark up this campaign?"[113] With the DFL coalition in shambles, Davis's only hope was to provoke Stenvig into committing a colossal error.

Known for moderation and even temper, Davis was ill suited for the role of campaign bulldog and bomb thrower. Nonetheless, in the campaign's final days, he accused Stenvig of racially motivated sins. Labeling the mayor "a lawbreaker . . . [for] condoning the brutality and sadism of some of our policemen," Davis accused his opponent of encouraging police brutality.[114] On the heels of this charge, he called the mayor a bigot, telling a crowd of supporters: "If you condone the people who misuse and abuse other people, then you have to be a racist."[115] Soon after, a Davis surrogate claimed that police dogs were trained to attack "high visibility" African Americans. Not stopping there, he compared Stenvig to Bull Connor, the legendary bigot and buffoon of civil rights lore.

Despite these accusations, there was little election night suspense. Building on white working-class support, Stenvig also captured the white-collar and professional vote en route to earning 71 percent of the vote.[116] The desegregation issue not only turned the mayoral race into a rout; it transformed the normally staid school board elections. Following Stenvig's lead, the T-Party's school board candidates, who opposed school pairing, swept to victory. Invoking Stenvig, T-Party nominees Marilyn Borea and Philip Olson said of their victory: "We feel the unheard voice of the public is now heard. We will function for the public by being responsible representatives."[117]

Despite the lopsided results, the 1971 campaign season marked a turning point for Stenvig and his nascent working-class movement. Demagoguing school pairing became a harbinger of the mayor's increasing unpredictability, irresponsible political maneuvering, and outright corruption. As mayor, Stenvig surely understood that desegregation was a fait accompli but that busing for integration was not necessarily a foregone conclusion. Indeed, Earl Larson, the federal judge charged with implementing the Minneapolis desegregation plan, was amenable to compromise. Larson, like Stenvig, came from a working-class background and graduated from Twin City public schools.[118] With him overseeing desegregation, the city was poised to integrate its public schools with minimal controversy.

Rather than provide leadership and quietly implement a fair desegregation plan, Stenvig opted for obstruction. Thereafter, his political career devolved into a farce. In his second term, his behavior, which had always been unorthodox, morphed into the realm of the bizarre. For the next two years, he alternately planned a run for governor and foreign adventures, until, in a fit of anger, he quit. Sadly, the maverick politician, known for his "just-plain-Chuck" stances, eventually used his public office for private gain.

In the winter of 1973, while the state legislature debated bills of considerable importance to the city, Stenvig planned an eighteen-day tour of Asia. Working with a local travel agency, he agreed to recruit travelers and act as an "assistant guide" in return for an all-expenses-paid trip. By soliciting trip customers on letters printed on the mayor's official stationery, Stenvig violated the very code of ethics he had signed into law two years prior.[119] After weeks of pressure from the city council and newspapers, he finally backed out of the venture. This episode signaled the start of a new behavioral pattern. Indeed, a city councilman presciently said of the "new" Stenvig: "The manner in which the mayor conducts himself is typified by the way he handled this. It's the same old thing. What's in it for me?"[120]

Increasingly erratic, Stenvig slowly lost working-class support. Consequently, labor leaders, who had been cowed by the mayor's popularity, criticized him for aligning himself with "ding-a-lings" and "reactionaries."[121] One early labor supporter said of Stenvig: "I don't mind if Charlie wants to listen to God. . . . But when he got God and the T-Party confused—well that was the end of it."[122] Specifically, labor leaders believed that a leading T-Party activist and conservative radio personality, Paul Helm, possessed too much influence with the mayor's office. During the United Farm Worker's grape boycott, one labor activist saw Helm taunt picketers by eating grapes. Thus, when Stenvig appointed the shock jock to a city post, the labor leader called it "the last thing we ever could stomach."[123]

In 1973, with his political fortunes in steep decline, the DFL stopped Stenvig's bid for a third term. In tandem with their leader, the T-Party also lost its school board seats and, with them, the desegregation battle.[124] As if losing were not enough, Stenvig resigned as mayor prior to his rival's inauguration. Citing the necessity of political "unity," he shocked city leadership with the abrupt resignation. Obviously worn down, Stenvig told council members: "I kind of feel, maybe, that I won't have a hard time getting this [resignation] accepted up here."[125]

Out of office, Stenvig joined the Republican Party in an attempt to revive his political career. At his coming-out party, he joined another recent Republican convert, Texas governor John Connally, at a St. Paul fund-raiser.[126] After years of attacking both parties, the partisan gloves and right-wing rhetoric fit Stenvig well. Explaining why he joined the GOP, he said: "We're all conservatives . . . and I'm not ready to pack my grip and take off because the super liberals with their super social welfare state are about ready to take over in this state."[127]

Running as a Republican, Stenvig sought a seat in the Minnesota state legislature. With his district located in the heart of his working-class neighborhood, Stenvig's victory seemed assured. Not only had he lived in south Minneapolis his entire life, but for three consecutive elections these blue-collar voters overwhelmingly supported him. Even in his unsuccessful 1973 race, Stenvig took these particular wards by a two-to-one margin. More importantly, this race measured his ability to bring working-class support-

ers from the DFL into the GOP ranks. In this instance, however, Stenvig
loyalists refused to cross over and vote Republican. In a stunning turnabout, a twenty-nine-year-old DFL'er soundly defeated the former two-term
mayor.[128]

Though Stenvig did recapture the mayor's office in 1975, any thoughts
or ambitions of moving to a larger stage or building a "Charlie Party" were
over. Within months of his inauguration, Stenvig sought to "trade" his office for a white-collar job. Using his relationship with the millionaire Deil
Gustafson, the mayor wanted a high-paying position in return for handing
the office over to the DFL city council president, Louis DeMars.[129] Citing
family reasons, a bad back, and boredom with city politics, Stenvig said he
wanted "some security" until he could draw his pension.[130] Though he eventually called his "job search" off, the episode reveals the sorry state of his
career and ambitions.

From the time of his 1971 reelection, Stenvig engaged in a series of
outlandish political theatrics that undermined his movement. Instead of finagling a free trip to Asia or a cushy golden parachute, he could have reori-
ented DFL liberalism back toward its working-class roots or moved these
voters into the GOP's ranks. Instead, he self-destructed. As a result, New
Politics liberals in Minnesota were spared any substantial soul searching.
Freed from this, they dismissed the Stenvig phenomenon as a meaningless
product of personality and circumstance. Consequently, Minnesota liberals, who had founded the DFL on white working-class support, followed
a national trend that saw liberals eventually lose white ethnics to Ronald
Reagan.

3

Too Big to Fail

Fred Harris and the New Populism

The jailers released the prisoner so he could to testify before the Senate. Clad in a plaid short-sleeve shirt, the sixth-generation farmer explained to the Washington powerbrokers: "You know, justice is not always brought and set in your lap. Sometimes, you have to stand up and reach for it."[1] Wayne Cryts should know. In February 1981, he faced down a slew of federal agents as his ragtag band of five hundred farmers liberated thirty-one thousand bushels of soybeans from a Missouri grain elevator.[2]

Igniting this entire episode was a grain company's bankruptcy. When the Puxico, Missouri, granary went belly-up, legal possession of the soybeans stored in its silos went to the banks rather than the actual owners— the farmers. Outraged, Cryts organized a fleet of three hundred trucks to take back the cultivators' property. When authorities jailed him on criminal and civil contempt charges, Cryts became an instant folk hero. With farmers picketing his Arkansas prison and planning "tractor protests" in support of the "Bean Day" action, Congress hurriedly rewrote bankruptcy laws.[3] Altering the insolvency statutes, however, failed to stanch the tumult.

During the early 1980s, high interest rates and sluggish commodity prices led to record farm foreclosures.[4] In the face of such adverse circumstances, farmers organized similar Bean Day revolts. One midwestern agriculturalist captured the essence of this nascent populist movement: "We're trying to unite the farmer, the small businessman and the urban American and tell them if we don't survive . . . they won't either."[5]

At the apex of this rural upheaval, a presidential election commenced. Pitting a wealthy Californian against a rural midwesterner, the match seemed a perfect opportunity to coalesce a populist coalition. Despite Wayne Cryts and a record spate of farm foreclosures, Ronald Reagan demolished Walter

Fred R. Harris clasps LaDonna Harris's arm during his presidential campaign, summer of 1975 (courtesy Carl Albert Congressional Research and Studies Center)

Mondale. Even more puzzling, the Gipper won farmers and the white working class. So much for Bean Day.

Fifteen years earlier, in 1969, Charlie Stenvig had signaled a white ethnic revolt. Simultaneous with and part of this upheaval was a wider white working-class defection from the Democratic Party. While white ethnics hail from cities in the North and the industrial Upper Midwest, the largely Protestant and nonunionized white working class, like Wayne Cryts, reside in the rural farmlands, small towns, and downscale suburbs of the South, Appalachia, and the Lower Midwest. Scarcely a neat and tidy demographic category, the white working class is real, nonetheless.

From "Nascar Dads" to "Reagan Democrats," psephologists regularly create media-savvy synonyms for the white working class en masse. Such a large grouping can scarcely be one cohesive thing. Unlike white ethnics, the white working class rarely, if ever, engages in recognizable identity politics. Instead of hyphenated Americans, low Protestant churches and Dale Earnhardt Sr. are their cultural markers. Though they eschew ethnicity, these Middle Americans share a common heritage and cultural bond: Scotch-Irishness and Jacksonian populism.

Jacksonian Populism

Scotch-Irish is an Americanism denoting backcountry settlers' mixed heritage and region. As Protestants from Northern Ireland and the Scottish lowlands, they bore a cultural legacy remarkably distinct from their fellow British colonists.[6] Emigrating in great waves throughout the eighteenth century, the Scotch-Irish flowed into the Appalachian and Allegheny backcountry before settling in West Virginia, Kentucky, southern Indiana and Illinois, Tennessee, Missouri, Alabama, Mississippi, and Texas.[7] A "folk community" bound by poverty, pride, and militant Christianity, this immigrant grouping established the cultural basis for what became Jacksonian populism.[8]

Extending far beyond those professing Scotch-Irish heritage and their original settlements, Jacksonian populism became the default ethos of what is now called *Red America*. Though populism remains an inchoate and protean movement, the Jacksonian variety originated as an expression of Scotch-Irish cultural and political values—an instinct more than an ideology. Jacksonian populists have long claimed that "the powers that be are transgressing the nation's founding creed."[9] In this way, they constantly see large institutions (government or corporate) as inevitably aligned against the interests of the majority.

Spawning copycats throughout the twentieth and twenty-first centuries, Jacksonian populism remains vibrant. As the imagined tribune of the people, these populists employ a changeable political rhetoric with deep historic roots.[10] Thus, during the Great Depression, Roosevelt used the "forgotten man" to bring these white working-class voters to his standard. During the 1970s, however, Jacksonian populists changed their partisan loyalties out of a mix of economic and cultural concerns.

Unlike the 1890s or the 1930s economy, the postwar economy produced a relatively affluent working class. Indeed, between 1950 and 1970, Americans' real incomes doubled.[11] Sharing in this broad-based prosperity were working-class whites—so much so that, by 1970, they constituted the most prosperous mass working class in human history. Neither "Alfalfa Bill" Murray nor Tom Joad of populisms past, these Jacksonian populists had mortgages, college tuition bills, and time-shares.

This demographic did not switch political allegiances solely owing to affluence. Cleaving the white working class from the Democratic Party were what observers called the *social issues*. From the counterculture to antiwar protesters and spiraling crime, these noneconomic matters cut to the very heart of Jacksonian populism. Fiercely patriotic, culturally traditional, and hardworking, working-class whites looked on these cultural developments with increasing alarm and disdain.

Hardly revolutionists, Jacksonian populists were (and are) more akin to restorationists. Emphasizing "true" American values of self-reliance, equality, and individualism, these activists yearned for a return to first principles. More succinctly, they sought a social, economic, and political order that would justly reward their prized values. Thus, a populism that inveighs against or violates these traditional ethics is scarcely an authentic movement (to the Jacksonians).

Walter Mondale was not the first contemporary liberal to conflate material interests with pure-and-simple populism. In the 1970s, the boy wonder of Middle American liberalism learned a similar lesson. As a senator, two-time presidential candidate and Democratic National Committee chairman Fred Harris hoped to negate a white working-class revolt through the "new populism." He did not succeed. Not only did he wind up leaving politics, but white working-class identification with the Democratic Party also dropped twenty points during the 1970s.[12]

Harris's new populism was not the revival of the "plain people's" revolt that he imagined. Socialists with a pitchfork in the minds of many contemporary liberals and leftists, the original Populists were not collectivists or radicals in the European sense. An authentic protest movement of the heartland, they pleaded for massive, even extreme federal intervention in American economic life. These intrusions were designed to support small farmers who sought a "fairer share of the national plenty."[13] This was a movement for hardy, self-reliant, and landowning individualists. In other words, the lumpen proletariat need not apply.

Making matters worse for himself, Fred Harris embraced a New Politics critique of American society. Hardly neutral on the social issues, the senator virtually endorsed the very cultural issues driving working-class whites out of the party.

Fred Harris, Populism, and Corporate Power

Born in Depression-era southwestern Oklahoma, Harris grew up in a sharecropping family picking cotton and baling hay. Known by the residents of his native Cotton County as "Freddie," he attended the University of Oklahoma on scholarships, earning his law degree from that institution in 1954.[14] Two years later, at age twenty-six, he became the youngest member of the Oklahoma State Senate, where he combined burning ambition with a populist's sense of moral righteousness.

Bucking the advice of Oklahoma senator Robert Kerr, Harris fought against a turnpike bill he considered "harmful to the people."[15] Though he knew his stance would injure his 1962 bid for governor, Harris told a reporter: "I'm just going to have to forget about that and vote the way I think is right."[16] This was merely one example of his innate populist sensibility. He not only came from a former hotbed of nineteenth-century Populist activism; he practiced a generic brand of the creed before reaching Congress. In this way, he embodies the tensions and divides within twentieth-century liberalism, especially as it concerns the primary bugaboo of latter-day populists: corporate power.

While the Populists were relegated to the dustbin of history, their ideological successors—insurgent Progressives—carried the banner. Accusing large-scale corporations of undercutting Jeffersonian values, opportunistic politicians, such as Woodrow Wilson, seized on insurgent Progressivism's concern with monopoly power. Calling his program the New Freedom, Wilson equated his presidential campaign to "a second struggle for emancipation" to free people from the bonds of monopolies. In this way, he borrowed heavily from insurgent rhetoric and the Populist tradition.[17]

Though many Progressives shared Wilson's fear of corporate power, New Nationalists, led by Theodore Roosevelt, sought accommodation with the new corporate order through state regulation. In this vein, they emphasized federal regulation and state building to restrain corporate power. Despite Wilson's defeat of Roosevelt in the 1912 presidential election, New Nationalist progressivism carried the day. Indeed, Wilson's antitrust program was largely rhetorical; thus, the New Nationalists remained dominant during his administration and into the 1920s.[18]

The Great Depression revived arguments over how to deal with corporate bigness and monopolies. New Freedom progressives interpreted the Depression as the logical result of "monopolistic rigidities" in which trusts had collapsed purchasing power, producing economic calamity.[19] They sought antitrust laws to enhance competition and revive the economy. At the same time, latter-day New Nationalists regarded antitrust rhetoric as hopelessly anachronistic. To their minds, bigness was an inevitable outgrowth of modernity and a necessity for efficient mass production, which meant permanent government regulation of economic life.

Ever the pragmatic politician, Franklin Roosevelt pursued both policies simultaneously. The journalist Dorothy Thompson observed that Roosevelt's contradictory strategy reflected a conflict residing deep in "the bosom of the American people."[20] For Thompson, egalitarian impulses caused Americans to revere the yeoman farmer and small businessperson. Concurrent with this reverence of all things small, Americans also enjoyed the fruits of the inexpensive and abundant goods produced through large-scale corporate enterprises. Consequently, Roosevelt pursued inconsistent policies—regulation and antitrust—in chorus.

In this way, a certain ambiguity came to define New Deal liberalism's approach to corporate power. Tacitly accepting big business while romanticizing smallness, liberals found that their hearts and their heads remained divided on the issue. By the early postwar era, this haziness ebbed. Because American industrial efficiency and capacity helped defeat fascism and counter Soviet totalitarianism, most liberals came to accept corporate bigness as an essential component of waging a hot and cold war. Encapsulating this long peace was JFK. Weeks into his presidential term, Kennedy reassured an audience of nervous business moguls: "Far from being natural enemies,

Government and business are necessary allies."[21] From 1945 through the mid-1960s, as the Cold War simmered, the economy boomed, and real wages blossomed, liberals made their peace with corporations.

This long peace was undermined by events: Vietnam, the civil rights movement, and an inflationary economy. If Vietnam revealed the folly of global anticommunism, it also prompted the questioning of other Vital Center liberal assumptions. Prior to the mid-1960s, most liberals believed that incremental reform would solve the nation's racial divide and assorted maladies. The violence and white intransigence associated with the struggle for racial equality convinced many liberals to take a second and more critical look. Thus, New Politics activists, like Fred Harris, turned a jaded eye toward American society and conventional Jacksonian populist norms.

Examining the corporate structure of the economy, Harris, like the Populists and insurgent progressives before him, concluded that corporate bigness was inherently unfair, undemocratic, and in violation of Jeffersonian principles. As a result, his "new populism" was merely a media-savvy tag for a traditional strain of thought within liberalism. Unlike his Jacksonian populist forebears, he employed a New Politics worldview that rendered the new populism alien to the white working class.

Harris climbed to national prominence by succeeding Robert Kerr as Oklahoma's junior U.S. senator. An Oklahoma political icon, Kerr was born in a fourteen-square-foot windowless log cabin in Indian Territory. Reared with the frontier value of self-reliance, he founded a highly successful oil exploration outfit, Kerr-McGee. Later, he won a Senate seat, and by the early 1960s he was known as the "uncrowned King of the Senate."[22]

The senator's sudden death from a heart attack on New Year's Day 1964 sparked a succession struggle. Most Oklahoma Democrats favored the temporary appointment of Kerr's son to give the party time to prepare for a special election. Oklahoma's Democratic governor, J. Howard Edmondson, appointed himself to the seat, setting off a firestorm of protest. By offending the Kerrs, Edmondson lost in the primaries to a relatively obscure thirty-three-year-old state senator, Fred Harris, whom the late senator's family had endorsed.[23]

In years past, Harris would have been a prohibitive favorite in the general election. Oklahoma being a one-party state by tradition, registered Democrats outnumbered Republicans by almost four to one. Nonetheless, Dwight Eisenhower and Richard Nixon had captured the state by wide margins in three consecutive presidential elections. Moreover, the Republican

Senate candidate, Charles (Bud) Wilkinson, was a state hero. As head foot-ball coach at the University of Oklahoma, Wilkinson had won three na-tional championships, coached six unbeaten teams, and compiled the best record of any active coach in college football.[24]

While a Texas-Oklahoma college football game was hardly D-Day for most Americans, Wilkinson's success made him an Eisenhower-type figure in the Sooner state. Indeed, Democrats had unsuccessfully drafted him for the governor's race in years past, while Republicans had nominated him for the vice presidency. In January 1964, Wilkinson finally threw his hat into the political ring. After resigning from the University of Oklahoma and quit-ting the Democratic Party, he announced his candidacy for the U.S. Senate as a member of the GOP.[25] Telegenic, fair-haired, and boyishly handsome, Wilkinson became the presumptive frontrunner to succeed Kerr.

Believing that celebrity would earn him victory, Wilkinson ignored con-troversial issues.[26] In a normal political year, his gridiron success might have guaranteed success: however, 1964 was no typical election. Barry Gold-water's nomination assured that reality. While Goldwater ran stronger in Oklahoma than elsewhere, LBJ's landslide victory carried scores of marginal Democrats into office.[27] Among them was Harris, who won the right to fin-ish Kerr's term on the strength of Johnson's coattails.

At first glance, Harris seemed a natural replacement for the hardscrab-ble and affable Kerr. Son of a sharecropper and relentless, Harris made an instant splash. The *Los Angeles Times* termed him "a master of Senate pro-cedure," while Senate majority leader Mike Mansfield cooed: "No one in such a short while has assumed such great responsibility and carried it out so auspiciously."[28] Scrambling up the ladder, he chaired a subcommittee during his first two years and in 1966 earned a seat on the prestigious finance com-mittee.[29] So complete was his seduction of the Senate, liberals, and the na-tional media that the *New York Herald Tribune* proclaimed: "Fred Harris is recognized as the new Bob Kerr of the Senate."[30]

The senator's meteoric rise was no individual achievement. Credit also belongs to his wife, LaDonna Harris. His chief aide and fully vested partner, LaDonna cut a striking figure. A Comanche Indian, her dark complexion and exotic features compensated for her husband's utter homeliness. De-spite appearances, she was not just a pretty face; she regularly filled in for her husband by making public appearances and speeches and even answer-ing questions at press conferences.[31]

As though taken from the pages of a fairy-tale romance, LaDonna and

Fred Harris hailed from the same hometown, where they lived on adjacent farms. Though a small creek separated their homes, LaDonna's Comanche heritage meant that she was raised in a profoundly different cultural environment. Reared by her grandfather, a peyote medicine man, and traditional grandmother, LaDonna was schooled in Comanche culture and language.[32] Moreover, her ethnic background had political advantages in a state where many claimed Native American roots. Teasing audiences that she was a "wild Comanche" and that she had been tamed by her husband, she used her ancestry to their combined political benefit.

The young, intellectual, and energetic senator and his attractive and bright Native American wife were an immediate hit on the Washington social circuit. Whether it was dinner on the presidential yacht, lunching with Joan and Walter Mondale, or socializing with Robert and Ethel Kennedy, the Harrises became a cocktail scene staple. LaDonna's activities went well beyond the social world. As vice president of the national Indian Opportunity Council, founder of Oklahomans for Indian Opportunity, and a member of mental health and antipoverty committees, she forged a uniquely modern role for herself.[33]

Always terribly ambitious, Harris successfully flattered the Senate's leadership and earned positions reserved for more senior colleagues. Following this career model, he supported the administration's Great Society and Vietnam policies and remained doggedly loyal to Johnson throughout his presidency. Unlike Robert Kennedy or Eugene McCarthy, with whom he cast his Senate votes over 90 percent of the time, Harris refused to break with Johnson on Vietnam.[34]

With Johnson in the White House, Harris had good reason to support the war. After eking out a narrow win over Bud Wilkinson in 1964, he faced potentially rough political waters in 1966. Though Democrats outnumbered Republicans in the Sooner state, Oklahoma was not a liberal bastion. Most Oklahoma congressmen were closely aligned with the conservative coalition, a loosely knit voting alliance composed of southern Democrats and conservative Republicans.[35] Realizing the political calculus, Harris was a leading proponent of Johnson's troop escalations and military policies, a stand that kept him in good stead with his constituents.

While inflation, riots, and Vietnam reduced the president's popularity, Johnson remained well liked in Oklahoma.[36] Consequently, Harris trimmed his sails and called LBJ's Vietnam critics "defeatists."[37] Once he won a full term in 1966, he began speaking to a more national and liberal constituency. Within months of his reelection, he intimated this changing political course. In a speech to the Oklahoma County Bar Association, he called for a vigorous reexamination of "old standards" and urged his audience to "face reality."[38] If constituents and journalists were left wondering what he meant, he wasted little time in charting a political course toward his new populism.

During the summer of 1967, a spate of urban riots swept through American cities, leaving death, destruction, and despair in their wake. In response, Harris and Walter Mondale took to the Senate floor and jointly called for a special commission to study the situation.[39] Prompted by these pleas, LBJ formed the eleven-member National Advisory Commission on Civil Disorders—the so-called Kerner Commission. Harris's relationship with LBJ earned him a spot on the body, a spot that came with a price. After appointing him to the commission, Johnson warned Harris what would happen if he forgot his allegiances: "I'll take out my pocket-knife and cut your pecker off."[40]

Despite this warning, Harris acted independently and to the president's great dismay worked closely with New York City mayor John Lindsay. Together, Harris and Lindsay formed the commission's most dynamic and aggressive duo.[41] By meeting clandestinely with black nationalists, the commission disproved Johnson's favored theory that Communists caused the riots.[42] Through these meetings, Harris encountered issues and characters he otherwise would not have, given Oklahoma's rural character and sparse minority population. In Atlanta, for example, one tenant of a slum told him that all federal studies on the poor amounted to little and were "a joke—like you're doing now."[43] Rather than disagree, Harris searched for radical alternatives.

Despite LBJ's threats, the Kerner Commission indicted traditional Democratic programs. In calling racial segregation and urban slums a system of "apartheid," it urged far-ranging federal action to promote significant change. Thus, the commission represented a watershed for many liberals.[44] No longer content to advocate piecemeal reform, many looked for new and far-reaching ideas.

The Kerner Commission also gave Harris enhanced national notoriety. In tandem with this, the senator played a distinctive role in an increasingly divided party. Aligned with Senate seatmates Robert Kennedy and Walter Mondale, Harris, nevertheless, remained a fixture at White House dinners.[45] In this way, his White House connections, youth (he was thirty-seven), liberal record, and border state credentials made him a natural conduit between the estranged party factions. Operating as an intermediary, he served as Humphrey's co–campaign manager and very nearly his running mate.

Within months of Humphrey's narrow 1968 defeat, the Minnesotan named his newfound protégé Democratic National Committee (DNC) chair. As party head, Harris allied himself with New Politics liberals and empowered party activists. In pursuit of this, he created two bodies: the Rules Commission and the Reform Committee. The former was intended to evaluate and change the party's convention policies, while the latter was designed to democratize the delegate-selection process.[46]

Of more immediate significance was Harris's new populism. Designed to win back the white working class, which fled to Nixon and George Wallace, the senator's plan was one of many cluttering the political firmament. From Kevin Phillips to Ben Wattenberg, political insiders plotted how best to lure a bloc of voters who had bolted the Democratic Party. Using the DNC chairman's post to trumpet his program, Harris claimed that his commonsense populist coalition "best characterizes the aims and purposes of the Democratic Party as it looks toward the 1970s" because it would bring working-class whites back to the Democratic fold.[47]

A populist program promised much for a Democratic Party riven by social divides. With inflation and unemployment on the rise, appeals to class could have, at the very least, papered over significant ideological disagreements. Unfortunately, Harris's new populism joined economic grievances with a New Politics social critique. Avowedly antiwar, and favoring radical voices from the black freedom movement, neopopulism antagonized the very voters it needed. Consequently, the senator's program never stood a chance of attracting white working-class support.

Freed from LBJ, by 1969 Harris called for an immediate withdrawal from Vietnam and publicly encouraged antiwar demonstrations.[48] As DNC chair, he led congressional Democrats in calls to take the "gloves off" with regard to Nixon's war policy. Taking a step further, he gave official sanction to the October 1969 Moratorium to End the War in Vietnam.[49] Organized by leading antiwar activists, the Moratorium culminated in protests across America and Western Europe. A significant moment in ending a senseless conflict, the demonstrations also won Vice President Spiro Agnew's ire.[50] Calling Harris and other leading Democrats "an effete corps of impudent snobs," Agnew's know-nothing pronouncements played well with Jacksonian populists.

Any DNC chair must elect Democrats, of any and all stripes, to office. Consequently, Harris would inevitably campaign for candidates who clashed with Oklahoma's conservative Democrats. The senator, however, spoiled for a fight and threw himself and the DNC into needless controversies. In 1970, for example, Harris endorsed a former Black Panther, Ronald Dellums, for Congress.[51] Overnight, an obscure congressional race in one of the nation's most liberal districts morphed into a national issue centering on the DNC chair's indirect endorsement of black radicals.[52]

Back home in Oklahoma, Harris's new populism and antiwar and Black Panther activities scarcely won any friends. The editors of Oklahoma's major paper, *The Oklahoman,* expressed "serious doubt [whether] the Populism 'scarecrow' will prove as effective as it once did."[53] *The Oklahoman*'s editorial page was a minor annoyance compared to constituents who called Harris "a blithering idiot" and the DNC, which fired him.[54]

After losing his DNC post, Harris published *Now Is the Time: A New Populist Call to Action.* The opening salvos of his 1972 presidential campaign, the book represented a reply to Kevin Phillips's *The Emerging Republican Majority* and Richard Scammon and Ben Wattenberg's *The Real Majority.* In the wake of the New Deal coalition's collapse, these authors offered competing theories on how best to construct a durable electoral majority. Of paramount interest to all were the "social issues": a euphemism for the counterculture, the antiwar movement, crime, and racial matters. According to Phillips and Scammon and Wattenberg, the social issues accounted for George Wallace's strong showing in 1968, Nixon's victory, and the Democratic Party's incipient collapse.

According to the Nixon aide Phillips, Wallace's showing in 1968 revealed the emergence of a conservative governing majority. For Phillips, the white working class's switch from the Democrats to the Republicans was all but complete. In contrast, Scammon and Wattenberg agreed that the social issues drove the white working class to Wallace and Nixon but felt that the realignment was scarcely inevitable. To forestall collapse and save the New Deal coalition, they urged liberals to heed white working-class concerns.

Discounting the social issues entirely, Harris termed *The Emerging Republican Majority* "immoral" and *The Real Majority* "amoral." Like the authors of those books, the Oklahoman took direct aim at George Wallace voters. Taking a position distinctly different from that of Phillips and Scammon and Wattenberg, Harris claimed that the Alabaman's positions on Social Security benefits and tax reform accounted for his popularity.[55] Somehow, the senator disregarded Wallace's populist stance on the social issues. In addition to his bigotry, during his presidential run the governor regularly delighted crowds with threats against hippies and protesters. One crowd-pleaser involved Wallace's promise that, if an "anarchist" attempted to block his car, "it'll be the last automobile they'll want to lie down in front of."[56]

Instead of social issues, Harris offered a pithy slogan: "Up with Those Who Are Down."[57] With economics as his glue, he sought a multiracial coalition of Wallace voters, "blacks . . . Indians and every other group and minority."[58] Huey Long or FDR could call for "wealth redistribution" during the Depression, but, when Harris sounded that populist theme, working-class whites heard the dog whistle of "welfare." Jacksonian populists inveighed against entrenched elites, real and imagined, but their populist remedies were intended for hardy and self-reliant individualists, not aggrieved minorities and assorted dissidents.

Undeterred, Harris took aim at corporations. Channeling his inner William Jennings Bryan, he called for the federal government to "bust" monopolies. Rather than Standard Oil or U.S. Steel, he set his sights on agribusiness. Claiming that monopoly represented the "great forgotten issue," the senator intended to make corporate power a primary issue and combine the Wallace vote with "blue collar workers, blacks, chicanos, old people, the activist woman, and the young activists."[59]

In 1971, Richard Nixon handed Fred Harris opportunity in the guise of a folksy loudmouth: Earl Butz. Born in rural Indiana, and reared on horse-drawn plows, as secretary of agriculture Butz came to oversee a revolution in American farming.[60] A staunch and outspoken advocate of free market agriculture, he pushed growing corporate control over the nation's farm economy. Indeed, in 1971, when Nixon tapped him for the cabinet position, farm-state Democrats very nearly defeated his nomination, a feat achieved just twice before in the twentieth century.[61]

Undaunted, Butz set out to dismantle New Deal price supports and subsidies in favor of a bold new policy: produce more and sell abroad.[62] During his tenure, commodity production, agricultural profits, and food prices shot through the roof. Big planters reaped profits, corporate farmers got rich, and small cultivators like Wayne Cryts increasingly got left behind. Despite this reality, Jacksonian populists adored Butz. Playing to their rugged individualism and aspirations, he prodded producers to refuse price supports and embrace an entrepreneurial future.

On paper, the secretary loomed as a perfect foil. Outspoken, and prone to rhetorical excess, Butz once said of African Americans: "The only thing coloreds are looking for in life are tight pussy, loose shoes, and a warm place to shit in."[63] Sharing the secretary's streak of self-reliance and likely his bigotry, farmers cast their lot with him. Though Harris failed to halt Butz's nomination, he developed a thoroughgoing analysis of modernity based on the secretary's agricultural policy. In this way, the senator connected, at least on paper, his disparate new populist coalition through a common thread.

To Harris, federal farm subsidies not only supported corporate farmers and agribusiness; they also sparked the urban crisis and inflationary food prices. According to this analysis, farm subsidies undermined small farmers, forcing the very mass urban migration that led to overcrowding, poverty, and urban riots.[64] Thus, neopopulists sought an end to agribusiness, which would save family farms and then solve the urban crisis by reversing the country-to-city population shift.[65]

To be fair, Harris's critique had one foot in reality. By 1970, the postwar era had witnessed the demise of approximately 2 million family farms.[66] Of the 2.7 million remaining family farmers, another million were predicted to cease operation by 1980.[67] Surely, the mass exodus to the cities lent fuel to the urban crisis fire. Moreover, Butz's emphasis on commodity exports did spark a rise in food costs and overall inflation.[68] Thus, Harris identified a common issue afflicting the rural and the urban alike. Unfortunately, his remedies were hardly mainstream.

With busting agribusiness as the keystone of his populist policy, Harris offered a legislative solution, the 1972 Family Farm Act. The bill offered a catchy slogan, let "farmers farm the land, rather than . . . corporations farm the taxpayers."[69] The pithy maxim obscured the bill's far-reaching policy prescriptions. Requiring businesses with more than $3 million in nonfarm assets to divest themselves of farmland, it directly attacked any and all forms of agribusiness.[70] In countering Butz's plan to grow the size of American farms with an arrangement to keep them small, Harris ran smack dab into economic realities. The expanding export markets and Soviet grain sales had created lucrative opportunities for farmers. In the early 1970s, they were in no mood to scale back their ambitions.

Scurrying to and fro, the senator increasingly delegated his duties to his staff. One lobbyist said of Harris's sustained absences from the Senate: "I just don't bother to see Harris anymore. There's no point to it."[71] Not surprisingly, Harris's standing in Oklahoma plummeted. With billboards and bumper stickers urging voters to "Shed Fred," a ten-term Democratic congressman, Ed Edmondson, challenged him in the primary.[72] With polls showing Edmondson leading by nearly two to one, Harris declined to run for reelection.[73]

Claiming that unpopularity in Oklahoma actually enhanced his qualifications for national office, Harris declared his presidential candidacy in September 1971.[74] He was the second antiwar liberal from the Midwest to enter the race, but he believed that his new populism rendered him distinct from George McGovern.[75] "No More Bullshit" was not only Harris's campaign slogan; it also captured his disregard for orthodox politics. Consequently, his campaign was run "entirely by those unscarred by past political campaigns and, therefore, unspoiled by political expertise."[76] Modeling this antipolitics stance, the aspiring president declared: "I think people are so damned tired of the wishy-washy, mealy-mouthed politicians they could puke—and so am I."[77]

Promising land reform, corporate tax increases, and antitrust suits, Harris believed that working-class whites and blacks would coalesce around his populist program.[78] He was so convinced of the new populism's efficacy that he considered George Wallace, not George McGovern, his principal opponent. As a result, his staff compiled an exhaustive list of Wallace's bouts with mental illness and Alabama's pitiful economic record.[79] Unlike the governor, who focused relentlessly on the social issues, the senator pursued the ghosts of populisms past.

The new populism was not limited to rural concerns. Realizing William Jennings Bryan's mistakes, Harris also appealed to urbanites. Promising antitrust suits against the steel, auto, aluminum, and farm machinery industries, he put General Motors (GM) at the top of his list. In capturing 50 percent of the American domestic car market, the company fit the senator's description of a monopoly. To stop the car company's "price-fixing" and alter its "dehumanizing assembly line," he planned for Congress to chop the carmaker into six to fourteen competing firms.[80]

According to the new populist blueprint, GM was not the only corporation undermining the American economy. In Harris's estimation, Coca-Cola, General Mills, and the big oil companies were run by "a few white male directors" and hence operated outside the public's control.[81] Owing to their monopolistic control, Coca-Cola overpriced its soft drinks, General Mills controlled children's diets, and the oil industry overcharged consumers. Mincing few words, Harris said of his state's second leading business:

"Oil is making us sick—sick with pollution . . . sick economically. Because the whole energy industry is itself sick with gluttony."[82]

Using the remaining days of his term to popularize the new populism, Harris and a colleague, Philip Hart, crafted antitrust legislation. Citing seven key industries—communication, computer, drug, steel, energy, electrical machinery, and automobiles—as sectors in need of dilution, their bill ranged far and wide.[83] As if taking on the auto industry was not enough, the duo attacked a Democratic mainstay, the United Auto Workers. Accusing labor of violating antitrust laws by collectively bargaining across one industry, Harris pestered friends and enemies alike in his quest to invigorate the new populism.[84]

Following a campaign swing through fifteen states, Harris officially opened his Washington, DC, campaign headquarters with a poorly attended open house. With only two hundred (of one thousand) invitees bothering to show, the event was a flop.[85] The open house revealed Harris's presidential bid for what it was, a quixotic quest by an ambitious politician with nothing to lose. Harris even admitted as much to a group of reporters, claiming: "[Since I have done] the Senate thing . . . [even] if I lose as President, I'll have had some effect on the race . . . and I can always go teach at Harvard."[86]

Realizing that George McGovern and Ed Muskie were unassailable in New Hampshire, Harris made the Florida primary his campaign's showcase event. The Sunshine state featured what he believed to be a showdown between two contending styles of populism: George Wallace's and the new populism. Harris relished the opportunity to finally challenge and confront the Alabaman's brand of "old turn-of-the-century populism."[87] Believing that a Florida victory would propel him to the front ranks of the presidential hopefuls, he poured his energy and campaign coffers into the state.[88]

Armed with an exaggerated country twang, Harris railed against the "bankers and profiteers." Ironically, these were among his staunchest supporters. Indeed, Bill Spohrer and Eli Timoner, the presidents of Florida-based Peruvian Airlines and Griffin Industries, bankrolled the senator's Sunshine state campaign.[89] On the stump, Harris mixed his old-time populism with Jesse Jackson and Dick Gregory quotes. Even less of a crowd-pleaser was his concern for prisoners. After a warden refused his request for a visit, he said: "I hope to get into some prisons . . . [because] my wife resents the fact that maximum security prisons are mostly peopled by blacks, Chicanos, American Indians, Puerto Ricans, and poor people."[90]

Six weeks into his populist presidential crusade, Harris abruptly dropped out. Explaining, "I'm broke," the senator refused to elaborate.[91] Thankfully, his contributors were more forthcoming. Indeed, it was the senator's self-described tendency to "get more radical when I spoke to a rich group" that killed his campaign before it even started.[92] In particular, his wonderment as to "why a government that could trace Angela Davis to a motel room couldn't stop the heroin traffic if it wanted to" led one wealthy contributor to exclaim: "When he [Harris] accused the FBI of being racist, that did it for me."[93]

Ironically, while Harris's campaign went nowhere, his populism dominated the Democratic primaries. The *Washington Post*'s David Broder noted six months after Harris's withdrawal: "You cannot scratch a Democratic candidate without his bleeding populist blood."[94] With an angry electorate eager, in the words of George Wallace, to "send 'em a message," Democrats staged photo ops with steelworkers, proposed populist tax reforms, and proffered anticorporate slogans. George McGovern's "demogrant" plan, for example, was predicated on capping inheritances at $500,000, while Ed Muskie pledged "to fight . . . the huge corporations that . . . practically run our lives."[95]

When he dropped out of the presidential race in November 1971, Harris still had over a year left in his Senate term. Despondent over his campaign's failure, he spent the Christmas season abroad. On his return, he sported hair to his collar, a moustache, and even a pair of sideburns that reached below his ears.[96] With his presidential ambitions spurned, the newly modish Harris patterned a post-Senate career on Ralph Nader. Planning to write and practice public interest law, he even worked on a deal for a syndicated talk show.[97] Though the television gig never came to fruition, his work in the Nader mold flowered.

In pursuit of championing populist reforms and influencing the presidential race, Harris founded the New Populist Institute, which sponsored Tax Action Day. Modeled after Earth Day, which was widely acclaimed for placing environmental issues on the political agenda, Tax Action Day, scheduled for April 15, 1972, the day federal income tax returns were due, was meant to publicize "how the special pleadings of high paid corporate lobbyists often overwhelm the common sense of the ordinary taxpayer."[98]

On its face, populist tax reform was a promising avenue. Indeed, opinion polls revealed that two-thirds of Americans were "fed up" with taxes.[99] Thus, the 1972 presidential campaign featured a constant drumbeat for changes in the tax code.[100] From George Wallace's refrain against "taxers and spenders" to George McGovern's denunciation of corporate tax cheats, the groundswell for reform prompted action across the political continuum ranging from the Nixon administration to Wilbur Mills.[101] In this way, Harris tried to channel the antitax torrent against corporations and the wealthy and empower the populist movement.

Unfortunately, the Tax Action Campaign reflected the continued relevance of the New Politics in Harris's new populism. Instead of building an organization comprising a cross section of American society, Harris created a strangely skewed one. For example, his advisory board consisted of the Black Panther–cum–congressman Ronald Dellums, the political gadfly John Kenneth Galbraith, and the Sears-Roebuck mogul Philip M. Stern.[102] Paradoxically, his heartiest populist benefactors were wealthy. Indeed, Charles Pillsbury (the great-grandson of the Pillsbury founder), the makeup mogul Max Factor, and the philanthropist Stewart Mott appeared on his donor list.[103]

Tax Action Day was emblematic of the course of and the contradictions within Harris's populism. Since Wallace and McGovern supporters were both "pissed off about taxes," Harris believed that they would coalesce around his populist program. Despite this wishful thinking, these two constituencies had little in common except disgust and disdain for the other.[104] One particular event reveals the quixotic nature of Harris's venture. Believing that music could tame the deep divisions within his nascent coalition, Harris commissioned a theme song, "Bad Taxes," and staged a bluegrass concert/fund-raiser at a working-class bar. The hope had been that the music would draw Wallace voters and that the new populism would lure the McGoverniks, but the fund-raiser drew only the latter while driving away the former.[105]

In much the same way, a latter-day populism driven by the New Politics not only failed to attract Jacksonian populists; it antagonized an already-agitated constituency. By repeatedly ignoring potent social issues, liberals pushed working-class whites out of the Democratic column, so much so that they have become, in the words of one GOP spokesman, "Bible-thumping, baby-saving, gun-toting conservatives."[106]

4

Good Intentions, Bad Results

Harold Ford and
Majority-Minority Redistricting

It all started in Harold Ford's Tennessee. And, though the political fight was over a seeming cliché, "one man, one vote," the brouhaha involved anything but. In 1962, this platitude scarcely reflected political reality in the Volunteer state or America. Indeed, for half a century, Tennessee's state legislators had simply refused to redraw their legislative boundaries and reapportion representation. As a result, of ninety-nine statehouse seats, sixty-six went to rural areas, 40 percent of the population, while urban Tennesseans claimed a mere thirty-three seats. In terms of representative impact, one rural vote packed twice the wallop of an urbanite's: so much for "one man, one vote."[1]

Hoping to render "one man, one vote" a reality, activists looked to Chief Justice Earl Warren for relief. Tennessee's rural Democrats relied on Felix Frankfurter. More specifically, they trusted that Frankfurter's *Colegrove v. Green* opinion would stand. In this 1946 decision, the justice restrained the court from entering the "political thicket" and forcing reapportionment. Fifteen years hence, Frankfurter still led the Court's conservative bloc. Three Nashville lawyers, however, sued Tennessee's secretary of state, Joe Carr, and called the question again.[2]

Tennessee was far from being the nation's sole reapportionment procrastinator; a majority of states featured outdated and, therefore, grossly malapportioned legislative districts. For decades, rural legislators had simply declined to redistrict and transfer political power to the cities. Thus, in 1960, cows and sheep routinely boasted more political representation than American urbanites.[3] Emphasizing this reality, in 1959 one rural California district of 14,294 people counted the same number of state legislators— one—as did six million Los Angelenos.[4]

Harold Ford Sr. (second from right) (courtesy Special Collections, University of Memphis Libraries)

Stopping the courts from intervening were mounds of judicial precedent. Though the forces of retrenchment might have owned tradition and Frankfurter, the Tennessee plaintiffs had Bobby Kennedy. Renowned for his dogged, personal loyalty, the attorney general maintained a close friendship with one lead plaintiff, John Jay Hooker. Hooker also possessed ties to the solicitor general, Archibald Cox. These prior relationships, joined with the plaintiffs' compelling case, earned the Justice Department's amicus brief in *Baker v. Carr.*[5]

Far from a slam dunk, *Baker v. Carr* pushed the judges and liberal legal theories to the limit. After hearing two oral arguments, enduring a yearlong debate, and losing one judge to stress, in 1962 the Court issued a stunning reappraisal of its own power. Ruling that individuals were entitled to comparable political representation under the "equal protection clause," the court established jurisdiction over apportionment and redistricting.[6] With the judiciary authorizing itself to enforce the principle of one man, one vote, the reapportionment revolution commenced.[7]

Always more hammer than scalpel, the one man, one vote doctrine offered a judicial solution for any number of political woes. While court-ordered reapportionment failed to ameliorate some of its intended targets, it did aid civil rights activists.[8] In conjunction with the 1965 Voting Rights Act (VRA), *Baker* empowered the court to oversee decennial redistricting and engineer the second generation of the civil rights struggle: legislative apportionment, vote dilution, and majority-minority redistricting. In turn, these were the issues spawning the final act in the South's political realignment.

Harold Ford Sr.

The controversial kingpin of an erstwhile urban political machine, Congressman Harold Ford Sr. blazed trails and burned bridges throughout his thirty years in public life. A one-man political Rorschach test, Ford symbolized racial progress to his black constituents while serving as an emblem of wanton political corruption to whites. Taking a majority-white congressional seat in 1974, early on Ford consciously, successfully, and by necessity appealed to white voters. Once he secured a majority-minority district, the congressman abandoned his early racial bridge building. Thereafter, he earned his reputation as a high-living political boss who maintained his power via reckless demagoguery.

Though the vast majority of black officials were hardly of Ford's ilk, his story symbolizes the unintended consequences of second-generation civil rights struggles. As African Americans gained political office, southern, white, and centrist Democrats lost their foothold and seats. In their place, white Republicans and black Democrats took what became increasingly uncompetitive seats. Without opposition, both the southern GOP and the Democratic Party moved steadily to the ideological margins—with significant consequences for American liberalism.[9]

The canned narrative of southern political realignment starts with Martin Luther King, continues with the voting rights revolution, and ends at the "backlash thesis." This theory follows the general contours of Lyndon Johnson's famous utterance to Bill Moyers, his fellow Texan and press secretary, following the passage of the VRA: "I think we just delivered the South to the Republican Party for a long time to come."[10] In this interpretation of southern history, bigotry and racism alone shifted the region from the Democrats to the Republicans.

Rather than the backlash thesis, a region-specific stew of white racism, well-intentioned legislation, and unintended consequences explains the South's move to the GOP. Rather than a sudden realignment caused solely by the civil rights revolution, the South's political evolution occurred in stages. LBJ's civil rights measure most definitely dissolved the "solid South," but the region's white voters split their tickets, voting GOP for president and Democratic in congressional, state, and local races until the early 1990s. The crucial time for the region's realignment was the early 1990s, which, not accidentally, coincided with the wide-scale inception of majority-minority redistricting.[11]

Majority-Minority Redistricting

Designed to enhance black (and Hispanic) political representation, majority-minority districts produced monumental gains in the numbers of African American elected officials. For white southern Democrats, however, these changes were vital. Losing a bloc of loyal black voters, white Democrats politicked (and lost) in progressively whiter and more Republican districts. Moreover, with African American legislators representing uncompetitive districts, they moved significantly to the left of the national party. Consequently, white Democrats were forced to market a political brand increasingly out of step with the South's white voters. Adding to this burden was racism. As southern Democrats increasingly became the party of African Americans, whites, not so coincidentally, fled.[12]

A narrative deprived of tidy morality tales, the 1982 VRA mandated majority-minority districts that most definitively buttressed black "descriptive" representation. From local and state to federal offices, majority-minority redistricting spawned a veritable revolution in the numbers of black officeholders. These African American politicians championed concrete legislative accomplishments; nevertheless, majority-minority districts undermined the Democratic Party in the South. And, as with *Baker,* the process, at least symbolically, started in Tennessee with Harold Ford.

One of America's most viciously segregated cities, Memphis in 1974 hardly seemed hospitable to biracial political coalitions. When Ford announced his candidacy for the city's congressional seat, he surely understood the improbability of taking a majority-white district. From a campaign theme, "Harold Ford: A Democrat for All the People," to campaigning with local, state, and national white Democrats, Ford struck a theme of racial conciliation out of political necessity.[13]

For Memphis, reconciliation could come none too soon. By 1974, the city's race relations had reached their nadir. Heaping local issues and events onto the steaming pile of American and southern racial strife, Memphis possessed a well-deserved reputation for racial turmoil. In the years just prior to Ford's congressional run, race relations had steadily worsened.[14] Court-ordered school integration resulted in the mass exodus of whites from the city's public schools.[15] Simultaneous with desegregation was the murder of a black youth by the Memphis city police.[16] After officials exposed a police cover-up, a five-day riot ensued.[17]

It was in this highly polarized racial milieu that Harold Ford ran to represent a majority-white congressional district. Newton and Vera Ford's eighth child (of twelve) came of age in an intensely close and hardworking family. The patriarch, Newton Jackson Ford, was named for his grandfathers, Newton Ford and Jackson Geeter, both of whom were veritable giants in the black community. While the Geeters donated the land for the city's leading black high school, church sanctuaries and major streets bore the Ford family name.[18]

With fourteen people crammed into a small, modest home, the Fords became a world unto themselves. Starting with the family enterprise, N. J. Ford and Sons Funeral Home, which they built into a community institution, the Fords later leapt into politics with Harold at the lead.[19] In 1970, he ran for and won a seat in the statehouse.[20] A relentless campaigner, Ford went door-to-door in the evenings and hit the bus stops in the mornings. In what was to become a common mantra, the defeated incumbent accused Ford of cheating. Despite the controversy, Ford took 73 percent of the vote in the general election.[21]

Sporting a trendy Afro, the tall and thin twenty-five-year-old was a charismatic and attractive candidate.[22] Despite representing a poor district, Ford sported designer suits and refined tastes but remained down-home enough to claim a "soul food" dish—black-eyed peas, ham hocks, and cornbread— as his favorite meal.[23] Combining ambition with political smarts, Ford became the majority whip in the statehouse, the first freshman legislator in Tennessee history to hold that post.[24]

In the early 1970s, Harold Ford developed into the leader of young, black Memphis. Brash and outspoken, he embodied the post–civil rights zeitgeist. In addition, he ambitiously eyed a congressional seat occupied by a white, conservative Republican, Dan Kuykendall. Elected in 1966, the former Proctor and Gamble executive represented Tennessee's Eighth Congressional District, which encompassed the city of Memphis and suburban (white) neighborhoods. Formerly a Democratic stronghold, the majority-white district had turned increasingly conservative during the 1960s.[25]

Swept into office in the Republican landslide of 1966, Kuykendall was no product of eastern Tennessee's moderate GOP. Instead, he boasted a sharp-tongued and bare-knuckled brand of southern conservatism. His rhetoric against the "rubber-stamping . . . federal extremists back in Washington" fit the temper of the 1966 conservative backlash.[26] A hawk's hawk, he called for the "all-out obliteration" of North Vietnam and a "rice war" to starve the Vietnamese to the peace table and even backed an all-volunteer task force to free American POWs from Vietnamese prisons.[27]

Rising inflation and unemployment coupled with Watergate and Nixon's resignation rendered Kuykendall vulnerable. Making matters worse, the incumbent maintained a cozy relationship with Nixon. Despite the circling impeachment buzzards, he remained a steadfast and outspoken ally. Displaying a hangman's noose on the House floor, he called Nixon's detractors a "legislative lynch mob" and said that his anti-impeachment stance "is one subject [constituents]" could not influence.[28]

Owing to *Baker* and Tennessee's consequent redistricting, the incumbent also faced a changed district.[29] The 1970 census provided the Democratic-controlled Tennessee statehouse with an opportunity to defeat the GOP incumbent. Losing one of their nine House seats, Democrats redrew district lines and gave Kuykendall the reconfigured (and renumbered) Eighth District. Over 40 percent African American and majority Democratic, the district was clearly designed to defeat the Republican and elect a white Democrat. Fearing for his political life, the congressman filed suit.

Kuykendall need not have worried. The GOP-controlled Shelby County Election Commission had already exploited a loophole in the Democrats' redistricting bill. The legislation specified certain precincts for an adjoining district and placed "all others" in Kuykendall's Eighth District. Using the vague language to their advantage, commissioners performed a neat trick. In the interim between the redistricting bill's creation and its enactment, the local body "created" seven new precincts, which qualified them for the "all others" category. Not coincidentally, these precincts placed in the congressman's district contained 18,474 whites and only 8 blacks.[30]

A clever and cynical ploy to save the incumbent, the gambit worked in 1972.[31] In 1974, statehouse Democrats attempted to shift the all-white precincts out of the Eighth District.[32] Vetoing the "Get Dan Kuykendall—Elect

Harold Ford" bill, the GOP governor, Winfield Dunn, left the congressional district 58 percent white.[33]

In the midst of this redistricting mess, Ford's campaign for Congress commenced. In addition to Harold, his two brothers and a brother-in-law also ran for state Senate and House seats, leading some to warn that the congressional candidate sought to become a "black Crump."[34]

In Memphis, *Crump* meant "bossism." Indeed, from 1909 until his 1954 death, E. H. (Ed) Crump had ruled Memphis and, through it, controlled Tennessee's Democratic Party.[35] The southern political baron looked the part. Sporting a white suit, a saucer-sized lapel flower, and a walking cane, Mr. Ed appeared as if he was sent straight from Hollywood's central casting.[36] At the time of Crump's death in 1954, few could have imagined that his successor would be African American.

Before Ford could dominate the city, he had to defeat Kuykendall. And to win he needed white votes. A biracial affair from the start, his campaign placed two prominent whites as cochairs and made race-neutral "vices and prices" a core theme.[37] Moreover, the younger and more dynamic Ford was better able to empathize with consumers' struggles. Recounting a recent excursion to the grocery store, he jokingly told audiences that he directed the bag boy to put his $29 worth of groceries "in the glove compartment" rather than the trunk.[38]

Ford, however, was no Pollyanna; he understood the racial dynamics shaping the contest. Avoiding television commercials, he realized that broadcasting a black face would merely elicit a greater white turnout. Admitting, "We don't want to bring them out to vote against us," Ford, nevertheless, tirelessly campaigned door-to-door in particular white neighborhoods.[39]

In contrast to his opponent's race-neutral campaign, Kuykendall employed billboards calling for voters to reelect "*your*" congressman.[40] Meanwhile, the challenger's door-to-door campaigning in white neighborhoods was curiously effective. Dominated by the Crump machine and then the GOP, Memphians seldom enjoyed competitive local elections. Thus, Ford's intensive canvassing and door-to-door campaigning resulted in enough whites thinking, "He's not as bad as they say he is," for him to build a biracial coalition.[41]

Fittingly, the campaign's conclusion was filled with intrigue and hints of corruption. At 9:00 P.M. on election night, the Memphis radio and television stations declared Kuykendall the winner. Ford, however, sensed that something was amiss.[42] Suspecting fraud, he went to the Republican-controlled election commission headquarters to observe the vote count. As he stood in the headquarters muttering, "Something must be wrong . . . I know I've got the lead," Kuykendall began his televised victory speech.[43] At that moment, a county election worker sidled over to Ford and gestured toward the basement, saying: "Harold, go down there and look in those ballot boxes . . . you might find what you're lookin' for."[44]

Racing down the stairs and into the basement, Ford found six unopened ballot boxes. In them were six thousand ballots from black wards and precincts. While Kuykendall delivered his victory speech, the election commission tallied the "lost" ballots. Just as the congressman was thanking his opponent's "people" for providing him with the margin of victory, a station official handed him a note reporting the turn of events.[45] Stammering under the weight of the television studio's klieg lights, Kuykendall sputtered: "I don't want that [note]."[46] With the cameras capturing the tension and humiliation of the moment, the congressman conferred with his press secretary and heaved a big sigh, claiming: "Well, I guess it's true."[47]

Though accounts vary as to how the ballots were misplaced, Ford accused the election commission of tossing black votes into "a garbage can."[48] The challenger's anger was short-lived as the enormity of his victory settled in. When news of the turnabout reached the Ford campaign headquarters, supporters chanted "party, party, party!"[49] Not only was Ford just the second black congressman elected from the South since Reconstruction; he was also the first African American to win a majority-white district in the South. By working eighteen- and twenty-hour days and being "willing to ask for a white man's vote," Ford won 17 percent of the white vote, an unprecedented amount for that era.[50]

Ford's triumph thrilled the black community of Memphis. In the days following the election, victory signs adorned the windows of black-owned businesses, and the newly elected congressman was greeted with standing ovations at local churches. With the city's black community claiming the dawn of a "New Memphis," white Tennessee Democrats believed that the election marked their party's revival.[51]

In addition to Ford, the 1974 election brought scores of reform-minded freshmen to Capitol Hill. These seventy-five freshmen Democrats, or Watergate Babies, set out to change the rhythm of national politics.[52] As the only African American among them, Ford received an inordinate amount of national media attention.[53] Rejecting the limelight, Ford worked quietly and behind closed doors and became a star of a luminous freshman class.[54] According to one freshman House member, Ford came to represent what the leadership wanted the American people "to think of" the Congress: efficient, respectful, and responsive.[55]

Cultivating a relationship with the leadership paid dividends. When freshmen Democrats demanded a "reform" seat on the Ways and Means Committee, it went to Speaker Carl Albert's favorite Watergate Baby, Harold Ford. An assignment to this powerful committee was a substantial coup for any congressman but represented an unbelievable stroke of fortune for a freshman. Rather than make the committee assignment a racial victory, Ford claimed that he was merely following in the footsteps of his fellow Tennesseans Andrew Jackson and Cordell Hull.[56]

Striking another correct political note, Ford established a biracial Citizens' Advisory Committee and very publicly returned a $1,000 contribution from Tennessee's First National Bank. In a press release, Ford claimed: "As a member of the House Banking and Currency Committee I can't accept it."[57] This sort of showmanship made for good politics.[58] Clearly, Ford had enormous talents and knew how to appeal to a biracial coalition.

As a freshman congressman, Ford worked hard and took constituent service seriously. Though he was afraid of flying, he flew home every weekend and walked his district every Saturday. In contrast to his high rate of absenteeism in the Tennessee statehouse, he was present for 90 percent of congressional votes.[59] Eventually, his office distinguished itself in the realm of constituent service, especially for his districts' previously ignored black voters.[60]

Largely winning the trust of the white business community and his white constituents—a necessity in a majority-white district—Ford cruised to reelection in 1976.[61] During his second term, his annual fund-raiser became a social event for the Memphis elite.[62] Signaling how he had changed the city's political culture was his annual "Christmas Luncheon." At these affairs, the Chamber of Commerce president and the black working class alike greeted the congressman, ate turkey, and enjoyed the entertainment of Rufus Thomas, the legendary "Funky Chicken" of Beale Street.[63]

In 1979, a federal extortion trial foreshadowed a turn in Ford's career. Testifying in the case, a Memphis-area strip club owner, Arthur Baldwin, claimed that he paid "protection money" to both Harold and his older brother, the state senator John Ford. In exchange for cash payments, the Fords, according to Baldwin, restrained the police from interfering with his business.[64] As Baldwin explained, Ford's political payoff system not only "took care of problems"; it was also distributed to high-level Democrats, including Jake Butcher, a politician and banker close to Harold Ford.[65] Though Ford declared, "I don't even know Art Baldwin . . . I've never met him a day in my life," federal officials launched an investigation.[66]

Following Baldwin's explosive charge was a scandal cutting to the heart of the congressman's power base. The nexus of Ford's political machine was its network of relatives occupying local and state offices, including Harold's younger brother, the state legislator Emmitt Ford. In the winter of 1977, Emmitt purchased thirty-four separate insurance policies and staged a hit-and-run accident in front of his home; making matters more suspicious, three weeks after the initial incident Emmitt convinced the police to change their report to reflect his wife's "injuries."[67]

The questionable accident, coupled with an altered police report, led the insurance company to investigate the $50,000 claim. The inquiry resulted in a fraud indictment brought against Emmitt and his wife, Earlene. In late 1980, a jury took all of five hours to convict them on nineteen counts of mail fraud and one count of conspiracy to commit fraud.[68] Though Earlene's prison term was suspended, owing to his prior insurance scams Emmitt was sentenced to twenty months in a federal prison.[69]

Ironically, the trial judge happened to be an old Ford rival, Harry Wellford.[70] In 1976, the congressman had led the fight against Wellford's nomination to the Court of Appeals for the Sixth Circuit.[71] Objecting to Wellford's stance on open housing laws and his membership in an all-white Memphis country club, Ford effectively stopped Wellford's nomination.[72] Six years later, Wellford sentenced Emmitt Ford to federal prison.

In spring 1982, as Emmitt Ford entered prison, a spot on the Sixth Circuit Court opened. By May, Ronald Reagan had nominated Wellford for the same Court of Appeals post that Harold Ford had denied him six years earlier.[73] Licking their chops, observers expected Harold Ford, civil rights groups, and liberals to defeat Wellford's nomination once again. There was one significant difference from the situation in 1976; Wellford now held the keys to Emmitt Ford's freedom.

With Ford possessing the power to squash his nomination, Wellford blinked. In late May, Emmitt Ford's lawyers refiled a motion to reduce his sentence, a request Wellford took "under advisement."[74] By August, when Wellford's nomination made it to the full Senate, the judge secured Ford's support in two ways. First, he had resigned from the all-white Memphis Country Club. Second, and more significantly, he reduced Emmitt Ford's sentence, making him eligible for immediate release.[75]

Not so coincidentally, Harold Ford lifted nary a finger to block the judge's confirmation. Conspicuously absent from the ranks of Wellford's opposition, he claimed that the judge's withdrawal from the all-white Memphis Country Club had satisfied his concerns. Incredibly, he maintained that his brother's commuted sentence "in no way relate[d] to" his actions on Wellford's nomination.[76]

This turn of events made the prosecutor, Dan Clancy, apoplectic. Begging the judge to reconsider, Clancy challenged him to show "that justice is not dictated by position, wealth, or influence."[77] Though Wellford claimed he had merely reconsidered the case's merits, clearly Ford had traded a judgeship for his brother's release. Adding to Clancy's umbrage, Harold Ford threatened the director of the federal Bureau of Prisons when Emmitt's release was slightly delayed.[78] Admittedly working "to do whatever we could legally to keep him [Emmitt Ford] incarcerated as long as we could," the federal attorney, Hickman Ewing, earned Ford's everlasting ire.[79]

With Ford publicly abusing his power, the GOP sensed opportunity.[80] Adding to this, in early 1983 John Ford announced his run for the mayor's office. In the aftermath of Emmitt Ford's foibles, John's quest for the mayor's office seemed especially odd. Indeed, of all the Fords, white Memphians reacted most viscerally to John Ford, owing to his public escapades and clashes with the city's white establishment. Even Harold once said of his older brother: "His name is just a bomb in this city."[81] Facing a crowded field of black candidates, and fueled by a 65 percent white turnout, the conservative (and white) Dick Hackett won by thirty points.[82] Accusing an African American candidate of taking "white money" to spoil his brother's bid, Harold Ford made a bad situation worse. Adding to these political woes, federal investigators officially launched a probe into the congressman's finances.[83]

At an "all-time low" with white voters, and begging for "a more exacting evaluation by" his black constituents, Ford was in 1984 susceptible to a challenge.[84] In what was still a fifty-fifty white-black district, insurgents needed a biracial coalition to topple Ford. Despite stereotypes, the early 1980s were propitious times for just such alliances.

The VRA and Ronald Reagan

Of all people and of all places, George Wallace and Alabama showed that biracial coalitions remained possible. In 1982, the black vote propelled Wallace back to the governor's mansion. On the night of his triumph, supporters might have claimed, "This is *still* Wallace country," but the governor-elect surely knew different.[85] Relying on a biracial coalition, the former racial demagogue defeated his pistol-packing and race-baiting GOP opponent. Few African Americans attended the victory celebration, but Wallace's open solicitation of the black vote signaled a sea change in southern politics.[86]

Adding to Wallace was Wayne Dowdy. In 1981, the white Mississippi Democrat stunned the political world by taking a rural GOP seat.[87] With 90 percent of the black vote and a third of the white ballot, the Mississippian cobbled together a multiracial coalition.[88] Hardly an isolated case, Mississippi's Fourth Congressional District was quite ordinary in a South where African Americans constituted at least 20 percent of the population in fifty-six congressional districts.[89]

In addition to Wallace and Dowdy, the 1982 midterms witnessed similar biracial coalitions electing Democrats across the South. More significantly, in winning back thirteen southern House seats and the Arkansas and Texas governorships, it was "national" Democrats, not conservative Boll Weevils, who claimed victory.[90]

The African American vote might have proved key in electing southern (white) Democrats, but whites failed to reciprocate. Indeed, by the early 1980s, there were comparatively few black elected officials in the South. In Louisiana, for example, African Americans constituted 26.8 percent of voters but merely 10.3 percent of officeholders. Texas and Virginia lagged far behind even that lackluster standard. In the former, African Americans made up 11 percent of voters but just 1.1 percent of officeholders, while in the latter they constituted 17.9 percent of voters but just 4.1 percent of elected officials.[91] Clearly, the VRA was no charm effecting the election of black officials in the South.

Considered the civil rights movement's crown jewel, the VRA combined Lyndon Johnson's legislative audacity with an issue impossible to ignore: black disenfranchisement. In 1940, an appalling 97 percent of southern black voters were unregistered.[92] By 1965, some Upper South states had slightly eased restrictions and allowed a steady trickle of blacks onto the voter rolls. The Deep South, however, remained mired in the Jim Crow era.

Realizing that sweeping legislation was the only possible solution, Johnson aimed big. Relatively simple yet entirely effective, the VRA employed a statistical formula to identify the worst offenders: Alabama, Georgia, Louisiana, Mississippi, South Carolina, Virginia, and North Carolina.[93] From there, the VRA's section 5 stripped the "worst offenders" of control over elections. Turning the "presumption of innocence" on its head, jurisdictions now had to prove to federal courts and lawyers that their rules were uncontaminated by racism.[94]

With LBJ's Justice Department overseeing all facets of elections in the "worst offender" states, black registration rates increased dramatically.[95] Incredibly, before Johnson even left the White House, his civil rights division believed that its efforts had substantially removed all legal barriers to voter registration. Segregationists, however, had hardly given up the fight. By altering candidate qualification rules, changing offices from elective to appointed, and converting single-member districts to at-large voting, white elites diluted the black vote and kept African Americans from public office.

Keeping pace with the segregationists was the Supreme Court and the Justice Department. Armed with fresh interpretations of the VRA's section 5, federal courts struck down sophisticated vote-dilution strategies.[96] Faced with vote-dilution schemes, in 1975 the Ford administration backed a seven-year renewal of the VRA. Significantly, the Congress and Ford armed the courts with section 5 powers to oversee the reapportionment and redistricting that followed the 1980 census.

In 1982, Congress not only faced section 5's expiration; it confronted new legal realities. In the 1980 *City of Mobile v. Bolden,* the Supreme Court redefined the scope of "suffrage enforcement." In vote-dilution cases, the court placed the onus of proving "racist intent" on the plaintiff. According to *Bolden,* courts could intervene only once plaintiffs proved that those devising the rules that resulted in vote dilution actually harbored racist objectives.[97]

As a result of *Bolden,* Congress and the lower courts were left almost powerless to redress many vote-dilution cases. And vote dilution most definitely pervaded the South. In 1980, African Americans constituted over half the population of eighty Deep South counties. Owing to at-large voting and multimember districts, more than a quarter of these counties had yet to elect one African American to any public office.[98] Many of these multimember districts were created during the Progressive era, and, since blacks could not vote at the time, racial animus played no role in their inception. Thus, in accordance with *Bolden,* the courts were powerless to act.

New Politics Liberals and Majority-Minority Redistricting

For civil rights activists, 1982 loomed as a most implausible time to strengthen the VRA and address *Bolden.* Indeed, at first the Reagan administration saw the expiration date as an opportunity to kill the legislation's temporary provisions: sections 5 and 2. Energized by Reagan's landslide, conservatives like Illinois congressman Henry Hyde lumped section 5 in with other "outrageous" examples of wanton federal power.[99] Their solution was to apply section 5 nationally or not at all.

New Politics officeholders, however, had other ideas. Fearing that Reagan would take aim at civil rights legislation, they launched the drive to renew the VRA far in advance of its August 1982 expiration. Moreover, they sought legislative avenues around *Bolden*.[100] Lucky for them they had Don Edwards as an ally. Hailed as an unfailing gentleman, the northern California congressman also came to be recognized as "Congress' foremost protector of civil rights."[101] More important than his beliefs was his chairmanship of the House Judiciary Committee.

With Edwards in the lead and section 5 partially negated, activists looked to skirt *Bolden*. They did so by transforming section 2, which had heretofore simply banned qualifications and procedures "denying or abridging" voting rights.[102] Their new section 2 called for federal action in elections "which result in a denial or abridgement of" voting rights.[103] In other words, a beefed-up section 2 provision could be utilized to redress vote dilution by building majority-minority districts.

Eager to build public momentum, Edwards took his committee hearings on the road. Held across the Deep South in the summer of 1981, the proceedings attracted significant media attention.[104] Over those months, witnesses publicly exposed a series of laws obviously designed to dilute the black vote. Some states required yearly reregistration. One locality, Burleson County, Texas, eliminated twelve of its thirteen polling places, leaving most of its black and Hispanic voters at least nineteen miles from the *only* voting booth.[105]

Fortunately for civil rights activists, Edwards had forged a close bond with a fellow committee member, the archconservative Henry Hyde. Though the Republican called his colleague a "Paleoliberal" who, according to the *New York Times,* remained "untouched by revisionism or self-doubt," his personal regard for Edwards was crucial in shaping the legislation's final outcome.[106] As for Edwards, he looked back on the halcyon days of the Johnson administration as a time when "we could pass anything if we labeled it civil rights."[107] Hardly stuck in the 1960s, the congressman eventually came to regard the next phase of the struggle as a "civil right for livelihood."[108]

In 1982, Edwards and his hearings changed Henry Hyde's mind. Entering the process firmly opposed to an extension of section 5, Hyde had believed that preclearance represented a violation of state sovereignty and compared the process to "sitting on the back of the bus."[109] Reminded of his city's infamous voting fraud, the former GOP precinct captain threw his total support behind an extension and backed the changes in section 2. Armed with Hyde's blessing, Democrats got their voting rights bill through the House.[110]

Reagan and the 1982 VRA

With voting rights opposition headed by the likes of Helms and Thurmond, adversaries never posed a realistic challenge to the act's renewal. Indeed, by late summer 1981, Reagan had committed himself, however vaguely, to the legislation's extension.[111] Though many African Americans believed that the White House ignored them, Reagan's strategists, Richard Wirthlin and John Sears, listened intently. Less interested in black concerns per se, advisers feared their impact on moderate Republicans and college-educated suburbanites. Owing to this political calculus, the administration avoided a protracted fight over the VRA.[112]

While Strom Thurmond and Jesse Helms loudly opposed the VRA's extension, many conservatives realized that the new section 2 provision actually buttressed their partisan cause. With blacks concentrated in a few noncompetitive districts, depressing minority turnout, most southern boroughs would become whiter and more conservative.[113] At first, the White House opposed the House revisions and simply called for extending the legislation "as is."[114] Stepping into the breach was Senator Bob Dole. Out to "save the Republican Party" from completely alienating the black vote, he negotiated a voting rights bill that satisfied all parties.

Addressing the *Bolden* decision, the 1982 VRA gave section 2 the teeth to address non–racially biased vote dilution.[115] In explicitly rejecting quotas, the beefed-up section 2 required the Justice Department and the judiciary to closely inspect redistricting maps and election laws for minority vote dilution. Later, the courts not only upheld the law's constitutionality but also interpreted section 2 broadly, paving the way for the inception of majority-minority districts. By 1992, fifteen black and ten Latino majority-minority districts were created under section 2 guidelines.[116]

On the surface, the drive for descriptive representation surely represents a civil rights triumph. Indeed, section 2 redistricting doubled the ranks of the Congressional Black Caucus by the mid- to late 1990s. While descriptive representation matters, the creation of majority-black districts across the South had huge implications for Democrats. Redistricting huge swaths of southern African Americans into majority-minority districts proved to be the "major shock to the political system" that led to the final act in the South's realignment.[117]

In 1950, Democrats held virtually every federal and state seat.[118] Fifty years later, the GOP controlled 13 of the South's Senate positions and 76 of the region's 131 House seats. This massive turnabout did not occur in the 1970s or even the 1980s. Indeed, as recently as the 1986 midterms, when Democrats toppled four incumbent GOP senators, liberals more than held their own in the region.[119] In 1990, fifteen of the South's senators were Democrats; by 2004, that number declined to four—the lowest number since Reconstruction.[120] The dean of southern political observers, Merle Black, explained realignment this way: "[First the Democrats] lost the white conservatives. They're now losing the younger, white moderate voters."[121]

For a generation after the civil rights revolution, moderate whites in league with African Americans had maintained Democratic majorities by electing centrist liberals. Majority-minority districts, however, deprived these white officeholders of black Democratic voters. As a result, the numbers of white congressional (and state-level) Democrats have declined precipitously. Ironically, as southern blacks' descriptive representation increased and an increasingly right-wing GOP dominated the region, African Americans lost "substantive" representation—a turnabout foreseen by the Georgia congressman and civil rights icon John Lewis, who predicted that majority-minority redistricting would weaken the region's fragile coalition of southern blacks and progressive whites.[122]

Harold Ford and the 1982 VRA

In Tennessee, the 1982 VRA coincided with a protracted court battle over redistricting. During the 1970s, Tennessee experienced a 17 percent surge in population. Ford's Ninth Congressional District, however, witnessed a 17 percent population decline. As a result, Memphians faced yet another racially tinged redistricting battle. In the first round, the Tennessee legislature placed significant portions of white and conservative east Memphis in the district. From his state Senate perch, John Ford pushed a bill ensuring a "fair drawing": meaning fewer whites and more African Americans.[123] As a result, the Ninth District became an overwhelmingly majority-black borough. Repeated throughout the South, black Democrats, like Ford, accepted safe, majority-minority districts. In return, Republicans took command of the burgeoning suburbs.[124]

Ensconced in a safe seat, Ford no longer had any reelection worries. Popular in the black community, he regularly captured 60–70 percent of the total vote. With his seat virtually unassailable, he simply stopped making the attempt to appeal to whites. Moreover, his corruption became more brazen. As a result, the remaining whites in his district revolted. In 1984, for instance, a blind political novice who spent no money and campaigned "over the phone" took nearly one-third of the vote—almost all of it white.[125]

In 1986, Ford ran for reelection while under a federal indictment for fraud. Ignoring his opponents, he took aim at the attorney general and local federal attorneys, claiming: "My opponent in this race is not those who might have filed on the ballots with signatures but Ed Meese, Dan Clancy, and Hick Ewing."[126] When speaking directly to the black community, Ford was even more forthright. In an interview with *Jet* magazine, he claimed that prosecutors sought "to destroy . . . black political power in Tennessee."[127]

Despite Ford's alleged corruption, his political position in Memphis remained airtight. As chairman of the House Subcommittee on Public Assistance and Unemployment, he had enormous power over social services and welfare legislation, which directly benefited his working-class constituency.[128] As his power peaked, he unfortunately engaged in shifty dealings and reckless shenanigans of personal finance. Writing 388 bad checks to the House of Representative's banks, the congressman compiled a $552,447 bill, rendering himself one of the institution's worst offenders in 1992's burgeoning House bank scandal.

The House bank sum was small potatoes compared to his personal debt, which climbed to over $1 million. In addition to his private liabilities, the family funeral business hovered on the edge of bankruptcy—another $1 million in hock.[129] Quite literally using his congressional and Ways and Means seats as collateral, Ford collected loans from ten Memphis-area bankers. Bankers understood that these credits would never be repaid or "called" so long as he held such a powerful position. Even more appalling, one senior bank officer claimed that Ford's family members indiscriminately bounced checks, and one financial institution simply wrote off a $10,000 unsecured loan made to another Ford. According to an additional executive, the boards of Memphis's largest banks understood the game. As one anonymous financier explained: "Suppose there is legislation that could hurt you real bad, or help you. It will probably originate in Ways and Means. So you talk to your congressman. And 10 days later he asks to arrange a little credit. What do you say?"[130]

With his family's financial solvency at stake, Ford cultivated a relationship with the Knoxville banker and Democratic politician Jake Butcher. In 1978, he endorsed Butcher's run for governor. Not so coincidentally, just a few months prior Butcher's bank had loaned the congressman $287,000.[131] By 1982, Butcher employed Ford's wife as a "consultant," for $21,600 a year.[132] Close friend, political ally, godfather, and namesake of Ford's second son, Butcher eventually extended to Ford a *third* mortgage on one home and a second on another.

While these dealings hinted at corruption, it was the Ford-Butcher jointly owned corporation Tenn-Ford that prompted the congressman's indictment. According to prosecutors, the corporation was established and used to "take care of" Ford's considerable personal debt.[133] At trial, a Butcher assistant claimed that the bank agreed to never "sue the congressman" for repayment. Instead, it would "take care of it."[134] Ford, however, was one small piece of Jake Butcher's larger conspiracy, arranging $17 million in fraudulent loans. One accounting expert called Butcher's abuses "the most flagrant" he had witnessed in a quarter century.[135]

In Ford's case, prosecutors alleged that Tenn-Ford enabled Jake Butcher to move and hide the congressman's debt throughout his banking empire. In the meantime, Butcher "invested" considerable sums in Ford's ailing funeral home business. Starting in 1982, Butcher-owned banks invested $350,000 in N. J. Ford and Son's Funeral Home. Simultaneously, the business also received a $137,000 loan from yet another Butcher institution.[136] Taking the loan money from the family business, Ford repaid his personal debts.

On November 1, 1982, the Ford-Butcher financial house of cards collapsed. On that day, federal examiners concurrently entered all thirty-four of Butcher's banks. With Butcher unable to move bad loans around, bank examiners uncovered the trail of sham corporations, shady loans, and financial misdeeds. Within months, the government forcibly closed Butcher's flagship bank, precipitating an old-fashioned bank run on his other institutions.[137] Upending east Tennessee's financial institutions overnight, the resulting investigation resulted in twenty-six indictments on wire, mail, and securities fraud and Butcher's guilty plea.[138]

In 1987, Ford's longtime foes Dan Clancy and Hick Ewing secured a nineteen-count indictment against the congressman. Accused of accepting nearly $1.5 million in bribes from Butcher, Ford was tried on charges of bank, wire, and mail fraud.[139] Charged with selling political influence to finance a profligate lifestyle, Ford cried victim. Blaming poor business acumen and Clancy and Hickman's vendetta, the congressman used his considerable political skills to wiggle free from jail.[140] To divide the jury, Ford and his defense team made racial issues a primary defense. From the very start, the congressman claimed: "If you can't see a racial indictment in this case, something is wrong."[141] Going one step further, Ford called one of the prosecutors, Dan Clancy, "a racist, a liar, and a coward."[142]

Despite the indictment, Ford's majority-minority district, 64.5 percent African American, virtually guaranteed him reelection.[143] Freed from concerns of a political backlash, during the trial Ford held daily press conferences outside the courtroom during which he critiqued testimony and the government's case.[144] Even worse, the African American judge Odell Horton accused the defendant of jury tampering, misconduct, and "treat[ing] [the trial] . . . like a political campaign."[145] That 1990 trial ended with a deadlocked jury, split along racial lines.[146] Owing to the defendant's unethical conduct, Horton ordered a new trial.

By choosing a venue one hundred miles from Memphis—Jackson, Tennessee—Horton hoped to keep Ford from contaminating the jury pool. In 1993, the Justice Department tried to move the trial back to Memphis. In reaction, the presiding judge angrily denounced the decision, which prompted Ford to leave "the court complaining of chest pains."[147]

Adding to the drama was the Clinton White House. When reporters discovered that Justice Department officials met with the Black Political Caucus the day prior to its pronouncement to move the trial back to Memphis, a political firestorm ensued. U.S. Attorney Edward Bryant called the meeting and "the whole concept of a congressman being able to call into play this kind of power to intervene and affect an ongoing trial . . . totally, totally improper."[148] In the face of public scrutiny, the trial remained in Jackson.[149]

During the trial, Ford admitted "financial embarrassment." However, proving that Butcher's malfeasance equated to bribes for Ford proved difficult.[150] Ultimately, the jury found Ford "not guilty" of fraud, at which time the congressman called for "racial healing."

In the six-year interim between his 1987 indictment and his 1993 exoneration, Ford lost his subcommittee chairmanship but retained his constituents' loyalty. Every day during Ford's trial, eighty-two-year-old Ruth Price drove downtown, walked several blocks to the courthouse, and sat in the courtroom to show her support. With obvious pride, Price said of the congressman: "Who would have thought a long time ago that we would have education enough to furnish a child to be congressman."[151]

Indeed, Ford appealed to those like Price, who grew up wondering "why the white children got to go to school nine months and we went four months and picked sprouts."[152] Most surely an outlier in terms of graft and corruption, Ford represents the unintended consequences of majority-minority redistricting. A well-intentioned civil rights measure that generates a social good—African American officeholders—the 1982 VRA also represented the final chapter in the South's realignment. Producing an increasingly right-wing and white GOP, majority-minority districts enhanced descriptive representation at the cost of substantive representation.

Rendering the dictum one man, one vote a reality via reapportionment, the VRA and majority-minority redistricting unquestionably made the South more democratic and just. The Jim Crow South, however, set a very low bar. Indeed, reformers would have been hard-pressed to make the region's politics more racially biased and inequitable. Owing to their reforms, thousands of African Americans have held local, state, and federal offices, undoubtedly a social good. The political costs for congressional and national Democrats were steep. Uncompetitive in large swaths of the South, liberals start any national, congressional, or local election by conceding most of the Old Confederacy.

In the realm of civil rights history, it is tempting to see historical actors engaged in a Manichaean struggle. By 1982, however, Jim Crow was dead. Reformers, both liberals and conservatives, faced an array of policy choices offering a plethora of unknown outcomes—none of which included reviving *Plessy v. Ferguson*. Well-intentioned New Politics reformers like Don Edwards opted for an admirable policy goal: black officeholders. They did so by rigging the system and forgoing the possibility of biracial political coalitions.

Ford's career reveals that opportunities for biracial coalition building, while difficult, existed. Moreover, once ensconced in a majority-minority district, the congressman behaved with impunity. Audaciousness without political consequences was hardly Ford's reserve. From Newt Gingrich's rhetorical bomb throwing to Congresswoman Cynthia McKinney's loony 9/11-conspiracy theories, uncompetitive districts breed poor public officials, bad policy, and noxious politics.[153] Moreover, for Democrats, majority-minority redistricting made their journey out of the wilderness that much more steep.

5

Liberal Interventionism

Senator Henry Jackson and the American Mission

The moral stakes were clear. By August 1978, the Khmer Rouge had murdered an estimated 1.5 million Cambodians. With nearly 20 percent of the country's population butchered, one observer claimed that Pol Pot's rampage made "Hitler's operation look tame."[1] Appalled at what he deemed "a clear case of genocide," Washington's most famous antiwar senator, George McGovern, did the unthinkable; he called for military intervention in Southeast Asia.[2] None other than William F. Buckley heartily endorsed the senator's proposal, which was met with a mix of alarm, confusion, derision, and surprise.[3]

In the wake of McGovern's bombshell, a motley coalition of liberals and right-wing conservatives pushed for action. Eventually, eighty senators approved a resolution calling for intervention to stop an ongoing genocide. With overwhelming bipartisan support, Jimmy Carter seemingly possessed the political backing to act. It was not to be. Instead of intervention, the president, who declared human rights the "cornerstone" of his foreign policy, sent a report on Pol Pot's crimes to the UN Human Rights Commission.[4] Meanwhile, the slaughter continued.

Befuddled at McGovern's seeming turnabout, the *Montreal Gazette*'s editors compared the senator's proposed humanitarian intervention to the Soviets' 1968 incursion into Czechoslovakia.[5] Claiming that no entity wanted "another war in Southeast Asia," they echoed the Carter administration's rationale for indifference.[6] Canadian journalists and American conservatives might have diverged on McGovern's proposal; they shared, however, a common bewilderment. How could the same senator who pushed to end one Southeast Asian war propose another just a few short years later? Buckley and the Canucks can be forgiven because most liberals, including McGovern, were similarly confused.

Henry M. Jackson playing baseball with John F. Kennedy and Mike Mansfield, ca. 1950s (courtesy University of Washington Libraries, Special Collections HMJ0738)

Long the noisy advocates for human rights and multilateral action, by the late 1970s liberals appeared bewildered about their core convictions. In this case, appearances did not deceive; liberals were confounded. The Vietnam War not only sowed destructive social divisions; it also muddied Democratic foreign policy. Prior to the conflict, most liberals embraced a type of liberal internationalism that assumed a degree of American foreign policy activism in the name of human rights and the promotion of democracy. The war, however, split liberals between old-style interventionists and New Politics global meliorists.

The tragedy that was Vietnam caused New Politics liberals to reject interventionism. Fearing that intrusions would lead to other Vietnams, they increasingly relied on nongovernment organizations to make their human rights claims across borders. In other words, liberals might have cared about human rights, but they declined to use the machinery of government to interfere in a sovereign state's internal affairs—even in the case of genocide.

Unlike New Politics liberals, Senator Henry (Scoop) Jackson maintained his liberal interventionism. Personifying early postwar liberal internationalism, Jackson believed that the United States was destined to spread liberal democratic values across the globe and duty bound to intervene to advance humanitarian aims.[7] Shaped by the exigencies of his age, his worldview began as a global meliorism, moved to a partiality for world government, and settled on what became liberal interventionism.

Liberal Internationalism

Liberal internationalism is no one single thing, theory, or idea. With a plethora of academics, practitioners, and politicians embracing this protean policy, the model possesses many different meanings over time. Indeed, the very term *liberal internationalist* came into vogue only in the early post-1945 era. As the "world stabilizer and repository of liberal values," liberal internationalists embraced America's role as the global hegemon.[8]

While liberal internationalists revolutionized American foreign policy tactics, they remained true to the nation's historic mission: redeeming the world.[9] The key to understanding the connection between mid-twentieth-century liberals and America's historic mission lies in the Puritans' "destinarian" zeal.[10] As a radical schism of a messianic outlier in Europe's Protestant movement, the seventeenth-century Separatists saw their march into the wilderness as nothing less than a journey to save the world.[11] Nearly four centuries later, liberal internationalism still bears this destinarian imprint.

Far from meek provincials fleeing the world stage, the Puritans believed that their "errand into the wilderness" would serve as a passive example to a fallen humanity. Secularizing the Puritans' original conceit and proselytizing ardor, the Founders were imbued with revolutionary zeal to "begin the world over again." Their internationalism was, nevertheless, tempered by a determination to remain aloof from the European scene.

It is clear that the makers of nineteenth-century American foreign policy avoided Thomas Jefferson's "entangling alliances"; however, it does not necessarily follow that nineteenth-century Americans were isolationist.[12] Rather than interpreting the federal government's reluctance to enter into alliances as proof of isolationism, recently scholars have looked beyond state officials in their assessment of U.S. foreign policy. According to them, during the nineteenth century individual Americans were thoroughly involved with and committed to transforming the wider world: the very definition of *internationalism*.[13]

Americans pursued their nation's historic mission in a variety of ways. From saving souls and expanding free trade to humanitarian interventions, their internationalism took many different forms. A transatlantic humanitarian movement, however, proved crucial in transforming U.S. foreign policy from individual, private crusades to a public and government project. Late nineteenth-century activists—all of whom came from the educated middle class—pushed and prodded their government to perform the yeoman work of humanitarian interventions. Feeding the starving in Russia, providing medical relief to Christians in the Ottoman Empire, and militarily intervening in Cuba were merely a few of the precursors leading to Woodrow Wilson's liberal internationalism.

The combination of humanitarian activists, American power, World War I, and Woodrow Wilson led to liberal internationalism's advent.[14] The original global meliorist, Wilson was convinced of America's "special role" in world affairs and renounced militarism, imperialism, and traditional power politics. In their stead, he believed, the League of Nations could create a "community of power and nations."[15] Reflecting a secularized version of the Puritans' mission, Wilson believed that liberal democracies offered the world salvation from war, poverty, and want.

An unabashed admirer of Wilson, Harry Truman shared a similar strategy but proffered different tactics. Truman also rejected traditional power politics and sought a world composed of free peoples and a community of liberal, democratic nations. Rather than pursue collective security via one international organization, the president opted for NATO and relied significantly more on force and coercive diplomacy. At root, liberal internationalists emphasized liberal democracy as the path most likely to safeguard American interests and promote democracy and human rights.

While postwar liberal internationalists, of all hues and stripes, agreed on ends, they differed on means. Old Wilsonians—global meliorists—invested much more faith in world organizations and assumed a more benign international system. In contrast, Truman-style liberal internationalists—interventionists—presumed conflict and the necessity of a robust American role.[16] From the Second World War's conclusion through the mid-1960s, global meliorists and interventionists were largely united under Truman-style liberal internationalism.

The tragic and senseless strategic miscue that was Vietnam revealed the deep and existing fissures within and among liberal internationalists. Fearing that interventionism would lead to other Vietnams, New Politics liberals turned to global meliorism.[17] In contrast, interventionists still foresaw a robust American role in safeguarding global stability and international human rights. During the 1970s, interventionists and global meliorists vied for control over Democratic foreign policy, a contest the latter won. Its policy merits aside, American voters hardly cottoned to global meliorism. From George McGovern and Jimmy Carter to Walter Mondale and Michael Dukakis, voters consistently rejected this brand of liberal foreign policy.

Henry Jackson and Liberal Internationalism

Political historians remember Senator Henry Jackson for his hard-line anticommunism and neoconservative protégés.[18] With neoconservatives invoking Jackson to justify the 2003 Iraq War, the senator's legacy became mired in contemporary political fisticuffs. In this way, his muscular liberal internationalism became an iconic symbol for many conservatives, neo and otherwise, who point to it as proof of modern liberalism's failings.

Jackson's liberalism and public philosophy are more complex than today's liberals and conservatives understand. A Truman-style liberal internationalist, Jackson believed that the United States was destined to spread liberal democratic values across the globe and duty bound to combat international communism.[19] Unlike many Democrats in the post-Vietnam era, he remained a liberal internationalist of an interventionist bent. Criticizing détente with the Soviet Union, he used Aleksandr Solzhenitsyn to illustrate realism's failings and in a failed attempt to revive his brand of liberal internationalism.

Born in a small mill town in Washington State's Puget Sound region, Jackson came of age in a veritable Norman Rockwell painting. The former paperboy earned his nickname, Scoop, from a comic strip character that possessed similar traits.[20] Adding to his all-American traits, as senator he earned infamy for his frayed suits and road-weary Chevrolet. Admirers rightfully claimed: "There is no such thing as an off-the-record Scoop. What you see is what he is."[21] He was no provincial simpleton, and a trio of global calamities—World War II, the Holocaust, and Stalinism—shaped his worldview.

In 1940, Jackson won a seat in the House of Representatives on a platform exclusively devoted to domestic issues. Despite best-laid plans, the young New Dealer was immediately thrust into a foreign policy controversy and confronted a major decision: support FDR's Lend-Lease proposal or break with his constituents. Though his "sympathies [we]re with England," the congressman followed his district's leanings and voted against Lend-Lease.[22]

With the economy slowly emerging from depression and domestic concerns foremost, the congressman, like a majority of his constituents, was "unalterably opposed to our country entering the European conflict."[23] One newspaper editor took issue with Jackson's vote, worrying that the congressman was "going to [be] a La Follette type," a progressive isolationist.[24] He need not have bothered; the congressman never entertained isolationism. He remained, like many liberal internationalists of his era, a global meliorist.

The Japanese attack on Pearl Harbor and Hitler's declaration of war earned Jackson's full-throated support for war. It was, however, the Nazis' savagery that proved decisive in his worldview's transformation. Visiting Buchenwald eleven days after the camp's liberation, Jackson left convinced of "how easily it could have happened to us if their program of world conquest had reached our shores."[25] He changed his prewar stance and now saw America's security as being intertwined with that of Europe.

Shaped by the Second World War and postwar Soviet expansion, Jackson's internationalism slowly evolved. In supporting American entry into the United Nations and NATO, Jackson, like millions of other liberals, sought to correct an earlier blunder.[26] As far as he and other UN advocates were concerned, the American refusal to join the League of Nations and exercise world leadership caused the Second World War.[27] To avoid a repeat of that mistake, Jackson heartily endorsed the Truman Doctrine, aid to Greece and Turkey, and the Marshall Plan.[28]

Global Meliorism and World Federalism

In the immediate postwar years, Jackson, like many other liberal internationalists, invested much hope in the United Nations. Hoping that it would develop into "a world federation of nations," he believed that the organization, along with the Atlantic Alliance, could enforce international law, prevent war, and stymie aggression.[29] Looking beyond the original intent of the United Nations, he hoped that the association of nations would function much like the American federal system; the central government would conduct foreign policy, while the states dealt with domestic affairs.[30]

Truly Wilsonian, Jackson's emphasis on institutions and international law represented the global meliorist side of the liberal internationalist coin. According to this view, poverty and oppression produced radicalism, aggression, and war. To prevent these maladies, global meliorists emphasized attacking, through international institutions, their socioeconomic roots.[31] They also emphasized the necessity of soft power in remedying the material roots of global problems.

Global meliorism heavily informed FDR's postwar vision, Truman's early foreign policy, and Jackson's worldview. For instance, as a member of the Joint Committee on Atomic Energy, Jackson extended his cooperative internationalism to the issue of nuclear weapons. Proposing to share America's nuclear secrets with Britain and France, he saw this as a first step toward his ultimate goal of the United Nation controlling the world's "atomic facilities."[32] As this showed, global meliorists possessed a deep and abiding faith in human rationality, the materialist basis of wars and social ills, and the promise of global collaboration.

Jackson was not alone in his heady, global meliorist optimism. Indeed, the carnage of the Second World War and the advent of the atomic age convinced many intellectuals and politicians that the times called for a world organization that could enforce international law and keep the peace.[33] By the late 1940s, a world federalist movement had gained considerable momentum and mainstream acceptance. Britain's Lord John Boyd Orr, for instance, won the 1949 Nobel Peace Prize for his scientific research and work as president of the Congress of World Federalist Organizations.[34]

Believing that world federalism would cause nations to "'pound our swords into plow shares' and offer the world a future of material welfare undreamed of," Jackson endorsed the movement.[35] In concert with the United World Federalists, whose leadership included the likes of Douglas Fairbanks, Albert Einstein, and Lewis Mumford, the congressman backed a constitutional amendment mandating American participation in a global federal government.[36]

The world federalist movement was not limited to Europeans, movie stars, and fuzzy-haired physicists. Both Frank Church and Alan Cranston, future senators from Idaho and California, were early backers of the idea.[37] Moreover, the state legislatures of California, North Carolina, Maine, Connecticut, New Jersey, and Florida all passed resolutions urging a constitutional convention on the subject.[38] Although editors at the *Seattle Post-Intelligencer* claimed that the proposal defiled and annulled the U.S. Constitution, Jackson pushed for the amendment aggressively.[39] With seven hundred chapters of the United World Federalists spread across the United States and backers spanning the globe, the congressman was not alone in dreaming of collective security through world government. Indeed, the newly written Italian and French constitutions contained clauses allowing for just such an eventuality.[40]

Reinhold Niebuhr and Liberal Interventionism

North Korea's June 1950 invasion of South Korea torpedoed Jackson's faith in world federalism.[41] Although wary of the Kremlin's intentions, two weeks before the incursion Jackson had declared disarmament and world federalism the keys to world peace. Indeed, the Soviets' development of a nuclear weapon and America's consequent hydrogen bomb had only deepened his commitment to world federalism.[42] Like many global meliorists, he believed that an effective system of UN-monitored disarmament would free defense dollars for the international aid and assistance that would eradicate the root causes of war.[43]

Like Truman, Jackson interpreted North Korea's aggression as part and parcel of the Soviets' drive for world power and hegemony in Eurasia. Drawing on the lessons of the 1930s, both thought it reminiscent of Germany's demands on Czechoslovakia at Munich.[44] On June 26, the day after the invasion, Jackson revealed his changing worldview by telling a radio audience: "For the first time, the two great powers of the world—Russia and the United States—come face to face in a direct conflict."[45] Never again would he declare that an era of peace and disarmament were within Americans' grasp.[46] Now, instead of disarmament, the congressman called for "augmenting the firepower of our Armed Forces."[47]

The Korean War transformed Jackson's liberal internationalism from global meliorism to interventionism. This evolution emerged in concert with Reinhold Niebuhr's theology and political thought. Niebuhr proved crucial in helping liberal internationalists formulate an interventionism that remained true to the American mission yet stopped short of conservative rollback and arrogant missionizing.

Attacking global meliorists for their starry-eyed cooperative internationalism, and steering clear of right-wing saber rattling, Niebuhr pursued a middle course.[48] With humanity's inherent sinfulness rendering millennial progress moot, the archetypal realist remained committed to the American mission to redeem the world.[49] Developing a more refined and sophisticated version of it, Niebuhr claimed that God had chosen the United States to defend "Western Civilization."[50] All the same, he fundamentally rejected any nation's or ideology's claim to transhistorical meaning. In other words, Niebuhr might have embraced America's "chosenness," but he contended that no individual or nation could fully act immanently.[51]

In this way, Niebuhr would intervene, or stage any foreign policy venture, only under certain circumstances. Recognizing that nations act from self-interest and individuals discern their motivations only with extraordinary difficulty, if at all, he called for multilateralism. With allies better able to detect hidden, selfish motives within their partner states, the theologian reasoned that America could maintain its responsibility to the world while restraining its messianic passion and inherent sinfulness.

The Soviets might have required containment, but for Niebuhr any superpower utterly convinced of its transhistorical role presented an international danger. In this way, his brand of liberal Protestantism offered a necessary rein on Americans' destinarian fervor. The theologian's restraints came none too soon. Whereas the Founders envisioned their work as a world-altering experiment, they possessed little power to pursue their grand project.

Few, if any, world leaders much noticed the braggadocio of the infant republic, then the geopolitical equivalent of a Chihuahua. One hundred sixty years later, however, America's greatly enhanced power rendered its foreign policy ardor a global concern. In terms of actual policy, Niebuhr's tempered vision found expression in the limited and achievable ends of postwar liberal interventionists.

While Jackson hardly read Niebuhr closely, the theologian's ideas most definitely influenced early Cold Warriors and their policy. Moreover, in 1953, the congressman, along with other seminal Cold War liberals like JFK and Mike Mansfield, won election to the U.S. Senate. Over the ensuing three decades, Jackson honed his worldview and became an iconic symbol of a Niebuhrian brand of liberal interventionism.

Eager to see the Soviet Union for himself, Senator Jackson joined a group of dignitaries for a tour. During his 1956 excursion, he noted, "Everywhere we went people were genuinely friendly," but he also recognized the human costs of a collectivized economy. Discovering that a physician's family shared a three-room apartment with two other families, he surmised that the Soviet Union made "military and foreign relations strides . . . by depriving its people of the goods and services Americans take for granted."[52] In this way, his ten-thousand-mile journey reinforced what he had already come to believe—that the Soviet Union was a totalitarian society that routinely trampled on human rights to achieve its revolutionary goals.

Scarcely the Dr. Strangelove his leftist opponents imagined, Jackson foresaw a long struggle that was unlikely to be won on a conventional battlefield. Thus, he backed increased defense spending, but in the spirit of George Kennan he also looked for less militarized means of waging and winning the Cold War.[53] Starting in the 1950s, the senator began attacking the Kremlin's abysmal human rights record. He did so to put the Soviets on the defensive and appeal to nonaligned countries.

During the 1960s, Jackson's worldview remained essentially what it had been since the Korean War. Claiming that the Kremlin would always "be tempted to pursue its imperial purposes," the senator might have seen the Soviets for what they were, but he failed to appreciate the changing complexities of the Communist world. As a result, he blindly backed the war in Vietnam and saw strategic parity as a recipe for disaster.[54]

To be fair, the Brezhnev-era Soviet Union called for a remarkably deft and subtle understanding of the Kremlin. Even Jackson realized that the Soviets' revolutionary zeal had abated.[55] The senator, nonetheless, failed to appreciate the implications of the Sino-Soviet split and the demise of a monolithic Communist world. In addition to its changing foreign policy, by the late 1960s the Soviet Union had reformed its human rights record. No longer indiscriminately murdering its dissidents, the Kremlin jailed them.[56] Given their distinctive worldviews, global meliorists and liberal interventionists vied over just how much the Soviet Union had changed.

For Jackson, the Kremlin remained committed to revolutionary tumult. As a result, he staunchly supported the American effort in Vietnam. In that one regard, he backed Richard Nixon; otherwise, he was appalled by the president's realism and pursuit of détente with the Soviet Union. Vietnam's social and economic shockwaves had pushed Nixon and his national security adviser, Henry Kissinger, to pursue a new era of strategic parity, a turnabout Jackson vigorously opposed.[57]

Though the president achieved arms limitation agreements, trade pacts, and improved superpower relations, Jackson remained unmoved. Convinced that the Soviets represented a global menace to stability, democracy, and human rights, he became the most significant opponent of détente. Looking to rally liberals to the interventionist standard, he made human rights his central theme. Indeed, he not only blasted détente for its amoral tolerance of Soviet human rights violations; he also claimed that the policy made Americans complicit in the Kremlin's brutality.[58]

Human Rights and U.S. Foreign Policy

The orthodox histories of the 1960s and 1970s see the eras as a study in absolute contrasts. Whereas the former witnessed liberal dynamism, the latter supposedly featured the total demise of these impulses. In terms of a broad reform movement making demands on an activist government, this caricature captures a semblance of reality. However, the 1970s did not witness the total demise of such activism. In the case of human rights, the era produced the emergence of a transnational human rights movement.

During the 1970s, the human rights movement found expression in the form of nongovernment organizations (NGOs). These transnational organizations, such as Amnesty International and Human Rights Watch, were dedicated to stopping the state-sponsored repression of human rights.[59] Activists utilized NGOs largely because Vietnam and the Cold War turned them away from state-sponsored interventionism. Hardly new, these human rights activists opted for a global meliorism that relied more on international institutions than the state. Preceding Woodrow Wilson and liberal internationalism, this type of advocacy began in the nineteenth century.

Humanitarianism does not usually play a significant role in most historical treatments of nineteenth-century American history. Indeed, the nineteenth century has a well-deserved reputation as the heyday of European and American imperialism and realpolitik. In spite of this reality, humanitarian sensibilities did influence Western foreign policies.[60] Initially catalyzed by the "teeming mass of ideas" linked to the American and French Revolutions, the humanitarian "association mania," as the London Times dubbed it, reflected the materialization of a humanitarian movement.[61]

Humanitarianism was a decidedly liberal project premised on the Enlightenment's fundamental hypothesis that all human life is equal.[62] The emphases of the American and French Revolutions on natural rights along with the emergence of the mass press, public opinion, and democratic (responsive) governments helped transform humanitarianism into a mass movement. More importantly, these ideological and institutional developments made humanitarian interventionism—governments acting to protect human life beyond its borders—both politically possible and popular.[63]

Contemporary observers have dubbed public outcry at images of human suffering and attendant calls for government action *the CNN effect*. However, media's ability to depict individual anguish, shape public opinion, and create calls for intervention existed prior to cable news. Indeed, rising literacy rates across Western Europe and America caused the proliferation of mass media in the form of newspapers and magazines, enabling nineteenth-century print media to perform the same function as television does today.[64]

Humanitarian intervention was not a top-down, White House–led endeavor. Instead, it was a grassroots movement emanating from the nation's educated middle class. Surprisingly, America's first humanitarian intervention emerged as a private (nongovernment) venture. In response to the 1892–1893 Russian famine, a Davenport, Iowa, newspaper editor, Benjamin Franklin Tillinghast, launched a national famine relief effort. Much more than simple charity, the Iowa Russian Famine Relief Commission represented the confluence of the transnational humanitarian movement with Americans' sense of mission in the world. Together, the mishmash created a new chapter in U.S. diplomatic history.

Quintessentially American, the Iowa Russian Famine Relief Commission emanated from American missionizing but was coordinated from Tillinghast's newspaper office. Lacking federal oversight, military transports, and bullets, what became a national famine relief enterprise, nevertheless, constitutes a humanitarian intervention. In foisting thirty-two thousand tons of food and hundreds of foreign observers, members of the media, and relief workers on a reluctant tsar, Americans effectively barged into the internal affairs of a sovereign state.

Trumpeted by governors, President Benjamin Harrison, and celebrities, the effort grew in popularity. Ultimately, the endeavor also helped condition voters and politicians to accept humanitarian intervention as a legitimate foreign policy expression of the traditional American mission. Within three years of the Iowa Russian Famine Relief Commission, Congress debated the merits of militarily intervening to stop Ottoman atrocities against its Armenian subjects.[65]

As with the Russian famine relief effort, private citizens stepped into the breach. Flanked by relief organizations and Tillinghast's Iowa Relief Committee, Clara Barton negotiated access to the Armenians and directed the American Red Cross's first humanitarian intervention on foreign soil.[66] Armenia not only remained a potent domestic issue; the Red Cross incursion also established yet another precedent for intervention.[67] In justifying the Spanish-American War two years later, McKinley referred to the "many historical precedents where neighboring States have interfered . . . to check the hopeless sacrifices of life by internecine conflicts beyond their borders." In this way, the president merely followed where the American people had already led.[68]

While the Spanish-American War had imperialist results, it was spawned from humanitarian motives, an irony fit for Reinhold Niebuhr. The war soured that generation's humanitarian activists on military interventions in the name of humanitarian ends—until Woodrow Wilson's "war to make the world safe for democracy." In a similar fashion, the Vietnam War turned humanitarians toward NGOs and away from state-sponsored interventionism.

Using human rights as political shorthand for Soviet oppression, Jackson sought to revive liberal interventionism in the post-Vietnam era. To do so, he relied on that most American of creeds: religious freedom. A longtime burr in his foreign policy saddle, the Soviets' "lip service to religious freedom" had been the object of his criticism for decades. In the mid-1970s, he stumbled on an issue that crystallized a humanitarian's reverence for individual freedom, exposed Soviet hypocrisy, and appealed to a religiously minded constituency.[69]

Human Détente

During the 1970s, rising anti-Semitism combined with the Kremlin's suppression of religious freedom caused thousands of Soviet Jews to apply for emigration visas. Using a combination of bureaucratic machinations and overt oppression, the Soviets actively squelched Jewish migration. Despite these machinations, applications for exit visas by Soviet Jews skyrocketed from thirty-one hundred in 1968 to sixty-eight thousand by 1972.[70]

In response to an emergent exodus of Jews, in September 1972 the Soviet Union essentially closed the door on emigration by imposing a steep "diploma tax."[71] Recognizing a potent issue when he found one, the senator pounced. Jackson proposed landmark legislation linking Soviet emigration policy to trade. Calling his bill the moral foundation of a "genuine détente," he made human rights and free emigration central to U.S.-Soviet relations.[72]

In fact, Jackson never truly believed that détente was possible. While

Nixon and Kissinger saw the policy as the recognition of Soviet military parity, Jackson believed that the Kremlin used détente to gain a strategic advantage.[73] In retrospect, historians realize just how far behind the Soviets lagged in science, technology, agriculture, and business management. Thus, Jackson's claim of Kremlin superiority in ICBM "throw weight" altering the "world's strategic balance" was hyperbole.[74] Nevertheless, the senator sincerely believed that realism gave the Soviet Union military superiority, undermining NATO's cohesion, and threatening the Western alliance.

While Jackson overestimated Soviet military capabilities, he understood that liberals lacked purpose in foreign policy. For better or for worse, most Americans see their nation pursuing a divinely ordained mission in the world. According to Andrew Preston, this missionizing leads activists to push U.S. foreign policy in a "moralist, crusading, and sometimes humanitarian direction."[75] For this reason, when Jackson called for a "clear movement of people and ideas across international boundaries," crowds rose to their feet in applause.[76] Thus, Jackson's use of human rights represented a useful attempt to imbue post-Vietnam liberal foreign policy with a sense of purpose that could appeal to American voters.

In 1975, the senator had bigger aims than simply reviving liberal interventionism. He intended to ride the human rights issue to the White House. Realizing that Soviet emigration policy remained more than a tad abstract for the average voter, he found a person to embody the issue: Aleksandr Solzhenitsyn. The renowned novelist and Soviet dissident was an unusual poster child for a presidential campaign.[77] Literary elites and Sovietologists knew him from his acclaimed novels and Nobel Prize for literature. Part Old Testament prophet and part literary genius, Solzhenitsyn was made by Jackson the symbol for what the senator called *human détente*.

Born to bourgeois, left-leaning parents in the shadow of the Bolshevik Revolution, Solzhenitsyn grew up a confirmed Leninist. A member of the Young Communist League, he earned degrees in mathematics, physics, and literature before serving as an artillery battery commander during the Second World War. During that stint, he wrote letters containing criticism of Stalin's leadership. Imprisoned for his thought crime, he labored in Stalin's infamous gulags, where his revolutionary certainty turned to doubt. On his release, he committed himself to publicizing the gruesome realities of Soviet communism.[78]

In his novels, Solzhenitsyn depicted how Soviet reality rarely conformed to the Kremlin's official line. Ironically, he became a living case study of this proposition. Throughout the West, he was regarded as "the only living classic Russian," writing in the tradition of Tolstoy, Dostoyevsky, and Chekhov.[79] In the Soviet Union, however, he was unemployable and unpublishable, and he survived on a meager pension.[80] Destitute in the Soviet Union, Solzhenitsyn possessed relative wealth from book sales in the West, a fortune he could neither access nor spend so long as he remained in the Soviet Union. Officially, his books were banned in the Soviet Union; in reality, all Russian intellectuals read Solzhenitsyn.[81] In theory and in reality, he soon became the Soviet Union's premier dissident.

In January 1974, Solzhenitsyn earned this status by allowing Western publishers to issue *The Gulag Archipelago, 1918–1956.* A history of the Soviet secret police, harsh labor camps, and Stalin's terror, the book represented a direct challenge to the Kremlin's authority. Indeed, Solzhenitsyn not only detailed Stalin's show trials, torture, and mass exterminations; he also committed a mortal sin in the theology of Soviet Communism—tracing Stalin's misdeeds back to Lenin.[82] By explicitly and graphically recounting Lenin's crimes, he staged a literary frontal assault on the entire Soviet system.[83]

The author's personal challenge to the Kremlin's leadership simply could not go without an official response. In fact, one of Solzhenitsyn's compatriots claimed: "If he gets away with this we will know that we live in a different country."[84] The very next day, this dissident discovered the Soviet Union remained a police state. On February 12, 1974, a team of Soviet secret police broke into his apartment and hauled him away for interrogation.[85] Twenty-four hours later, Solzhenitsyn resurfaced in West Germany, a victim of expulsion from his own country.[86] Jackson now had his human rights icon.

Pouncing on the publicity associated with the Soviet expulsion of their Nobel Prize–winning citizen, Jackson accused the Nixon administration of narrowing "its conception of détente to exclude issues of human rights."[87] Nixon's resignation merely fueled the political storm aimed at détente. Freed from Watergate and from defending the president from his critics, conservative Republicans renewed their attacks on Kissinger's realism. As a result, Gerald Ford was forced to defend an inherited foreign policy from a decidedly weakened political position.

Jackson shared with right-wing Republicans a distaste for détente, but with that their commonalities ceased. In this way, liberal interventionists starkly diverged from conservatives. For instance, Jackson worked with Ohio congressman John Ashbrook and North Carolina senator Jesse Helms on the issue.[88] However, Ashbrook regularly accused "liberals in collaboration with big business" of supporting détente and undermining American national security. Similarly, Helms defended U.S. relations with Chile by claiming that Augusto Pinochet's dictatorship was "not much different from what we have here."[89] Avoiding rhetorical excess, insults, and outright slander, Jackson prized human rights, not hypernationalist chauvinism.

Marshaling his motley coalition of conservatives and liberal interventionists, the senator attached his Jackson-Vanik amendment to the 1974 omnibus trade bill. According to the legislation, in return for most-favored-nation trade status, lower tariffs, and import-export bank credits, the Soviet Union would significantly ease its emigration restrictions.[90] The specter of the amendment's political strength was so powerful that Ford shared his first White House breakfast with the leading Senate Jackson-Vanik sponsors, Jackson, Abraham Ribicoff, and Jacob Javits.[91]

Realizing that the administration could not stop the legislation, Kissinger had by October reached a compromise with Jackson that made the Jackson-Vanik amendment law. The "Pact of the Two Henrys" provided for an eighteen-month trial during which the Soviets would receive trade benefits in return for emigration reform.[92] If they restricted emigration, Congress could revoke most-favored-nation status.[93]

Not coincidentally, by early 1975 Jackson was gearing up for a presidential campaign. Making international human rights a major theme, he hoped that his human détente would bring Jewish groups, the educated middle class, and organized labor to his standard. Since a vast number of Soviet dissidents were Jewish, American Jews, a key Democratic constituency, agitated for greater attention to their plight.[94] As a result, Jackson hoped that human détente would put Ford on the defensive and garner Jewish primary votes and campaign contributions.[95]

In addition to Jewish voters was a newly significant Democratic bloc, the educated middle class. To woo these voters, Jackson pursued opinion leaders who would second his call for greater freedom in the Soviet Union. From socialists (e.g., Michael Harrington) and liberals (e.g., James MacGregor Burns) to neocons (e.g., Irving Kristol) and conservatives (e.g., George Will), the senator's basic premise won wide ideological backing.[96] Embracing his formulation, these opinion leaders claimed that détente must be more than an absence of military confrontation or the exchange of vodka for Pepsi-Cola.[97]

With intellectuals firmly behind him, Jackson reached out to his most ardent supporters—organized labor. The AFL-CIO's George Meany was not only a staunch anti-Communist; he was also interested in blocking free trade with Russia, or any other country, to protect American jobs. Delighted to support a Jackson presidential campaign, he helped organize an April 1975 Solidarity Day rally in New York City. There, Meany, Jackson, and 100,000 protesters denounced détente Soviets and the Kremlin's repeated human rights violations.[98] Following this successful action, the AFL-CIO invited Solzhenitsyn to tour the United States and give his first major public address since his expulsion.[99]

Claiming that he was in no "position to undertake long journeys," Solzhenitsyn had spent his first year in the West finishing a novel.[100] His spring 1975 American tour posed a major political problem for Gerald Ford. As a matter of courtesy and smart politics, George Meany had invited the president to the banquet honoring Solzhenitsyn. Kissinger believed that Ford's attendance could irritate the Kremlin and torpedo détente for good. If the president refused the invitation, Jackson received a potent issue. As the Ford administration was wont to do, it bungled the entire matter in just about every way imaginable.

Three days prior to Solzhenitsyn's long-awaited speech, the White House canceled Ford's appearance at the banquet. Citing a "heavy schedule of commitments," officials claimed that the president could neither attend the dinner nor even meet privately with the author.[101] Unfortunately for the president, his scheduled obligations amounted to a dinner with his daughter that came on the heels of meetings with a "Cotton Queen," the soccer star Pele, and an artist who had "sculpted the . . . Alaska pipeline."[102] Pilloried for this decision, the administration first questioned Solzhenitsyn's mental health and then claimed that the author merely wanted publicity to sell more books. In this way, Solzhenitsyn's American debut had become a media event and a White House headache.

Addressing an enthusiastic crowd of twenty-five hundred at the AFL-CIO banquet, Solzhenitsyn bitterly attacked détente and the entire Soviet system. Referring to Khrushchev's infamous threat, "We will bury you," he called it shorthand for "détente."[103] As if he was eager to prove that Kissinger's fears were well founded, he begged for continued interference in Soviet internal policies. The Kremlin's pleas of "Don't interfere in our internal affairs," he declared, really meant "Let us strangle our citizens in peace and quiet."[104]

Administration hopes that Solzhenitsyn would vanish from the headlines were quickly dashed. Following the AFL-CIO banquet, the writer embarked on an American tour during which he pilloried détente in the direst manner imaginable. Calling détente an illusion, he declared: "The Cold War is still going on, but from the other side. I can assure you the Cold War has never stopped for one second in the Soviet Union."[105] "Soon they will be twice as powerful as you . . . and then 10 times," he breathlessly warned. "Some day they will say to you: 'We are marching our troops into Western Europe, and if you act, we shall annihilate you.'"[106] Not surprisingly, these grim predictions made headlines.

The "Solzhenitsyn Affair" earned the Ford White House considerable bad press. From Russell Baker and George Will to the *Washington Post's* Pulitzer Prize–winning political cartoonist Herb Block, pundits excoriated Ford's snub. Will complained that détente gave the Kremlin veto power over the "appointments calendar of the President."[107] Block's syndicated cartoon was even harsher. The cartoonist drew Ford hiding under his Oval Office desk as Solzhenitsyn departed, the caption featuring Kissinger telling the President: "It's all right to come out now. If you had met him, Brezhnev might have disapproved."[108]

Provided with a national spotlight, Jackson pressed his advantage, as did Solzhenitsyn.[109] When Jackson could not finagle enough support for the author to address a joint session of Congress, he used the Senate office building as a speaking venue.[110] Serving as Solzhenitsyn's host while he toured Capitol Hill, Jackson accused Ford of "cowering" in fear of the Soviets and, as a result, "sid[ing] with the Soviet rulers against the American commitment to freedom."[111]

Solzhenitsyn's Capitol Hill speech sparked even wider denunciations of Ford's rebuff and détente. The *New York Times* editorial staff, for instance, accused the president of confusing détente with appeasement. Jackson took up this charge in speeches delivered across the country. Claiming that "Congress . . . knows the difference between détente and appeasement," he repeated his call for human détente based on freedom and reciprocity.[112]

Meanwhile, the administration was scrambling to repair the political damage. Though White House officials were divided, Ford finally listened to his chief of staff, Dick Cheney—in a clumsy sort of way. During a staged "informal chat" with reporters, the president claimed that he was willing to meet Solzhenitsyn.[113] Dutifully taking Ford's cue, they reported the policy reversal and the president's "open invitation." Unfortunately for Ford, Solzhenitsyn did not play along. Refusing the bait, he never asked for a meeting, which only added to the administration's woes.[114]

The Solzhenitsyn Affair metastasized from a small public relations gaffe into a full-scale controversy. In weakening domestic support for détente, the episode displayed the political potency of Jackson's interventionist brand of liberal internationalism. A staunch multilateralist, Jackson did not allow for unilateral adventurism in his interventionism. Grounded in a Niebuhrian sense of humility, limits, and tragic optimism, liberal interventionists made human rights claims across borders. Most significantly, they were willing to use the machinery of government to communicate and, at times, act on these concerns.

In contrast, global meliorists increasingly channeled their human rights activism through NGOs and international institutions. A byproduct of Vietnam, these liberals saw danger in government intrusion into the internal affairs of other states. In this way, they betrayed an understandable aversion to the excesses of American missionizing. They did, however, forget one key point that their fellow global meliorist, George McGovern, had understood in the case of Pol Pot and Cambodia. Because America was a global hegemon, its leadership remained vital for those hoping to advance the cause of human rights.

Despite the power of his message, Jackson saw his presidential ambitions flounder. A poor public speaker who garbled applause lines, his campaign slogan, "The charisma of competence," merely reminded voters of his limits.[115] Moreover, New Politics liberals deemed the senator a reactionary. Without the educated middle class, the senator's campaign believed that a very crowded field would split the New Politics vote and leave the political center open. This might well have happened if not for Jimmy Carter.[116]

With a chameleon-like ability to convince both liberals and conservatives that he was one of them, Carter took the political center from Jackson, the right from George Wallace, and a share of the New Politics from the rest.[117] Moreover, by promising to make international human rights the cornerstone of his foreign policy, he effectively stole Jackson's main issue. The senator might have made human rights political shorthand for Soviet oppression, but Carter reaped the benefits. Indeed, the seminal moment of the 1976 presidential election occurred when, in a nationally televised debate with Carter, Ford claimed that Eastern Europe was not under Soviet domination.

As president and a foreign policy novice, Carter pursued his "corner-

stone" with decidedly mixed results. Pinballing between the global meliorists and the liberal interventionists, he failed to forge a consistent human
rights strategy. The Solzhenitsyn Affair and the role that human rights
played in the 1976 campaign reveal that Jackson's legacy consists of more
than a smattering of impulsive, neoconservative unilateralists.

The senator's political inheritance aside, for a generation liberals wandered the foreign policy wilderness. They did so because American voters
sought a worldview that responded to their sense of mission in the world.
That the redeemer nation motif leads to unnecessary conflicts is all too, and
tragically, true. It is, nevertheless, a theme that liberal policymakers must
heed.

6

The Middle East
of Domestic Politics

Jimmy Carter and Welfare Reform

Linda Taylor wore many hats. A voodoo doctor, bigamist, suspected child nabber, and overall con artist, the forty-seven-year-old Chicagoan also earned infamy in the 1976 presidential campaign.[1] Identified as the nation's most notorious "welfare queen" by Ronald Reagan, Taylor found herself in the governor's standard stump speech. Though the Gipper failed to capture the GOP nomination, "welfare cheats" became customary boilerplate for the New Right.

Ronald Reagan understood the power of an anecdote. Cutting through the highfalutin fog of details, a well-told and -timed yarn emotionally connected voters to abstract issues. As he was wont to do, Reagan stretched the truth by claiming that Taylor possessed eighty aliases, thirty addresses, and twelve Social Security accounts—but only a little.[2] In addition to fraudulent cash payments, which paid for her Lincoln, Chevrolet station wagon, and Cadillac, Taylor also collected benefits for her "deaf, retarded, and totally disabled" daughter, a claim that investigators discovered to be totally false.[3]

Critics sneered and rolled their eyes at Reagan's "anecdotage," but voters responded.[4] By making welfare queens the symbol of the liberal welfare state, Reagan and the New Right slowly turned voters against it. In fact, during the 1970s no single domestic issue damaged liberals more than welfare.[5] Whether it was food stamps or cash assistance, state aid to the nonworking poor became political kryptonite for liberals. With Reagan using a few high-profile cheats and fudging the facts, Republicans led voters to believe that "people . . . have it to[o] easy on Welfare better than those that work."[6]

America's individualistic political culture has always produced popular

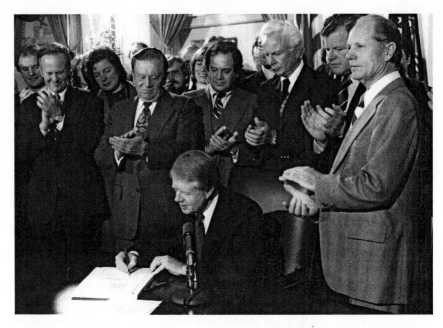

President Jimmy Carter signing Air Transportation Reform, October 24, 1978
(courtesy Jimmy Carter Library and Museum)

antipathy toward a thoroughgoing welfare state. The flaccid economy during the 1970s, coupled with expanding social service spending for the nonworking poor, rendered voters even more hostile to welfare. Moreover, the
economic woes of the 1970s, namely, stagflation, were particularly traumat-
ic when experienced against the still-fresh memories of the 1960s. As late as
1969, the U.S. economy boasted 3.3 percent unemployment and 6.4 percent
growth rates. By the early 1970s, those economic times had surely passed.

An economy burdened by inflation reached a crisis point when the
1973–1974 Arab oil embargo spawned spiraling prices and unemployment.
Together, this mishmash made economic history and caused economists to
invent a new term: *stagflation.* Prior to the 1970s, economists presumed that
high unemployment and rising inflation violated basic economic principles.
In 1975, however, unemployment and inflation reached near-historic levels,
8.5 percent and 11 percent—hence, the new coinage.[7] Consequently, American workers faced an economy in which their dollar's buying power was cut
in half from 1970 to 1980.[8] Encouraged by Reagan and their tax bills, many
turned their ire toward welfare recipients.

Whether it was because of welfare queens or supposedly posh public housing, conservatives tapped into voters' belief that the nonworking poor were bleeding them dry. The burgeoning costs of welfare were not merely a figment of taxpayers' imagination. Owing to Great Society programs instituted in the mid-1960s, social services for the nonworking poor increased precipitously in the 1970s. Moreover, the costs borne by the federal government had to be matched by states and localities. For example, New Jersey reported that state funds spent on welfare rose from $35.7 million in 1966 to almost $501 million in 1976 while the number of people enrolled rose by only 13 percent.[9] As a result of spiraling expenditures, states and localities either increased taxes or reduced other public services.

The most controversial of all welfare programs was Aid to Families with Dependent Children (AFDC). As a direct cash benefit to the nonworking poor, AFDC became synonymous, in the public mind, with welfare. As the number of single female-headed households skyrocketed throughout the 1960s and 1970s, the AFDC budget increased, and so did public ire at liberals.

Entitlement versus Opportunity Liberals

Ironically, Franklin Roosevelt's New Deal coalition was being undermined by a welfare policy he would have abhorred.[10] Indeed, FDR always felt that relief was akin to a subtle narcotic suppressing the human spirit. According to this premise, Social Security was established on the principle that recipients paid into the system and were not simply entitled to a pension. To receive a monthly Social Security check, individuals must, in theory, have worked for it.

Establishing a welfare state that remained true to the nation's individualist political culture was one of FDR's unnoticed yet signature achievements. With Social Security establishing the paradigm, opportunity liberals followed the Roosevelt example. In this way, federal activism commanded public support so long as programs called on recipients to labor in return for benefits. Following FDR's lead, New Deal, Fair Deal, New Frontier, and early Great Society activisms were founded on an opportunity liberal ethos.

By the 1970s, this New Deal governing philosophy had been supplanted by the New Politics–inspired philosophy of entitlement liberalism. In contrast to opportunity liberals, entitlement liberals clamored for income redistribution and cut the tie linking work to benefits. Starkly rejecting the New

Deal's work for benefits calculus, activists even pushed for a guaranteed income for all Americans.

For entitlement liberals, the federal government had an obligation to raise all Americans above the poverty level, no questions asked. Indeed, every citizen possessed an inherent right to benefits. In contrast, New Deal liberals adhered to the nation's individualist political culture. Consequently, they pushed economic growth, jobs, and education, not guaranteed incomes, as the cure for poverty.[11] By the 1970s, however, the guaranteed income had become the touchstone of entitlement liberal welfare policy. Thus, Department of Health, Education, and Welfare (HEW) bureaucrats designed welfare policies reflecting these principles and pressed the Nixon, Ford, and Carter administrations for their enactment.[12]

Surprisingly, Nixon's welfare reform plan, the Family Assistance Plan (FAP), contained generous guaranteed-income provisions. Despite this apparent victory, entitlement liberals deemed FAP "medieval and cruel" because it mandated work in return for welfare benefits.[13] They pressed, instead, for a guaranteed-income bill that was more generous and less onerous for recipients. In so doing, they signaled how far entitlement liberals had traveled from their New Deal roots.

Jimmy Carter and the Middle East of Domestic Politics

On paper, the peanut farmer–turned–submarine officer–cum–politician appeared perfectly suited to quell the entitlement liberal tide. Tapping into growing antipathy against "big government," on the campaign trail Carter called the tax code "a disgrace to the human race" and the federal bureaucracy "totally unmanageable" and "incompetent."[14] As a result, in contrast to the supporters of his New Politics opponents, the typical Carter Democrat was younger, white-collar, Protestant, and from a rural area or small town.[15]

During his 1976 presidential campaign, Carter consistently vowed to reform welfare. His promises to purge 1.3 million people from the welfare rolls elicited murmurs of approval from audiences. Unlike Reagan, the Georgian did not inveigh against welfare cheats. Instead, he promised that, if recipients refused employment on completion of a training program, he "would not pay them any more benefits."[16]

As president, Carter fully intended to implement his campaign pledge to reform welfare. Unfortunately for him, the combination of ideological in-

fighting and his own ineptitude undermined this promise. More importantly, this failure revealed a much more significant issue: liberals' inability to
reform their increasingly unpopular creed. Carter's own secretary of health,
education, and welfare might have called welfare "the Middle East of domestic politics," but Democrats controlled the White House, the Senate, and
the House; therefore, Carter's welfare reform was possible.[17] Moreover, welfare reform remained an enormously popular proposal. With both the power and strong incentives, liberals, somehow, squandered the opportunity.

Full Employment

While entitlement liberals possessed momentum, their opportunity liberal
rivals proffered a legislative alternative to a guaranteed income: full employment.[18] With Rooseveltian roots, full employment represented a politically
viable alternative to unpopular New Politics welfare programs. In his 1944
State of the Union address, FDR unveiled his "second bill of rights." Declaring rights to education, health care, a home, and even reasonable farm
income, he claimed: "The most fundamental right is to a useful and remu-
nerative job."[19] The speech established postwar liberalism's basic parame-
ters and made full employment basic Democratic policy for decades.

Though full-employment legislation had been proposed before, after
FDR's death proponents wrapped themselves in his mantle, rendering resistance tantamount to opposing a dead martyr. Pushing the issue was Secretary of Commerce Henry A. Wallace. In the fall of 1945, he published *Sixty
Million Jobs* to pressure the new president, Harry Truman, to make FDR's
full employment a reality.[20]

Pushed from the left, Truman endorsed the Employment Act of 1946,
which, among other things, established the Council of Economic Advisors.[21]
A disappointment to Wallace, the bill, nonetheless, helped institutionalize
the fuzzy goal of maximum employment as national policy. Moreover, one
of the council's first chairmen, Leon Keyserling, became a leading voice for
full-employment policy well into the 1970s.

Like nearly all economists of his era, Keyserling believed that "high
buying power" remained the key to preventing economic calamity.[22] With
full employment still seen as an economic elixir, the 1974–1975 recession
reignited liberal cries for FDR's "most fundamental right."[23] As a result, the
old New Dealers Senator Hubert Humphrey and Congressman Augustus
Hawkins, aligned with the AFL-CIO, rolled out their perennial answer to

any economic woe—full-employment legislation. This iteration of Democratic orthodoxy was titled the Humphrey-Hawkins "Full Employment and Balanced Growth" bill.[24]

As Jimmy Carter assumed office, two major domestic dilemmas confronted his administration: unemployment and public antipathy to liberal activism. His attempt to solve both with a comprehensive welfare reform bill, the Program for Better Jobs and Income (PBJI), revealed the divergent impulses tearing liberalism apart. In PBJI, Carter tried to fuse the entitlement liberal policies of a guaranteed income with New Deal liberalism's dream of full employment. The resulting legislation was a confused jumble that only confirmed what voters suspected—liberals could not reform their creed.

The bill's short life—from its February 1977 inception, to its public presentation in August 1977, to its eventual death in committee in December of the same year—reveals much about the Carter presidency. Always ambitious, the president wanted to propose and pass welfare reform in his first year in office. His expedited timetable was based on HEW secretary Joseph Califano's estimate. In an informal telephone conversation between the two, Califano suggested that welfare reform could be crafted and passed within the administration's first year.[25]

Welfare reform was not the only domestic item on the president's agenda. Carter also pushed an energy policy and national health insurance. Two weeks after taking office, he delivered a fireside chat in which he outlined these policy goals. Dressed in a yellow cardigan sweater, and seated next to a roaring fire, he presented his broad welfare reform objectives: minimizing abuse, strengthening families, supporting the disabled, and providing jobs and training for the able-bodied.[26] Though he had scarcely moved into the Oval Office, he promised to unveil his plan by the first of May.

Curiously, the president's point man on welfare reform was an entitlement liberal, Joseph Califano. For Carter, *reform* meant curbing fraud, aiding the disabled, and training workers—all at no additional expense. The president came to office pushing a zero-based-budgeting management approach. According to this doctrine, executives budgeted programs annually by starting at zero without assumptions of a funding increase. Thirsting for the Great Society's renewal, Califano assumed that welfare reform would involve enhanced expenditures.[27] Thus, from the start, administration liberals had quite different ideas about what welfare reform entailed.

Carter's choice of HEW secretary was odd for someone who campaigned against the liberal governing class. A former LBJ official and the ultimate Washington insider, Califano spent the Nixon-Ford years practicing law with a powerful Washington firm. The veteran journalist Hugh Sidey noted the contradiction of a reformer naming Beltway insiders to a key cabinet post by suggesting: "Grafting the head of this administration to its body is going to be one of the most fascinating bits of political surgery of this century."[28]

Adding to issues stemming from an internally divided administration was an unruly Senate. Ostensibly controlled by the president's party, the Democratic caucus featured the same opportunity versus entitlement liberal divide that racked the White House. As a result, the freshman senator from New York, Daniel Patrick Moynihan, emerged as the administration's most formidable welfare reform foe.

A babe in terms of congressional seniority, Moynihan was a grizzled veteran when it came to social welfare legislation and political controversy. After serving in the administrations of four successive presidents, the streetwise yet scholarly Moynihan had built a career out of his prescient opposition to liberal orthodoxy.

Holding a Ph.D. in international relations, Moynihan had risen from hardscrabble roots to a position as assistant secretary of labor in the Kennedy and Johnson administrations.[29] In service to LBJ, he first sparked national controversy through his 1965 "The Negro Family: The Case for National Action." The Moynihan Report, as it was dubbed, blamed the social pathologies of northern black ghettos on the disintegration of the African American family.

Though he attributed the breakdown of black family life to centuries of institutionalized racism, Moynihan also faulted AFDC payments for accelerating this dynamic. According to the Moynihan Report, since cash payments went only to single (usually) female-headed households, the federal government unwittingly incentivized family disintegration. While many scholars later deemed his thesis prophetic, at the time his conclusions rendered him a heretic.[30] Embracing his role as an apostate, he lambasted New Politics liberals as "professional reformers, elite academicians, and intellectuals" who failed to understand the key issues of welfare reform.[31]

After a stint at Harvard University, in 1969 Moynihan returned to the White House as an adviser to Richard Nixon. Within a year, he sparked another controversy when he counseled that race relations could benefit from a period of "benign neglect."[32] Since Nixon hardly lacked for hullabaloo,

Moynihan was eventually (in 1973) convinced to accept the ambassadorship to India. After a brief return to the academy and a stint as Gerald Ford's ambassador to the United Nations, he won a hotly contested New York Senate seat. Once there, he earned a Senate Finance Committee position and chaired the Senate Subcommittee on Public Assistance.[33]

With seats on two bodies possessing direct oversight over welfare reform, Moynihan played an outsized role. Despite the senator's power and public excoriation of entitlement liberalism, Califano chose two entitlement liberals, Ben Heineman and Henry Aaron, to pen the administration's legislation. Born seven years apart in the same city, Heineman and Aaron earned Ivy League degrees and wide respect as policy intellectuals. Aaron, an economist and expert on welfare reform, and Heineman, a financier who dabbled in welfare policy, joined the administration as assistant secretaries for planning and evaluation at HEW.[34]

The primary author of PBJI, Aaron was especially unsuited for his role as Carter's welfare reformer. For instance, he urged observers to ignore social science highlighting the policy failures of Great Society programs. Instead, he argued that research tended to be a "conservative" force because it fostered skepticism and caution.[35] To his mind, a moral commitment to social equality was what mattered most in the arena of social policy.[36] Not surprisingly, he believed that comprehensive welfare reform was impossible without dedicating more resources to the task.[37]

To be fair, the policy intricacies of welfare reform were frightening to behold. For instance, HEW wanted a nationally uniform welfare program despite the reality in which welfare payments dramatically differed from state to state. Though HEW financed large portions of AFDC payments, benefit levels were largely dependent on a state's matching fund. Thus, there were stark disparities in benefits, from a low in Mississippi of $60 a month to a high in New York of $430.[38]

Welfare reform was further compounded by Carter's campaign promises to curb federal spending. From the start, Carter and Califano had different ideas of what constituted welfare reform. Indeed, contradiction was the only consistent theme in the administration's winding path toward its legislation. Other than fiscal concerns, the president proffered no clear idea of what he wanted, nor was there any consensus within the administration.[39] The secretary of labor, Ray Marshall, demanded that any bill include a full-employment jobs program, which he would administer. Califano balked at Marshall's proposal because he wanted a guaranteed-income package.[40]

The initial welfare reform debate revolved around cost. However, it was not until March 25, 1977, that Carter explicitly informed Califano that welfare reform would be achieved without additional expenditures.[41] Weeks later, on April 11, Califano presented Carter with three options but concluded: "Mr. President, I don't think that any of these plans is really adequate unless we increase present spending." Carter responded: "In that case, to hell with it."[42]

Though Carter had promised to present a welfare reform program by May 1, he also insisted that Califano seek "wide input into the evolution of our welfare proposals."[43] As a result, instead of having Califano work closely with the congressional leaders who actually passed the legislation, the president allowed him to sponsor a ten-week-long series of roving public hearings.[44] One HEW official optimistically called the process "policy analysis in the sunshine."[45] Hoping to rally and educate interest groups about the administration's choices, the secretary sought to win over skeptical liberals.[46]

The president's call for "wide input" came with good reason. Primarily, Carter was concerned that HEW, which had the principal responsibility for social welfare legislation, would leave others out of the loop. In the administration's short life, HEW had already earned a reputation for trying to "sneak" policy past the White House. According to the domestic policy adviser Joe Onek: "If we didn't call meetings, if we didn't circulate the papers and if we didn't force HEW to do it they'd be perfectly glad never to talk to anybody in the policy formulation."[47] To prevent this, Carter actively involved himself in the legislative muck of welfare reform.

Unfortunately, its focus on HEW caused the White House to ignore Congress. Rather than consult a Senate or House committee chair, officials made a fetish of interadministration consultation. As the assistant economic policy adviser Van Doorn claimed: "[If anything the president's policy process] may be a little too open in that there is kind of an invitation for a wide set of options, and the options may not be narrowed very rapidly sometimes."[48] Leading the way was the president, who involved himself in meetings with lower-level staffers. An assistant director of science policy, Benjamin Huberman, recalled Carter attending a meeting and debating "a fellow fairly far down in OMB."[49] Meanwhile, congressional leaders and assorted experts were kept outside the policy process.

Despite or more likely owing to the "wide input," by mid-April the administration still possessed no consensus on its welfare reform plan. Faced with a self-imposed May 1 deadline, a deeply divided administration, and no legislation in sight, Carter presented a twelve-point outline. Admitting that welfare was "worse than we had anticipated" and that "the complexity of the system is almost incomprehensible," he maintained his promise to pass comprehensive reform with no funding increases.[50]

As HEW and the Department of Labor vied over welfare reform, congressional leaders questioned Carter's ambitious timetable. Senate majority leader Robert Byrd flatly warned: "We can't do welfare reform in this session of Congress."[51] Instead of stalling the process until 1978, the administration pressed forward. Consequently, HEW spent the summer of 1977 hammering out its version of welfare reform. By July 25, Califano informed the president that his department had completed PBJI.

Because Marshall and Califano vied over guaranteed-income levels for the disabled and able-bodied, they split the difference. Consequently, the legislation established two tiers of recipients and consolidated AFDC, Food Stamps, and Supplemental Security Income into one single cash payment program. Recipients were further categorized according to family size and income. Tier 1 was for the disabled and certain single parents. This group included the aged, the blind, the disabled, single parents with children under the age of seven, and single parents with children aged seven to thirteen if a job and day care could not be found.[52]

Tier 2 was for the poor who were expected to work full-time: two-parent families with children, single parents whose youngest child was over thirteen, single people, and childless couples. If recipients could not locate a job, 1.4 million public service jobs and training slots were to be provided at the federal minimum wage of $2.30 per hour.[53] By making a massive jobs program and a federal commitment to full employment the keystone of PBJI, Carter accepted increased spending as an inevitable consequence of welfare reform.

In this way, the legislation compromised between entitlement liberalism's guaranteed income and opportunity liberalism's full employment. All the same, the 1.4 million public service jobs program angered both camps and was controversial for several reasons: it was going to be costly; unions balked at the public service job competition; and some liberal groups charged that the pay, set at minimum wage, was too low.

For Califano, PBJI—which featured a simpler administrative system, work incentives, inducements for two-parent families, and uniform benefit levels—was superior to the old system. He was partially correct.[54] The bill, however, possessed significant shortcomings. For one thing, PBJI did not meet one of the president's primary benchmarks—it cost more money. HEW officials estimated that the program would cost $2 billion more than prevailing welfare expenditures.[55] When the Congressional Budget Office (CBO) calculated funding levels, it did so in 1982 dollars, 1982 being the year PBJI would have gone into effect. According to the CBO, the legislation cost $14 billion more per year.[56]

As the administration readied itself for the legislation's unveiling, Tom Joe dashed its optimism. A policy intellectual who had pioneered the universally revered Earned Income Tax Credit, Joe understood welfare and Washington. Blind since birth, he was also one of the few insiders who clearly saw PBJI's deep problems.[57] Calling the legislation "misguided" and "unworkable," he claimed that the administration failed to understand its own bill.[58] In his estimation, PBJI would cause welfare rolls to skyrocket by 67 percent and bring 14.2 million more Americans onto public relief. In states such as Mississippi and Georgia, over one-third to one-quarter of the population would be welfare eligible.[59] This scenario promised a fiscal and political nightmare.

Begging Carter's domestic policy adviser Stu Eizenstat to revise the legislation, Joe warned that the welfare reform bill was "divisive, punitive, administratively complex and conceptually confusing." Worse than a bad bill, PBJI could "make a mockery" of the Carter White House if the legislation was offered as the administration's first major domestic initiative.[60]

Undeterred, the administration planned for Carter to give a nationally televised address to introduce his welfare reform. Meanwhile, policymakers were still writing the bill and had not agreed on a media-savvy title for the legislation. At the last minute, Carter personally instructed Eizenstat to "get [a] better name" for the bill. The result was the awkward moniker the Program for Betters Jobs and Income.[61]

On August 6, 1977, Carter unveiled PBJI. Choosing Plains, Georgia, rather than the Capitol for his speech venue, the president tried to unveil welfare reform suited to Middle American tastes. In this path, he described legislation the American people wanted rather than the bill his administration designed. Vowing that PBJI provided tax relief and "strong incentives to keep families together" and was designed to deter dependency, he hit the right notes.[62] In contrast to the president's happy talk, HEW's press release revealed the plan's true programmatic aims, trumpeting PBJI as the "largest jobs program since the Great Depression." HEW's comfort with the language of big government was noticeably absent from Carter's address.[63]

Given Carter's rhetoric, PBJI received an overwhelmingly positive reception. Editorial boards from the *New York Times* to the *St. Louis Post-Dispatch* endorsed the proposal. At first, Moynihan lauded the bill. Joining the senator were the National Urban League and the National Governors Association.[64] Significantly, a Lou Harris poll showed that 70 percent of Americans approved the legislative effort while only 13 percent disapproved.[65]

Carter sold PBJI as comprehensive reform that would bring widespread tax relief, though he knew the opposite to be true. Indeed, the bill's supposed tax relief received as much fanfare as did welfare reform itself. The day following the president's speech, a *St. Louis Post-Dispatch* headline bellowed: "Welfare Plan a 'Tax Relief for Millions.'"[66] In his campaign, Carter had promised to be frugal and to "never tell a lie." With PBJI, he failed on both counts.

The president failed to offer the reform he promised because opportunity and entitlement liberals remained divided. Thus, PBJI married New Deal liberalism's full employment with entitlement liberalism's guaranteed income and commitment to statism. The product of this union promised to be the largest government jobs program since the Great Depression.[67] Quite literally merging the two ideologies, PBJI became a guaranteed jobs program—and an expensive one at that.[68]

The president made welfare reform all the more difficult by his ham-handed conduct of congressional relations. Three key Democrats—House Ways and Means chair Al Ullman, Senate Finance chair Russell Long, and Moynihan—became increasingly unhappy with the bill, and all three possessed the power to kill it. From the start, Carter refused to stroke congressional egos. The administration's liaison to Congress, Frank Moore, compared Carter's tact to Gerald Ford's. According to Moore, Ford spent hours "deciding which congressional trip went where and who got which airplane and the makeup of his delegation." In contrast, Carter declined to invest time in such picayune yet hugely important matters.[69]

The president did try to charm the Senate majority leader, Robert Byrd. Like a love-struck teen, he sent personal notes to the Senate baron hailing him for his "splendid" leadership and claiming: "I need your help."[70] Unlike others, Byrd and his family spent time at the White House engaged in "leisurely conversations" and intimate family dinners.[71] Carter's youngest child, Amy, played with Byrd's grandchildren, all of them often watching movies at the White House theater. One of those movies, Disney's *Boatniks,* starring Stefanie Powers in a madcap cops-and-robbers adventure, particularly engaged the kids. Unfortunately, neither Stefanie Powers nor Robert Byrd could save Carter's welfare reform.[72]

Unlike the Senate majority leader, Moynihan, Ullman, and Long had considerable personal interest in the welfare issue. In addition, because they served on such powerful committees, any welfare reform bill simply had to receive their explicit approval.[73] Despite this foreknowledge, the administration somehow managed to anger all three. Long, the son of the legendary Louisiana politician Huey Long, ruled the powerful Finance Committee without regard to presidential prerogative, a lesson Carter had already learned the hard way.

Intending to demonstrate his commitment to sound fiscal and environmental policy, in one of his first acts as president Carter summarily rescinded nineteen water projects. Since four of these projects were in Louisiana, Carter needlessly provoked Long.[74] Calling the move "dumb, dumb, dumb, dumb," the senator later sarcastically introduced himself to the president's aides: "My name is Russell Long, and I am the chair of the Senate Finance Committee."[75] Bert Lance called the president's decision to challenge the federal water projects "the worst political mistake he made," adding that "its effects lasted the rest of his term and doomed any hopes we ever had of developing a good effective working relationship with Congress."[76]

Adding to Carter's problems, Long desperately wanted to field test his own welfare plan, which emphasized work requirements for single mothers, even those with small children, and strict child support enforcement. The administration understood the contours of the senator's ideas.[77] Nevertheless, it offered a welfare reform plan that ignored Long's beliefs. He not only had ideas; Long also possessed power and a willingness to use his authority against the administration, a propensity that led Carter to claim: "I never knew what he was going to do—except screw me most of the time."[78] Regrettably, for the president, this forecast proved correct.

In contrast to Long, Al Ullman was theoretically more amenable to Carter's welfare reform plan. Rising to the House Ways and Means chairmanship after Wilbur Mills's infamous nocturnal adventures with the "Argentine firecracker" Fanne Foxe, Ullman was an effective chair—so successful that he had been mentioned as a possible vice president for Carter.[79]

Unlike Long, the soft-spoken Ullman did not have a contentious relationship with the White House. Nonetheless, he opposed PBJI. An opponent of full-employment legislation, cash assistance, and comprehensive welfare reform, he disagreed with PBJI on every plane possible.[80] Moreover, like

Long, the congressman had his own welfare reform plan, REACH. Within weeks of PBJI's unveiling, Ullman pronounced the White House legislation "totally unworkable."[81]

Because Carter came to office apparently echoing a neoconservative critique of welfare, Moynihan seemed a natural ally. Furthermore, as chair of the subcommittee with oversight over welfare proposals, he became by default the administration's point man on welfare reform. It was he who officially introduced PBJI to the Senate. In his speech, the senator described the bill as "the most important piece of social legislation since the New Deal."[82] Despite the clear and present need to mollify Moynihan, the administration did anything but. First, Carter vigorously opposed a Moynihan bill that provided $1 billion in fiscal relief to the states and cities.[83] This was a particularly sensitive subject for the senator because his own New York City was teetering on the edge of a fiscal abyss.

In addition to blocking this bill, White House officials told several reporters that Moynihan "was a heavy drinker." Another writer used a White House staffer to corroborate fallacious stories in his unauthorized biography of Moynihan.[84] Not surprisingly, the senator traced these rumors back to Pennsylvania Avenue. Adding to the bad blood, the senator complained that "he had never really been consulted on appointments and none of his suggestions have ever been accepted."[85] When the administration stopped the inclusion of state and city fiscal relief in PBJI, Moynihan reversed course and opposed the president's bill.[86]

Weeks after comparing the legislation to the New Deal, the senator pronounced the bill "grievously disappointing."[87] He not only found it lacking but also claimed that it ruined the "climate for welfare reform."[88] Citing opposition to PBJI from interest groups ranging from the AFL-CIO to the Congressional Black Caucus, Moynihan accused the president of spoiling an opportunity to build a broad coalition around a welfare reform package.

Strangely, Moynihan's turnabout failed to ring alarm bells in the White House. Carter's domestic policy adviser Stu Eizenstat counseled that Moynihan's opposition did not "call for any precipitate action on our part."[89] Within weeks of its introduction, the legislation earned Long's, Ullman's, and Moynihan's hostility. Other congressional Democrats deemed PBJI either too complex or insufficiently ambitious. Indeed, it was so complicated that very few officials outside HEW really understood it. As far as the administration was concerned, complexity was a byproduct of the political climate. Public anger at welfare cheats and high taxes had grown so precipitously that, the administration believed, nothing short of comprehensive reform could muster mass support.

In this way, Carter's comprehensive approach was politically sound. Other than that, the legislation served merely to agitate both opportunity and entitlement liberals.[90] The cosponsor of the Humphrey-Hawkins Full Employment Act, Augustus Hawkins, feared that PBJI subverted his quest for a full-employment economy.[91] Hawkins and other African American legislators were especially keen on employment programs. In the summer of 1977, black unemployment equaled its post-1945 high of 14.7 percent, while African American youth joblessness reached a staggering 40.4 percent.[92]

With his highly anticipated welfare reform bill floundering and the economy stagflated, the president found congressional Democrats turning on him. On returning from Britain, Carter attended a fall fund-raiser at which Capitol Hill Democrats treated him so coolly he joked that his "influence in Britain may be more than in Congress."[93] Regrettably, he was correct. By placing administration prestige behind PBJI without bringing key members of Congress into the policymaking process, he made himself, as Tom Joe warned, look feckless.

Adding to the liberal carping were Republicans and centrists. Senator Carl Curtis, a Republican from Nebraska, groused: "Working men and women across America want fewer people on welfare, not millions more."[94] Meanwhile, Richard Nathan, of the Brookings Institute, smartly posited that, in contrast to PBJI, "multiple incremental reforms present more flexible and realistic solutions than by forcing all welfare cases into a single system."[95] With organized labor, big city mayors, and governors jumping into the fray, Carter got the worst of all political worlds, a bill that earned the enmity of the entire known political universe.

The fall of 1977 offered the best opportunity to achieve comprehensive welfare reform. The Carter administration's bumbling efforts fumbled that opening and revealed its utter incompetence. Consequently, PBJI died a quiet death in congressional committees. Vice President Walter Mondale did not even list the legislation among the administration's top twenty legislative priorities for 1978. Instead, he urged Carter to "sharp[ly] limit" the number of bills he was sending to Congress and concentrate on issues of peace and prosperity.[96] To Mondale's mind, Carter haphazardly overloaded Congress, invested presidential prestige in failed initiatives, and offered no large vision or theme for his presidency.

Despite Mondale's admonitions, the president did not immediately shelve his bill. Instead, he urged Speaker Tip O'Neill to place the issue at the top of his agenda, form a special welfare reform committee, and pass PBJI "this year."[97] Within weeks of Congress reconvening for 1978, Ullman pushed PBJI aside entirely and introduced his own bill. Echoing candidate Carter, Ullman said of PBJI: "The administration has fallen into a trap. It is convinced that we can make poor Americans happy and secure by giving them a guaranteed national income. . . . To accept that concept is to perpetuate the 'welfare syndrome.'"[98] Thus, within a year of taking office, "Carter the reformer" had become "Carter the defender of the liberal status quo."

Liberalism's confused state was reflected in Carter's attempt at hybridization in PBJI. During the 1970s, liberalism moved from the concept of welfare as a necessary means of survival, that is, a means to fend off starvation and to keep roofs over the heads and clothes on the backs of small children. It became instead a mechanism to redistribute income to groups seeking equality of condition. Entitlement liberals clung to these policy goals despite overwhelming public opposition and rising anger at the basic components of their ideology.

In addition to advocating misconceived legislation, Jimmy Carter mismanaged his working relationship with congressional Democrats. In sum, he struggled to translate his gubernatorial political tactics to the political culture of Washington. In Georgia, he had gotten his legislation by methodically and doggedly overwhelming the opposition. Confident in his ability to render government manageable and bureaucracy competent, he saw himself as an engineer charged with the task of routinizing big government.[99] Unfortunately for him, Washington was not Atlanta, and Congress was not composed of part-time state legislators.

Even if the president had been a more skillful tactician, PBJI was doomed owing to entitlement liberals' regard for welfare: whether people were poor for reasons beyond their control or as a result of their actions made no difference; whether poverty was a temporary condition or a chronic situation was irrelevant; whether opportunities were plentiful or scarce was beside the point. Entitlement liberalism, embraced by policy elites, ignored America's dominant ideology—liberal individualism.

Moreover, PBJI showed little promise of reducing the number of poor people. The additional billions to be spent on welfare would have raised a relatively insignificant number of families above the poverty line. When fully implemented in 1982, PBJI would have left 5.7 percent of families in poverty, compared to a projected 8 percent if no changes were made in the existing programs.[100] Furthermore, PBJI required the handful of southern and midwestern states where the majority of the poor resided to set higher standards for aiding the needy. These states already had every opportunity to increase welfare funding and gain generous federal matching grants; they did not do so because welfare spending remained unpopular.

The trajectory of PBJI illustrates Carter's failure to heal the rift between New Deal and entitlement liberals and his inability to move the Democratic Party back into the political mainstream. As a candidate, he promised welfare reform imbued with fiscal restraint that adhered to the dominant ethos of individualism. These efforts were doomed from the start because entitlement liberals at HEW, such as Califano, Heineman, and Aaron, professed policy goals that were antithetical to Russell Long, Daniel Patrick Moynihan, and Al Ullman. Political ineptitude exacerbated the administration's problems. Carter was the ultimate expression of this confusion; his vacillation created a lasting image of futility and indecisiveness.

7

"America Ain't What's Wrong with the World"

Ben Wattenberg, the Vital Center, and Neoconservatism's Liberal Roots

The "Little Flower" understood schisms. Acknowledging, "The trouble with us liberals and progressives is that we're not united," Fiorello La-Guardia confessed: "Let's not fool ourselves—we have more than fifty-seven varieties."[1] If anyone realized liberalism's voluminous categories, it was LaGuardia. Indeed, the son of Italian and Jewish immigrants inhabited an extraordinary number of these varieties all by himself. Born in bohemian Greenwich Village, he grew up in the Arizona Territory, worshiped as an Episcopalian, worked in Italy, and joined the GOP—all before serving three terms as mayor of the multiethnic stew that was New York City.

Taking full advantage of the Left's divides, in 1947 the "Little Flower" and Henry Wallace launched the Progressive Citizens of America (PCA). Through organizing liberalism's dissidents into the PCA, they hoped to unseat Harry Truman. To buttress the president, Arthur Schlesinger and Eleanor Roosevelt formed Americans for Democratic Action (ADA). In the time before the 1948 election, these two entities vied to attract LaGuardia's fifty-seven varieties to their cause.

Days prior to the PCA-ADA split, these very progressives and liberals met to mend political fences. Before the afternoon had expired, their get-together turned into a political brawl. Entering their summit, each side proffered contending interpretations of the nascent Cold War. LaGuardia and Wallace believed that Stalin merely desired secure borders, while Schlesinger and Roosevelt regarded Kremlin intransigence as evidence of its revolutionary nature.[2] When a Wallaceite accused Schlesinger of being "obsessed

Ben J. Wattenberg (second
from right) (courtesy
Hobart and William Smith
Colleges Archives and Special
Collections)

with the Communist problem to the neglect of all the great fascist and war-
making forces," reconciliation talks broke down.[3]

The fisticuffs revealed the profound divisions separating postwar liberals. With Schlesinger and the ADA pushing for containment and Wallace
and the PCA wanting to share global leadership, a showdown appeared inevitable. The 1948 election produced just such a confrontation, an alter-
cation that decided postwar liberalism's trajectory. More than a triumph
for containment, Truman's victory also bequeathed a liberalism that united
many of LaGuardia's fifty-seven varieties under a common banner: Vital
Center liberalism.

Vital Center Liberalism

Born from international events, Vital Center liberalism was much more than
a foreign policy impulse. While the Soviet Union represented an international challenge, communism also posed a domestic problem that all Western
leftists faced: cooperate with or oppose the Stalinists in their midst. Vital
Center liberals opted for battle. Their resulting transatlantic alliance of liberal capitalists, deradicalized socialists, and moderate rightists moved all
those creeds to the center. Far from a mushy middle way, the Vital Center
represented a profoundly cosmopolitan and sophisticated reply to the challenges of midcentury political extremism.

Vital Center liberals saw the stakes as nothing less than the survival
of democracy. Rocked by the democratic Left's prewar failures, the Nazis'
wartime atrocities, and the Soviets' postwar aggression, they searched for
a viable path between Stalinism and rightist reaction. Arthur Schlesinger
found that course in the person of Leon Blum. The French socialist who lan-

guished in a Nazi prison during the war had sensed the very same issues that so hounded Schlesinger: the survival of democracy in an age of extremes.[4]

Blum and Schlesinger worried with good reason. Hamstrung by the Depression, Western democracies had watched helplessly as the fascists engulfed Europe in war. During the early postwar era, it appeared that history might repeat itself. Unhindered by democratic procedures, Communists offered easy remedies to economic calamity and disorder. Rightists, in turn, proposed their own radical agenda. Fearing a reprise of prewar Europe's political vertigo, Blum called for a fundamental reformulation of the modern political order. As he saw it, the Nazis and Soviets had rendered the French Revolution's Left-Right continuum obsolete. As a result, he called for a "third force."[5]

Dispensing with a "united Left," Blum and Schlesinger cast their lot with a centrist alliance of democratic socialists, liberal capitalists, and moderate rightists. To Schlesinger's mind, this coalition promised consistent political action to counter the big issues of the day. In so doing, the Vital Center would imbue liberal democracies with the "fighting faith" they lacked a generation prior.[6] By trading socialist utopias for gradual reform within a democratic and capitalist system, Vital Center liberals also built a lasting moderate coalition that offered a viable path between the radicalisms of the Left and the Right.

Schlesinger most famously explicated his ideas in the 1949 *The Vital Center: The Politics of Freedom,* but he was not alone. A scad of like-minded authors published similar works in the late 1940s. Max Ascoli, for one, not only penned *The Power of Freedom;* he founded a journal, *The Reporter,* to propagate this new liberal temper.[7] Stopping short of prescribing particular policies, Vital Center liberals expressed a mood. Skeptical of human nature, and dismissive of utopian schemes, these activists combined a progressive penchant for reform with an understanding of humanity's limits.

A refugee from Mussolini's fascism, Ascoli represented this novel and chastened Left. Embracing Edmund Burke and Alexander Hamilton, the Italian proffered conservative-sounding notions of human nature.[8] In this way, Vital Center liberalism, or, as Schlesinger preferred to call it, the new "radicalism," was a reformist impulse undergirded by traditionalist notions. Acknowledging humanity's dark side, fearful of disproportionate concentrations of power, yet fully in support of a limited welfare state, Vital Center activists merged the liberal inclinations of the past with the stark political lessons of the present.

Not surprisingly, Henry Wallace did not agree with Schlesinger's formulation. Accusing the Vital Center liberals of dividing "the world into two camps," the former vice president used the PCA as a base to found the Progressive Party and mount his own presidential campaign.[9] In winning re-election, Truman relegated Wallace to the margins and turned Vital Center liberalism into the American Left's dominant creed.[10] Though a smattering of Progressive Party disciples remained wary of this centrist coalition, the ADA maintained an alliance of liberal elites, deradicalized socialists, and organized labor well into the 1960s.

Ironically, Vital Center liberalism was killed by the very organization that once spawned it—the ADA. During the mid-1960s, New Politics activists gained effective control of the ADA. Using the organization's considerable heft as a launching pad, these activists slowly took over the Democratic Party. With this power, New Politics liberals dispensed with Vital Center liberalism and consigned it to the periphery.

Seeking to refight and rewin the battles of 1947, Vital Center liberals established a successor organization to the ADA, the Coalition for a Democratic Majority (CDM). Designed to revive Vital Center liberalism, the CDM waged the same battles over similar issues that the ADA had once fought in the 1940s. Unlike its predecessor, the CDM failed.

Ben Wattenberg

The primary force behind the CDM was the former presidential speechwriter, author, and political commentator Ben Wattenberg. Born in the Bronx to Jewish parents at the height of the Great Depression, Wattenberg came naturally to his political activism. The grandson of Simha Alter Guttman, a poet and the cofounder of Tel Aviv, Israel, Wattenberg grew up in a milieu of leftist politics and Zionism.[11] A writer by trade, Wattenberg parlayed his keen interest in demography and public affairs into significant political influence.

In 1965, Wattenberg and his longtime collaborator Richard Scammon published *This U.S.A.*[12] Using the 1960 census report as their source, the two transformed raw data into a well-crafted tableau of mid-1960s American life. Written from a Vital Center liberal perspective, *This U.S.A.* paints a picture of an affluent and democratic society fully capable of reforming and solving its social and political woes.[13]

After using portions of *This U.S.A.* for a well-received presidential speech, LBJ's press secretary, Bill Moyers, invited Wattenberg to join his staff. His clear and optimistic prose was especially welcome in an administration dealing with urban riots and Vietnam. Rejecting "crisis mongering," Wattenberg's speeches emphasized: "America is still a pretty good place to live."[14] Through this tone and style, Wattenberg earned the president's trust and quickly became the press secretary's "left hand man."

During the 1970s, Wattenberg battled New Politics activists in a war to define liberalism for the post–New Deal era. Succeeding where Henry Wallace had failed, New Politics liberals defeated Wattenberg's Vital Center and left the New Deal coalition for dead. Instead of that alliance, New Politics liberals believed, a union of educated professionals, African Americans, the poor, and young activists would constitute a new Democratic majority. Conspicuous for their absence were the white working class and organized labor. It was no accident that New Politics activists saw organized labor as a relic of the past and deemed it no longer central to a liberal coalition.[15]

By marginalizing the white working class, New Politics liberals took away their opponents' key bloc of support. Indeed, for Vital Center liberals to maintain their place in the political firmament, they simply had to keep organized labor and the white working class in the Democratic coalition. In pursuit of this, Wattenberg did what he knew best—he wrote a book.

Neoconservatism and *The Real Majority*

The 1968 election revealed the New Deal coalition's implosion. Consequently, a number of psephologists penned their analyses, offering a myriad of paths toward a new, lasting, and permanent majority. In 1969, Kevin Phillips published *The Emerging Republican Majority*. In it, the young Nixon aide forecasted an era of GOP dominance that ran through the Sun Belt. One year later, Wattenberg and Scammon offered their reply, *The Real Majority*. Their work proposed an alternative path toward an enduring Democratic coalition: Middle America.

As a liberal critique of the Great Society's welfare state and New Politics foreign policy, *The Real Majority* also represents a foundational text of the early neoconservative movement. Contradicting forecasts of a nascent liberal majority just waiting to be coalesced, Scammon and Wattenberg maintained that the bulk of the American electorate remained "un-young, un-poor, and un-black."[16] With Middle America constituting the nation's "real majority," the authors argued, any lasting Democratic coalition must heed basic demographic reality while also focusing on the social issues.

A Middle American backlash to the youth rebellion, the urban riots, and the general cacophony of the era, the social issues were to the 1960s what economic matters had been to the 1930s. From spiraling crime rates to drug use and evolving sexual mores, Scammon and Wattenberg claimed, social issues had become coequal with bread-and-butter concerns.[17] On the basis of reams of quantitative research, the authors introduced their proto-typical American voter: a forty-seven-year-old wife of a Dayton, Ohio, trade union machinist. A lifelong Democrat who increasingly worried about the drug culture and crime, she tiptoed toward the GOP owing to the social issues.

Scammon and Wattenberg saw the 1968 election as a clear defeat for the New Politics, but Gene McCarthy's troops believed that they opposed a senseless war and confronted a racist society. To the Dayton housewife, however, these activists symbolized the "ideal of confrontation politics, of confusing cops with pigs, of justifying riots, of sympathy for muggers and rapists, of support of the drug culture."[18] In this way, the New Politics promised to antagonize the working class and bring nothing but defeat.

The Real Majority not only became regarded as a classic of its genre; it also constituted Wattenberg's first literary contribution to neoconservatism. A critique of the Great Society and the New Politics, and a clarion call for a return to traditional liberalism, the work encapsulated nascent neoconservative themes. Later in his career, Wattenberg deemed *The Real Majority* a neoconservative brief.[19] At the time of its publication, he remained a self-identified liberal and intended his work to serve as a political primer for Democrats.

As did Schlesinger in the late 1940s, Wattenberg rejected the dictum, "No Enemies on the Left."[20] To his mind, demographic and political reality meant that any Democratic victory must follow a centrist path, which entailed purging recalcitrant leftists from the Democratic Party. In contrast to this, New Politics liberals, like the Wallaceites before them, sought a united Left. Though their coalition hardly included the Stalinists and their fellow travelers of the 1940s, New Politics liberals did crave a similar goal—domestic liberalism with a social democratic tinge and a less robust foreign policy.

Ironically, Wattenberg and Vital Center liberals also supported a vigorous and thoroughgoing welfare state. However, as staunch anti-Communists with roots in the anti-Stalinist crusades of the 1930s, they were conditioned to question orthodoxy.

A sober worldview permeated with doubt, Vital Center liberalism pushed Wattenberg and his compatriots to ponder the Great Society's excesses and programmatic efficacy. Consequently, they differed with the New Politics on ways to achieve greater equality.

In addition to domestic issues, Scammon and Wattenberg examined the Vietnam War's influence on the domestic political scene. As far as they were concerned, the antiwar movement merely exacerbated and fed the social issues. Moreover, since they were forged in the anti-Stalinist wars of the mid-twentieth century, Vital Center liberals looked on any departure from the nation's overseas commitments with deep suspicion. With New Politics liberal domestic and foreign policies antagonizing the Democratic base, Scammon and Wattenberg intended *The Real Majority* as a road map toward liberal reform that would be acceptable to Middle America.

The McGovern Party Reforms

Undeterred by the Vital Center pushback, New Politics activists planned for their new coalition by making wholesale changes to the party's nominating process.[21] In 1969, the Democratic National Committee (DNC) chair, Fred Harris, appointed George McGovern to head the Commission on Party Structure and Delegate Selection. With a mandate to "open the Party to wider rank-and-file participation," McGovern stacked the commission with allies and expanded the body's mission to recast the whole delegate selection process.[22]

The body's ensuing "McGovern Reforms" featured two rule modifications of special significance: quotas and participatory democracy. In an effort to democratize the party, the commission mandated that every state delegation to the national convention be composed of women, young people, and racial minorities "in numbers bearing a reasonable relationship to their share of a state's population."[23] Though activists denied that this constituted a quota, the commission's vice chair, Senator Harold Hughes of Iowa, admitted: "We have, in fact, established something which you might call a quota system."[24] McGovern later acknowledged: "The way we got the quota thing through was by not using the word 'quota.'"[25]

To achieve the second reform, participatory democracy, activists called for the rank and file to elect the party's leadership and nominees. In other words, Democrats would choose their leaders and nominees through the ballot and various democratic procedures. While this reform sounded innocuous and profoundly Jeffersonian, it gave New Politics liberals effective control over the nominating process.[26]

Prior to the McGovern Reforms, national convention delegates were not bound to cast their votes according to their state primary's results. Most states, in fact, did not even bother to host presidential primaries, which were little more than beauty contests. In 1968, Hubert Humphrey totally ignored them and racked up delegates in nonprimary states. Moreover, at the convention, delegates from states that hosted primaries that other candidates won cast their votes for Humphrey anyway. Consequently, the 1968 Democratic nominee earned the fewest primary votes of any serious contender.

The McGovern Reforms fundamentally altered the nominating process. Taking authority away from party bosses and insiders, the modifications transferred power to primary voters and caucus-goers. From the national to the county and local levels, grassroots activists possessed significantly more power in choosing the party's nominees. Advertised as an innovation in democratizing the party, the reforms also empowered the educated middle class, which possessed the flexible schedules and leisure time for grassroots politicking. Thus, participatory democracy gave New Politics liberals a clear advantage in electing the party's leadership, selecting its nominees, and controlling its machinery.

Displacing working-class Democrats was no unintended consequence. In the 1968 convention's aftermath, activists publicly labeled the white working class an obstacle to reform. Indeed, John Kenneth Galbraith believed, organized labor was expendable because its gains came at the expense of the poor, African Americans, and the elderly—the very constituencies that New Politics liberals so prized.[27]

The Hard Hat Riot

Adding to the nascent class war within the Democratic Party was the May 1970 "Hard Hat Riot." In late April, Richard Nixon announced an American incursion into Cambodia. Scores of American college campuses erupted in a frenzy of protest. On May 4, 1970, Kent State University students confronted the Ohio National Guard, which resulted in the shooting deaths of four students. This event merely fueled an already combustible environment.

On May 8, thousands massed in New York City's Wall Street district to protest the war and demand the release of "all political prisoners in Amer-ica."[28] At noon, just as hungry Wall Street employees emptied into streets already crowded with protesters, a horde of construction workers, wear-ing their signature yellow hard hats and carrying American flags and met-al pipes, bore down on the demonstration. Chanting, "Love it or leave it" and "All the way, USA," the hard hats beat and pummeled the protesters.[29]

After crushing the demonstrators, the hard hats set their sights on the American flag at City Hall. Angry that Mayor John Lindsay had ordered the flag be flown at half-staff to honor the Kent State dead, they surged toward it, overwhelmed the police, and screamed, "Lindsay's a red," until the flag was hoisted to full staff. As the flag moved up the pole, the rioters belted out "The Star-Spangled Banner" and ordered the police to "get your helmets off."[30] Dubbed the Hard Hat Riot, the event merely confirmed what many New Politics activists already believed: working-class whites were "super-patriotic hawks" who were "hostile to blacks and racial integration" and various liberal causes.[31]

The 1972 Democratic Nomination

The Hard Hat Riot notwithstanding, George McGovern used the reforms he had championed to forge a national profile. Consequently, the Senate backbencher and vocal anti-Vietnam activist became a bona fide contender for the party's presidential nomination. The resulting Democratic primaries hardly produced a definitive winner: McGovern, Humphrey, and George Wallace were essentially tied in raw vote totals.[32] In fact, the triumvirate of Humphrey, Wallace, and Edmund Muskie received nearly 60 percent of all primary ballots.[33] Awarding delegates in proportion to their percentage of a state's vote rather than on a winner-take-all basis enabled the South Dako-tan to consistently suffer defeat in key states but take the nomination any-way. After losing to Muskie in New Hampshire and Illinois, to Humphrey in Pennsylvania and Ohio, and to Wallace in Florida, Maryland, and Michi-gan, McGovern nevertheless captured the nomination.

Fred Harris had originally created the McGovern Commission to re-dress grievances dating back to the 1968 convention. The body, however, failed to alter the bare-knuckle politics governing the nominating conven-tion. Thus, instead of organized labor controlling the meeting, in 1972 New Politics activists flexed the very political muscle they had once decried. For example, despite receiving 30 percent of West Virginia's primary votes,

George Wallace received no Mountain state delegates. Even more egregious was the California delegation. Though McGovern took only 44 percent of the Golden state's primary votes, he earned all 271 of the state's delegates.[34]

With New Politics activists in charge, the fruits of the McGovern Commission's reforms were on display at the Miami convention. Though the keynote speaker, Florida governor Reubin Askew, claimed that the assembled delegations "looked like the country," this was hardly the case. At a time when a mere 4 percent of all Americans possessed a postgraduate degree and only 5 percent earned as much as $25,000, 39 percent of the Democratic delegates held a postgraduate degree, while nearly one-third had incomes in excess of $25,000.[35] In describing her California delegation as "a couple of high schools, a grape boycott, [and] a Black Panther rally," the movie star Shirley MacLaine unwittingly confirmed the convention's unrepresentative nature.[36]

Though New Politics activists claimed to represent the poor and the oppressed, it was wealth and celebrity that were conspicuous at the convention. In addition to the young millionaires bankrolling the McGovern campaign, the senator also counted the cosmetics mogul Max Factor III, the General Motors' heir Stewart Mott, Art Garfunkel, Jack Nicholson, and Warren Beatty among his staunch supporters.[37] In contrast to Hollywood, organized labor seethed with resentment. Complaining that New Politics liberals portrayed union workers as "crude, narrow-minded bigots who can't see beyond their own paychecks," the AFL-CIO's George Meany refused to endorse McGovern.[38]

With Hollywood representing the oppressed, McGovern's forces punished their symbol of white working-class power, Richard J. Daly. After ousting Daly's Illinois delegation from the convention, New Politics activists tapped the Reverend Jesse Jackson to lead the state's replacement group. This was the same Jackson who had been so busy denouncing the Illinois Democratic Party during the primary season that he failed to vote.[39] Using the McGovern Commission's quotas, Jackson organized a delegation that included African Americans and women but excluded white ethnic Chicagoans.[40]

It was not just Richard Daly and Chicago's white ethnics who were pushed aside. McGovern's forces systematically marginalized organized labor, treating union officials like unreconstructed conservatives. One AFL-CIO leader, Jim Murray, groused: "I'll be a son of a bitch! I'm only 37, and I've always been a liberal. And there I was . . . being made out as some kind of old conservative. Me, who has been called a Communist! Old! A conservative! Christ!"[41] After New Politics activists nominated a two-term Texas state legislator, Sissy Farenthold, for vice president, the journalist and Mc-Govern delegate Jimmy Breslin had seen enough. Screaming, "They're fuckin' crazy, the fuckin' reformers. I'll never vote for another fuckin' reformer in 100 years," he voiced the sentiments of many Democrats.[42]

While McGovern secured the nomination, Wattenberg organized a counterattack. Sensing and "hoping that a big enough . . . loss would move the party" back to its roots, Wattenberg recruited academics, labor leaders, and socialist intellectuals to found his new ADA.[43] Conscious of the parallels between the intraparty politics of 1947 and those of 1972, he wanted the CDM to revive and rebuild the Vital Center.

The most obvious link between 1947 and 1972 was the Democratic nominee himself. As a graduate student at Northwestern University, McGovern enthusiastically supported the Progressive Party's Henry Wallace. Echoing LaGuardia and the PCA, in 1948 the future senator had claimed that U.S. policy was "needlessly exacerbating tensions with the Soviet Union." Backing his rhetoric with action, he joined the Illinois delegation to the Progressive Party's 1948 convention.[44]

As a Wallaceite, McGovern always questioned Cold War orthodoxy. This nondoctrinaire outlook produced both simpleminded and prescient observations. Disregarding the Kremlin's role in the Cold War and the arms race entirely, he claimed that arms reduction would naturally thaw U.S.-Soviet tension. By contrast, in 1965 he was the first senator to publicly accuse the administration of "tak[ing] us into a major land war on the Asiatic mainland."[45] As a presidential candidate, McGovern was no different. While many Democrats merely railed against the war, the South Dakotan promised to remove every American soldier from Vietnam within ninety days of his inauguration.[46] As a result, Wattenberg believed that McGovern's ascendance represented the return of Henry Wallace's neoisolationist ghost.

While Democrats nominated McGovern, Wattenberg convened a secret meeting in a Miami Beach hotel suite. United by "a sense of common outrage," Wattenberg along with DNC treasurer Robert Strauss, James Roosevelt (FDR's son and vice chairman of Democrats for Nixon), representatives of the AFL-CIO, several governors, and top aides to Henry Jackson, Hubert Humphrey, and George Wallace planned their "struggle for party control." It was a fight in which Wattenberg would play a significant role.[47]

In the days after the convention, the McGovern campaign was rocked by revelations of Thomas Eagleton's bouts with depression and electroshock therapy treatment. After backing his running mate "1,000 percent" and then dropping him from the ticket, in desperation McGovern appealed to organized labor through his new vice presidential nominee, Sargent Shriver. Ignoring the New Politics and its novel coalition, Shriver called for Democrats to "build again the coalition . . . of Poles, Italians, [and] Irish." George Meany, however, had seen enough and kept the AFL-CIO officially neutral in the 1972 presidential election.[48]

New Politics liberals accused Meany of "dictatorial practices" for declining to endorse McGovern. The labor leader, however, was merely responding to the overwhelming sentiment of labor; polls not only revealed weak support for McGovern but also showed that 49 percent of union workers actively supported Nixon.[49] Moreover, many working-class Democrats sensed the party's emergent class conflict. The president of the United Steelworkers, I. W. Abel, angrily cried: "Tens of millions of ordinary working Americans are sick and tired of being called racists and reactionaries by slick Madison Avenue hucksters—or by alleged liberal politicians who couldn't get elected without them."[50]

While Meany shared Abel's sentiment with regard to domestic issues, McGovern's foreign policy also prompted labor's neutrality. From the time of Samuel Gompers, mainstream American labor leaders were adamantly anti-Communist. Following in the Gompers tradition, Meany condemned the Kremlin's domination of Eastern Europe. Indeed, decades before Aleksandr Solzhenitsyn's *Gulag Archipelago,* he had a map of Soviet concentration camps tacked to his office wall.[51] An ardent Vital Center liberal, he considered McGovern an "apologist for Communism" and an example of the "so-called sophisticated people" who turned their backs on basic American principles.[52]

Reenacting the Wallace-Truman split, McGovern and Meany's disagreements were fundamental.[53] This schism, in conjunction with the senator's considerable campaign gaffes, led to Nixon's overwhelming victory. The president not only exceeded FDR's 1936 margin over Alf Landon; he also stood the Roosevelt coalition on its head. Taking over 60 percent of the vote, Nixon won every state except Massachusetts.

The CDM

Within days of the election, Wattenberg officially founded the CDM. Given the organization's eighty-one high-profile charter members, its launch received national media attention. From politicians (e.g., Hubert Humphrey and Henry Jackson) and civil rights activists (e.g., Bayard Rustin and A. Philip Randolph) to intellectuals (e.g., Seymour Martin Lipset and Daniel Bell) and movie stars (e.g., Gregory Peck and Charlton Heston), the CDM boasted a range of high-profile members.[54] In this way, it possessed relevance from its very inception.

Tweaking McGovern and his campaign slogan, "Come Home, America," the CDM used "Come Home, Democrats" as a motto for its initial fund-raising appeal. While the motto was playful, the organizers also meant business. Not content to merely show that "no political party will ever take us for granted again," George Meany threatened: "Who says there shouldn't be recriminations?"[55] Taking direct aim at the New Politics, Wattenberg declared: "All this New Politics talk is a lot of crap. What's new about it isn't left and what's left isn't new."[56] Accusing his rivals of having "contempt" for organized labor and "sneering" at American greatness, he blamed them for allowing "the party of privilege [Republicans]— to represent itself for the first time as the champion of . . . [working-class] values and concerns."[57]

In May 1973, Dean Acheson's venerated widow, Alice Stanton Acheson, hosted the CDM's public debut at her Georgetown home. Exceeding Wattenberg's expectations, the occasion drew over 350 labor leaders, politicians, and policy intellectuals.[58] With the liberal establishment's backing, Wattenberg's strategic vision seemed achievable.[59] In the short term, this meant ousting the McGovernik Jean Westwood from the DNC chairmanship, controlling the Commission on Rules, and eradicating the party reforms.[60] Or as the AFL-CIO's Al Barkan succinctly put it: "The reforms must be wiped out—the crazies have got to go."[61]

McGovern's loss, coupled with the CDM's successful launch, gave Wattenberg the muscle to help oust Westwood and install a CDM ally, Robert Strauss, as DNC chair.[62] With the McGovernik gone, the CDM targeted the McGovern Commission's reforms. Fortunately for them, the former chair had created the Charter Commission to evaluate the reform's effectiveness. More importantly, because Westwood was trying to save her job when she appointed the new commission, the body was relatively balanced between New Politics and Vital Center liberals.[63]

To influence the Charter Commission, Wattenberg appointed a CDM task force on party reforms. Headed by two veterans of the original McGovern Commission, Congressman James O'Hara and the political scientist

Austin Ranney, the task force produced its own proposed reforms, reporting them in a document called "Fairness and Unity in '76."[64] In terms of specific changes, the CDM's plan called for abolishing the quota system and installing Democratic officeholders as voting delegates to the national convention.

Turning elected officials into delegates at nominating conventions was central to the CDM's overall critique of the McGovern reforms. To Wattenberg's mind, "participatory democracy" simply privileged an "activist elite" at the expense of working-class Democrats. Rather than rely on activists to express grassroots sentiments in caucuses, primaries, and various party functions, Vital Center liberals urged the Charter Commission to consider general elections an expression of "participatory democracy."[65] By a bare two-vote margin, the Charter Commission eventually accepted "Fairness and Unity in '76" as the party's blueprint.[66]

The CDM's offensive did not deter New Politics activists. One young organizer, Lanny Davis, deemed McGovern's 1972 loss a product of "attitude and approach" rather than an outgrowth of his movement's flaws. He, like other like-minded activists, continued to believe that the Democrats could win with or without working-class votes.[67] Adding to this brewing class war were the socialists.[68] During the 1972 election, they were divided between leftists sympathetic to the New Politics and those still aligned with the Vital Center. Eventually, the Social Democrats U.S.A. (SDUSA) endorsed McGovern. The hubbub and infighting over the endorsement splintered the party into contending factions.[69]

Leading the socialist charge against the New Politics were Penn Kemble, Bayard Rustin, and Joshua Muravchik.[70] As self-described "defenders of the organized working class," they feared that New Politics liberals threatened to displace labor's position in the Democratic Party in favor of an activist elite. Their fears were well founded. One leading socialist who was sympathetic to the New Politics, Michael Harrington, questioned "the indispensability of organized workers" as the foundation of the socialist caucus within the Democratic Party.[71] As these activists saw it, the "New Class" of affluent yet alienated professionals had replaced organized labor as the leaders of a new reformist coalition.[72]

Realizing the CDM's significance, Harrington organized. Through sponsoring the National Conference on the Democratic Left, he tried to outflank Wattenberg and convince labor and socialist intellectuals to move "beyond liberalism" toward a New Politics–led socialist movement.[73] Progressively in agreement with New Politics liberals, Harrington had become an increasingly lonely voice within the SDUSA.[74] Thus, in the summer of 1973, he officially resigned his party membership, claiming that its "obsessive anti-communism" and opposition to the New Politics had rendered it a conservative force in American politics.[75]

Believing that the SDUSA had isolated itself from the new currents of the American Left, Harrington founded the New Politics–friendly Democratic Socialist Organizing Committee (DSOC). Though he realized that the DSOC was "the defeated remnant of a defeated remnant," he hoped to use it as a base from which he could build a new coalition to support the New Politics.[76] Unimpressed, Wattenberg presciently claimed that Harrington's preference for middle-class New Politics came "at the risk of wrecking the [Democratic] Party's working class base."[77]

Tiny in comparison to the major political parties, the DSOC and the SDUSA possessed influence well beyond their numbers. Indeed, significant figures across the political spectrum, from Irving Howe of *Dissent* to *Commentary*'s Norman Podhoretz, heeded what these key American thinkers had to say.[78] Thus, when Harrington termed the CDM *neoconservative*, his political coinage reached far into the popular culture. Indeed, *neoconservative* became a popular tag for leftists of all stripes who opposed New Politics liberalism.[79] Moreover, the socialists' schism mirrored the quarrels within the mainstream Left of the Democratic Party. As the socialists splintered into two competing factions, they battled over which would become most influential within the Democratic Party.[80]

With organized labor and the SDUSA firmly behind the CDM, the organization flexed its muscles at the 1974 Democratic midterm conference. Billed as a "mini-convention," the meeting—held in the immediate aftermath of Nixon's resignation—was intended to establish clear rules and procedures for delegate selection for the 1976 convention. Democrats had every reason to establish unity and avoid a repeat of 1972. On the surface, the midterm meeting appeared markedly different.

The meeting's very site—that most Middle American of cities, Kansas City, Missouri—prompted a different mood. At the 1972 convention, the California delegate and movie star Warren Beatty had worn jeans and long hair. Two years later, he sported short hair and a tweed suit, which, according to one observer, made him "look like a Whiffenpoof [i.e., like a member of Yale's clean-cut singing quartet]."[81] Nonetheless, Beatty and his New Politics liberal acolytes arrived in Kansas City ready to battle Wattenberg and the CDM for control of the party.

Prior to the midterm convention, Wattenberg discovered that Washington, DC, New Politics activists had secretly elected their own slate of delegates—a direct violation of party rules. Not only was this breaking the regulations, but this was the very delegation representing the CDM, which was based in Washington. Though Wattenberg successfully challenged this delegation, the episode reveals how quickly the former insurgents had become adept party insiders.[82]

On top of that victory, the labor-liberal coalition eventually constituted 60 percent of all delegates at the Kansas City meeting.[83] In noting that they "looked like the leadership of their own state [and] not like a bunch of interlopers," DNC chair Robert Strauss underlined the apparent decline of New Politics liberals.[84] The CDM failed to return the presidential nominating system "to the smoke-filled room," but it controlled the miniconvention. Despite this victory, significant issues remained.[85]

The divisive matters confronting the party were dramatized at the 1975 issues convention. Unlike the midterm convention, the Louisville, Kentucky, gathering was controlled by New Politics liberals. Thus, at this meeting John Kenneth Galbraith discussed his plans to nationalize the railroads and oil companies. Meanwhile, five thousand protesters marched outside the hall clamoring for Democrats to reverse court-ordered busing.[86] Seizing the floor, Wattenberg pleaded for conventioneers to heed the obvious: voters cared more about busing than owning the means of production.[87] Pushed by the CDM, New Politics liberals allowed *one* Kentucky Democrat to speak to the convention on behalf of the protesters—for two minutes.

Despite the issues convention, by 1976 the CDM had won over the Democratic Party's leadership. Thus, to Wattenberg's great surprise, the CDM greatly influenced the party platform.[88] Along with Jeanne Kirkpatrick, Wattenberg helped draft a "set of tough-minded ideas" guiding Democratic foreign policy. Moreover, he was particularly pleased with Jimmy Carter's human rights proposals, which he termed "morally and strategically sound—and politically potent."[89]

While domestic issues such as national health insurance and full employment reflected the CDM's conception of the "progressive center," foreign policy remained its central concern. High on its list of targets was détente. Believing that the policy signaled a retreat from traditional U.S. foreign policy, the organization routinely sparred with the Ford administration on the issue.[90] In this vein, the CDM opposed trade agreements, insisted on the right of free emigration, and continued to refer to the "Soviet imperialist conquests in Eastern Europe."[91]

With Ford on the defensive, Jimmy Carter sensed an advantage and gave lip service to the CDM's foreign policy line throughout his presidential campaign. For example, when in a nationally televised debate Gerald Ford famously claimed that the Soviets did not "dominate" Eastern Europe, Carter's response could have been lifted from one of Wattenberg's speeches for Senator Henry Jackson. In one of the most dramatic moments of an otherwise dull election, Carter challenged the president to "convince the Polish-Americans and the Czech-Americans and the Hungarian-Americans in this country that those countries don't live under the domination and supervision of the Soviet Union behind the Iron Curtain."[92] This brief exchange encapsulated the CDM's distaste for détente and helped buttress Carter's foreign policy bona fides.

The Carter Administration

Originally intended by Michael Harrington as a dig, the tag *neoconservative* was enthusiastically embraced by Wattenberg and the CDM. As old Vital Center liberals, they remained staunchly committed Democrats who sought a return to the ADA's original foreign policy principles. More than advocating or opposing specific defense budget items or treaty negotiations, they sought to advance human freedom. What Wattenberg called the "Liberty Party" entailed a foreign policy vision that was "mildly messianic and nonjingoistic in tone."[93]

Hardly a warmonger or foreign policy simpleton, Wattenberg endorsed engaging the Soviets, the Chinese, and the Communist world. To his mind, the "essential strategy is morality." Thus, neoconservatives wanted Carter to make the distinctions between the Communist and the non-Communist worlds quite clear. Wattenberg's attendance at Mao Zedong's funeral neatly typified this neoconservative stance. Accepting the necessity that an American delegation attend the funeral for a genocidal megalomaniac, he objected to those who approved of Mao's ruthless rule by claiming: "Maoism is just a Chinese solution to a Chinese problem."[94]

During the Reagan era and beyond, neoconservative foreign policy and political philosophy evolved significantly. On the cusp of the Carter administration, however, the CDM's variety of the creed called for rhetoric and action that recognized the abnormality of Communist regimes and their inherent and fundamental hostility to human freedom and dignity. In other words, negotiate, host summits, and engage the Kremlin, but always recognize the brutality, in rhetoric and action, of Soviet reality.

After successfully wading into the battle over party reforms, the CDM had helped nominate and elect a president who purportedly supported a platform that Wattenberg had helped draft.[95] Claiming that he was "very happy" with Carter, Wattenberg prepared to disband the CDM, believing that its very success had rendered it obsolete. As Wattenberg contemplated his organization's quiet demise, Carter began making appointments to his State Department and foreign policy team that George McGovern termed "excellent [and] quite close to those I would have made myself."[96] Consequently, Wattenberg's mood changed from happy in November 1976 to "dumb-struck" by January 1977.[97]

Wattenberg was hardly alone in his anxiety with Carter's foreign policy orientation. The CDM members Eugene Rostow, Seymour Martin Lipset, and Paul Seabury felt that the president had assembled "a bunch of McGovernistes" whose worldview reflected a "form of innocence which was fashionable in the mid-1930s."[98] Though Wattenberg was more circumspect, he shared their concerns. Believing that the dichotomy between "hawk and dove" was too simplistic, he nonetheless claimed that the new administration's foreign policy team lacked a proper balance between the two. Describing that team as a mix between neutral technicians and advocates of the "soft argument," he wanted Vital Center views represented in the Oval Office and the State Department.[99]

Wattenberg's caution turned to alarm when Paul Warnke was mentioned as a nominee for a top Defense post. An original member of Robert McNamara's "whiz kids," Warnke was also George McGovern's chief national security adviser in 1972. Advocating "unilateral disarmament" to end the nuclear arms race, he equated the two superpowers. Calling them "apes on a treadmill," he believed that the Kremlin's defense spending amounted to little more than a "pathetic desire" to imitate the United States rather than a push for global hegemony.[100]

The CDM helped stop Warnke's nomination to the Pentagon.[101] Undaunted, Carter tapped him to head the Arms Control and Disarmament Agency. The fight, however, convinced Wattenberg that the CDM possessed the power to influence events.[102] Believing that the president valued pragmatism over a coherent foreign policy, he decided to use the CDM to push Carter into honoring his tough campaign rhetoric. With a newfound organizational purpose, the CDM resumed a full pace of activities in the winter of 1977.[103]

Intending to press the administration, the CDM named Henry Jackson and Daniel Patrick Moynihan as cochairs to increase its visibility.[104] The organization's revival occurred in concert with the rejuvenation of the Committee on the Present Danger (CPD). Formed in 1950 as a "citizen's lobby" of eastern establishment types, the CPD had successfully lobbied for Harry Truman's defense posture.[105] By the mid-1970s, as McGovern urged Americans to "come home" and Kissinger peddled détente, the CPD was resuscitated. Since its leadership was composed of the CDM fellow travelers Paul Nitze, Jeanne Kirkpatrick, and Eugene Rostow, the CPD became a natural ally of the CDM in opposing Carter's increasingly Janus-faced foreign policy.

Though his campaign rhetoric and service as a naval officer had suggested that Carter would embrace the CDM's worldview, in his first months in office he was alternately a dove and a hawk. This split was symbolized by his choice of the hard-liner and CDM member Zbigniew Brzezinski as his national security adviser and the dovish Cyrus Vance to be secretary of state.[106] Throughout the summer of 1977, the CPD and the CDM pressured the administration for a consistent hard-line policy. With sniping coming from formerly stalwart supporters, in August Carter convened a meeting with CPD leaders, Paul Nitze, Eugene Rostow, and the AFL-CIO's Lane Kirkland, all of whom also belonged to the CDM.

Rather than allaying their concerns, Carter further aggravated matters. When he cited public resistance to higher defense expenditures to justify his policies, Nitze, an early Carter-for-president supporter, loudly muttered, "No, no, no." Hearing Nitze's frustration, the president snapped: "Paul, would you please let me finish."[107] Sensing the obvious frustration, Carter created an official link between the CPD and the Pentagon. In return for its public silence, the CPD would now have its defense policy recommendations heard at the administration's highest levels.[108]

Unlike the CPD, Wattenberg and the CDM remained administration outsiders and were free to air their criticisms publicly. Terming Carter's policy one of "unilateral restraint," Wattenberg begged the president to press the Soviets on their arms buildup, crackdown on internal dissidents, and foreign aggression.[109] Even Carter's hallowed commitment to human rights, a key area of agreement between the CDM and the president, ceased to impress Wattenberg. Frustrated that the president would pressure South Korea on the issue while claiming, "Our concept of human rights is preserved in

Poland," Wattenberg declared that Carter's policy had "degenerated to the point where it is no longer supportable."[110]

In the spring of 1978, Joshua Muravchik called for a "new posture toward the Administration."[111] As part of its critical stance, the CDM began issuing a congressional scorecard identifying how members aligned themselves on national defense and bread-and-butter liberal issues.[112] By May, Wattenberg began raising money and cultivating candidates who would reflect the CDM's worldview.[113] The organization made the 1978 Illinois Senate race a showcase for its novel strategy.

In this contest, the CDM's candidate, Alex Seith, faced a liberal Republican and incumbent senator, Charles Percy.[114] Joining the CDM in support of Seith were major labor unions, the Polish American Political League, and the Jewish Council for Good Government. With this backing in a Democratic state, Seith was seemingly positioned for victory. In the weeks prior to the election, a bizarre coalition of Ronald Reagan, Gerald Ford, Muhammad Ali, and Jesse Jackson barnstormed the state on Percy's behalf, helping the incumbent defeat Seith.[115] Jackson, a New Politics icon, did not back a GOP incumbent without reason. Indeed, his active role in defeating a Vital Center liberal reveals the hostile political space in which Wattenberg and the CDM operated.

In tandem with its independent electoral tactics, the CDM moved from critiquing particular administration policies toward outright denunciation of its overall strategy. To Wattenberg's mind, Carter's amiability encouraged Kremlin policy that sowed instability, revolution, and coups. This volatility was especially pronounced in an area stretching from the Indian subcontinent to the Horn of Africa that observers termed "the arc of crisis."[116] According to the CDM, Carter's "weakness" led to the arc of crisis and made America appear to be, in the words of the Ayatollah Khomeini, "a defeated and wounded snake."[117]

In addition to the sharpened critiques, the CDM edged toward outright revolt. When asked whether the organization remained committed to the Democratic Party, Wattenberg replied: "For the time being."[118] A year into its rhetorical offensive, events seemingly proved the CDM's assessment correct. When the shah of Iran's pro-American government fell in January 1979, the administration dispatched Brzezinski for a summit in Algeria. Four days after the meeting, Khomeini's students took the American embassy, sparking the Iranian hostage crisis, which lasted for the duration of Carter's presidency—444 days.

Adding to the sense of crisis, on Christmas Day 1979 the Soviets invaded Afghanistan. Jarring the administration, the Kremlin's move also offered a rare opportunity. With any semblance of détente destroyed, Carter possessed the political space to fundamentally reverse course. Indeed, he initially claimed that the Kremlin's actions "have made a . . . dramatic change in my own opinion of what the Soviets' ultimate goals are."[119] Matching his rhetoric with action, Carter ramped up defense expenditures by 5 percent, imposed a grain and technology embargo, and boycotted the 1980 Moscow Olympics.[120]

Wary that Afghanistan had changed Carter for good, Wattenberg feared that the president's actions simply constituted more "tough ad hoc gestures from which we will later retreat."[121] Pronouncing the Soviet invasion a "moment of national humiliation," the CDM called on Carter to finally root his foreign policy in military strength.[122] More importantly, Wattenberg hoped that the crisis represented "a critical turning point in American political life."[123] Realizing that the impending 1980 election offered leverage, he convinced Walter Mondale to convene a meeting between Carter and the CDM.

Concerned that the president would not be reelected without the CDM's support, Mondale arranged for a January 31, 1980, get-together.[124] Bridging the divisions between the CDM and Carter would prove difficult. Jeanne Kirkpatrick, for one, wanted Carter to fire "almost everybody" at the assistant secretary of state level and demand the Soviets withdraw from Cuba.[125] Moreover, the CDM was divided between multilateralists such as Seymour Lipset and unilateral nationalists like Norman Podhoretz. The organization's members, however, were united in a hope that Carter had finally changed his fundamental opinion of the Soviets and the Cold War.

More than three decades after the PCA-ADA schism, the CDM prepared to bring Carter into its tent or leave the Democrats altogether. After initial pleasantries, the president emphasized his dedication to human rights as the foundation of his foreign policy and the seriousness with which he regarded the Soviet invasion of Afghanistan. Wattenberg took the lead in explaining his deep disappointment with the president's policies but offered his unqualified support for the grain embargo, Olympic boycott, and increased defense spending.[126] Pressing the administration to go further, he probed Carter for his fundamental assessment of the Soviets.

Instead of seeing human rights as a major ideological weapon in the Cold War, Carter asked for the CDM's help in advancing the issue in Ecuador. Utterly confused that the president was more interested in the CDM's assessment of a small Latin American nation than the Soviets, the meeting devolved into acrimony. After the president departed, Mondale, who well understood the organization's stance and concerns, attempted to contain the damage.[127]

Mondale's entreaties notwithstanding, Wattenberg and the CDM pronounced Carter "hopeless." While Wattenberg remained committed to the Democrats, many CDM members embraced Ronald Reagan. In April, when the Carter White House called on Jeanne Kirkpatrick to participate in the Democratic Convention, she replied: "I already have a date."[128]

While the CDM was officially neutral in the 1980 election, many of its members privately, and even publicly, hoped that a Reagan victory would remind liberals of the potent traditions they had so blithely discarded.[129] When president-elect Reagan appointed Kirkpatrick to be ambassador to the United Nations, the irony was not lost on Wattenberg. Noting that the CDM had unsuccessfully lobbied Carter to appoint Kirkpatrick to a diplomatic post, Wattenberg conceded that he and like-minded liberals "don't seem to be a [Democratic] majority any longer."[130]

In losing the Vital Center liberals–cum–neoconservatives, Democrats forfeited a significant group of thinkers and policymakers. The New Politics' quest for LaGuardia's united Left stripped the party of intellectual firepower and rendered it unable to build mainstream policy and attract Middle American votes. Indeed, for all their faults, the early neocons challenged liberal orthodoxy and shibboleths—a necessity for liberalism to remain relevant. Without these neoconservative thinkers, Daniel Patrick Moynihan explained: "The Republicans simply left us [Democrats] behind. They became the party of ideas and we were left, in Lord Macaulay's phrase, as 'the stupid party.'"[131]

8

"Everybody Is People"

Bella Abzug and the New Politics of Feminism

Bella jumped right in. For decades, the House swimming pool had been an all-male reserve. By tradition, the old pols and congressional bulls swam naked. To compensate for this inhospitable environment, Congress built a women's gym—sort of. Lacking a swimming pool and other amenities, the facility was, in the words of one congresswoman, "ten hair dryers and a ping pong table."[1] Never shy about confronting hypocrisy and inequality, Bella Abzug donned a swimsuit and dove into the pool, naked men and all. Shaming chauvinists into wearing swim trunks was merely a prelude to the congresswoman's antics to come.[2]

During the 1970s, New Politics activists like Bella Abzug transformed Congress and pushed their issues onto the national agenda. A mix of reformist impulses, the New Politics also counted feminists among its adherents. While New Politics liberals did not spark the women's movement, their moralism and activism helped shape it. A three-term congresswoman, professional insurgent, and feminist leader, Abzug embodies the intersection of the New Politics and the women's movement.

Combining the moralism, activism, and issues of the New Politics with second-wave feminism's aims and sensibilities, Bella Abzug's New Politics feminism promised to advance both agendas by forging a broad political alliance. Claiming to have become a feminist "the day I was born," Abzug was ideally situated to bridge and blend second-wave feminism and the New Politics into one coherent impulse—New Politics feminism.[3]

Abzug was born in 1920, and her activism and feminism were shaped by the leftist milieu of her Depression-era Jewish community. Channeling the Zionist and antifascist sentiment of the 1930s Jewish Left into the political struggles of her adult life, she fought for civil rights in the 1940s, battled Joseph McCarthy in the 1950s, pushed for a nuclear test ban treaty in

Bella Abzug (photo by E. A. Schwartz, used with permission)

the 1960s, and called for an equal rights amendment in the 1970s. Audacious and bold, her combative style not only characterized the typical New Yorker for a generation of Americans; it also imbued the New Politics and the women's movement with her spirit and moral sense.

The product of Russian-Jewish émigrés, Bella was reared in a devout Orthodox household in the South Bronx "Jewish Ghetto."[4] As a young girl, she routinely attended synagogue with a doting grandfather and delighted onlookers with precocious recitations of traditional prayers. Even at this early age, her feminist sensibilities were evident. She not only objected to the women-only seating in her temple's balcony, but in the months after her father's death twelve-year-old Bella trudged to synagogue every morning to say kaddish, a ritual reserved for sons.[5]

It was after her father's death that Abzug discovered Zionism. In contrast to her sister, Helene, who polished her piano skills, she joined a left-wing Zionist youth organization, Hashomer Hatzair. Spending her early teenage years raising funds for Zionist causes, she dreamed of life on a kibbutz in Palestine.[6] Though she never moved to Israel, this charged atmosphere shaped her romantic politics and activism.[7]

While Bella threw herself into Zionist causes, her mother, Esther Savitsky, maintained the family's middle-class lifestyle by working as a department store saleswoman.[8] Following in these footsteps, Abzug was expected "to be something" rather than simply marry and raise children.[9] As a result, she enrolled at Manhattan's Hunter College and joined in the roiling political fray of the 1930s.

In addition to Zionism, the Left's Depression-era ideological struggles shaped Abzug's worldview. From her post as president of the Hunter College student council, Abzug joined the battle against fascism and graduated into the larger political world that lay beyond Zionism.[10] Zionism and her Jewish identity nonetheless always informed her worldview. Universalizing the Jewish experience as a quest for social justice, she once declared: "The Jews are a parent whose son goes to Vietnam, [or] a tenant who doesn't have decent housing."[11]

Though Abzug joined her contemporaries in the day's political fisticuffs, she always remained doggedly independent and unorthodox, even for the famously nonconformist New York Left. For example, while the vast majority of young Jewish radicals replaced God with utopian politics, Abzug clung to her religious roots and even studied Hebrew at the Jewish Theological Seminary.[12] Abandoning the kibbutz, kosher eating, and Orthodox Judaism, she remained observant nevertheless.[13] This religiosity underlines Abzug's extraordinary individualism, which was necessary as she strived to "be something" in what was definitely a man's world.[14]

Like millions of other women during the Second World War, Abzug took advantage of newfound opportunities. As one of seven women at Columbia University's law school, she thrived and was named editor of the *Columbia Law Review*. While in law school, she met and married Martin Abzug.[15] As subdued as his wife was tempestuous, Martin shared his spouse's worldview. Starting his career as a garment cutter, he later became a stockbroker and penned two novels while supporting his wife's decidedly unconventional activism and career.[16]

After graduating from law school in 1945, Abzug struggled to find her niche. Early in her career, during a meeting with clients and other lawyers, someone would inevitably ask the "secretary," meaning Bella, to "run out for coffee."[17] Tiring of this routine, Abzug took to wearing hats so that others would recognize her as a peer. Her wide-brimmed and colorful hats not only distinguished her from the clerical staff; they also became a trademark.[18] Once she became a national figure, more than one passerby knew her as "that Abzoooog woman": "You know the one who wears the crazy hats."[19]

As a labor lawyer, she represented various unions and was on the front lines of the 1948–1949 New York City longshoremen's strike.[20] By 1949, she had turned to civil rights cases and found an outlet for her passion—fighting for the disenfranchised. Ever the lover of lost causes, the twenty-nine-year-old Abzug served as chief counsel for Willie McGee, an African American facing the death penalty in Mississippi for raping a white woman.[21]

Seven months pregnant, Abzug traveled to Mississippi to appeal McGee's death sentence.[22] Not surprisingly, the presence of a young, pregnant Jewish lawyer defending a convicted African American rapist drew considerable media attention and local scrutiny. Owing to the additional coverage of McGee's plight, Mississippi officials were inundated with telegrams pleading for leniency. As a result, McGee's life was not the only one at stake. With threats to lynch the "white lady lawyer" and no motel willing to rent her a room, Abzug slept in a bus station bathroom stall.[23] Despite these efforts, in 1951 McGee was executed, which pushed Abzug further into civil rights law.

Following McGee's execution, Abzug collaborated with the leftist-oriented National Lawyers Guild. Drafting civil rights legislation, and fighting for the implementation of the landmark 1954 *Brown* decision, Abzug became well regarded in what was then a narrow circle of civil rights law. Indeed, she carved a niche for herself as a tireless champion of free speech and so repeatedly used a defense based exclusively on First Amendment rights that it became known as the "Bella line."[24]

Women's Strike for Peace

By the mid-1950s, Abzug turned her attention to nuclear disarmament and political reform in New York City. These activities strategically positioned her to become a leader of the nascent New Politics movement. In 1961, she reemerged on national radar as a leader of the Women's Strike for Peace (WSP).[25]

A grassroots organization dedicated to promoting peace, disarmament, and nuclear nonproliferation, the WSP organized an estimated fifty thousand women across sixty American communities to protest the Kennedy administration's resumption of nuclear testing. As its national legislative chairwoman, Abzug pushed the organization into what many considered the "male political culture" of traditional party politics.[26] Convincing WSP leaders that a viable peace movement must offer "specific legislation," she pushed the organization to back and help pass the 1963 Nuclear Test Ban Treaty.[27]

While gendered politics gave the WSP and its issues a modicum of mainstream respectability, the organization failed to fully reflect Abzug's political instincts and agenda. Thus, her devotion to the WSP and willingness to work behind the scenes reveal a pragmatic political streak existing alongside her insurgent tendencies. The political culture of the early 1960s was not conducive to a national movement with Abzug as its public face—a situation she seemingly understood and accepted. In the meantime, she turned her attention to local politics and helped lead a reform impulse that foreshadowed, influenced, and launched the New Politics.

The Reform Democrats

During the 1950s, New York City's infamous political machine, Tammany Hall, staged a comeback under the auspices of its new boss, Carmine DeSapio. Born and raised in Greenwich Village, DeSapio climbed the rungs of political power to become the Democratic leader of First District South (Greenwich Village) and later the chair of the New York County Democratic Committee, the traditional power base of the Tammany Hall boss.[28]

To reformers, DeSapio embodied an anachronistic and decidedly undemocratic style of government. He not only sported a decidedly unfashionable pompadour; because of an eye disease he wore dark prescription glasses as well. The eyeglasses, combined with his dated fashion, made him appear sinister, obsolete, and even comical. In reaction to the "image of bossism," young middle-class liberals formed "grassroots" Reform Democrat clubs from which they battled Tammany Hall.[29]

While the reformers depicted themselves simply as good government activists, the struggle between DeSapio's old-liners and the Reform Democrats was fundamentally a power struggle between the social classes and ethnic groups of Manhattan's rapidly changing neighborhoods. The well-heeled and highly educated Reform Democrats were usually WASPs, assimilated Jews, or "liberated" Catholics who lived in Manhattan's tonier neighborhoods. In contrast, DeSapio's supporters were working-class and decidedly ethnic—Irish, Italian, and observant Jews. These lower-class Democrats were unmoved by abstract issues of party reform. Moreover, they perceived charges of bossism as veiled ethnic slurs.[30]

While New York's Reform Democrat clubs were at first a local response to a particular issue, the ambitious activists peopling them eventually turned their attention to the wider political world. Indeed, the New Politics movement in many ways reflected the ethos of New York's Reform Democrats. Calls to rid New York of the "invisible government of the bosses" were the exact type of rhetoric later employed by New Politics liberals against the Democratic establishment.[31] Moreover, both groups called for a politics founded on mass participation, activism, and public integrity.

With DeSapio gone, Reform Democrats turned their attention to the city's congressional delegation. Running a slate of "reform" candidates against the "Democratic regulars," they sought to replicate their local successes on the congressional level. Starting in 1964, they set their sights on Congressman Leonard Farbstein. No conservative, Farbstein was targeted for his "mechanically liberal" voting record and past ties to DeSapio.[32]

As Reform Democrats squashed the remnants of the Tammany machine, events conspired to help them control New York's state Democratic Party. Starting in 1965, the Vietnam War's unpopularity swung the political momentum their way. Armed with that momentum, New York's Reform Democrat clubs were among the first liberal organizations to call for American withdrawal from Vietnam and for the party to "dump Johnson."[33]

With leadership roles in WSP, Reform Democrat clubs, and the dump Johnson movement, Abzug was ideally situated to channel the zealous energy of New York's reformist Left into the antiwar and women's movements. As its legislative director, she also moved the WSP into direct political activity. In this way, the Vietnam War fundamentally changed the WSP, which, in turn, helped spawn and shape the women's movement.

Sensing opportunity, Abzug used the domestic implications of the Vietnam War as a "women's issue" to bring formerly politically inert women into the fight. One activist, Elinor Guggenheimer, explained how the war became for her a "women's issue." Claiming that "the first person to be hurt [by war] is the woman," Guggenheimer believed that, "as the fabric of our society bursts at the seams, the first thing destroyed is the warm family life."[34] For Guggenheimer and other activists, since the war treaded on their domain, it became a women's issue.

For Abzug, convincing women to join the antiwar movement was only an initial step. By 1970, she was calling for female candidates to run for public office and end the war themselves.[35] As usual, Abzug was prescient. Indeed, 1970 became a watershed moment for women in American politics. Before, they were usually elected to Congress only as replacements for their deceased husbands. The *widow's mandate,* as it was called, was responsible for thirty-three of the seventy-five congresswomen elected prior to 1970.

By 1970, the tradition of the widow's mandate was on the wane. Of the eleven female members of the Ninety-first Congress, only three served in their deceased husband's stead. Some observers associated the declining numbers of congresswomen with increased campaign costs. Senator Maureen Neuberger, herself a political widow, speculated that many women felt that they lacked the foreign policy credentials necessary for the job and, thus, had refrained from running.[36] Vietnam, however, changed these perceptions of foreign policy elites.

In conjunction with altering women's political roles, Vietnam also spawned the proliferation of disparate yet loosely connected groups: the antiwar, women's, and New Politics movements. Many significant figures, such as Bella Abzug, were involved in all three. These organized responses to the social and political tumult of the era fed into and influenced one another. The New Politics might have represented an organized response to the Vietnam War, but its agenda transcended foreign policy.

Rather than merely calling for the withdrawal of U.S. troops, these new liberals sought a "reconstruction of the Democratic Party" because they genuinely feared "genocidal repression and fascism" at home.[37] To fend off this nightmarish outcome, New Politics liberals sought a new Democratic Party, one composed of "authentically" liberal businessmen, youth activists, teachers, trade unionists, the poor, and racial minorities.[38]

To build this coalition, New Politics activists needed a "connecting thread" that tied distinct issues of war, civil rights, and domestic reform into a coherent narrative. Since Abzug had been engaged in this particular project throughout her entire career, she was unusually suited to weave this story. In 1969, she had advised New York City mayor John Lindsay to "convert passive grievance bearers" into supporters and activists by making "urban priorities" the central uniting thread of his reelection campaign. As chairwoman of the Taxpayers Campaign for Urban Priorities, she tried to render urban priorities shorthand for the Vietnam War's domestic impact on health care, civil rights, environmental, and consumer affairs.

Whether it was the WSP's "human needs" or the Taxpayers Campaign's "urban priorities," Abzug made the domestic implications of the Vietnam War the common theme of her activism. Fortunately for her, she timed her political machinations with the fiftieth anniversary of the passage of the Nineteenth Amendment, the constitutional amendment guaranteeing women the right to vote. With this date in mind, the recently formed National Organization for Women (NOW) launched the Women's Strike for Equality. Scheduled for August 26, 1970, the event was intended to channel antiwar sentiment into a new "crusade for [women's] equality."[39]

If anything, NOW's Strike for Equality was lagging behind the pace of social change. Nationally, a record number of female candidates had filed to run for Congress, promising the largest number of congresswomen since 1961. Unlike the situation in 1961, however, these female candidates were not running on a widow's mandate. Rather, most came from the ranks of the New Politics and the emergent women's movement, including Bella Abzug.

Congresswoman Abzug

After years of trying and failing to unseat Leonard Farbstein, New York's Reform Democrats finally turned to Abzug. With sterling reformist credentials and grassroots support, she was a formidable candidate. At stake was New York's Nineteenth Congressional District. Heavily Jewish, this gefilte-fishhook-shaped district encompassed a bubbling stew of ethnic neighborhoods stretching from New York's financial district to Greenwich Village. Among these blocks and wards was Manhattan's Lower West Side—a Reform Democratic stronghold.[40]

Weaving the New Politics, antiwar issues, and the women's movement into the fabric of her congressional campaign, Abzug appealed to antiwar activists, inflation-squeezed taxpayers, and women by offering a common salve for what ailed all three constituencies—New Politics feminism. According to the candidate, New Politics feminism offered a grassroots movement that would force Congress to channel tax dollars away from Vietnam and toward "human priorities."[41]

Abzug recognized that Farbstein's "me-too" record rendered him vulnerable to an insurgent challenge.[42] Rather than opting for the *Village Voice's* suggested motto, "Support me or I'll make you deaf," Abzug's theme, "This Woman's Place Is in the House," struck a feminist note.[43] Moving beyond appeals to gender, she labored to bridge the distance between the New Politics and working-class bread-and-butter issues.[44] With her distinctively hoarse Bronx accent, native New Yorker swagger, and trademark "Hello-I'm-Bella-Abzug" handshake, she hit the campaign trail with all the subtlety of a speeding freight truck.[45]

Roaming her district's ethnically diverse neighborhoods, the multilingual Abzug spoke Yiddish, Spanish, Hebrew, French, and Italian to win over wary voters. Even as she appealed to a diverse constituency, she promised to "raise holy hell" and did just that. In the weeks prior to the Democratic primary, she took her campaign to Farbstein's literal doorstep. Riding atop a sound truck with Barbara Streisand, she canvassed the predominately Jewish neighborhoods of the Lower East Side, coming within earshot of her opponent's home.[46]

With the issues in perfect alignment, and through the sheer force of her personality, Abzug handily defeated the seven-term incumbent.[47] Months later, she won the general election and became the nation's first ever female, Jewish member of the House of Representatives. When the Ninety-second Congress convened in January 1971, the body's composition revealed the nation's swirling political winds. In addition to Abzug, New Politics acolytes such as Connecticut's Ella Grasso, Massachusetts's Robert Drinan, and California's Ron Dellums were elected as well. The nation's political zeitgeist was not uniform. The ascendance of Boston's antibusing crusader Louise Day Hicks to Congress revealed the complexity of the national mood. Ignoring this, Abzug believed that the winds of change were wholly at her back.[48]

Perpetual motion machine that she was, Abzug hit the capital like a force of nature. Taking the oath of office while brandishing an "Uppity Women Unite" button, she also took a "people's oath" of office on the Capitol steps while supporters shouted, "Give 'em hell!"[49] Organizing a staff that reflected her "spirit and approach to life," she hired young women with little direct congressional experience.[50] With a typical workday that began at 6:30 or 7:00 A.M. and lasted until 1:30 or 2:00 in the morning, she drove herself and her staff to the limit.[51]

Garrulous, demanding, and often abrasive, Abzug drove the thin-skinned and sleep deprived from her office. Her first personal secretary, Frances Cash, quit, opting for a more pleasant and less noisy job: directing traffic at construction sites. Cash's claim that "these machines couldn't make as much noise" as her former boss was echoed by Congressman John Breaux, who compared sitting near Abzug on the House floor to "living next to an airport."[52]

At her noisiest and most bellicose during her first few months in office, Abzug refused to comply with accepted conventions. Calling the allotment of committee assignments by seniority "the [same] old bullshit" and the trade of one's vote for a committee seat "selling your soul," she demanded a spot on the House Armed Services Committee—on the nationally televised *Dick Cavett Show.*[53]

Not surprisingly, the freshman congresswoman's antics failed to win over the House Democratic leadership. Alone among freshmen Democrats, Abzug was relegated to the Siberia of congressional committee work—Government Operations and Public Works.[54] If the leadership believed that handing her subpar assignments would muffle the rabble-rouser, they were sorely disappointed. From her Government Operations post, she personally investigated American oil companies and U.S. military activities in Laos.[55] Exclaiming, "The hell with it, I'll hold my own hearings," she hosted ad hoc inquiries from her office and promised more if tepid colleagues failed to act.[56]

Thanks to these antics, Abzug developed a national constituency that believed that she was, as one admirer put it, "one neat-ass dude."[57] Some politicians might have simply reveled in the attention, but Abzug founded the National Constituents for Bella Abzug (NCBA).[58] With a mailing list of approximately six thousand, the NCBA became an additional resource devoted to advancing the New Politics.[59] Recognizing her emergent political power, the National Press Club invited her to address the organization; she was the first congresswoman ever asked to do so. In typical fashion, she used the venue to announce the formation of yet another political organization, the National Women's Political Caucus (NWPC).[60]

Established July 1971, the NWPC was led by Abzug, Gloria Steinem, Fannie Lou Hamer, and Betty Friedan.[61] With a rallying cry of "Make Policy, Not Coffee," the self-described "multi-partisan" organization was designed to increase women's political power and representation. In 1971, a measly twelve women were among the nation's top seven hundred elected and appointed offices.[62] Believing that women were bound by "conscious unity," Abzug claimed that the NWPC could right the nation's "lopsided priorities and distorted values" by displacing the "masculine mystique['s] . . . obsession with militarism" and ending the Vietnam War.[63]

While the NWPC was officially nonpartisan and cochaired by Republicans, the issues the organization confronted—abortion, racial equality, sexism, and the Vietnam War—rendered it a potentially powerful interest group within the Democratic Party, so much so that the NWPC forced DNC chairman Lawrence O'Brien to open the party to female delegates at the 1972 convention.[64] In contrast to the 1968 delegation, which was 13 percent female, the 1972 slate of conventioneers was 38 percent female. By electing Jean Westwood chairwoman of the Democratic Party and including the Equal Rights Amendment (ERA) and abortion rights in the party's platform, the NWPC helped shape the party's agenda.[65]

Never one to compromise core principles, Abzug nevertheless sought a middle ground.[66] Chiding feminists who refused to back male candidates, she sought more than an end to the Vietnam War and abortion rights.[67] Rather than pursuing a single-issue politics, she believed that women's political power promised to reorder national priorities. In this way, she remained a visionary even as her movement became mired in controversial social issues.[68]

Abortion

In the years immediately preceding the Supreme Court's 1973 *Roe v. Wade* decision, NOW had organized a grassroots movement to liberalize abortion laws. Before NOW's national office had even formulated its official stance, in 1967 its New York chapter had penned and submitted an abortion rights state constitutional amendment.[69] While Albany lawmakers failed to pass the amendment, abortion rights sentiment in New York led to the dramatic passage of the state's landmark 1970 abortion reform law,[70] which legalized abortion up to the twenty-fourth week of pregnancy. At the time of its adoption, the law became the nation's most permissive abortion statute.[71]

Reasoning that antiabortion sentiment represented "one of the few leftovers from our sexually sick Puritanical past," NOW's national organization followed its New York chapter and endorsed abortion rights, organizing accordingly.[72] To build a national movement, in the summer of 1971 the Women's National Abortion Action Committee (WONAAC) was founded. Working with WONAAC and NOW, Abzug introduced the 1972 Abortion Law Repeal Act. Reasoning that a woman's right to "not be compelled or required to carry or bear a fetus or child against her will" rendered abortion a "natural right," Abzug's bill would have repealed all state and federal laws restricting the procedure.[73]

Abzug's proposal became a rallying point for abortion rights activists, and its introduction became the climactic point of WONAAC's Abortion Action Week. During the first national abortion rights rally, demonstrators called for public hearings on abortion rights, high school contraception programs, and mass protests against forced sterilization.[74] *Roe v. Wade* might have rendered Abzug's legislation obsolete, but her activism played a crucial role in creating the proper climate of opinion for the Court's decision.

While some feared that abortion would divide the women's movement, gay rights proved just as troublesome. From NOW's very inception in 1966, the "lesbian issue" had threatened to undermine the organization's unity. Abzug railed against the "sexual McCarthyism" of those who used lesbianism to discredit the movement, but even NOW's own leadership lacked accord on the issue. The organization's founder, Betty Friedan, was widely known to be a "conservative on the lesbian issue" and avoided confronting the matter whenever possible.[75] Even Bella's husband, Martin, remained cold to the movement's sexual politics.[76] By 1975, the issue threatened to split the organization even as NOW was making a final push for the passage of the ERA.

Though the women's movement identified the ERA as its primary goal, some more militant feminists believed that the constitutional amendment would barely make a dent in a "fundamentally corrupt, compassionless, [and] dehumanizing [society]."[77] Calling themselves the Majority Caucus, in the fall of 1975 these radicals took effective control of NOW. While the Majority Caucus publicly pushed for the ERA's passage, one South Dakota NOW board member, May Lynn Myers, believed that the new leadership's more radical goals were akin to "going after the frosting . . . without ever having achieved the cake."[78] Hence, in Myers's estimation, the radicals were no longer "dedicated to passing the ERA."[79]

Ironically, while the *Roe* decision was heralded by many, including Abzug, as a watershed victory for women's rights, it indirectly led to the defeat of what had been the movement's highest priority—the ERA. Proposed in every Congress since 1923, forces backing the ERA reached a crescendo in the early 1970s. With the women's movement and the President's Commission on the Status of Women, the Citizens' Advisory Council on the Status of Women, and several state commissions endorsing the ERA, Congress passed the amendment in 1972.[80]

From there, activists needed thirty-nine state legislatures to ratify the ERA for it to become a constitutional amendment. Within five years, backers convinced thirty-seven state bodies to endorse the measure.[81] Conservative women's groups responded. Using opposition to abortion rights as a wedge issue, they coalesced and elected prolife slates dedicated to fighting prochoice feminists at national women's political gatherings.[82] With politically active women divided between prochoice and prolife forces, the push for the ERA slowly lost steam.

While many critics used abortion rights to pigeonhole the women's rights movement, Abzug's feminism was never the single-issue variety. In Congress, Abzug introduced and battled for a number of bills, amendments, and issues beyond abortion and the ERA. For example, the Abzug-Chisholm child-care bill, which provided $800 million in funds and income tax deductions for child-care expenses, became law in 1972.[83] Not above allying with an old enemy, Abzug made common cause with Vivian Kellems, a conservative activist, to pass legislation granting single women "head of household" tax benefits. Kellems might have been "that old reactionary battle axe," but in this one case Abzug declared "Vivian Kellems a women's libber on taxation."[84]

Even while Abzug gave a national voice to women's issues, she paid heed to local issues. Aiming her verbal barrage at Governor Nelson Rockefeller and the Republican-dominated state legislature, she accused Albany of "disenfranch[ising]" New Yorkers and placing the city in a "master-slave relationship."[85] Despite Abzug's hyperbole, she touched a raw political nerve. Albany not only returned a mere eighty-two cents of every tax dollar New York City sent to the state, but the city's Reform Democrats were also routinely marginalized by a coalition of Republicans and old-line Democrats.[86] Without sufficient electoral muscle to defeat Albany's conservative coalition, the congresswoman pushed for secession and backed a referendum on New York City statehood.[87] Unfortunately for Abzug, Rockefeller and the legislature pushed back.

The 1970 census revealed such significant shifts in national population that New York lost two congressional seats to booming Sun Belt states. Owing to her rabble-rousing, state legislators chose Abzug's Nineteenth Congressional District for elimination. Treating the district like a stolen car, the legislature chopped it into bits and added them to every surrounding congressional borough.[88] Abzug had long suspected that she would lose her congressional district and had decided beforehand to follow "the people's mandate" and run for reelection.[89] Proving that her political enemies possessed a sense of irony, the largest proportion of Abzug's old district was placed in Manhattan's Twentieth District, which essentially compelled her to run against a political and ideological soul mate, William (Fitz) Ryan.[90]

The affectionately nicknamed "Wild Bill" Ryan was the Reform Democratic movement's original rising star. In 1960, he had first taken on and defeated DeSapio's machine in a local congressional race. Like Abzug's, his seat was redistricted after one term, but he managed to defeat another one of DeSapio's lieutenants and return to Congress in 1963.[91] While there, he pushed civil rights and civil liberties and was the first House member to speak out against American involvement in Vietnam.[92]

Ryan's redrawn district not only contained 30 percent of Abzug's constituents; it also included Manhattan's West Side, the heart of the Reform Democratic movement. Thus, the Abzug-Ryan primary promised to split the city's New Politics liberals. With few substantive differences separating the two, Abzug made "activism" her campaign theme. Claiming that her activism and national profile promoted the issues her constituents cared about, she rummaged for an issue to highlight the nonexistent differences between her and Ryan.[93]

Slowed by cancer surgery, Ryan remained in Washington churning out legislation and publicizing his accomplishments.[94] He also countered Abzug's claims to a monopoly on activism by pointing to his early collaboration with the civil rights movement and fight against the Vietnam War. Lacking an issue, Abzug did what came naturally—she made a commotion. Walking the Twentieth District canvassing for votes, she alternated between Spanish, English, and Yiddish, booming: "I'm Bella. . . . A vote for Bella is a vote against Nixon."[95]

Despite its energy and pizzazz, Abzug's campaign faltered from the start. Never able to answer effectively why she was "running against a good man in his own district," the congresswoman was thrown on the defensive.[96] As the campaign wore on, her high-profile celebrity supporters abandoned her. Still, her diverse constituency transformed campaign events into colorful affairs. At one fund-raiser, a drag queen attracted considerable attention. Journalists might have gawked at this symbol of gay liberation, but Abzug shrugged it off, claiming: "Everybody is people."[97]

Backed by labor and high-profile supporters, Ryan remained formidable.[98] The battle of the New Politics titans never lived up to its billing as the congressman trounced Abzug by a two-to-one margin in the Democratic primary. In what was otherwise a good primary season for New Politics liberals, Abzug's congressional career was seemingly stopped cold.[99]

As the congresswoman licked her wounds, Ryan's cancer very suddenly and unexpectedly ended his life. On his death, speculation raged over who would take his place on the November ballot. One embittered Ryan acolyte hollered that he would not merely oppose Abzug but "wouldn't even let Bella *live* in the district."[100] Though some pushed for Ryan's widow, Priscilla, to succeed him, Abzug received the nod and won a decisive victory in November's election.[101]

In the midst of this especially chaotic season of Abzug's life, her office became the center of intrigue as a quieter and more insidious scandal developed. During the height of the 1972 presidential campaign, Abzug was engaged in a late-night telephone conversation when she and the party on the other line both overheard a voice say: "Keep the tape going. I want to get all of this."[102] Because similar reports had put Abzug and her staff on the alert for electronic surveillance, she immediately hired a private investigator, Nicholas Beltrante, to assess the situation.

A veteran Washington, DC, policeman, Beltrante conducted a thorough sweep of Abzug's congressional office and uncovered startling evidence of electronic surveillance. Indeed, when he tested one of the office's lines, he clearly heard a voice on the other line state: "Bob—they're dialing a Washington number—start monitoring."[103] While he found no "tone-activated microphones" or "hidden eaves-dropping devices," his conclusions were profoundly jarring. According to Beltrante, the absence of rudimentary bugging devices indicated that professional political spies had employed a highly sophisticated network of surveillance equipment to access the Capitol Hill telephone system.[104]

In 1973, Abzug reentered Congress with a tempered and sobered perspective. While she remained an outspoken activist, she had in the words of Speaker Carl Albert "learned that she doesn't have to get out in front on every issue."[105] Realizing that many conservatives enjoyed voting against any "Abzug amendment," she let others take the lead. When Congresswoman Leonor Sullivan objected to the formation of a women's political caucus, Abzug settled for a weekly women's lunch instead. These lunches laid the groundwork for what eventually became the Congressional Women's Caucus.[106]

A mellower Bella did not translate into inactivity. In addition to her board memberships with the ACLU, ADA, NOW, B'nai B'rith, and the Lambda Legal Defense and Education Fund, Abzug was the first member of Congress to call for articles of impeachment against Nixon.[107] Realizing that her comparisons of Nixon to Adolph Hitler and of the Vietnam War to "the horror of the Nazi years" would undermine the impeachment process, she let other, less incendiary voices take the lead.[108]

Nixon's resignation changed the zeitgeist regarding women and politics. By souring voters against traditional elected officials, Watergate boosted the prospects of female politicians, who were regarded as more honest than men.[109] The 1974 midterms saw a record number of women run for the

Congress (108), state legislatures (nearly 700), and governorships (10).[110] In the aftermath of the watershed event that was Watergate and the midterm elections, Abzug was transformed from a divisive backbencher into one of the most powerful and effective members of the Congress.

Abzug thrived in the post-Watergate era. The 1974 midterms, held a mere three months after Nixon's resignation, brought seventy-five liberal "Watergate Babies" to the House. Many of them looked to Abzug for inspiration and, according to the journalist Mary McGrory, constituted a veritable "Bella Abzug Fan Club."[111] With "the kids" as allies, she was no longer fighting a lonely uphill battle.[112]

In the years following Nixon's resignation, Abzug worked to make government more transparent and less prone to Watergate-style abuses. In that vein, she coauthored the 1974 Freedom of Information Act, which gave citizens further rights to uncover government secrets. From her chairwomanship of the Government Information and Individual Rights Subcommittee, she oversaw the implementation of the Freedom of Information and the Privacy Acts.[113] She also pushed for the release of Warren Commission documents and introduced "sunshine bills" that opened the records of federal agency meetings.[114]

Even as Abzug safeguarded the republic, she brought billions of federal dollars to New York City. Whether reimbursing the city for protecting the United Nations or proposing mass transit bills, she focused her considerable energy on the yeoman work of legislation and pork barrel spending. As the coauthor of the groundbreaking Urban Mass Transportation Act, she ensured that, for the first time ever, federal dollars directly funded mass transit. The bill sent an estimated $1 billion to New York City's transit system, thereby guaranteeing the continuation of thirty-five-cent subway fares, a boon for her working-class constituents.[115]

While she stressed traditional bread-and-butter issues, Abzug had several staff members tend solely to women's issues. Using Title VII of the 1964 Civil Rights Act, she made accepted civil rights law work for women. For example, when a public works bill lacked employment protection for women, she grafted a "Title VII provision" onto the final piece of legislation.[116] Because Title VII provisions had been institutionalized by the 1964 Civil Rights Act, an Abzug add-on amendment would usually pass without significant controversy. With legislative assistants constantly seeking opportunities for add-on amendments, Abzug provided women with federal civil rights protection in scores of bills.

Abzug's Title VII add-on maneuver underpinned the Equal Credit Opportunity Act. Passed in 1974, Abzug's bill prohibited creditors from discriminating against applicants on the basis of sex, religion, race, or marital status. In addition to this piece of legislation, she forced the New York Stock Exchange to exclude discriminatory questions in its application forms.[117] This legislation provided single and divorced women the access to credit and financial independence they had heretofore lacked.[118] The add-on amendments not only became Abzug's alternative to direct confrontation; the maneuver also reveals her maturation as a legislator. Indeed, in 1976 her colleagues named her the third most influential and effective member in the House.

The 1976 Senate Race

Though Abzug seemed atypical, like other House members she also coveted a Senate seat. In the months and years leading up to the 1976 election, New York's junior senator, James Buckley, appeared vulnerable.[119] Running as New York's Conservative Party nominee, the older brother of the *National Review* founder, William F. Buckley, had eked out a narrow win. Widely seen as too conservative for New York, Buckley attracted a number of potential challengers. *Monday Night Football*'s controversial anchor, Howard Cosell, pondered the race before opting to remain in the broadcast booth. Among those who did challenge Buckley were former U.S. attorney general Ramsay Clark, New York City Council president Paul O'Dwyer, and the policy gadfly and former ambassador to the United Nations Daniel Patrick Moynihan.[120]

Despite the crowded field, most observers considered Abzug the front-runner.[121] In reaching out to the New York that lay beyond Greenwich Village, Abzug realized that the electorate wanted little of the activism and histrionics that had so animated New York's Left-liberal politics of the 1960s. Understanding that the public perceived her as abrasive and aggressive, a new, "nice" Bella emerged during the 1976 campaign.[122]

Defining her candidacy as something more than an extension of the 1960s and the women's movement proved even more difficult when New York's lieutenant governor, Mary Ann Krupsak, challenged Governor Hugh Carey for the Democratic nomination. With Krupsak and Abzug both running for statewide office, the primary season featured two high-profile insurgent female officeholders challenging male incumbents.[123] This development transformed the Democratic primary into a referendum on the feminist movement. And, in typical fashion, Abzug took the bait.

In so doing, she had her campaign overemphasize gender at the expense of the bread-and-butter issues that had made her into a formidable congresswoman. Modifying Senator Buckley's 1970 campaign theme, "Isn't it about time we had a Senator," Abzug adopted as her unofficial slogan, "Isn't it about time we had a woman Senator."[124] Using the template from her House races, the congresswoman hit the campaign trail. Surrounded by handlers and the media, Abzug would make her way down crowded streets with her trademark hat seemingly floating above the maelstrom as supporters and the curious called out: "Hey, Bella!"[125]

Abzug's maturation during her three terms in Congress earned her the endorsement of many in the Democratic Party's establishment. Breaking with his rule against endorsing non-Massachusetts candidates, the Speaker of the House–to–be Tip O'Neill spoke on Abzug's behalf at a fund-raiser.[126] In addition to O'Neill, Averell and Pamela Harriman surprised many with their very public endorsement of Abzug. Spurning Moynihan, who had worked for the former governor, the Harrimans called the congresswoman a "true Democrat" and implored their friends to "give Bella the chance she so richly deserves."[127]

The support of these establishment figures and their wealthy friends was vital in what became a hard-fought and expensive primary. Sporting Diane von Furstenberg's iconic clothing, and moving from Fire Island soirees to a benefit hosted by Elizabeth Taylor, Abzug raised money from Manhattan's most elite company. The Broadway doyenne Kitty Carlisle-Hart not only cohosted a fund-raiser with Pamela Harriman; she even donated "my two girls and an extra someone to help wash the glasses."[128] Objecting to those who called their gathering "some kind of upper-class radical chic party," Carlisle-Hart and Harriman claimed that they simply wanted to educate critics who said: "You? You're for Bella?"[129]

With plenty of money and the backing of establishment Democrats, Abzug seemed poised to win the nomination and defeat a vulnerable incumbent. Standing in her way was the equally verbose and camera-friendly Daniel Patrick Moynihan. The academic turned policy intellectual had served in cabinet and subcabinet posts in four successive presidential administrations (Kennedy, Johnson, Nixon, and Ford). While he identified himself as a staunch Democrat, Moynihan was a hawk in foreign policy matters and a neoconservative in domestic issues. As a result, the Abzug-Moynihan showdown served as a microcosm of the civil war splitting liberalism asunder during the 1970s.

Though both maintained similar positions on the Israeli-Arab dispute, inflation, and unemployment, Abzug nevertheless questioned her opponent's Democratic bona fides. Attacking Moynihan's service in the Nixon and Ford administrations, the congresswoman declared that she would not support him as the party's nominee.[130] When Moynihan called on voters to repudiate her "rule-or-ruin" attitude, Abzug's longtime enemies saw an opening.[131]

During an address to AFL-CIO conventioneers, the president of the American Federation of Teachers, Albert Shanker, called Abzug a "scab." Dredging up an old rumor, Shanker claimed that the congresswoman had once crossed a picket line of striking teachers by serving as a substitute.[132] With many labor activists jeering at Bella, Shanker's late parry effectively swung AFT and AFL-CIO members to Moynihan.

In addition to Shanker's charges, the *New York Times*'s shifting endorsement of Abzug proved decisive in a tightly contested election. The newspaper's nod to Moynihan, however, was controversial in itself, revealing the ideological fault lines permeating New York's liberal community. In a dramatic move, the publisher of the *Times*, Arthur Sulzberger Sr., overruled the editorial board's initial support for Abzug and forced it to endorse Moynihan. In the wake of Sulzberger's strong-arm tactic, John Oakes, the venerable and visionary editorial page chief, resigned his post.[133] Shanker's charges and the *Times* endorsement most likely provided Moynihan with a crucial edge in an election decided by less than 10,000 votes out of more than 850,000 cast.[134]

While Moynihan's victory was hardly decisive, Abzug's primary defeat in the New Politics stronghold of New York revealed the changing political climate of the mid-1970s and the limits of the New Politics appeal. Though Abzug polled well with New York City's Puerto Ricans, African Americans, and liberal activists and even showed surprising strength in some upstate counties, her signature issues, and those of the New Politics, failed to resonate with voters.

Despite Abzug's raw political talents and relentless energy, she failed to win a statewide race. In so doing, she exposed the rough political seas confronting the New Politics. In the years following the epic 1976 battle, Abzug went on to lose a congressional race and a mayoral race, while Moynihan became a Senate icon and a New York political institution beloved for his heterodox and centrist liberalism.

Abzug's New Politics feminism fundamentally altered the Congress. A generation hence, hundreds of women have served in both the House and the Senate. Scores have wielded committee chair gavels, and one woman, Nancy Pelosi, served as speaker. Institutional change is not synonymous with a popular mandate. Abzug's brand of feminist issues and insurgent politics came to define the women's movement and liberalism. The Reagan era revealed the rough seas awaiting Abzug's New Politics feminism.

9

Leave Us Alone

Morris Udall, the Sagebrush Rebellion, and the Reagan Revolution

Apparently, Democrats hated baseball—so much so that in Nevada, where the federal government owned 87 percent of all the land, the townsfolk of tiny Alamo had to petition Washington just to construct a Little League baseball field.[1] Located in the sparsely populated Lincoln County, Alamo was also situated near Area 51. The security needs of the experimental military airfield meant that the federal government controlled 98 percent of the county's land, a reality causing bureaucratic headaches. Indeed, two and a half years after Alamonians asked for the building permit, it literally took an act of Congress before Little Leaguers could play ball.[2]

In the face of such bureaucratic nightmares, conservatives launched the 1979–1980 "Sagebrush Rebellion." Calling for the transfer of federal lands back to the states, the Sagebrush Rebels exploited westerners' growing ambivalence toward the federal government by offering a succinct program: leave us alone. Campaigning for the presidency in 1980, Ronald Reagan promised a new relationship between the federal government and western states. While Reagan never fully delivered on this pledge, the Sagebrush Rebellion and Reagan's campaign effectively rendered the West a conservative stronghold.

Although leading Sagebrush Rebels, such as Republican senators Orrin Hatch (Utah), Alan Simpson (Wyoming), and Pete Domenici (New Mexico), saw their movement as a novel political undertaking, it was the latest installment of a continuing melodrama pitting western states against the federal government over control of the region's land. In this particular episode, the 1964 Wilderness Act sparked a political uprising.[3]

A watershed in federal land management legislation, the Wilderness Act revealed a shift from conservationist to preservationist policies. Since the

Morris Udall at the Capitol
(courtesy University of Arizona
Libraries)

Progressive Era, conservationists had emphasized the planned use of natural resources. In contrast, preservationists valued the aesthetic and ecological value of wilderness areas. The preservationist-inspired legislation created a National Wilderness Preservation System that banned farming, logging, grazing, mining, road building, and motorized vehicles in wilderness areas. Sixteen years after its enactment, conservatives mounted a counterattack.

Morris Udall and the Alaska Lands Act

Swimming against the political stream of the Sagebrush Rebellion was Arizona's Democratic congressman Morris Udall, a preservationist. Tall, lanky, and athletic, the six-foot, five-inch Udall had gained national renown for his humor, presidential campaign, and legislative prowess. Chairman of the House Interior Committee during the Carter administration, he was the key figure in the passage of the 1980 Alaska Lands Act. A logical extension of the Wilderness Act, the legislation doubled the size of the national park system and tripled the acreage of the national wilderness system; it also prompted the Sagebrush Rebellion.

A major player in every significant battle over environmental legislation from the mid-1960s through the 1980s, Udall symbolizes liberalism's evolving environmental policy. Prior to the 1960s, liberals promoted western economic development via federal projects that ranged from dams and roads to a variety of water projects, literally building the region's infrastructure. By the 1970s, New Politics liberals turned against development in favor of wilderness preservation. Once Democrats ceased allying themselves with westerners in developing infrastructure and resources, conservatives took the region.

Though Udall's impressive record of green legislation has rightly earned him accolades, for conservatives the Alaska Lands Act was the culmination of a century's worth of heavy-handed federal domination and typified the preservationists' agenda. Indeed, it was opposed by every member of Alaska's congressional delegation, raised the ire of most western politicians, and fueled the Sagebrush Rebellion.

Conservationism and Preservationism

During the 1960s and 1970s, New Politics liberals like Udall had become interested in environmental issues. Concerned about humanity's harmful impact on ecosystems, they opted for preservationism, which favored the permanent protection of wilderness as a partial solution to the burgeoning issues of pollution and ecological imbalance.

Though Henry David Thoreau, Lewis Mumford, and Aldo Leopold had popularized environmental sentiments, Rachel Carson catalyzed a movement. Her 1962 best seller *Silent Spring* communicated scientific concerns about humanity's ecological impact to the informed public. A marine biologist by trade, the author claimed that insecticides and other pollutants threatened both the natural and the human environments.[4]

With this impetus, an educated, middle-class constituency rallied to the environmentalist banner. In response to this groundswell, throughout the 1960s and 1970s presidents of both parties signed landmark environmental legislation. From Johnson's 1966 Clean Water Act to the Nixon administration's creation of the Environmental Protection Agency, environmentalists' concerns found expression at the highest levels of the federal government.[5]

In tandem with the burgeoning environmental movement were record numbers of Americans who flocked to national parks. Formerly remote and barely accessible areas such as Utah's Zion National Park witnessed enormous increases in tourism. In 1919, for example, fewer than 2,000 people

visited Zion; by 1964, over 750,000 travelers trekked to the park for vacation.[6] By spurring extensive road building and development in wild and
primitive areas, this tourism helped prompt the Wilderness Act's passage.[7]

The 1964 Wilderness Act was the culmination of an evolution in federal western land policy. Originally, federal policy was designed to dispose
of public lands rather than conserve resources or preserve wilderness.[8] This
initial strategy was short-lived. It was the explorer and academic John Wesley Powell who altered Washington's policy and helped spawn the conservation movement. In his landmark 1878 *Report on the Lands of the Arid
Region,* Powell argued that the West's arid environment rendered eastern
settlement patterns obsolete. Calling for the "intelligent development of the
West" based on environmental sense, the explorer pleaded for the conservation and efficient use of natural resources.[9]

Taking the baton from Powell, President Theodore Roosevelt placed
public lands and national forests under Gifford Pinchot's Forest Service. He
also used the Antiquities Act to place western lands under permanent federal control.[10] As a conservationist, the president believed that public lands
and resources should be managed for efficient use. Decades later, his cousin,
FDR, expanded the conservationist model. Partnering with westerners, the
federal government developed infrastructure and enabled the exploitation of
natural resources. As a result, the region became a Democratic stronghold.

Not all were pleased with Teddy or Franklin Roosevelt's actions. Indeed,
preservationists objected to the conservationist ethos from its inception.[11] In
1964, they finally gained the upper hand. With the 1964 Wilderness Act,
preservation became a central component of federal policy.[12] With Washington already controlling 96 percent of Alaska, 87 percent of Nevada, 66
percent of Utah, 63 percent of Idaho, 54 percent of Oregon, 47 percent of
Wyoming, 45 percent of California, and 42 percent of Arizona, the Wilderness Act treaded into sensitive territory.[13] Locals, who had looked to Washington as a partner, now began resenting their absentee landlord.[14]

From the start, the federal government's massive landholdings had
shaped the West's identity and defined the region.[15] Bound together by the
common influence of the frontier, economies based on agricultural and extractive industries, and dependence on the federal government, the western
states had developed a distinct political culture.[16] Alternately dependent on
and resentful of federal largesse and control, many westerners had long believed that regional economic development had been hindered by onerous
federal regulation leaving them in near colonial dependence.[17]

While the Alaska Lands Act constitutes the most significant piece of preservationist legislation in congressional history, it also fueled the Sagebrush Rebellion. Angered by preservationist-inspired regulations and the specter of Udall's legislation, in 1979 a Nevada state senator, Norman Glaser, authored a bill "requiring" the federal government to return forty-nine million acres of land to the Silver state. Complaining that westerners "were tired of being pistol-whipped by the bureaucrats and ambushed and dry-gulched by federal regulations," Glaser convinced the state legislature and the governor to sign his bill into law.[18]

Following this opening salvo, similar legislation and state referendums calling for the return of federal land to the states were passed in the West's remaining twelve states.[19] In the midst of a hotly contested presidential election, Ronald Reagan jumped on the bandwagon, telling Alaskans in a December 1979 campaign speech that they could "count me in as a rebel."[20]

Mo Udall

Despite these political currents, Udall continued to press for the Alaska Lands Act's passage. Born to Mormon pioneers, the one-eyed and whip-smart Udall grew up in rugged and rural St. Johns, Arizona. Under orders from Brigham Young, Udall's grandfather, David King Udall, founded the eastern Arizona town. After polygamy landed Bishop Udall in a federal prison, Grover Cleveland's presidential pardon freed him. This act made his branch of the Udall clan into Democrats.[21]

David King Udall's third son and Morris's father, Levi, fulfilled Brigham Young's hopes for Mormons in Arizona. After marrying in Salt Lake City's Mormon Temple, Levi oversaw a thriving farm and a growing family while embarking on a successful career in law and politics.[22] He was not the only Udall engaged in state and local politics; the family name became a fixture in both major political parties across Arizona. Both Democratic and Republican Udalls served as state legislators, judges, mayors, cabinet secretaries, and congressmen.

Raised in the harsh high-desert environment of eastern Arizona, Morris Udall was a natural-born son of the West. Situated on a six-thousand-foot-high plateau, St. Johns offered a short growing season, scarce water, and poor soil, making farming very difficult.[23] The high-desert environment, coupled with its rural locale, caused Morris to recall that, if St. Johns was not the end of the Earth, "you sure as hell could see it from there."[24] Diligent and upwardly mobile, Levi and his wife, Louise, "taught and prodded and hollered that [their children] had to get an education to succeed."[25] Dinner-table debates on political issues were the norm, while the family's entertainment consisted of reading newspapers and novels.[26]

From an early age, Udall developed an affinity for the outdoors. As boys, Stewart (the eldest), Morris, and Burr (the youngest) spent hours exploring their desert landscape. After their mother packed them a lunch, the boys would wander the desert, hike along the Little Colorado River, and explore mesas.[27] As a child, Morris was unusually accident prone. At age five, he broke an arm after falling off a horse. One year later, a friend accidentally punctured his right eye with a rusty knife. A botched surgery spread an infection, which necessitated the removal of his right eye.[28]

Within months of the operation, Udall contracted a near-fatal case of spinal meningitis. The doctor performed "excruciatingly painful" spinal taps that required three men to restrain him, prompting Udall to later recall: "It was a miracle I survived."[29] Bouncing back from the meningitis was relatively easy compared to growing up with one eye. Udall's gawky frame and the nicknames "Cyclops" and "Old-One-Eye" rendered him extremely self-conscious. He recalled: "[Being the school freak] had a profound effect on my life, my sense of self and my dealings with people."[30] It led him to develop his wit, which he wielded as an emotional shield throughout his life.

Despite the trauma, Udall's tight-knit family cushioned the blow. When Morris periodically replaced his eye, the entire family would gather and sift through the regular shipment of glass eyes looking for just the right one.[31] Rather than a tragedy, within the confines of the Udall household Morris's injury became a topic of humor and jokes.[32] With the help of strong and loving parents, he overcame his personal tragedy. He also developed into an unusually mischievous boy who continually tried his stern father's patience.

Though Udall describes his relationship with his father as distant, he credited him with providing "much of my philosophy and outlook." His penchant for challenging conventional wisdom was certainly influenced by his father's constant search for "a new and better way."[33] Moreover, Levi Udall's dictum, "If good men don't run for office and try to make things go, the bad men will," also profoundly shaped his son's career path.[34] Following Levi's example, both Morris and Stewart pursued a life of law, politics, and public service.

When not in trouble with Levi, Udall was a star student and athlete at tiny St. Johns High School. With a graduating class of thirty, "Mo," as he was called by his friends, was class president, an all-state basketball player, and valedictorian.[35] When not quarterbacking the football team, playing in the marching band, or editing the yearbook, he was also developing a passion for politics as a columnist for the *Apache County Independent News*.[36]

After high school graduation, Udall enrolled at the University of Arizona in Tucson, where he joined his brother, Stewart, on the basketball team.[37] One year into college, Udall found his life path altered by Pearl Harbor and the Second World War. Missing an eye prevented him from immediate induction. In the summer of 1942, he served in Lake Charles, Louisiana, where he led a segregated air force squadron of three hundred African Americans.[38]

Udall's two years in what he called "the heart of redneck country" were formative.[39] In addition to honing his leadership skills, Udall experienced the Jim Crow South at its most brutal. Despite lacking a bachelor's degree, he was enlisted to defend a black airman accused of murdering a white guard. Working against an experienced prosecutor and without any significant legal training, he lost the case. His client paid with his life, a result that haunted him for decades.[40]

After returning to the University of Arizona in the summer of 1946, Morris enrolled in an accelerated academic program that would grant him an undergraduate and law degree by January 1949. Over the course of three years he made up for time lost during the war. As cocaptain of what the head coach Fred Enke called the "best [team] I ever coached at Arizona," Udall led the Wildcats to a conference championship. In his spare time, he also served as student body president.[41]

As Udall neared graduation, the Denver Nuggets from the National Basketball League offered him a one-year, $8,000 contract. After making arrangements to complete his studies at the University of Denver's school of law, Udall joined the team for the 1948–1949 season. Playing basketball in the evening and studying late into the night from the seat of a chartered DC-3, he somehow managed to ace the Arizona bar exam.[42]

Though Udall never received the promised salary and his team set a record for consecutive losses, he did meet his first wife, Pat Emery, while living in Denver.[43] After marrying Emery, in April 1949 Morris moved to Tucson, Arizona, where he and Stewart opened a small law office handling "anything . . . that came through the door."[44] Realizing that wit and charm won jury cases, Udall made use of his humor. The wit he had originally developed as the "one-eyed boy" made him a formidable trial attorney.[45]

Udall's standing in the Tucson legal community led to his election as Pima County attorney in 1952.[46] In late 1953, the Democratic House member from Tucson, Harold Patten, announced his retirement, setting off a succession struggle between the Udall brothers. Despite Morris's early political success and his older brother's relative disinterest in elective politics, Levi tapped Stewart.[47] Though Morris later admitted that he believed "if any Udall was going to run it should've been me," in the interest of family harmony he stood aside.[48] As a consolation prize, Morris announced his candidacy for the position of superior court judge.

In years past, the Udall name and the Democrats' advantage in voter registration would have guaranteed Stewart and Morris easy victories. Arizona's postwar economic boom, however, had lured conservative southerners and midwesterners to the state, changing the region's political makeup. Revealing the altered landscape was the Phoenix businessman Barry Goldwater's 1952 defeat of Arizona's incumbent senator and the Democratic majority leader, Ernest McFarland.[49]

Despite the choppy political waters, in 1954 Stewart won his House race. In contrast, Morris lost in the Democratic primary.[50] With Stewart off to Washington, Morris threw himself into his law practice, claiming that he was out to "be the best lawyer you could find."[51] Breaking his own verdict award record on three separate occasions, he amassed significant personal wealth and became regarded as a master of courtroom theater throughout the Southwest.[52]

Bored with personal injury cases, Udall decided to write a book on Arizona case law. Over the course of three summers, he researched and penned his 510-page tome, *Arizona Law of Evidence*. The product of his labor became the definitive work on state evidence law.[53] Though Morris campaigned for Adlai Stevenson in 1956 and cofounded a local savings and loan, his burning ambitions were not satisfied. Sensing this, Levi planned for his son to succeed him on the state supreme court.

On Memorial Day 1960, Levi died suddenly of a stroke. With Udall's father's influential voice gone, Arizona's Republican governor, Paul Fannin, appointed Morris's Republican uncle, Jesse Udall, to the state supreme court. Cursing the ironies that were sinking his political future, Morris despaired.[54] His pain was short-lived. In 1961, John Kennedy appointed Stewart to be his secretary of the interior, and Morris finally found his opportunity.

Udall's first congressional race was to be the toughest and tightest of his career. Despite the family name and his opponent's crude racism, Udall won by just 2,107 votes.[55] After nearly a decade of waiting, in the spring of 1961 Morris Udall finally arrived in the nation's capital. The tall and gangly lapsed Mormon made an immediate impression. Ambling the halls of Congress sporting a crew cut, a wide leather belt with a big silver buckle, a bow tie, and a bawdy sense of humor, he was impossible to ignore.[56]

As the product of a special election, Udall also possessed the least seniority of any House member, which meant lackluster committee assignments. These positions notwithstanding, he instantly made his mark by transforming that timeworn communication method, the congressional newsletter, into a work of literature. Fretting over his incapacity to communicate with constituents, Udall developed a "four-page essay format" in which he walked the reader through a particular issue or vote. Originally intended for newspaper editors, academics, and party officials, the newsletter eventually went to twenty-five thousand recipients. In 1972, these essays were compiled in a well-regarded book, *The Education of a Congressman*.[57]

After barely eking out a win in the 1961 special election, Udall won in 1962 by a solid ten-thousand-vote margin.[58] Emerging as a leader of young House liberals, he served as a whip during the House debate over the 1964 Civil Rights Act. As he learned the system and made friends, his constituents profited from federal dollars flowing to Arizona's Second District. By 1971, federal defense expenditures in the district climbed to $625 per person, nearly three times the national average.[59]

In the meantime, Udall's work habits and political ambition took a toll on his family. In 1965, Pat filed for divorce and returned to Tucson with the children.[60] Because divorce was quite rare in the mid-1960s and rarer still among Mormons, Udall's frayed personal life threatened to undo a promising political career. Despite this personal setback, 1964 and 1965 were defining years. With a post on the Interior Committee, Morris worked for the passage of the 1964 Wilderness Act. This landmark legislation withdrew millions of acres of primitive wilderness from development and empowered the federal government to more closely regulate public lands.[61]

The Central Arizona Project

Ironically, while the Udall brothers were passing the 1964 Wilderness Act and overseeing its implementation, they were promoting opposite policies in Arizona. From his post on the Interior Committee, Udall diligently pushed the mom and apple pie of Arizona politics, the Central Arizona

Project (CAP).[62] Using the water from the Colorado River Basin, located on the state's border with California and Nevada, the CAP was intended to economically develop central and southern Arizona.[63] The project required a complicated series of dams, reservoirs, aqueducts, and pipelines to pump water up and over mountains and through hundreds of miles of harsh desert.[64]

In pursuit of this, Arizona signed onto the Colorado River Compact, which gave it and California, Colorado, Nevada, New Mexico, Utah, and Wyoming legal access to the river's water. The Colorado River Compact had sparked a decades-long legal fight among western states as each vied for control over precious water resources.[65] In 1963, the Supreme Court finally ruled in Arizona's favor, granting the state access to 2.8 million acre feet of water.[66] On the heels of this victory, Arizona's congressional delegation, led by the eighty-six-year-old dean of the Senate, Carl Hayden, immediately proposed legislation to fund the CAP.

As western states arranged their forces to block the CAP, the secretary of the interior, Stewart Udall, stepped into the middle of the brewing political storm. To increase its chances of passage, Udall rolled the CAP into his Pacific Southwest Water Plan, making it one of many proposed hydroelectric dam and water projects intended for western economic development.[67] Since the CAP was the holy grail of Arizona politics, if Stewart's plan failed, it was Morris who would pay the political price.

Unfortunately for the Udalls, the Pacific Southwest Water Plan prompted an unexpected political firestorm. Environmentalists posed the greatest obstacle because the CAP called for the construction of two new hydroelectric dams, one at each end of the Grand Canyon. Though Morris later called his support of the Grand Canyon dams "one of the most wrenching decisions I've faced," he advocated it nonetheless; if Stewart's plan failed, the 90 percent of Arizona voters who backed the CAP would inevitably punish him.

The fight over the Grand Canyon dams was a central event in the modern environmental movement's formation. When the Wilderness Society, the National Parks Association, and the Sierra Club successfully blocked the proposal, it represented the environmental movement's first major victory against dam building. In years prior, environmentalists had accepted dam building as inevitable. Frustrated by this acquiescence, the Sierra Club's David Brower vowed to fight any further dam projects.[68]

Faced with the specter of dams in the Grand Canyon, Brower unleashed a powerful and effective media blitz. With full-page ads in the *New York Times,* the *Washington Post,* and the *San Francisco Chronicle* telling readers, "Now only you can save Grand Canyon from being flooded—for profit," the Sierra Club spurred an avalanche of popular protest. So many letters poured into congressional and federal offices that they had to be delivered by dumptrucks.[69]

Realizing that Carl Hayden and Stewart Udall's power would not last forever, Morris feared that the Eighty-ninth Congress, and the summer of 1966 in particular, represented the CAP's best chance for passage. Incensed by Brower's media blitz, Udall denounced the Sierra Club's "dishonest and inflammatory" ad. Following his speech and a lunch with a Treasury official, the IRS announced an investigation into the Sierra Club's tax-exempt status.[70] Despite Udall's hardball tactic, Brower's agitation, combined with the public uproar over the IRS investigation, effectively killed the Southwest Water Plan.

As if losing the CAP were not enough, Udall had grown to oppose the war in Vietnam. Worried that an antiwar position would imperil his congressional seat and embarrass his brother, he waited until the fall of 1967 to publicly declare his opposition. Coming from the brother of a cabinet member, Udall's antiwar pronouncement made headlines from the *Nogales Herald* to the *New York Times.*[71]

Concerned that his controversial headlines and Carl Hayden's and Stewart's looming retirements spelled doom for his career, Morris was especially eager to pass the CAP. Even with a "stripped-down" bill lacking the controversial Grand Canyon dams, the congressman and Brower continued to butt heads over the Sierra Club's no-dams-anywhere policy.[72] Brower successfully stopped the construction of additional hydroelectric dams, but Udall got the CAP passed and signed into law by September 1968.[73]

The National Scene

With the third rail of Arizona politics out of the way and Carl Hayden and his brother both leaving Washington, Morris was finally free. Other milestones quickly followed. In 1969, Udall remarried and published a second book, *Job of a Congressman.* Unlike Pat Udall, who detested politics, Morris's second wife, Ella, was a native Washingtonian who had worked in Congress.[74] Nicknamed "Tiger" for her sassy style and outspoken ways, Ella Udall became the perfect political companion as Morris entered his prime.[75]

With the Democrats out of the White House, Udall turned his attention to institutional reform. Always critical of the House seniority system, he decided to challenge the seventy-seven-year-old John McCormack for the speaker's post.[76] When Johnson was president, McCormack's strength as a behind-the-scenes dealmaker was ideal. With Nixon in the White House, many House Democrats privately groused about his tight-fisted rule and worried that the septuagenarian was ill suited for the Sunday morning television circuit.[77]

While Udall never actually expected to unseat McCormack, his symbolic challenge was intended to "breathe new life into the House . . . and into [the] Democratic Party."[78] His distinction between a symbolic and a real challenge was lost on McCormack. Though he easily defeated Udall, the speaker never forgave him.[79] While Udall correctly believed that his race had "pushed the frontiers of reform," Tip O'Neill called it "the biggest mistake Mo ever made" because any hopes for a House leadership position had evaporated with his challenge.[80]

Even though his stock fell in the Congress, Udall had become more popular back home. Named Tucson's Man of the Year in 1968, he had secured his political base by scoring well with independents and Republicans.[81] With a safe seat and his leadership aspirations stymied, he was forced to look toward the national scene.[82] In 1972, he was rumored to be a potential presidential running mate. Two years later, he considered challenging Barry Goldwater. Despite their friendship, a sputtering economy and Watergate made 1974 an ideal circumstance. The congressman's stance on busing, gay rights, and abortion, coupled with Arizona's conservative political environment, forced Udall to reconsider.[83]

Looking toward the national political scene, Udall sought a policy niche to burnish his ambitions. He had to look no further than the line of cars at his neighborhood gas station. Though the roots of the energy crisis were muddled, the results—spiraling gas prices and lines at service stations—were clear.[84] In the wake of the 1973 Yom Kippur War, the Organization of Arab Petroleum Exporting Countries had imposed an oil embargo against the United States, Western Europe, and Japan. As a result, oil prices spiraled by 400 percent, producing fuel shortages. Long lines at gas stations, sometimes snaking for miles, produced near panic.[85]

Combining humor with straight talk, Udall built a national constituency. Pitch perfect for the burgeoning New Politics movement, Udall's wit and casual nature earned him accolades from educated, middle-class liberals.

Unlike New Dealers who promoted quantitative liberalism, which pushed economic expansion as its key domestic policy, the New Politics proffered qualitative liberalism. More interested in the quality of American culture than quantitative progress, they embraced the environmental movement and were drawn to Udall's take on the energy crisis.

In place of feel-good rhetoric and the New Dealers' push for quantitative progress, Udall claimed that the energy crisis signaled the arrival of the "Age of Scarcity." In this era, the congressman claimed, spiraling housing costs and even blue jeans rationing would become commonplace.[86] This Age of Scarcity prompted Udall to consider electric cars and the adoption of the squirrel as the nation's conservation symbol. He also further developed solutions that had been gestating for years.[87]

Starting in the early 1960s, Udall had embraced a neo-Malthusian interpretation of demography that predated Paul Ehrlich's 1967 bestseller *Population Bomb*. Indeed, he had warned his constituents that a "population bomb" would shape American life and politics in the years to come.[88] Believing that "all our problems . . . of poverty and racial strife stemmed from overpopulation," the congressman claimed that the energy crisis merely foreshadowed the shape of things to come.[89]

With what he thought was a clear understanding of the issues plaguing the American economy, Udall planned his presidential campaign. Although no House member had won the presidency since James A. Garfield in 1880, when House Democrats, led by David Obey and Henry Reuss, petitioned him to run, he immediately took to the idea.[90] Since Gerald Ford was buffeted by the political storms of Watergate and stagflation, Democrats queued up to challenge the vulnerable incumbent.

Surrounded by a field of like-minded liberals and antiestablishment candidates, Udall nonetheless stood out. His first obstacle was his relative obscurity. Realizing that retail politicking was the key to success in the New Hampshire primary, the congressman ambled into a local barbershop and introduced himself, "Hi, I'm Mo Udall and I'm running for president," to which the barber replied, "Yeah, we know. We were just laughing about that this morning."[91] Just like the one-eyed kid who had deflected teasing with his humor, Udall used this vignette to disarm audiences and introduce himself as a modest antipolitician.[92]

Despite razor-thin second-place finishes in the New Hampshire, Wisconsin, and New York primaries, Udall could never get over the hump. Saddled with a bickering staff and a bout with pneumonia, he remained "second place Mo."[93] In losing, however, he finally found the national political limelight. Popular with Linda Ronstadt, Robert Redford, and Arthur Schlesinger Jr., he was satirized by Johnny Carson, lampooned in *Doonesbury*, and six-down in a *New York Times* crossword.[94]

While 1976 brought Udall national recognition, 1977 was a year of despair. After breaking both arms in a fall from his roof, he entered the new year with both arms in slings and casts.[95] His two broken arms, however, were rendered a relatively minor annoyance in comparison to a Parkinson's diagnosis. A progressive neurological disorder with no known cure, Parkinson's results in the loss of muscle control, causing slurred speech, loss of balance, and steep physical decline.[96] Though Udall did not publicly divulge this diagnosis until October 1980, his deteriorating condition was apparent to those close to him. Much as he had done after losing his eye, he pressed forward—this time in search of a proper legislative legacy.

The Alaska Lands Act

After years of waiting, Udall was poised to become chairman of the House Interior Committee. With his presidential hopes gone and Parkinson's disease diagnosed, he was also prepared to make the most of his situation. Setting his sights on enacting the boldest legislation of his career and the most significant environmental act since the founding of the National Forest System, he looked to the Alaska Lands Act as his legacy.

Udall had planned for this legislation. Ever since Alaska had gained statehood in 1959, the federal government and the state's aboriginal population had been negotiating the control of federal lands. In 1971, Congress finally passed legislation, the Alaska Native Claims Settlement Act, "solving" Alaska's land disputes. This bill, however, contained Udall's amendment, section D(2). The clause authorized the secretary of interior to designate new "national conservation systems" in Alaska by no later than December 1978.[97] Udall thought that D(2) would "fulfill the promise of the Wilderness Act of 1964" by establishing a vast Alaskan wilderness forever free of development.[98]

During the Nixon and Ford administrations, there was no action on D(2). With Carter in the White House and Udall as chairman of the Interior Committee, the issue was reborn. Udall's D(2) amendment became so reviled that Alaska's congressman, Don Young, once refused to board an airplane through a gate marked D-2.[99] After earning Carter's endorsement of his amendment, Udall created the special Subcommittee on General

Oversight and Alaska Lands with Ohio's John Seiberling, a devoted preservationist, as chair.[100]

More than anyone else, Udall understood that placing additional lands under federal control was a very sensitive subject among westerners. Indeed, when he had originally endorsed the Wilderness Act in 1964, he had praised the legislation for "neither add[ing] nor reduc[ing] the amount of federal land in Arizona."[101] Like other westerners, both Alaskans and Arizonans had a complicated and ambivalent relationship with the federal government, especially with regard to Washington's control of public lands.

Alaska

Among all western states, Alaska had the most land under federal control, 96 percent. Moreover, in the two decades following statehood, bitter disputes over nuclear weapons testing and dam building had soured relations between the state and federal officials. Featuring vast uninhabited spaces that dwarfed the arid and empty basins of Nevada and Utah, Alaska was a natural choice for the Pentagon's weapons testing programs. As a result, many Alaskans believed that Washington considered their state "a wasteland suitable as a dumping ground, as a test-site for dangerous technologies, and a practice bombing range."[102]

This belief had not always been prevalent. During the early 1960s, federal development projects such as dams and road building had engendered good relations between Alaskans and Washington, DC. Indeed, John Kennedy had kicked off his "New Frontiers" presidential campaign in Anchorage by promising to support development projects such as the Rampart Dam.[103] Slated to be the world's largest hydroelectric project, the Rampart Dam would have produced twice as much power as the Grand Coulee Dam and created a reservoir larger than Lake Erie.[104]

When Kennedy took office, Alaskans, led by Senator Ernest Gruening, were confident that the Rampart Dam would finally be constructed. To Gruening's mind, the dam was absolutely crucial to the state's economic development. It not only promised to provide Alaskans with cheap electricity; the project would also supposedly fuel the rise of aluminum industries.[105] On the strength of a 1962 Senate report declaring the project feasible from an engineering and fiscal perspective, and with Alaska's labor unions and the state's Democratic leadership firmly behind the $1.3 billion plan, the proposal was seemingly headed for passage.[106]

Instead of bulldozers and cranes heading into the state's vast interior, however, the Rampart Dam project was scuttled by an environmental impact statement. Warning that "nowhere in the history of water development in North America have the fish and wildlife losses anticipated from a single project been so overwhelming," biologists concluded that the dam would inflict unacceptable devastation.[107] When Stewart Udall officially killed the project in 1967, Alaskans like Gruening complained that the federal government was "more concerned about the alleged future of a duck than in the future of the people." In this way, they no longer saw Washington as an ally helping the state move toward economic self-sufficiency.[108]

In conjunction with the Department of the Interior's turn against development projects, Alaskans also began waging campaigns against the Pentagon's weapons testing program in the state. The advent of nuclear weapons and the Cold War had turned Alaska into one of the Pentagon's most valued assets. The state's close proximity to the Soviet Union and sparse population made it an obvious choice as a weapons testing site. This status went relatively unopposed until 1958, when the Atomic Energy Commission (AEC) announced Project Chariot.

Planned as a showcase for the peaceful use of atomic energy, Project Chariot was intended to detonate a massive nuclear explosion and, thus, create a harbor in northwest Alaska. In response to this audacious proposal, the state's first significant environmental group, the Alaska Conservation Society, formed, and a native rights movement coalesced. By the summer of 1962, Project Chariot was dead, but the progenitors it spawned—Inuit political consciousness, an environmental movement, and greater suspicion of the federal government—lived on.

When the Pentagon announced plans for nuclear tests on Amchitka Island, Alaskans moved one step closer toward political revolt. One of the most remote islands in the Aleutian chain, Amchitka was a three-mile-wide and thirty-five-mile-long barren military outpost located closer to Russia's Far East than to Anchorage. Starting in 1965, the AEC and the Defense Department detonated three nuclear devices thousands of feet below Amchitka's surface. In August 1970, the Defense Department announced plans to detonate the most powerful underground nuclear explosion in the nation's history. Alaskan political officials finally revolted.

Fearing that the tests would upset the Aleutian ridge fault lines and trigger earthquakes and tsunamis, Alaska's state legislature considered banning nuclear testing altogether.[109] Claiming, "Virtually 100 percent of my constituents are against blasts of any sort," one state legislator, Carl Moses, led an odd and ungainly coalition opposed to the tests. Joining Moses in his opposition were environmentalists, the state political establishment, and the staunchly conservative editorial board of the *Anchorage Times*.[110]

As the federal government and state officials battled, environmentalists joined the fray. One multinational group sailed from Vancouver, British Columbia, toward Amchitka to demonstrate against the blast. Though their vessel, the *Greenpeace,* was forced to return to port, it marked the beginning of an activist environmentalist organization that took the name of the vessel as its moniker. Despite these protests, the Pentagon detonated a five megaton bomb in the summer of 1972. While officials claimed that the blast caused few side effects, the explosion did trigger at least twenty-two "small" earthquakes in the geologically sensitive area and produced radioactive and chemical pollution that would later cost billions to clean up.[111]

Amchitka was one incident in a series of many that fueled Alaskans' growing resentment of the federal government. By the 1970s, many had come to believe that Washington stymied economic development while using the state as a dumping ground for radioactive waste. It was within this highly charged political context that Morris Udall proposed his Alaska Lands Act.

The Alaska Lands Act Redux

With large congressional majorities and the president's backing, and given his chairmanship of the Interior Committee, Udall had every reason to be optimistic. Indeed, Carter's secretary of the interior, Cecil Andrus, called Udall's bill "the most important land conservation program in the history of this country."[112] Unfortunately, the manner in which the chairman pursued the legislation only fueled the Sagebrush Rebellion.

For years, Udall had begged his fellow environmentalists to excise elitism from their ranks so that the movement could gain mainstream political success. To his mind, the cause of environmentalism had suffered because activists had utterly failed to connect their issues to "the gut issues of American life."[113] With national attention focused on his legislation and the opportunity to connect environmentalism to "gut issues," Udall ignored his own advice. By failing to address the "gut issues," he invited charges of elitism and further opposition.

While Alaska featured the most national parkland of any state in the

Union, only a relative handful of its residents could afford to access their state's natural treasures. Because of the state's extreme climate and immense size, most parkland was accessible only through air travel, which even Udall's own staff admitted meant "only a very few, elite, or rich will enjoy." The relative inaccessibility of Alaska's remote wilderness rendered it less a national park than an extreme habitat where only truly "special people" could travel.[114] In this way, few Americans, or Alaskans, could conceivably enjoy Udall's wilderness preserve.

In terms of gut issues, jobs were far more important than accessibility. The subjects of the economy and jobs were especially timely in Alaska; in the late 1970s, Fairbanks, one of the state's largest cities, experienced a depression following the end of the Trans-Alaska Pipeline's construction.[115] Rather than arguing that his legislation would spark growth in the state's tourist industry, Udall ignored the issue. From the start, his staff had warned him that the bill's opponents were certain to highlight job losses as the legislation's primary shortcoming.[116] Rather than taking this advice seriously, he discounted the issue as nothing but a "spook show."[117]

Yet the Alaska Lands Act was certain to result in some job losses. For example, the legislation effectively restricted the lumber industry from harvesting in Southeast Tongass National Forest, which heretofore had provided 96 percent of the state's timber harvest.[118] Udall's decision to ignore the bill's economic impact is especially puzzling because the legislation offered the state a potential economic boon. Boosting the state's tourist industry to the billion-dollar plateau, the bill enabled residents to escape the "boom-bust-cycle" that had characterized an economy based solely on extractive industries.[119]

In addition to his myopic treatment of the bill's economic pitfalls and benefits, Udall never constructively appealed to Alaskans' strong environmental consciousness. Polls revealed that an overwhelming percentage of state residents—61 to 20 percent—favored permanently protecting Alaska's public lands.[120] In 1974, Alaskans had elected a GOP environmentalist, Jay Hammond, as governor largely owing to his opposition to unrestrained development.[121] The bearded poet-homesteader turned politician had prevailed over a popular former governor, Walter Hickel. In calling for a cooperative approach to environmental issues that treated "fish and wildlife as our first concern," Hammond revealed Alaskans' nascent environmental sense.[122]

Udall, however, never intended to cultivate Alaskans' support for his legislation; he had always planned to nationalize the issue. His key legislative ally, John Seiberling, actually declared: "If all 400,000 Alaskans were against [the legislation], it would be insignificant."[123] Following this statement, Udall and Seiberling continued to ignore Alaskans. The latter hosted a series of hearings across the nation to focus public attention on the legislation. Reflecting the growing interest in the environment, citizens from all walks of life testified before the committee. From college professors to fourth graders, thousands voiced their support for the Alaska Lands Act.[124]

In 1978, Udall went to Alaska for a series of public hearings. On finally visiting Alaska, he was even less disposed to compromise. After landing in the snow-covered peaks of the Wrangell Mountains, he leapt out of the helicopter and exclaimed in reference to what he surveyed: "I want it all!"[125]

Standing in Udall's way was Alaska's congressional delegation, Republican senator Ted Stevens, Republican congressman Don Young, Democratic senator Mike Gravel, and a smattering of congressional conservatives. With a congressionally imposed 1978 deadline looming, private developers and Alaska state officials sought a court order severing federal jurisdiction over the state's public lands.[126] Fearing that the courts would side with developers, Carter declared 110 million acres off-limits to development and established seventeen national monuments encompassing 56 more acres of land.[127]

Carter's executive action, while resolute, was a stopgap measure intended, as he said, "[to] preserve for the Congress an unhampered opportunity to act next year [1979]."[128] With the president securing him a second chance, Udall seized the opportunity. Looking to give his bill a bipartisan look, he enlisted the support of the independent-minded Illinois Republican John Anderson as a cosponsor. After the bill cleared the House, Alaska's congressional delegation was inclined to let it pass. Years of uncertainty led developers and investors to seek some sort of resolution. With victory in sight, a measure to add twenty-three million more acres to the bill led to yet another impasse.[129]

After three years of congressional finagling and delay tactics, 1980 loomed as the decisive year for the Alaska Lands Act. The final act of the drama could not have occurred in a more combustible political environment. Not only was 1980 a presidential election year, but Carter also faced a primary challenge by Edward Kennedy, the Iranian hostage crisis, and the Soviet invasion of Afghanistan. Meanwhile, the Sagebrush Rebellion raged across western states.[130] Sensing this, Republicans included a strong endorsement of the Sagebrush Rebellion in the party's 1980 platform.[131]

After Udall reached a compromise with Senators Stevens and Gravel, in July 1980 the Senate finally took up the bill. With Carter calling the legislation the "most important decision on conservation Congress will face this century," the Alaska Lands Act enjoyed the full support of the White House.[132] Following the Democratic and Republican conventions, in August 1980 the Senate passed its version of the Udall-Anderson Alaska Lands Act.[133]

With the presidential election looming, Udall negotiated a middle way between the more liberal House bill and the Senate's version. While most environmentalists argued against Udall's compromises, the practical politician within told him that 1980 was the last best chance for his bill. With the Republican nominee, Ronald Reagan, campaigning in the West and promising to return federal lands to the states, Udall realized that the political tide was turning against wilderness preservation.[134]

The 1980 election not only ushered Reagan into the White House; the president-elect also brought a Republican-controlled Senate with him. Many Sagebrush Rebels believed that a new era of state-federal relations was imminent.[135] In this political milieu, Udall understood that the time to pass the bill had come. In the interim between the election and Reagan's inauguration, Democrats convened a lame-duck Congress, which passed the Alaska Lands Act.

Sagebrush Rebels were apoplectic. One Alaskan claimed that the bill's passage meant that "the blue-jeaned backpackers . . . and silver spoon crowd" had won.[136] Likewise, many environmentalists were unhappy with a bill that theoretically allowed oil exploration in the Arctic Wildlife Range. They even urged Udall to reject the compromise legislation. Wisely, he settled for an act that doubled the size of the nation's national park, wildlife refuge, and scenic river systems and tripled wilderness areas.[137]

The bill represented an unqualified victory for Udall, environmentalists, and preservationists. It also served as a potent symbol for liberals' changing western policy. A generation prior, big government liberals developed the West, built infrastructure, and provided jobs. By 1980, liberals stymied western economic development. The Sagebrush Rebellion failed to return the region's land to the states, but the GOP effectively took the region, which proved crucial in Ronald Reagan's conservative realignment.

10

"Zero, None, Zip, Nada"

Lindy Boggs and Gender Gap Politics

In 1984, Ronald Reagan roared to a reelection victory. The Democratic nominee, Walter Mondale, struggled to win even his home state. And, though prognosticators had predicted the landslide, Geraldine Ferraro had also promised that a "silent [women's] vote" would save the day.[1] Hardly a quip by an undisciplined candidate, Ferraro's forecast referenced the Democrats' strategy to defeat Reagan: women. On election night, however, the "silent vote" amounted to, in the words of Dan Rather, "zero, none, zip, nada."[2]

A wave of undetected female voters not only failed to emerge; the Gipper also won the very groups Ferraro supposedly represented: Catholics, Italians, *and* women.[3] Losing the latter was especially painful because, in 1984, the "gender gap" was supposed to spell the difference. Shorthand for Reagan's lagging popularity with women, the gender gap was the Democrats' sole silver lining from the 1980 electoral debacle. With Jimmy Carter and a third-party candidate, John Anderson, splitting the female vote, Reagan rolled to victory on the strength of male voters.

As the first time the male and female vote had significantly diverged in a presidential election, the 1984 election represented a political opportunity.[4] Indeed, since among registered voters women outnumbered men by four million, Democrats banked on the gender gap for good reason. Tellingly, feminists were divided over how to exploit it. Symbolizing this split were Lynn Cutler and Eleanor Smeal. A party insider and the Democratic National Committee (DNC) vice chair, Cutler emphasized pocketbook concerns as the avenue to best develop the gender gap. In contrast, Smeal, the president of the National Organization for Women (NOW), named reproductive rights and the Equal Rights Amendment (ERA) "bottom-line" campaign themes for women.[5]

Lindy Boggs and Tip O'Neill (courtesy Hale and Lindy Boggs Papers, Louisiana Research Collection, Tulane University)

Geraldine A. Ferraro (Collection of the U.S. House of Representatives, Photography Collection, used with permission)

Buttressing her case, Smeal also claimed personal responsibility for creating the gender gap.[6] Famous for her rhetorical excess and organizational acumen, the slight, five-foot, five-inch dynamo had led a march on the 1980 GOP convention to publicize Reagan's ERA and abortion positions. Flanked by former first lady Betty Ford and twelve thousand activists, the demonstration, according to Smeal, had peeled women from the GOP.[7] She not only claimed the credit; Smeal also coined the term, changing what journalists had called "Reagan's problem with women" into a media-friendly tagline. The gender gap was born.[8]

Ebullient at the election's result, Smeal and NOW trumpeted 1980 as a watershed moment where a "feminist bloc emerge[d]."[9] As far back as the passage of the Nineteenth Amendment, feminists had longed for just such an eventuality.[10] In the decades following women's suffrage, the sexes rarely diverged in statistically meaningful ways or for lasting periods of time.[11] Starting in the mid-1960s, however, men and women slowly began to go in different directions. And, throughout the Reagan era, polls repeatedly reaffirmed that the gender gap was real.[12]

To Smeal and NOW, women had finally become a bloc of voters ready-made for Democratic interest group politicking. Echoing Smeal was the DNC's Ann Lewis. Calling the gender gap "the grand canyon of American politics," Lewis claimed that a "continental divide" now separated women from the "cowboys."[13] Reinforcing this trope were the 1982 midterms. On the strength of female voters, Democrats took key governorships—Texas and New York—and twenty-seven House seats.[14] Adding to this were the polls. In the summer of 1983, the gender gap had reached twenty-four points.[15]

Unfortunately for Smeal and Lewis, the gender gap hardly heralded a feminist voting bloc. Typically, an identifiable ethnic voting bloc or interest group uniformly prefers candidates from its community or those who support matters directly buttressing its parochial concerns.[16] Rather than constituting an interest group, a majority of women voters simply differed from men on two key and specific public policies: defense and social welfare. Significantly, men and women did not substantially vary on supposed "women's issues": abortion, the ERA, and female candidates.[17]

Complicating the issue even more were men. Indeed, despite Smeal's earnest hopes, the gender gap emerged because men's voting behaviors had changed much more than women's. In 1952, men and women identified as Democrats at almost identical rates: 59 and 58 percent. Over the ensuing four decades, it was white men who switched parties and changed public policy attitudes, while women remained comparatively constant in their support of Democrats.[18]

Instead of signaling a hardened partisan interest group, the gender gap meant that a clear and constant majority of women backed Democratic social welfare and foreign policies. After Reagan, this breach became more pronounced and politically meaningful.[19] Eventually, Democrats, led by Bill Clinton, learned to more fully exploit conservative weaknesses with female voters.[20] Indeed, by the late 1990s, gender trailed only race, social class, and religiosity as a predictor of party preference.[21]

In 1984, the gender gap offered Mondale a partial path to parity. If Democrats could woo women and white ethnic "Reagan Democrats," then Mondale could wage a competitive race. In winning just one state and 40 percent of the vote, Mondale had clearly failed in both endeavors. Despite the lopsided defeat, most Democratic leaders understood that the women's vote represented a route back to political relevance. In the interim between the New Deal coalition's collapse and the 1990s, liberals experimented with gender gap politics; in 1984, they did so poorly. Nowhere was this more apparent than Pennsylvania.

Pennsylvania, Abortion, and the Catholic Vote

The heart of America's industrial heartland, Pennsylvania had long been a linchpin of the New Deal coalition. Dominated by major urban centers, midsized industrial cities, and white ethnics, demographically Pennsylvania was ripe for Mondale's taking. To win the state and others like it, he turned to Geraldine Ferraro. Believing that the congresswoman's gender, ethnic background, and compelling biography would attract women *and* old New Deal constituencies, Mondale put her on the ticket.

The Reagan campaign team, however, read the same polling data and recognized the importance of the white ethnic vote. Ethnic voters—that is, those hailing from Eastern, Southern, or Central Europe—were historically a Democratic mainstay. By the 1980s, white ethnics were up for grabs. The journalist Theodore White, along with Reagan's pollster, Dick Wirthlin, considered blue-collar ethnics, and Italians and Poles in particular, the "most dynamic element in American politics."[22] Overwhelmingly situated in the Upper Midwest and the Northeast, the ethnic vote, along with gender, figured greatly into both campaigns' strategies.[23]

A chip off the old New Deal block, Ferraro appeared well suited to court the Archie Bunkers of ethnic America. The daughter of Italian immigrants was no limousine liberal. Attending law school at night while working and raising three children, Ferraro entered politics as a law-and-order prosecutor.[24] Once in the House, the congresswoman became a Tip O'Neill protégé. A latter-day ethnic pol, she seemed a perfect combination of the New Deal and the New Politics. Unfortunately for Mondale, she was also prochoice. And, though Mondale favored abortion rights and Reagan's vice president, George Bush, had zigged and zagged on the issue, Ferraro was the only Catholic and white ethnic nominee.

Pennsylvania's Fifteenth Congressional District was ground zero for the Ferraro experiment. Located in eastern Pennsylvania, and dominated by Bethlehem and Allentown, the Fifteenth had elected a Democrat to represent it throughout the New Deal era. In 1984, however, a Republican, Don Ritter, held the seat. Designated "the number one race in the nation," the Fifteenth featured an incumbent "slightly to [Reagan's] right," double-digit unemployment, and a Democratic registration advantage. As a microcosm of their national strategy, Democratic strategists hoped to exploit the gender gap, induce traditional constituencies to "come home," and take back the Fifteenth.[25]

The core of Pennsylvania's Democratic Party—white ethnics—might have voted for Reagan in 1980, but the recession caused many to reconsider their vote.[26] Given the Rust Belt's unemployment rates and the Democratic Party's registration advantage, the ticket should have taken the region. Realizing that Catholics were drifting to Mondale, the White House dusted off its main ethnic strategy from 1980: shared values. With Reagan widely perceived as supporting "God, country, neighborhood, and family," operatives hoped that ethnics would once again respond to these wholesome themes.[27]

While liberals scoffed, the shared-values strategy proved politically decisive in the Fifteenth (and nationally). Fielding Jane Wells Schooly to oppose Ritter, Democrats believed that synergy with the Mondale-Ferraro ticket would result in winning the House seat. With a million-dollar war chest, two thousand volunteers, and celebrity endorsements, the college professor and former NOW vice president seemed poised for victory—until the social issues interceded.[28] The candidate's advocacy for gay and abortion rights led to charges that she was "antifamily" and a lesbian. Largely conceding the shared-values theme to Ritter and Reagan, Schooly, like Mondale-Ferraro, lost badly.[29]

In a similar fashion, Ferraro's abortion stance yielded shared values to Reagan. The administration treaded lightly on the subject of abortion, an issue about which the president cared deeply. Aware that prolifers experienced "despair" and "dashed hopes" over the White House's halfhearted push on the issue, officials understood that the subject cut both ways.[30] Indeed, the White House feared that an extended push on abortion would exacerbate the gender gap. Communicating its position through press releases and opinion pieces placed in select newspapers, the administration quietly appealed to prolife Catholics.[31]

More important than particular policies was tone. White House officials assumed that the white ethnic community's respect for authority and aversion to "confrontational politics" buttressed the shared-values theme.[32] They felt that, if Catholics believed Reagan embraced their values, the GOP would take the white ethnic vote. Whether it was Schooly, Ferraro, or Reagan, all three deviated from the church's teachings on the troika of abortion, the arms race, and economic justice. Unlike Reagan, however, Democrats directly and publicly challenged the church. By confronting religious authority, the Mondale campaign unwittingly supported White House strategy: to portray Reagan as a "reasonable man with values similar to those of most Catholics and ethnic Americans."[33] This eventuality was not only avoidable; it was also altogether predictable.

During the early 1980s, the American Catholic Church had waded into the political thicket as never before.[34] Blazing the trail was Chicago cardinal Joseph Bernardin. With a "peace church" as his goal, Bernardin tied hot button issues—abortion, poverty, war, and capital punishment—into a coherent theological stance.[35] Proposed in a 1983 U.S. bishops' pastoral letter, "The Challenge of Peace," the "seamless garment of life" doctrine was officially unveiled by Bernardin in a 1983 speech at Fordham University.[36] Hardly a liberal apostate, the cardinal chaired the Bishop's Prolife Committee, and his pastoral letter eventually garnered the pope's tacit approval.[37]

In strictly domestic political terms, Bernardin's critique threatened the nascent alliance between evangelicals and Catholics. United on abortion rights, southern evangelicals and northern Catholics diverged on social justice matters and the nuclear arms race. Phyllis Schlafly, for one, understood the stakes and termed the seamless garment proposal "very divisive."[38] By 1984, the newly installed bishops of New York and Boston, John O'Connor and Bernard Law, might have overtaken their Chicago colleague.[39] The doctrinal conservatives nevertheless backed Bernardin's doctrine.[40]

For Mondale, the seamless garment of life offered a viable inroad to the Catholic vote. Opposing Reagan's defense buildup, Cold War rhetoric, and slashes in social spending, many Democrats implicitly embraced Bernardin's ethic—except for abortion rights. Moreover, in trailing a popular incumbent, Mondale needed a vice presidential nominee to jump-start his campaign, attract women, and court Catholics. Because Ferraro was a practicing Catholic, her prochoice position rendered this strategy unworkable. For some reason, Mondale had passed over a congresswoman more capable of achieving this trifecta: Lindy Boggs.

Ferraro

At first glance, Marie Corinne Morrison Claiborne Boggs hardly represents modern feminist aspirations. Religiously devout, feminine to a fault, unfailingly charming, and equipped with an aristocratic southern drawl, in 1984 Lindy Boggs was also the most powerful woman in Congress. Unlike her fellow Catholic congresswoman, Boggs combined deep and wide-ranging experience with a liberal and prolife record. In choosing Ferraro instead of Boggs, Mondale and the Democrats learned the perils of exploiting the gender gap while ignoring divisive cultural issues.

Initially, Ferraro ignited Mondale's campaign. As a result, Mondale briefly believed that his plan could work.[41] Revelations of Ferraro's sloppy tax records and her husband's shady business dealings might have tarnished the nominee's image. But it was the abortion issue that helped transform Mondale from plucky underdog into George McGovern. During the fall homestretch, Mondale's mistake in opting for a prochoice Catholic became devastatingly clear. This outcome should not have surprised anyone. With the church increasingly vocal on public policy matters and a doctrinal conservative, John O'Connor, heading America's flagship diocese, Democrats, like the crew of the *Titanic,* ignored the signs of looming disaster.

The Jeanne Kirkpatrick dissertation advisee and former naval chaplain boasted an unambiguous prolife record. As bishop of Scranton, O'Connor issued a twenty-three-page directive instructing his underlings to "give total support to the pro-life movement."[42] Following on that edict, he publicly warned Catholic politicians: "I will give no support . . . that could be in any way construed in favor of any politician . . . [who] takes refuge in a so-called prochoice position. I categorically reject the evasion."[43] Named archbishop of the New York City dioceses, O'Connor predictably used his position to sharply and publicly condemn Ferraro's abortion stance.

In the weeks following Ferraro's nomination, bishops largely offered muted and studied comments regarding her prochoice politics. Surprisingly, it was the Democrats who took the simmering feud public. Led by Ted Kennedy and New York governor Mario Cuomo, these high-profile Catholic Democrats claimed that the seamless garment of life allowed for their prochoice stance. Directly confronting church hierarchy, however, merely added fuel to an already combustible situation.

The week following Labor Day, the traditional start of the presidential campaign, the abortion controversy surged to the forefront. With Ferraro touring Ohio and Pennsylvania to woo white ethnic voters, Kennedy and Cuomo delivered major addresses on Catholicism and abortion. At Notre Dame University, Cuomo argued his Catholic prochoice case.[44] Eloquent, rational, and deeply pious, Cuomo's remarks were well received in South Bend but not so in Altoona, Pennsylvania.

Responding to the Democratic offensive at a Pro-Life Federation convention in Altoona, O'Connor took direct aim at Ferraro. In reference to the congresswoman's claim that "the Catholic position on abortion is not monolithic," the bishop accused her of "misrepresenting the teachings of the church." Clearly angered by attempts to nuance the church's stance on abortion, O'Connor argued that the statement could even land her "in trouble with the Pope."[45]

Publicly indicted for near heresy, Ferraro found that the issue dominated her Pennsylvania campaign swing. Worrying that abortion would "get in the way of the message we're trying to deliver," the nominee finally, if awkwardly, addressed the subject in a speech in Scranton, Pennsylvania.[46] If the nominee sought a high-profile venue to offer a full-throated rebuttal, then Scranton fit the bill. The seat of O'Connor's former diocese, the city was, according to its mayor, James McNulty (a Ferraro supporter), the "heart of prolife country."[47]

By choosing a candidate in part for her ethnocultural appeal, Mondale had essentially invited the abortion controversy. Moreover, it was the Democrats who first launched the national and very public debate. Once that debate was under way, Ferraro and other Democrats refused to fully participate. Instead, they continually invoked John Kennedy's 1960 line: "I do not speak for the church and the church does not speak for me." Relying on a refrain from a markedly different political era, liberals apparently hoped that the abortion issue would go away. In this vein, when a reporter asked Ferraro, "What does your religion mean to you?" the devout Catholic replied: "I'm not going to discuss that with you. My religion is very, very private."[48]

Thus, in her most important speech since the convention, Ferraro simply refused to expound on her faith. Inserting a last-minute allusion to the controversy, remarkably the candidate even declined to directly mention abortion by name. Confronting a sea of protesters screaming, "Vote prolife," while waving "Excommunicate Ferraro" signs, the nominee invoked JFK while promising to never "impose my own religious views on others."[49] Simultaneously wooing white ethnics as a coreligionist while also pledging to keep her Catholicism out of the White House, Ferraro undercut her very appeal. So much for shared values.[50]

The Mondale campaign having failed to stanch the controversy, the issue dogged it to the vice presidential debate in Philadelphia. While Bush and Ferraro argued inside Pennsylvania Hall, outside the venue prochoice and prolife activists screamed at one another. With feminists chanting, "Mommies, mommies, don't be commies, stay at home and fold pajamies," and prolifers jeering, "16 million dead! You bloody Nazis," the scene devolved into a farce.[51] What was supposed to have been a bold move to exploit the gender gap and bring Reagan Democrats home had, most definitively, bombed.

With so much carnage left in its wake, the ticket is still remembered more as political punch line than prescient trailblazer. While the campaign fundamentally failed, its strategy remained sound. In the 1990s and beyond, gender gap politics aimed at economic concerns finally bore fruit for Democrats. To defeat a popular and charismatic incumbent, Mondale needed a politically savvy and experienced feminist to jump-start his campaign and woo women and disaffected Reagan Democrats. To thread this needle, the nominee had to be a coreligionist, prolife woman who offered a feminism fit for Middle America. Lindy Boggs was not only the ideal choice for that election; her career foreshadowed the effective gender gap politicking of the Clinton era and beyond.

Lindy

Literally born on a plantation, Boggs married into politics.[52] Entering Tulane University at fifteen, she met her future husband—the eventual House majority leader—Hale Boggs.[53] As editors of, respectively, Tulane's two campus newspapers and later leaders of a political reform organization, the People's

League, Hale and Lindy formed a political dynamo from the start.[54] With Hale serving as People's League chair, organizers asked Lindy to serve as a precinct captain. Wondering, "Don't the police do all that?" Boggs nonetheless learned the art and science of Louisiana politics—all while pushing a baby stroller.[55]

Elected to Congress in 1941, defeated in 1943, and then reelected in 1946, Hale became a Sam Rayburn protégé and quickly ascended the leadership ranks. From the outside, Hale and Lindy appeared conventional. The two, however, "shared all . . . congressional responsibilities and the privileges" and at night divided receptions to literally double Hale's social reach.[56] Running her husband's campaigns, cochairing inaugural balls, and befriending nearly every Washington insider, Boggs was no typical congressional spouse. As a result, politics became a total family affair. Rayburn not only presided over a pet's burial, but Hale and Lindy also hosted an annual garden party—a staple of the Washington social calendar.[57]

Unfortunately, a twin engine Cessna interrupted their charmed life. In October 1972, Hale traveled to Alaska to stump for Congressman Nick Begich's reelection effort. While flying from Anchorage to Juneau, the duo's plane crashed. Following a fruitless two-month search, in late December 1972 Hale Boggs was declared deceased. Since he had been reelected while "missing," Louisiana scheduled a special election to replace the congressman. Understanding that these sorts of contests often began in the funeral parlor, Lindy quickly committed to run. A power broker before she won one election, Boggs rounded up the votes for Tip O'Neill to replace Hale as the new majority leader before she became a congresswoman in her own right.[58]

Coming to Congress in the most traditional and timeworn manner for a woman, the widow's mandate, Lindy Boggs nevertheless forged a decidedly feminist path. Moreover, she arrived at a significant juncture in the institution's history. With only sixteen women in the House and none in the Senate, in 1973 Congress remained a male-dominated institution. During Boggs's tenure, women slowly, yet steadily, climbed to power. By 1991, the 102nd Congress, women held thirty House and five Senate seats. Twenty years later, the 112th Congress, there were seventy-six women in the House and seventeen in the Senate.[59] Though not the most vocal, Boggs was easily the most powerful, influential, and effective congresswoman during an era of enormous transition.

Outwardly traditional, yet inwardly progressive, Boggs used her prior relationships with congressional barons and her relentless charm to ren-

der a woman's power more palatable. Ever manners conscious, she "tried
. . . not to assume too much from my relationships with the more senior
members." Nonetheless, realizing that her district depended on urban development monies controlled by the Banking and Currency Committee, she
turned to "dear old friends," Tip O'Neill and Gerald Ford, for help. Passing a rare joint resolution to add an extra seat to the Banking and Currency Committee, the Speaker and the minority leader added their institution's
newest member to the body.[60]

A tireless worker, Boggs began every day with a 7:15 A.M. mass, labored
until "[her] eyes refuse[d] to cooperate," and returned to her district nearly every weekend.[61] Once she landed a coveted position on the House Ap-
propriations Committee, she, like Hale, funneled projects to New Orleans.
Recognizing that she could never duplicate her husband's agenda or influence, she focused on urban renewal, poverty, and especially women's issues.[62] From founding the Congressional Women's Caucus to establishing
the Select Committee on Children, Youth, and Families, Boggs institutionalized feminist concerns while making women's political power about as
threatening as a Tupperware party.[63]

Responding to the issue of spousal abuse, Boggs pushed the 1977 Domestic Violence Assistance Act.[64] Aimed at establishing a clearinghouse of
information regarding spousal, elderly, and child abuse, the bill also connected victims to services and provided federal support for shelters and
counseling.[65] Incredibly, when she and her Democratic compatriot George
Miller first introduced the legislation, they were openly mocked. In addition
to "snickers" and "sniping," one congressman *jokingly* accused Miller of
"taking the fun out of marriage."[66]

Scrambling for some rationale to oppose the legislation, opponents finally dubbed the bill an unnecessary "federal intrusion into domestic family affair[s]."[67] Faced with this sort of obtuse sexism, Boggs refused to rant
and rave. Instead, she used a popular television movie on the subject, *Battered,* to publicize the issue. Filling a congressional hearing room, she hosted an evening with the film's stars, *Mash*'s Mike Farrell and *Little House
on the Prairie*'s Karen Grassle, during which onlookers met the actors and
discussed the issue.[68]

As Boggs worked to pass her "pet project," a sex discrimination case
exploded onto the scene that both tested and revealed her savvy. Three years
prior, in 1974, Louisiana congressman Otto Passman had fired his depu-
ty administrative assistant, Shirley Davis, claiming that the "heavy work

load . . . and diversity of the job . . . required a man . . . instead of a woman."[69] While Title VII of the 1964 Civil Rights Act protected women against employment bias, Congress had exempted itself from this very provision.[70] Three years later, in 1977, Davis's suit against the "congressional exemption" finally reached the Supreme Court. Though Patricia Schroeder and Morris Udall filed briefs on Davis's behalf, Boggs refused to weigh in. Insisting, "I can't take a position opposite to what the Justice Department is taking when a case is pending in court," she declined to make unnecessary enemies. Letting the Court void the congressional exemption, she pushed her domestic violence legislation instead.[71]

After saving the bill from certain death in 1978, Boggs revived it for 1979. Overcoming past obstacles, the House finally approved her project. In appropriating $65 million, Congress funded temporary housing for abused women. Moreover, the legislation clarified the law on a timely and sensitive subject. With divorce rates spiraling, so had cases of divorcees, usually men, kidnapping their noncustodial children. Designating these crimes "federal felonies," the bill buttressed women's custodial rights.[72] Though the legislation was later lost in the Senate, Boggs paved the way for the next Democratic president, Bill Clinton, to finally sign her bill into law.[73]

By 1982, Boggs and Miller realized that Congress would never respond to women's needs unless members were duly informed and issues publicized. Using her access to Tip O'Neill, Boggs convinced the speaker to create the Select Committee on Children, Youth, and Families. Modeled on Claude Pepper's Select Committee on Aging, which successfully focused public attention on the elderly, the body reflected Boggs's consensus style. Indeed, with conservatives worried that the committee would be used for partisan attacks, Boggs, who was famous for convincing "non-progressive men" to back feminist issues, personally recruited Henry Hyde and James Jeffords to serve.[74] Because of this, the legislation officially creating the body boasted 229 cosponsors.[75]

With Miller as its chair and Boggs heading a committee task force, the two used their posts to "hold up a mirror for Congress to see the American family."[76] High on Boggs's agenda was child support. By the early 1980s, higher divorce rates made the problem of fathers refusing to support their offspring a national crisis. In 1983, for instance, over half of all divorced parents simply refused to pay court-ordered child support.[77]

Though some states boasted hearty enforcement mechanisms, most lagged behind. Moreover, it was the cases of interstate enforcement that begged for congressional action.[78] Discovering that $4 billion worth of child support went uncollected, Republican congressman Carroll Campbell claimed: "The statistics [provided by Boggs's committee] were so shocking they woke everybody up."[79] This was not always the case.

In early 1983, Congresswoman Barbara Kennelly had first introduced a bill to force court-ordered child support. The male-dominated Ways and Means Committee was so disinterested the congresswoman could not even schedule a hearing for her bill. With Miller and Boggs publicizing the issue through the Select Committee, the House finally paid heed and approved the beefed-up Child Support Enforcement Amendments of 1983. Passed unanimously in the House and Senate, the bill established strong mechanisms for child support enforcement—legislation reflecting Boggs's influence and power.[80]

In tandem with the child support issue, rising divorce rates and households headed by single women brought renewed attention to the income gap separating men and women. With 45 percent of all poor families headed by single women, legislative efforts to repair the income breach gained fresh salience.[81] To tackle the issue, Boggs and her congressional allies trumpeted the Economic Equity Act.[82] Addressing retirement benefits and discriminatory insurance practices, the bill guaranteed pensions for widowed spouses and banned gender-based actuarial tables, which resulted in higher premiums and lower remuneration for women.[83] For workingwomen, the bill made employee-provided child care a tax-free benefit—akin to health insurance—and lowered the age at which workers were eligible to vest themselves in company pension plans. Eventually, significant dribs and drabs of the Economic Equity Act even earned Reagan's grudging approval.[84]

First proposed in 1981, the legislation gained additional momentum as congresswomen earned seats on the House's main fiscal committees. Endorsed by three ranking Republican senators, Mark Hatfield, Dave Durenberger, and Robert Packwood, and the Congressional Women's Caucus, the act represented, according to its backers, "the instrument by which we will write the next chapter of equality."[85] More significantly, the Economic Equity Act buttressed women's equality while also fitting the Reagan era. Rather than proposing government-run day care or additional bureaucracies, the bill simply offered "individuals new ways of caring for themselves."[86]

In addition to achieving assignments to powerful committees for women, Boggs's style helped move the bill along. In the long, slow slog of legislating, her methodical persistence proved effective. Unlike sister feminists who pushed and shoved, Boggs cajoled and suggested. A study in contrasts, the congresswoman combined southern gentility with ardent feminism. Living on Bourbon Street, where neighbors called her "Mrs. Lindy," she was known to prepare meals for fifteen hundred and soothe persnickety grandchildren all while dictating a speech over the phone.[87]

Truly beloved by colleagues and staff, Boggs developed a charming yet utterly devastating legislative technique. Compared to the "drip-drip-drip of Chinese water torture," she was a relentless legislator who earned a reputation for "getting things done."[88] Making her skills more valuable and her legislative feats possible was her unique access to the speaker. Moaning, "If she wants something done, she can go whisper in Tip O'Neill's ear," John Breaux complained: "If I tried that, I'd get a punch in the nose."[89] Indeed, it was the congresswoman who convinced O'Neill to reintroduce the ERA.[90]

The ERA

First proffered by Alice Paul and the suffragettes in 1923, the ERA lived several political lives. Simply worded, and divided into three concise sections, the amendment's first and most significant clause read: "Equality of Rights under the law shall not be denied or abridged by the United States or any state on account of sex." The additional two segments gave Congress the power to enforce the amendment via legislation and established a time line for enactment.[91]

Continually upended by claims that its passage would eradicate women's protective labor laws, exemptions from military drafts, child custody rights, and alimony, the ERA gained new momentum from the feminist movement. With NOW pushing from the outside and Congresswoman Martha Griffiths clamoring for action, in 1970 the House and Senate finally approved the amendment by a 352–15 and 84–8 vote.[92] In January 1972, the ERA went to the states for ratification. Given seven years to earn the endorsement of thirty-eight legislatures, when thirty states approved it by March of the same year, passage seemed certain.

The pungent atmosphere of Middle America's backlash against the counterculture and feminism enabled Phyllis Schlafly to organize STOP ERA (Stop Taking Our Privileges). Calling feminists "anti-family, anti-children, and pro-abortion," Schlafly touched a nerve, spawned a grassroots movement, and stopped the amendment cold.[93] She did so by using high-profile events to define feminism as a fight for abortion and gay rights. The

1977 International Women's Year (IWY) conference represents just one example of Schlafly's showmanship and political acumen.

Schlafly organized a "Pro Family Rally" to counter the IWY conference and ensure maximum media coverage. With the IWY's proceedings televised on the major networks, viewers watched as delegates passed abortion and gay rights planks. Adding to the substance was the sideshow. As the delegates cheered their victories, television cameras zoomed in and captured their buttons and banners: "Mother Nature Is a Lesbian" and "The Pope Has Clitoris Envy."[94] Editors of the *Washington Star* remarked that these scenes legitimized Schlafly's outlandish claims: "Phyllis Schlafly didn't have to make it up. Feminist Leaders put the package together for her."[95]

With the media gobbling up the hullaballoo, Schlafly claimed that she "sealed [the ERA's] . . . doom by deliberately hanging around its neck the albatross of abortion [and] lesbianism."[96] The months following the IWY conference proved her correct as the ERA went down to defeat in Georgia, South Carolina, Alabama, and Florida.

With the seven-year window for passage scheduled to close in 1979, ERA advocates remained three states short. The ERA had always been nationally popular, and Congress granted amendment backers a thirty-nine-month extension to win the necessary state endorsements. Instead of easing the path to passage, however, the reprieve allowed time for the Tennessee, Idaho, Nebraska, Kentucky, and South Dakota legislatures to annul their earlier ratifications. By 1983, when the congressional extension expired, activists had failed to earn even one of the needed three additional state ratifications.[97]

Reagan's "Women Issues"

Though the ERA fight ended with a thud, Reagan breathed life into the issue.[98] Indeed, the 1982 midterm elections revealed the electoral consequences of Reagan's "women issues." In that year, women preferred Democrats to GOP candidates by seventeen points, fifty-seven to forty, a breach handing Democrats the governor's mansions in Texas, Michigan, and New York along with significant gains in Congress.[99] One year later, polls showed a startling 24 percent gap between men and women as to whether Reagan "deserved a second term."[100] Warning that the GOP risked becoming "the party of men," in the spring of 1983 the White House political director, Ed Rollins, rang the alarm.[101]

Rollins's warning came none too soon. Weeks prior, Muriel Siebert had offered a similar admonition. A leader in New York's GOP and a Wall Street icon, Siebert accused Reagan of "alienating women more intentionally and effectively today than at any time since we won the right to vote."[102] Disregarding the president's high-profile female appointees, she claimed that female Republicans "have as much to do with the leadership of the party as a mannequin has to do with the management of Bloomingdales."[103] While Siebert's broadsides produced ripples, when the project director for the attorney general's Gender Discrimination Agency echoed these sentiments, a media tsunami lashed the White House.

Reagan's alternative to the ERA, the Interagency Task Force on Women's Legal Equity, was charged with correcting discriminatory federal and state law and quieting the Gipper's women problem. Launched with much fanfare, the project blew up in the administration's face when a director for a task force review group, Barbara Honneger, publicly pronounced the entire enterprise a "sham."[104] Publishing a scathing critique in the *Washington Post,* Honneger alleged that with regard to gender discrimination: "Frankly, my dear, I don't think Ronald Reagan gives a damn."[105]

Adding fuel to the political fire was the administration's ham-handed response to Honneger's claims. Contending that the project director position never existed and that her venom stemmed from an obsession with "titles" and job security, the Justice Department simply dismissed the allegations. Meanwhile, the White House spokesman, Larry Speakes, ripped the *Washington Post* for publishing a piece from such "a low-level Munchkin" and joked that he had last seen Honneger wearing an "Easter Bunny [costume] at the White House Egg Roll."[106] Dripping with chauvinist contempt, the administration risked making Reagan's gender gap even wider.

In a sense, Honneger was more correct than she probably realized. While the administration remained greatly concerned about the politics of the gender gap, officials faced an impenetrable dilemma. Reagan slashed social welfare spending and raised defense expenditures, which, in turn, exacerbated the gender gap. In an unusual moment of clarity, the president's special assistant, Michael Uhlmann, admitted as much: "The greater part of the gender gap is caused by reactions which are a direct consequence of policies which lie at the heart of the President's agenda."[107]

Even Republican women *supportive* of Reagan privately agreed with Honneger and Siebert. In 1982, when the administration reached out to television and movie stars—Debbie Boone, Shirley Temple, and Ginger Rogers—and assorted conservative women to tout Reagan's record on gender issues, *all* of them complained that the "administration has done very little (compared to previous ones) to serve women."[108] Realizing that women were key, the White House, under Ed Rollins's direction, worked to repair the damage.[109] Months before Honneger's public tantrum, Reagan made women's issues a theme in his 1983 State of the Union address and had appointed Margaret Heckler and Elizabeth Dole to serve in his cabinet.[110]

An experienced White House special assistant and the wife of Senator Bob Dole, Elizabeth Dole seemed a natural choice for Transportation secretary. It was Heckler's selection that revealed the administration's genuine concern.[111] The Massachusetts Republican, an ERA supporter and former cochair of the Congressional Women's Caucus, brought an authentic feminist voice into the White House.[112] Armed with a clear understanding of the gender gap, and sufficiently motivated to respond, the administration nevertheless consistently fell short.

Try as the administration might, Rollins's changes remained cosmetic in nature. At root, most high-level White House staffers considered the gender gap a result of communication problems, not substantive issues. Making matters worse was the president. Inhabiting a cultural world far removed from modern women's concerns, Reagan struggled to connect with women. The president's August 1983 appearance before the International Federation of Business and Professional Women reveals this cultural breach. Usually expert at winning an audience, the Great Communicator's quip, "I happen to be one who believes if it wasn't for women, us men would still be walking around in skin suits, carrying clubs," fell flat.[113] Prompting hisses and boos, and called "degrading" by the organization's president, Reagan's attempt at flattery came off as demeaning.[114]

Though Rollins might ameliorate the damage and even push Reagan to embrace certain pieces of legislation, the president's hidebound conservatism and old-fashioned norms created political opportunities for Democrats. Sensing this, Boggs convinced the speaker to give the ERA the honorary legislative pole position, "House Joint Resolution 1," for 1984.[115] While the amendment had no chance of earning ratification, the ERA remained popular in national polls and was especially so among women. Looking to make the GOP pay a political price for the White House's unpopular stance, Democrats used it as an opening salvo in the 1984 campaign.

In this instance, Boggs's instincts served her well. Making Reagan the face of the amendment's opposition, rather than a few stubborn state legislatures, would surely help Democrats woo educated women from "wine-and-cheese" districts.[116] To win downscale, single, and working-class women, however, Mondale needed another tactic. In 1984 and beyond, economic issues were the sine qua non of the gender gap. With only 1 percent of women earning $25,000 or more and a majority of all workingwomen making less than $10,000, in 1984 economic concerns were by definition women's issues.[117] Moreover, core economic matters offered Democrats an occasion to expose the sharper edges of Reagan's conservatism and disrupt his shared-values theme.

Education Equity: Title IX

With the numbers of career women and households headed by single women spiraling, by 1983 women's access to higher education emerged as a top-shelf issue. Swimming against the tide was Ronald Reagan. Imbued with basic conservative principles to restrain government, he instructed his secretary of education, Terrell Bell, and the Justice Department to battle Title IX of the 1972 Education Amendments.[118] Title XV of the 1972 Education Amendments amended Title IX of the 1964 Civil Rights Act by banning gender discrimination in "any [educational] program or activity receiving Federal financial assistance."[119]

In the years following Title IX's enactment, the Nixon, Ford, and Carter administrations interpreted "program or activity" broadly. As far as these administrations were concerned, a university benefiting from federal funds of any sort placed the entire institution under federal civil rights laws. Under this interpretation, Title IX offered broad and expansive protections for women at nearly every American university.

The act, however, received most of its public accolades for blazing trails in the realm of sports. Before 1972, colleges offered no athletic scholarships to women and spent almost nothing on women's athletics. By 1984, 10,000 women had earned athletic scholarships, which helped underwrite the 160,000 female athletes participating in collegiate sports.[120]

The expansion of opportunity sparked a veritable revolution in women's sports. A decade after Title IX, 35 percent of high school athletes were women, up from a paltry 7 percent in 1972.[121] Moreover, the legislation spurred the Amateur Sports Act of 1978, which mandated equality for women's events in the Olympics.[122] As one of the most high-profile and popular legislative accomplishments of the women's movement, Title IX enjoyed broad support across the political spectrum.

Believing that student grants and loans scarcely established a sufficient basis for federal jurisdiction over entire colleges, conservatives battled Title IX's "institution-wide coverage." Their plaintiff, Grove City College, offered a nice, tidy morality tale: a small liberal arts institution, David, versus the Department of Education, Goliath. Coeducational from its founding, the institution's lone Title IX violation was its refusal to sign the standard "assurance of compliance" form.[123] Refusing direct government aid in any form, Grove City did enroll a small number of students who paid tuition via federal grants. Claiming that Title IX applied only to those programs directly receiving federal funds—in this case the financial aid office—the college found an ally in Reagan and, eventually, the Supreme Court.[124]

The Supreme Court's March 1984 *Grove City v. Bell* decision marked the administration's first civil rights victory. Technically ruling against Grove City, the Supreme Court upheld Title IX but called for more legislative clarity regarding "institution-wide coverage." Until the Congress revised Title IX, the court claimed that it applied only to those departments directly receiving federal funds.[125] Since no federal monies went directly to athletic departments, Title IX, in the popular understanding of the legislation, was void. Sensible on paper, and reasonable in theory, the ruling greatly curtailed federal oversight and lawsuits, the threat of which had moved universities to accommodate a vulnerable and not particularly litigious population: female college students.[126]

While the administration claimed that the *Grove City* decision merely enabled a "private citizen to order his or her life," high-profile examples of obtuse sexism simply overwhelmed this philosophical justification.[127] For example, the week following the court's decision, the Department of Education issued its report on the University of Maryland's Title IX violations, which ranged from the expected (inferior women's athletic facilities) to the controversial (discrimination charges against the men's basketball coach). However, because of the Court's ruling, the infractions had become meaningless.

In this way, the case of a student manager being denied a promotion evolved into national news. According to the female student, the University of Maryland's coach, Charles (Lefty) Driesell, denied her promotion and a scholarship "because she was a woman."[128] Driesell hardly possessed a sterling record on gender issues. Simultaneous to the student manager's charges, he was fighting to reinstate a star basketball player accused of sexual assault. Ignoring protocol and good taste, he phoned the female victim on three separate occasions.[129] With his star suspended for the team's final game of the season, the coach implored: "How could you do that to me? Don't you know what tomorrow is?"[130] Once his entreaties escalated into threats and attempts to discredit the victim's reputation, the university's women's center intervened. Asked to explain his actions, Driesell deadpanned: "I don't care about the Women's Center, I'm the Men's Center."[131]

As the Democratic primary season heated up, Lefty Driesell and the now toothless Title IX beckoned as campaign issues.[132] Far from a tragedy, for Democrats this was political manna from heaven. Given an ideal issue through which to exploit the gender gap, Boggs and her congressional allies immediately launched legislative proposals to clarify Title IX language and reinstate institution-wide coverage. Armed with a 414–8 vote on a resolution condemning the *Grove City* decision, House leaders had every confidence they could pass a bill, elicit a veto, and bludgeon Republicans with the issue.

In late June, the House passed its legislative remedy, the 1984 Civil Rights Act.[133] Approved by a 375–32 supermajority, the legislation reinstated "institution-wide coverage" and extended antidiscrimination protections to include the aged and the handicapped.[134] Cosponsored by GOP Senate leaders Howard Baker, Ted Stevens, and Bob Dole, and backed by a bipartisan grouping of Republican women and congressional liberals, the bill seemed destined for quick passage.

With the politics pushing one way and conservative principles pulling another, early on the administration sent mixed signals. In March, the assistant attorney general for civil rights, William Bradford Reynolds, claimed: "I don't have any personal problem with Congress changing the law if it wants to."[135] By June, Reynolds and the administration changed their tune and readied themselves for a costly political fight.

Leading the charge was the special assistant to the attorney general, Charles Fried. Annoyed at the bill's extension of Title IX protections to the handicapped and aged, Fried warned that the legislation betrayed an "excessive and undiscriminating zeal to spread the federal anti-discriminatory net as widely as possible."[136] Fearing for the GOP Senate majority and sincerely committed to reversing the Court's decision was Bob Dole. To his mind, the bill merely restored Title IX to its pre–*Grove City* status. Meanwhile, Republican moderates begged the White House: "We must not allow protection against discrimination to be a Democratic [campaign] issue."[137] Reagan, unsurprisingly, held firm.

With sixty-two cosponsors and an estimated seventy votes in the Senate, the bill was expected to pass, and Reagan's veto, and a high-profile override vote, loomed.[138] The vote occurring just in time for the fall political homestretch, its backers employed every publicity stunt to bring these hopes to reality. In September, senators invited female gold medalists from the 1984 Los Angeles Olympics to trumpet Title IX's importance. Standing with Mary Lou Retton, the four-foot, nine-inch gymnast–cum–folk hero, advocates begged for action.[139] With America's sweetheart pushing from the outside, it was up to Senator Orrin Hatch to quietly battle in the legislative trenches. With almost no public support, Hatch did possess two allies: a fast-approaching election and a looming government shutdown.

As September moved toward the October recess and campaign season, Congress had yet to pass a budget. A temporary stopgap resolution kept the federal government open while leaders crafted a comprehensive spending package, onto which Democrats hoped to attach their bill. Hatch, however, had other plans. Threatening to attach thirteen hundred amendments to the bill, grinding the Senate to a halt, and shutting the federal government down, the senator stopped the 1984 Civil Rights Act cold.[140] And, though Barry Goldwater believed that "the Senate . . . look[ed] like a bunch of jackasses," the overwhelmingly popular legislation failed, Congress adjourned, and Reagan sailed to victory.[141]

Jackasses or no, Democrats missed an opportunity. Obscured by abortion, and overwhelmed by a superior candidate, Mondale-Ferraro failed to use the 1984 Civil Rights Act to exploit the gender gap. Better equipped to make political hay out of Title IX was Boggs. Breaking with tradition, she had even actively campaigned for the vice presidency. With a comprehensive plan outlining media, fund-raising, and administrative strategies, the congresswoman used her southern charm, as usual, to camouflage her ambitions.[142] In early 1984, she promised to endorse the Democratic presidential candidate "smart enough to pick me as vice president."[143]

Combining raw ambition with political smarts, Boggs understood that she offered Democrats something beyond the vogue of a woman's candidacy. Indeed, the 1984 election revealed that most liberals misunderstood both the gender gap and the travails that high-profile female candidates faced. Despite Ferraro's missteps and Mondale's considerable weaknesses, Lou Harris and George Gallup correctly identified the gender gap.[144] However, Ferraro contributed less than one percentage point to Mondale's overall tally. Most observers were confused by the seeming contradiction; Raymond Strother was not one of them.

A pioneer in the political consulting field, Strother ran Bill Clinton's Arkansas campaigns, Al Gore's Senate contests, and Martha Layne Collins's and Evelyn Gandy's gubernatorial races in Kentucky and Mississippi.[145] By 1984, thousands of hours of focus groups had taught him that "generations of sexism and prejudice" made winning top-of-the-ticket races very difficult for women.[146] With older women doubting a woman's executive abilities and blue-collar men peppering their observations with gender stereotypes, the focus groups converted the self-described redneck into a feminist.

Convinced that women needed "the best research, the best media, the best polling, the best strategy, and the most hours and the toughest skin" to simply remain competitive, Strother warned Mondale against a female running mate.[147] Nevertheless, a woman vice president represented, in the words of Louisiana governor Edwin Edwards, the Democrats' "last, best hope."[148] Echoing Strother and Edwards was the dean of presidential political journalism, Theodore White, who joked that only Florence Nightingale or Joan of Arc could save Mondale. Ironically, Democrats had the political equivalent in Lindy Boggs.[149]

Accepting the rank inequities and obstacles confronting her, Boggs understood how to exercise power without rankling tender male egos or upsetting tradition-minded women. Still paying homage to Hale, whom she called "my [political] teacher," she sprinkled her speeches with, "Hale used to say . . . Hale always thought." In this way, Boggs simply came across as "less threatening" than other female candidates.[150] Equipped with a national image as a lady, and moving into politics in the most socially acceptable manner of any female candidate, Boggs as a vice presidential candidate broke the fewest gender norms and appealed to the widest possible variety of voters.[151]

As a result, almost all Democratic presidential contenders consistently named Boggs to their short list of potential nominees. Going one step further, Michigan lieutenant governor and "mother" of the ERA, Martha Griffiths, speculated that Ohio senator John Glenn had "already struck a deal" with Boggs for the number two slot.[152]

While many observers claimed that Boggs's prolife stance rendered her unacceptable to feminists, this was just not the case.[153] From the National Women's Political Caucus and the Women's Equity Action League to Ellie Smeal, feminists generally made their peace with Boggs's abortion record. Some, perhaps, even recognized the substantial difference between antiabortion conservatives and prolife liberals.[154] A staunch foe of *Roe v. Wade,* in the tradition of Bernardin's seamless garment of life, Boggs sought a "total environment—cultural, economic, social, and physical—in which a woman would not feel compelled to seek so drastic a solution."[155] In contrast, New Right antiabortion rhetoric and thought merely banned the procedure without any concomitant obligations to the newborn.

Reflecting her gentle and consensus style, Boggs generally balked at prolife constitutional amendments and held "no grief with anyone who does anything legally permissible and morally acceptable to herself." She was, nevertheless, one of only five members of Congress to speak at the 1983 March for Life, an event marking the tenth anniversary of *Roe*.[156] Ironically, those most zealous to protect the right to individual conscience also refused to grant to her what Boggs called that "same dignity." Indeed, the day before the 1984 Democratic convention convened, NOW mandated that all future speakers at national meetings "must be supportive of all NOW priority issues."[157] Clearly alluding to abortion, the organization banned the recipient of the New Orleans chapter's "Sweetheart Award" from speaking at upcoming functions.

The Civil Rights Restoration Act

Little wonder that prolife delegates at the Democratic convention complained: "We just feel we have no place in the party."[158] After nominating Boggs for vice president, one leader, Stella Lundquist, shrugged: "We are beginning to think there's been a certain amount of shutout of prolifers and their issues."[159] Abortion not only hounded and dogged the Democrats in 1984; the issue also undermined their efforts to reinstate Title IX. As it had in 1984, a huge bipartisan majority backed what had been renamed the Civil Rights Restoration Act. Stopping its progress was an old foe, Orrin Hatch, and a familiar bugaboo, abortion.

Using a tactic earlier honed by Schlafly, Hatch associated Title IX with something totally unrelated yet controversial, abortion. By attaching the Hyde amendment, a prohibition against federal funding of abortion, to the Civil Rights Restoration Act, Hatch might have created "a howling irrelevancy," but feminists nevertheless took the bait.[160] Thus, from 1985 to 1988, NOW, the Women's Equity Action League, and congressional liberals, in effect, battled their own bill over a symbolic issue.

Prior to *Grove City*, federal regulations technically mandated that religiously affiliated hospitals or universities offer a health-care plan covering abortions. However, the regulations also offered exemptions so that organizations would never be forced to violate their "religious tenets."[161] In 1985, the U.S. Catholic Conference, a supporter of Title IX's reinstatement, asked for slight changes in the Civil Rights Restoration Act's language. In return for its full support, officials requested that waiver rules be liberalized and that abortion be removed from the health-care section of the bill's regulations, to reflect the church's belief that the procedure "is [not] like everything else."[162]

With women's groups declaring their opposition to the U.S. Catholic Conference request, the Civil Rights Restoration Act remained stalled in Congress for three more years. Meanwhile, women's legal remedies against workplace and educational discrimination remained weak.[163] Without the threat of federal investigations, universities refused to settle suits and forced its young claimants to wait years for redress. Stuck in this legal limbo since 1980 was the former Temple University student Rollin Hafer. The lead claimant in a class-action lawsuit against her alma mater, Hafer alleged that Temple University had engaged in system-wide discrimination against its female athletes.[164]

Outraged that the football team ate "steak and shrimp" at specially catered after-hours dinners while women athletes were locked out of cafeterias if their practice ran late, Hafer and her teammates filed suit.[165] Originally falling under the jurisdiction of Title IX, Hafer's suit was limited in scope to scholarship allocations. Echoing the thoughts of many, Hafer said of this: "I felt stabbed in the back. . . . I thought Title IX was the answer to sex discrimination."[166] With hundreds of like suits either dismissed or waiting for their day in court, the congressional debates over nonbinding abortion language seemed increasingly frivolous.

In early 1988, Republican senator John Danforth broke the impasse with a compromise amendment. Reaffirming accepted and settled federal policy, the amendment allowed religiously affiliated hospitals to refuse abortion services and religious institutions to offer health plans without abortion coverage.[167] Resenting the antiabortion language in a bill designed to buttress women's rights, feminists pushed against the deal, but to no avail. Passed 315–98 in the House and 75–14 in the Senate, the Civil Rights Restoration Act went to the White House, where Reagan vetoed it.

Slightly revising his administration's objections to the 1984 Civil Rights Act, the president called the bill a "threat to religious liberty."[168] Joining him was the Moral Majority's Jerry Falwell. Adept at scare tactics, Falwell called the legislation the "Sodom and Gomorrah" bill. Not so skillful with the truth, he warned that the bill gave Washington the power to run churches and force them to hire "a practicing active homosexual drug addict with AIDS to be a teacher or youth pastor."[169] Though the demagoguery generated angry phone calls from Falwell's legions, the U.S. Catholic Conference and other mainline religious organizations remained staunchly in favor of the Civil Rights Restoration Act. Given ample political cover, Congress overrode the president's veto by significant margins.[170]

During the 1980s, the politics of abortion most definitively hurt Democrats in national politics. From Ferraro's imbroglio with the Catholic bishops to the ludicrous struggle over the Civil Rights Restoration Act, the abortion issue constantly undid carefully constructed coalitions. Though liberals might have agreed with Congresswoman Mary Rose Oakar's solemn wish that "the abortion issue would just go away," even the prolife Democratic congresswoman understood: "But it never will."[171]

As a general rule, pollsters recognize that prolifers rank abortion as a much more relevant issue than do prochoice voters. As a result, the subject definitively shapes their voting and partisan behavior. With this in mind, throughout the 1980s and 1990s, prolife Democrats were significantly more likely to switch or merely cross party lines than were prochoice Republicans. Adding to this reality, most considered *Roe v. Wade* relatively secure and settled law, meaning that proabortion Republicans could more safely ignore the issue and vote their party line.[172]

The 1992 presidential election proves the salience of abortion and its disproportionate impact on Democrats. Though the Clinton-Gore campaign is rightly remembered for its "it's the economy, stupid" mantra, abortion played a significant and highly suggestive role in the Democrats' victory. In that election, only one-fourth of GOP and Democratic voters were even aware of their candidates' abortion position. Disproportionately white, affluent, and educated, these voters were a distinct yet highly informed minority. However, among these voters, the issue played a stronger role in determining a voter's choice than did the economy.[173]

Unlike 1984, in 1992 the abortion issue helped the Democratic ticket. This time, educated and affluent voters, who were overwhelmingly prochoice, supported Clinton-Gore or Ross Perot. Significantly, Democrats gained further support from prolife Democrats who were simply unaware of their nominee's position on abortion. Indeed, Clinton-Gore scored its highest support, 88 percent, with Democrats favoring a total ban on the procedure.[174] Thus, as 1992 suggests, Democrats performed best in an environment in which only the most informed voters were aware of their abortion position.

In stark contrast, Ferraro's stance on abortion became a central campaign issue in the 1984 presidential race. Clearly alienating the very white ethnic Catholics she was nominated to woo, the congresswoman, and the ticket, could never effectively exploit the other intended bloc: women. While Ellie Smeal's women's rights organization believed that the gender gap emanated from supposed women's issues—abortion and the ERA—polls definitively revealed that the gender gap resulted from defense and social welfare. Thus, in fighting over abortion, Democrats not only alienated white ethnics; they also stopped their candidates from discussing the very issues that mattered to women voters.

With the economy in recovery and his own party divided, and opposing a talented and polished incumbent, Walter Mondale had very little, if any, margin for error. In retrospect, 1984 marked the final temporal burial place for FDR's coalition. Barring some unforeseen catastrophe, Mondale's real hope lay not so much in defeating Reagan as in laying a foundation for a new electoral coalition. In that sense, the vice president's failure was doubly so. Ferraro was a disastrous choice because it revealed how much Democratic elites fundamentally misunderstood the gender gap and white ethnics—both of whom were, and remain, crucial to the Democrats' national strategy.

11

"There Is Nothing for Nothing Any Longer"

Dave McCurdy's Quest for National Service

Jesse Jackson yearned for relevance. Fresh from earning 6.9 million primary votes and electrifying the party faithful at the 1988 nominating convention, he nevertheless felt his political influence ebb. Denied the vice presidency, and then ignored by Michael Dukakis, he might have claimed that the "full scope of [his] leadership has yet to blossom and flourish," but he sensed otherwise.[1] Dave McCurdy similarly burned with ambition. Unlike his rival, however, the Oklahoma congressman had political momentum and an organization, the Democratic Leadership Council (DLC).[2]

Founded in 1985 and composed largely of southern and midwestern officeholders, the DLC originated from the Reagan Revolution's ashes. Following the 1980 election, Congressman Gillis Long, Al From, and Will Marshall first organized the House Democratic Caucus into what eventually became the DLC. At one time, the caucus had chosen presidential nominees and enforced strict party discipline. By 1981, however, it hosted perfunctory and poorly attended meetings. Long as caucus leader and From as its executive director transformed the organization and with it American liberalism.

A distant relation of the legendary Kingfish, Huey Long, Gillis Long survived the Reagan Revolution and remained popular with his rural Louisiana, socially conservative, yet decidedly Democratic constituents.[3] With the caucus's House Committee on Party Effectiveness (CPE) as a political test tube, Long searched for a liberalism based on ideas rather than interest groups.[4] In pursuit of these ideas, he hosted a weekly political-intellectual kibitz in his seventh-floor office.[5] It was core CPE affiliates like McCurdy who convened each Thursday in Long's suite to plan and strategize. Eschewing "blood oaths" to party orthodoxy, House moderates studied, learned,

Josh McCurdy, Dave McCurdy, Pam McCurdy, and Cydney McCurdy sitting together on the floor of a living room, playing video games (courtesy Carl Albert Congressional Research and Studies Center)

and offered programs so that other Democrats would understand the "nitty-gritty intricacies" of particular legislation and issues.[6]

While Long nurtured young centrists and the CPE developed policy papers, these were ancillary to his central task: modernizing liberalism. Generations prior to and through the New Deal, FDR had made Democrats dominant by turning formerly unorganized voters into interest groups: African Americans, white southerners, farmers, union members, and senior citizens. While even Alexis de Tocqueville witnessed citizen associations demand government munificence, before Roosevelt only the GOP and big business had practiced this form of client-patron governance. Doling out programs and government largesse to diverse constituencies, FDR founded his electoral coalition on a novel creation: interest group *liberalism*.[7] Dominating American politics for generations, the coalition among these disparate factions had been undone by the cultural and political wars of the 1960s.

As Long saw it, FDR's creation had not only unraveled; it had also failed to adapt to an increasingly globalized and technological world. Seeking a liberalism with the "compassion to care and the toughness to govern," he attempted to move beyond the Great Depression and the Great Society's interest group liberalism.[8] In search of that vision, in 1982 the CPE published *Rebuilding the Road to Opportunity: A Democratic Direction for the 1980s*. A summation of economic policy designed to stymie inflation and spur growth, the document represented the Democrats' first coherent and unified response to Reaganomics.[9] It was intended to serve as a "general direction" for a party divided, according to one Democrat, into "five factions," but as Long cautioned: "Nobody is bound by it. It is not the bible, it is not a platform, but it is not pabulum."[10] It was, however, a start.

Dave McCurdy

A start is all Dave McCurdy required. Embodying the Democratic Party's frontier roots, the great-great-grandson of Sooner homesteaders made the most of every opportunity. The son of a singer–rancher–crop duster–turned–electrician loaded flour sacks into boxcars, served in the air force ROTC, and painted signs to put himself through college.[11] Relentless at politics and love, in 1971, after nine proposals, McCurdy finally convinced his college sweetheart to marry him. While he studied law, Pam (Plumb) McCurdy attended medical school. Four years later, both earned advanced degrees from the University of Oklahoma.[12]

"Bored stiff" by the state attorney general's office and private practice, McCurdy leapt into elective politics.[13] Revealing a penchant for boldness bordering on audacity, the twenty-nine-year-old McCurdy challenged a sixteen-term Democratic incumbent, Tom Steed. Quitting his job in 1979, he spent the next fourteen months campaigning.[14] Once Steed retired, the fifth-generation Oklahoman vied with six other candidates for the party's nomination. Though his family was firmly rooted in Oklahoma's Fourth Congressional District, the sprawling eight-thousand-square-mile area hardly offered any candidate a home court advantage.[15]

Youthful and hardworking, McCurdy eventually took the nomination. In normal political times, the Democratic nominee would have easily captured the south-central Oklahoma district. Stretching south from suburban Oklahoma City to the Texas border, the sprawling and historically Democratic Fourth District encompassed mostly small towns, rural communities, and the scattered cities of Norman, Lawton, and Ardmore.[16] Though Oklahoma Democrats retained a decided registration advantage, the state and the region were in the throes of realignment. Running against a strong GOP headwind, McCurdy also faced a formidable challenger, Howard Rutledge.[17]

Rutledge was a former Vietnam prisoner of war and career naval officer, and his service played well in a district with three major military installations.[18] Entering the race very late and for a seat that had last gone Republican during Woodrow Wilson's administration, he was very nearly carried to victory by Reagan. Indeed, the Gipper's 59 percent Fourth District vote very nearly negated his Democratic opponent's twelve-month head start and four-to-one party registration advantage. Squeaking to victory, McCurdy won by 2,906 votes—out of nearly 150,000 cast.[19]

Representing a district and a state that went overwhelmingly for Reagan prompted McCurdy to accept Tom Steed's advice: "The campaign isn't over."[20] During his first term, he nabbed a coveted seat on the Armed Services Committee and returned home from Washington forty-nine times.[21] Moreover, within weeks of taking office, he stopped the ACLU from closing a district cultural treasure: "The Holy City of the Wichitas" Passion play. The ACLU had filed suit because the play was located on a sixty-thousand-acre federal preserve. Filing a bill to change the designation of the ninety-acre Holy City site from federal land to private property, McCurdy, with elegant simplicity, defused the controversy.[22]

The episode helps reveal that McCurdy was no Boll Weevil. Composed of southern and border state Democrats who voted in lockstep with Reagan, the Boll Weevils signaled conservative realignment.[23] With the president on many defense issues, and against "severe cuts [in] . . . school lunches and school impact aid," McCurdy rejected easy labeling. Claiming, "I don't see myself as a conservative," he called Phil Gramm, Richard Shelby, and other

Boll Weevils mere "extensions of the Republican Party."[24] Bucking liberal and Boll Weevil orthodoxy alike, he explained: "Some of us didn't come here to be taken for granted."[25]

McCurdy's centrist liberalism was much more than the triangulation or the vapid pragmatism that some critics claimed. Indeed, despite his district's three military installations, the freshman refused to shill for the Pentagon or blindly back Reagan. Pushing the issue of Defense Department waste, McCurdy was named chair of a special military procurement panel. Using that position to investigate bureaucratic inefficiencies, he coauthored the 1982 Nunn-McCurdy Amendment, which forced the Pentagon to report all significant cost overruns.[26] Hardly stopping at faceless bureaucracies, Mc-Curdy claimed that it was the president's defense policies and lack of "clear goal[s]" that led to senseless and wasteful weapons systems.[27]

Rather than bolt for the GOP, House moderates, led by Gillis Long and the CPE, saw 1984 as an opportunity to, as McCurdy put it, "inject reality into the party."[28] To influence the 1984 election, in July 1983 they founded the National House Democratic Caucus (NHDC).[29] Armed with *Renewing America's Promise,* a booklet of policy statements and new ideas, the NHDC took its plans directly to local Democrats. Titling these conferences "Choices for Change: Democratic Directions for America's Future," Long openly, yet respectfully, challenged party elites.[30] With the *Blueprint* sprinkled with calls to reduce the "Reagan debt" and even "review . . . entitlement systems," Long, McCurdy, and other centrists sought federal activism within defined spheres, a noticeable departure from reigning liberal convention.

In conjunction with the NHDC's *Blueprint,* centrists hoped that the Hunt Commission would significantly reform the Democrats' presidential nominating system. Indeed, since the 1970 McGovern-Fraser party reforms, the activist fringe had controlled the Democrats' presidential nominating process. To counter this, the Hunt Commission transformed congressmen, big city mayors, and governors into "superdelegates."[31] These superdelegates having been given significant power to influence the nominating and platform-writing process, centrists believed that 1984 signaled a new beginning.

Though Walter Mondale gave Long, From, and the CPE an audience, he nonetheless believed that a scaled-down interest group appeal could bring victory. More damning to Mondale's quest was his refusal to break with the AFL-CIO on even *one* issue.[32] Declining to buck interest group orthodoxy one iota created an opening for Senator Gary Hart. An unlikely vessel for moderates' hopes, George McGovern's former campaign manager nevertheless emerged as the candidate with "fresh, new ideas."[33] Though the vice president eventually captured the nomination, Hart and Jesse Jackson won enough delegates to prolong the campaign. The ensuing intraparty civil war, which masqueraded as a political campaign, revealed that the Democrats remained, in the words of the journalist Elizabeth Drew, little "more than a loose and uneasy collection of its interest groups."[34]

Rather than allay these critiques, the 1984 Democratic convention merely reinforced the stereotype. With Hart still hoping for Gillis Long to lead a superdelegate rebellion and Jackson clamoring "cultural racism," the convention teetered on the edge of anarchy.[35] Adding to this was Mondale's vice presidential selection process. Allowing it to devolve into the most base form of interest group appeasement, Mondale interviewed representatives from every party faction—African Americans, women, Hispanics, and southerners. One *Newsweek* cartoon captured popular sentiment regarding the selection process: "Did you get a shot of me with the woman? Good! How about the black guy? Great! Okay, send in the Indian and after that the midget."[36]

Ironically, Tip O'Neill, Gillis Long, and McCurdy held the eventual vice presidential nominee, Geraldine Ferraro, in very high esteem. Her selection was nevertheless widely viewed as Mondale pandering to constituency groups. Indeed, with the National Organization for Women threatening a divisive floor fight unless he chose a female running mate, the vice president had few good options. Choosing Ferraro because she "represent[ed] what this country is all about," Mondale realized that many still saw him as someone "who was [not] strong enough to make history but a man who gave in."[37] Though a postconvention *Newsweek*-Gallup poll showed Mondale-Ferraro leading Reagan by two points, one party insider presciently claimed: "I'll bet seventy-five percent of the delegates here don't think we have a prayer in November."[38]

With Long leading the fight against yet another set of presidential nomination rule changes, this time Jesse Jackson and Gary Hart's Fairness Commission, it was left to Virginia governor Charles Robb to offer an alternative vision for the party.[39] Delivered to a distracted, resistant, and altogether subdued crowd, Robb's warning against "cling[ing] to ghosts of a time now vanished" fell on deaf and bored ears.[40] Because of this milieu, McCurdy avoided the main convention hall altogether. Telling one reporter, "Those people in here don't represent Oklahoma," he cast the lone superdelegate vote against Mondale and for Gary Hart.[41]

McCurdy and Oklahoma's entire Democratic congressional delegation might have rolled to victory in 1984, but Reagan steamrolled Mondale. Capturing nearly 60 percent of the national vote, the president earned almost 70 percent of the Sooner state tally. As the smoked cleared, Oklahoma Democrats, led by Senator David Boren, clamored for the party to recapture the "mainstream."[42] Boren's call came none too soon. With Reagan capturing the white, youth, and independent vote, every index screamed realignment. Psephology aside, one lifelong southern Democrat summed up in words what numbers clearly showed. Explaining Mondale's crushing defeat, he claimed that his friends simply "thought it was un-American" to vote Democrat.[43]

Sensing the coming landslide, Long had convened a meeting of centrist dissidents during the convention. Arizona governor Bruce Babbitt, Virginia governor Charles Robb, Georgia senator Sam Nunn, Florida senator Lawton Chiles, and Missouri congressman Richard Gephardt met upstairs while party activists careened toward yet another electoral disaster.[44] Fearing that "there wasn't going to be a Democratic Party . . . in [his] state," Chiles, along with his southern and midwestern brethren, looked to name the next Democratic National Committee (DNC) chair or found an extra-party organization.[45]

The DLC

Gillis Long's January 1985 death left centrists leaderless. But, once Ted Kennedy's longtime special assistant, Paul Kirk, was named to head the DNC, they knew their next move. In late February, Al From and Long's House protégés defied the DNC by formally establishing the DLC.[46] Their meetings bearing a remarkable resemblance to Gillis Long's original seventh-floor skull sessions, the DLC's forty-three original members, including McCurdy and its first chair, Richard Gephardt, mostly hailed from the CPE and the NHDC. Moreover, the DLC remained true to Long's essential vision, developing a centrist, yet liberal, middle way between the New Politics and the Reagan Revolution.

Derided as a "good dog and pony show" by some, the DLC had two initial goals: showcase centrist Democrats and alter the presidential nominating process.[47] While the DLC worked on the outside, McCurdy expanded on Long's inside game. Looking to shape Democratic foreign policy, he led a very public and risky gambit to replace the doddering eighty-year-old chair of the House Armed Services Committee, Melvin Price. In deposing a chairman for only the fifth time in sixty years, McCurdy launched a generational and ideological assault on the House leadership.[48] Indeed, antagonizing House Democratic leaders had already become a McCurdy habit. Described by colleagues as a "quiet revolutionary," a "radical moderate," and someone who roamed the House with "a grenade in one hand and a pen in the other," the Oklahoman aggressively pushed his centrist agenda.[49]

Rather than follow McCurdy's confrontation of party orthodoxy, the "DLC Cavalry" toured the Sun Belt. In producing the inevitable "Democrats steer new course" headlines, strategists hoped to build enough momentum to influence the presidential nominating process.[50] While Arizona governor Bruce Babbitt praised the DLC's "flash and energy," that was exactly the problem.[51] The organization's big tent efforts were, by design, sparkle with little substance. Hoping to attract a broad spectrum of lawmakers, the organization emphasized *projecting* a moderate image rather than building substantive centrist policy. From truly conservative Democrats and moderates to those merely looking for political camouflage, the DLC mirrored the national party's diversity and convention: nearly half the organization's House members scored at least a 75 on the Americans for Democratic Action's rating. In this way, the DLC might have been relevant, but it also failed to leave a centrist imprint on the party.[52]

Believing that they could reform the party purely from above, From and Marshall jiggered the 1988 presidential primary calendar. In turning the second Tuesday of March into a southern primary, the so-called Super Tuesday, they hoped to propel one of their own to the White House.[53] Focusing organizational energy on this goal, the DLC hosted three presidential debates and launched the Super Tuesday Education Project. In 1988, the DLC cofounder and Tennessee senator Al Gore followed the organizational road map. Ignoring Iowa and New Hampshire in favor of Super Tuesday, Gore invested all his electoral hopes in Texas, Florida, Tennessee, Louisiana, Oklahoma, Mississippi, Kentucky, Alabama, and Georgia voters. Ironically, it was the DLC's archnemesis, Jesse Jackson, who benefited; while the crowded field divvied up the white vote, Jackson took 96 percent of the black tally and captured three states and a significant delegate count.[54]

Even more telling was Richard Gephardt's campaign. The DLC cofounder and former chair abandoned the organization's centrist positions from the very start. Basing his shifting positions on trade, abortion, and defense on a simple "I have to win in Iowa" calculus, Gephardt appealed to an old FDR base: organized labor.[55] Thus, despite the DLC's emphasis on free trade, he ran as a protectionist. Reeking of "yellow fever," the St. Louis congressman claimed: "[Koreans] invade our market with Hyundais sold cheap because we are paying dearly for the tanks defending their borders." By whacking Japan, Taiwan, and South Korea while ignoring Europe, Gephardt struck an emotional, decidedly dated, and slightly bigoted chord.[56]

In failing on terms, strategy, and candidates set by itself, the DLC could hardly have seen a more disastrous year than 1988. Ironically, the only organization faring worse was the national party.[57] Following a unified convention, Massachusetts governor Michael Dukakis led Vice President George H. W. Bush in some polls by as much as seventeen points. With both candidates running to the electorate's middle, Bush used social issues—flag burning and the death penalty—to portray Dukakis, or at least his ideas, as something "born in Harvard Yard's boutique."[58] When Sam Nunn suggested that the DLC's national service plan could blunt attacks on the governor's patriotism, Dukakis demurred, ultimately endorsing the program only three days after the election.[59]

Cast as an elitist, distant from Middle American values, the governor saw his one-time lead evaporate into yet another GOP presidential cakewalk: Bush's 53.4 percent and 426 electoral votes versus Dukakis's 45.7 percent and 111 electoral votes. Democrats yet again were left with postelection soul-searching. Despite losing five of the last six presidential contests and four of those five by landslides, party elites proffered the same excuse as they did in 1972: low minority turnout, paltry voter registration drives, and an agenda aimed at middle-class whites had cost Democrats the election.[60] Pointing to one study, activists claimed that, *if* African American voter participation equaled that of whites *and* Dukakis had won 5 percent more of the white southern vote, *then* the Democratic nominee would have won the South (but still lost the election).[61] In the face of such obtuse conjecture and yet another defeat, centrists realized that their task was bigger than they had first anticipated.[62]

With the Super Tuesday and big tent strategies in obvious shambles, the 1988 election had at least produced a definitive direction for Al From. In the three years prior, he had avoided pointed critiques of the party. But, when Jesse Jackson's convention manager and yet another Kennedy protégé, Ron Brown, won the DNC chairmanship, the DLC finally pushed back.[63]

Forgoing "broad-based participation" in favor of developing an alternative governing philosophy, the DLC founded a think tank, the Progressive Policy Institute (PPI).

Led by Will Marshall, PPI was nimble and aggressive from the start. Unlike the Brookings Institution and the American Enterprise Institute, which regularly produced five-hundred-page tomes, Marshall employed the "briefcase test": all policy briefs had to fit into a satchel. Most importantly, PPI was liberated from the constrictions placed on the DLC, which remained an elected officials' organization. Thus, Marshall believed that PPI was inoculated against the Democrats' "allergy to new thinking." Freed from these conventions, Marshall's first policy paper attacked a Democratic shibboleth: raising the minimum wage. Terming it "regressive . . . anachronistic . . . and not terribly relevant to men and women working in today's economy," Marshall took direct aim at liberal orthodoxy.[64]

Using the DLC's March 1989 annual conference as their platform, From and Marshall launched a multipronged offensive against the Democratic establishment. Unlike past gatherings, this meeting was less fund-raiser and wonk-fest than a nationally broadcast intraparty civil war.[65] The meeting was held in Philadelphia, and organizers arranged special travel plans so that scores of national journalists could cover the fireworks. To ensure conflict, they scheduled a keynote and a roundtable sure to spark discord.

Setting the tone was the political theorist Bill Galston.[66] An unlikely bomb thrower, the curly headed academician might have looked professorial, but he was the DLC's bloodless Trotsky. His analysis of the 1988 election, "The Politics of Evasion," took direct aim at the New Politics and was the roundtable's discussion point. According to Galston, "liberal fundamentalists" were to blame for the Democrats' woes. Because they "transform[ed] government programs into the political counterpart of a sectarian movement," Galston equated party elites to ideologists. Blinded by their quasireligious faith in liberal orthodoxy, they hardly noticed (or even cared) that most voters believed that Democrats were soft on defense, indifferent to moral issues, and incompetent in economic affairs.[67]

Forecasting continued electoral routs, realignment, and a conservative takeover of Congress, Galston challenged Democrats to forgo interest group politicking and woo the white middle class. As Galston and the DLC saw it, the issue was simple. Whites constituted 80 percent of the American electorate, of which Democrats won only 40 percent in 1988.[68] Since a white, forty-four-year-old male swing voter spelled the difference between winning and losing, Democrats must change.[69] With cameras rolling, and in full view of the press, a roundtable of party leaders debated Galston's searing indictment. Featuring Robb, Gephardt, Virginia governor Douglass Wilder, and Jesse Jackson, the forum was hardly designed for scholarly discussion and accord.[70]

Jesse Jackson

Most responsible for the combustible atmosphere was Jackson. After brokering an end to a Howard University student revolt and calling for a 500,000-person "Children's March," he had spent early 1989 bobbing and weaving from one controversy to the next.[71] The latest hullaballoo involved a toxic stew of race, politics, and Jackson's own ambitions. When the first black mayor of Chicago, Harold Washington, died in November 1987, the fight to name his successor revived temporarily dormant racial and ideological tensions. While Washington's coalition proffered its successor, Alderman Timothy Evans, the city's Democratic political machine installed its candidate, Eugene Sawyer, to finish the mayor's term. Adding to the injury, in March 1989 Richard J. Daley's son, Richard M. Daley, won the Democratic nomination for mayor over Sawyer.[72]

In using Washington's death to reestablish its power and reverse black political gains, the Chicago political machine drew Jackson into a fight. Smarting from Daley's nomination and his own declining political clout, Jackson turned an already tense situation into a racially polarized event. Leading black leaders in chants of "keep the keys" (to City Hall), he bolted the party. He not only supported Timothy Evans's independent campaign; he also leapt across the rhetorical line. Comparing Daley to the former Ku Klux Klan wizard and Louisiana legislator David Duke, he made even close associates wince.[73]

Leaving Chicago as controversy swirled and Election Day neared, Jackson arrived in Philadelphia to picket with striking airline workers before going to the DLC's roundtable. Engulfed in tumult, and itching to fight, he understood the stakes. Galston's "Politics of Evasion" offered a stark choice for Democrats: the white middle class or Jackson's "Rainbow Coalition."[74] If Democrats embraced Galston, then Jackson's 1992 presidential hopes vanished. Humbly calling himself "just a member of the panel," Jackson was, nevertheless, incredulous. And he rightly revealed his overwhelming significance to the party when he claimed: "I'm a Democrat who registered

more Democrats to vote than any other Democrat in America. I've supported more Democratic officials for election than any other Democrat in America."[75] In the minds of the DLC, that was exactly the problem.

Once the roundtable disbanded, Jackson and Robb engaged in an im-
promptu showdown crystallizing the issues and ideas determining the Democrats' future. While reporters clustered and cameras rolled, Jackson and
Robb went toe-to-toe. Calling the DLC's centrism "ill-defined, indecisive
[and] kind of like warm spit," Jackson, who towered over the much short-
er Robb, challenged Democrats to "determine which side of history we're
on."[76] Uttering maxims—the "minimum wage people have the maximum
vote" or unregistered blacks provided the margin for George Bush's defeat—however, hardly dented reality; Democrats had lost five of six presidential elections, and centrists feared that they were next.[77]

With the party's family squabble made public and New Politics liberals thrown on the defensive, centrists relaunched their effort to construct
"liberalism . . . as a vibrant force in achieving broad national purposes."[78]
To exemplify this effort, Marshall and From made McCurdy's national service program their cornerstone.[79] Undoubtedly pleased by this decision, Mc-
Curdy saw national service as a harbinger of a new political era. To his
mind, the Cold War's demise, the consequent "peace dividend," and economic prosperity meant fewer congressional "zealots," promising a bipartisan and moderate congressional era.[80] Poised to take advantage of this,
McCurdy and the DLC used national service to advance "opportunity liberalism," which addressed issues dear to conventional liberals, mainstream
voters, and disaffected Democrats: urban poverty, crime, and rising college
tuition costs.

National Service

Far from a novel concept, national service had been debated by policymakers and political elites for decades. The issue finds its roots in William
James's iconic antiwar speech "The Moral Equivalent of War," FDR's Civilian Conservation Corps, and an unimplemented Great Society scheme to
end the youth rebellion. It was neoconservative and neoliberal policy intellectuals and journalists, however, who revived the issue. They had more disparate ends for it, however, than to end war, solve economic depression, or
quell the New Left.

Chairing the Coalition for a Democratic Majority's Task Force on Foreign Policy and Defense, McCurdy first came to national service from the neoconservative "military preparedness" perspective. The neocons saw national service as an elixir to the all-volunteer force's (AVF) woes: manpower costs, force readiness, and low-quality and racially unrepresentative recruits.[81] As they saw it, the AVF's recruitment costs siphoned money from weapons system development, sparked skyrocketing manpower expenditures, and produced a weaker military. By the mid-1980s, however, the Montgomery GI Bill and the army's two-year enlistment program had greatly enhanced the AVF's efficacy.[82] Thus, by 1989, few seriously called for mandatory military service. Nevertheless, military service remained a crucial component of McCurdy's legislation.

Like its infamous ideological soul mates, neoliberalism also emerged in the 1970s. Fostered by the *Washington Monthly*'s founding editor, Charles Peters, neoliberals embraced the neoconservative critique of the New Politics. They, however, adhered to "old liberal goals" and remained Democrats. Early and ardent national service advocates, they yearned for a patriotic liberalism eschewing "phony . . . flag waving" and emphasizing national service "where everybody does his part."[83] Keeping the issue alive, neoliberals emerged as an intellectual force during the 1980s.

Stepping into this rich and contradictory stew of national service advocacy, McCurdy and the DLC used the issue to bludgeon opponents, coopt adversaries, and loudly proclaim: "There is nothing for nothing any longer."[84] High on McCurdy's list were entitlement liberals. Rooted in the guaranteed-income movement of the 1970s, they had come to dominate Democratic social welfare policy. Explicitly eschewing liberal individualism's equality of opportunity, they sought instead a social democratic equity in results. In contrast, New Deal–era Democrats, and now McCurdy and the DLC, reembraced opportunity liberalism, which made equal opportunity central to social policy.[85]

By tying student aid to national service, McCurdy promoted a liberal activism espousing America's individualist ethos. National service, however, represented more than sugarcoating progressive policy for a conservative body politic. Service advocates believed that the program could salve the nation's emergent citizenship woes. Indeed, by the late 1980s, academics and opinion leaders of all stripes, from E. J. Dionne and David Broder to William F. Buckley, worried that the baby boomer's rights-based liberalism and me-first conservatism had severed rights from obligations.[86] One commonly cited survey revealed that three times as many young Americans valued "success in job or career" over "making the community . . . a better place" while only 12 percent defined "good citizenship" as "voting or other forms of political involvement."[87] Worried that America's civic glue had come undone, backers believed that national service taught the reciprocal duties and responsibilities that bind democratic societies together.

To wit, in 1989, Congress appropriated $9 billion in Pell Grants and loan subsidies for 3.9 million students in higher education; for Charlie Moskos, who penned the DLC's national service program, Americans had created a GI Bill without the GI. The Northwestern University sociologist hoped that tying service to education benefits could alter a liberalism heretofore too dependent on rights and ignoring duties and mutual obligations.

In league with McCurdy and a hodgepodge of neoliberal and neoconservative academics and journalists were communitarians. A school of political philosophy popular with dissident academics, communitarianism was deeply critical of contemporary liberalism's value-free and rights-based notions.[88] Balancing the common good with individual rights, communitarians believed that rights-based liberalism had as much to do with the "celebration of individual cunning in the single-minded pursuit of wealth and status" as did Ronald Reagan.[89] For Charlie Moskos and other communitarians, connecting responsibility (service) to entitlements (Pell Grants and loan subsidies) promised to "move us beyond the sort of something-for-nothing, every-man-for-himself, me-first philosophy that has been prevalent" during the 1980s.[90]

With the presidential race concluded, McCurdy finally convinced the risk-averse DLC chair, Sam Nunn, to cosponsor the 1989 Citizenship and National Service Act. Armed with a high-profile cosponsor for the DLC's highest legislative priority, Speaker Jim Wright and Majority Leader George Mitchell gave the bill top priority.[91] One part GI Bill and one part JFK, the program offered a civilian and military track in a proposed Citizen Corps.[92] Promising a $10,000 tuition credit for every year served ($12,000 for the military track), the legislation mandated service in exchange for federal financial aid. Exempting single mothers and adults (those over twenty-five), the Citizen Corps replaced a $9 billion grant and loan bureaucracy with a nimble Corporation for National Service. Matching grants would be provided to state and local agencies and nonprofits, and these agencies, not Washington, DC, would administer the program—yet another way in which the DLC broke from liberal orthodoxy.[93]

Rather than highfalutin philosophies, rising college tuition and the nation's "social deficits" made national service jive with voters' concerns. A play on Reagan's soaring budget deficits, *social deficits* referred to the poor and needy hit hardest by the president's domestic cuts. McCurdy believed that national service tutors, hospital orderlies, street cleaners, policemen, and teachers could rectify these gaping social deficits.[94] In conjunction with the social deficits was soaring university tuition, which had risen by 40 percent while median family incomes rose by a meager 6 percent in the same time frame. As a result, low- and middle-income students were pushed out of elite institutions, saddled with student loan debt, or driven from higher education altogether.[95] McCurdy and the DLC positioned national service to address an array of issues. It would be required for students to receive federal aid, offer vocational training for non-college-bound youths, broaden the military's recruitment pool, and address the nation's social deficits.[96]

Hardly the warmed-over Reaganism that critics claimed it to be, McCurdy's legislation offered generous universal benefits while promoting a federal activism consistent with Middle American sensibilities.[97] Moreover, the ensuing national service debate enabled McCurdy and the DLC to battle congressional lions and liberal interest groups and, eventually, change the party. Predictably, Ted Kennedy balked, Senator Claiborne Pell (he of the "Pell" Grants) called the legislation "cruel," while Congressman William Ford accused national service of "hold[ing] the educational aspirations of the poor hostage."[98]

Joining the liberal lions was the Pentagon. Leading the charge was Congressman Sonny Montgomery, who had authored the updated 1984 Montgomery GI Bill. Mincing few words, he dismissed the Citizen Corps's military track out of hand.[99] Conservatives, meanwhile, tarred national service with both sides of the totalitarian brush. Milton Friedman compared the idea to "the Hitler *Jugend* [Youth]," while the *Washington Times* branded it "one of the bureaucracies Mikhail Gorbachev wants to kill."[100] In the face of such organized and powerful bipartisan opposition, the Nunn-McCurdy bill stalled in the House Education Committee.

Realizing that it would take years to pass sweeping legislation, McCurdy and Marshall looked to leverage the national service buzz into a tangible piece of legislation. Luckily, William F. Buckley and President Bush were drawn to the issue. Buckley not only endorsed national service; he also published *Gratitude: Reflections on What We Owe to Our Country* to popularize it. The president, meanwhile, offered a meager bill.[101] Competent and experienced to a fault, Bush and his inner circle, according to one insider, regarded "idealism of any sort [as] a sign of naïveté."[102] Thus, he opposed the McCurdy-Nunn bill's daring. Trumpeting the Youth Engaged in Service to America and Points of Light programs as alternatives to McCurdy's "bribes and penalties," Bush called his initiatives real national service.[103]

Rueful that "at least [Bush] came up with an idea unlike the Duke [Michael Dukakis]," Moskos saw the president's interest as opportunity.[104] With the president and Senators Daniel Patrick Moynihan and Kennedy pushing their service legislation, Marshall urged, and McCurdy accepted, a compromise.[105] A mishmash of nine pet service projects, the National Community Service Act of 1990 included Bush's Thousand Points of Light and the DLC's altered pilot program.[106] Reasoning that earned benefits, as opposed to entitlements, would eventually garner public support, Marshall believed that the compromise bill "b[ought] time to test the program and build a political base."[107]

The DLC's newfound assertiveness and the community service bill's passage seemingly boded well for the DLC's moderate liberalism. The Reagan Revolution and the 1988 presidential campaign, however, brought a new breed of conservatives to the House. Tired of the GOP's seemingly permanent minority status, Sun Belt conservatives adopted new tactics. In stark contrast to stuffy New England and plain midwestern Republicans, a new generation, inspired by Lee Atwater and led by Newt Gingrich, waged guerrilla war.

The architect of George H. W. Bush's bare-knuckle takedown of Michael Dukakis, Atwater turned Richard Nixon's "Southern Strategy" into GOP reality. Realizing that the Solid South would remain so as long as "Republicans . . . talk[ed] about issues," he cast Democrats as the "bad guy" through personal attacks.[108] One outrageous antic typifies his use of innuendo. After planting a false rumor involving a Democrat and electroshock therapy treatment, he told a reporter that he refused to "comment" on someone who used to be "hooked up to jumper cables."[109] Perfecting his dark arts, Atwater regularly turned rumor into reality and erased old boundaries separating hard-boiled politicking from the tacky, tasteless, and downright racist.

As Bush's campaign manager in the 1988 election, Atwater made a dark-skinned violent criminal named Willie Horton synonymous with Michael Dukakis. Indeed, the convicted murderer who raped a woman while on weekend furlough from a Massachusetts prison became a stand-in for all Democrats. Flashing the African American's mug shot along with the words *kidnapping, stabbing,* and *raping* across the television screen, Atwater's "Willie Horton" ad was brutally effective. Leaving nothing to chance, he also sent mailers that veritably shouted: "You, your spouse, your children and your friends can have the opportunity to receive a visit from someone like Willie Horton if Mike Dukakis becomes president."[110] Such a blatant appeal to white racial fears might have angered media elites, but Bush named Atwater Republican National Committee chair, a move that promised Democrats more of the same.

In tandem with Atwater was Newt Gingrich. Born in Pennsylvania, the army brat came of age in the post–civil rights South. Earning a Ph.D. in history from Tulane University in 1971, he taught at West Georgia State University before entering Congress in 1979. Running as a Republican in the solidly Democratic South, he soon learned the same lessons as Atwater: discredit Democrats so voters would feel compelled to "split their ticket."[111] Once in Congress, he honed this logic. Leading a cadre of young House firebrands, he painted Democrats as "morally illegitimate" so that they would soon be "politically illegitimate."[112]

Using the newly launched C-SPAN as a platform, Gingrich made what were perfunctory opening, closing, and special order speeches into spectacle. That these speeches were given to an empty chamber was irrelevant. The estimated 200,000 viewers saw only a close-up, leaving them to believe that the House was in full session.[113] The daily verbal broadsides against Democrats reached a crescendo in spring 1984. In what had become a nightly televised ritual, Gingrich claimed that Democrats "sounded like Communists" and defied the vacant chamber to "come down here and disagree with us."[114] The next day, an angry Tip O'Neill took to the House floor and thundered: "You [Gingrich] deliberately stood in that well before an empty House . . . and challenged their Americanism and it is the lowest thing that I have ever seen in my 32 years in the House."[115] Violating House rules against personal attacks, the speaker's words were stricken from the record, the first time since 1795 that such an event occurred.[116]

Though the amicable Bob Michel maintained his minority leader post, the incident, according to the House historian Ray Smock, marked "the passing of the older order and the honing of this new, confrontational spirit."[117] Increasingly relevant, by 1989, Gingrich was elected House whip and turned his sights on O'Neill's successor, Speaker Jim Wright. Unfortunately for Wright, who privately called his nemesis "a shrill and shameless little demagogue," he fatally underestimated Gingrich.[118] Focusing on the speaker's lucrative book deal, Gingrich convinced the House Ethics Committee to investigate Wright's financial record. Uncovering sixty-nine House rule violations, the probe and ensuing controversy forced the speaker's resignation in June 1989.[119]

While Wright asked that his resignation be "total payment for the anger and hostility we feel toward each other," Gingrich had other ideas. In charge of the political action committee GOPAC, he used the organization to recruit and train Republican candidates in his slash-and-burn mold. Thus, a whole generation of young Republican officeholders came to Washington and scattered state capitols with one strategic target: convince Americans that Democrats were "sick," "radical," and "traitors."[120]

Once Wright was gone, the House whip (and his minions) aimed at the Democratic House majority's soft underbelly: Middle America.[121] Already saddled with a national party often at odds with rural, southern, and midwestern voters, moderately blue districts, Gingrich figured, would turn ruby red in the face of a frontal assault on the party's moral legitimacy. Because the GOP's rhetorical bomb throwers targeted its rank and file, the DLC counterattacked.[122] Launched at its annual 1990 conference, the "New Orleans Declaration" was a self-described "turning point" in the organization's history. In pronouncing the "ideas and passions" of the 1930s and 1960s outdated, the DLC ignored the ghosts of liberalism past. Trumpeting equality of opportunity while downplaying divisive social issues, From and Marshall once again made McCurdy's national service their organization's centerpiece.[123]

Reinforcing the sense of a watershed moment was Jesse Jackson. Unlike the 1989 meeting, Jackson came to New Orleans and gave the DLC a "political bear hug."[124] In his speech, "Delighted to be United," Jackson congratulated his rivals for joining him in the "new mainstream." Claiming the DLC's domestic and defense policies as his own, he declared that the "people" and the DLC "are moving our way."[125] Raising a few eyebrows, and annoying Al From to no end, Jackson was a sideshow to the real attraction: Bill Clinton. As the incoming DLC chair and the organization's unofficial presidential candidate, the Arkansas governor employed a new tactic. Using state DLC chapters as a counterweight to liberal activists, he built a national network of elected officials to buttress his presidential campaign.[126]

With Clinton minding the national scene, McCurdy continued to battle for the House. Fighting the "screamers" who "pound the podium [and] get the clip on the evening news," he founded the Mainstream Forum.[127] Intended to offset Gingrich's C-SPAN antics, the seventy-member Mainstream Forum was more *Andy Griffith Show* than the whip's guerrilla theater.[128] Being "boring on purpose," McCurdy threatened to talk about his kids' softball team to show that Democrats were hardly "Ted Kennedy clones" but were much like the average American voter.[129]

The forum was more than a Gingrich antidote. In taking his cause and the caucus to the airwaves, McCurdy explicitly told Democratic House leaders and the White House: "[Moderates] are not going to stand by and let them [the Republicans] dictate the agenda."[130] Indeed, he believed that the House leadership and the Bush White House suffered from a similar malady: both avoided "the big issues."[131] Deriding the president's proposed constitutional amendment against flag burning, McCurdy offered the DLC's agenda as a serious alternative to GOP wedge issues.

The early 1990s were a propitious time for new thinking. McCurdy, for one, realized in political terms that, "when the Cold War ended, so did the 20th Century."[132] Indeed, apartheid's collapse, the 1991 Gulf War, and the Soviet Union's peaceful dissolution merely reemphasized the scale of global change. Communism's disintegration had already spawned significant innovation within Western Europe's social democratic Left. Thus, the DLC's battle against liberal orthodoxy was no longer a lonely and American struggle. Rather, with West European socialists accepting "unequal rewards" as the sine qua non of an economic system, the DLC was now merely part and parcel of the Western Left's innovations.[133]

Ironically, the global pace of change not only overtook and consumed the Kremlin; the Bush White House also fell victim to history. The savings-and-loan debacle, national debt anxieties, and the president's innate caution created a popular impression that, in the words of Elaine Kamarck, "official Washington is losing it."[134] Hopelessly pragmatic, and saddled with what he called "the vision thing," Bush hardly had grand themes to pronounce grandiloquently, even if he could. More importantly, the GOP was coming apart at the seams. The president's 1990 budget deal, which included a modest tax increase, precipitated a conservative rebellion. In typical fashion for him, Gingrich accused the administration of "declar[ing] war on the entire Reagan wing of the party." Even shriller was the conservative activist Richard Viguerie. Claiming, "The shelling of Fort Sumter has begun," Viguerie and the conservative movement declared war against a Republican White House.[135]

The president's tax increase notwithstanding, the ur-neocon, Irving

Kristol, identified Bush's "traditional conservatism" as the real culprit causing the right-wing's revolt. To Kristol's mind, conventional Republicans like Bush doubted whether conservatism required an "identifiable agenda at all."[136] As a result, they governed as a natural right and did so competently but always lacking "the vision thing."[137] Thus, even in the midst of his greatest triumph, the First Gulf War, Bush auditioned rationales for war.[138] From "war against aggression" and "Hussein-as-Hitler" to "jobs," it was only America's overwhelming victory that erased the president's foibles.[139] Without the Cold War or Saddam Hussein, the Bush White House simply lacked an overriding rationale for governance.

The Cold War's conclusion might have undone Bush's second term, but it also gave national service a second life. Indeed, for all the president's talk of a "new world order," the world-weary American voter anticipated a peace dividend to address long-ignored domestic issues. Searching for policies, even conventional liberals gave national service a second look. Leading the way was one of McCurdy's staunchest foes: the Congressional Black Caucus. Realizing that the military's drawdown shrank one avenue for black social mobility, Augustus Hawkins and Major Owens backed Mc-Curdy's bill.[140]

Given the opportunity to win further liberal support, McCurdy promoted service as a policy addressing spiraling crime rates and urban poverty. Early 1990s America was a crime-ridden society. Statistically, eight of every ten Americans were victims of some sort of violent offense.[141] The proliferation of crack cocaine, handguns, and high-rise public housing units and the demise of low-skilled manufacturing jobs and the welfare state had created inner-city ghettos wracked with drug abuse, homicides, and black-on-black violent crime. In 1951, for example, the New York City police investigated 244 homicides and 904 rapes; by 1989, reported murders and rapes rose to 1,900 and 3,912 even though the city had lost 700,000 residents.[142] New York was a mere reflection of national trends; between 1960 and 1988, violent crime had increased fivefold.[143]

Spiraling violent crime had bedeviled policymakers since the late 1960s. Whether it was Richard Nixon's War against Crime or Ronald Reagan's Say No to Drugs campaign, the efforts to quell crime and epidemic drug abuse failed. By the late 1980s, liberals paid greater heed to the interrelated issues of crime and poverty. Alex Kotlowitz's 1987 *Wall Street Journal* piece "Urban Trauma" and consequent 1991 bestseller *There Are No Children Here* helped draw renewed attention to the issue. Focusing on twelve-year-old Lafayette and nine-year-old Pharaoh Walton and their struggles to survive in Chicago's infamous Robert Taylor Homes, Kotlowitz humanized the gritty and violent world of urban poverty.[144]

Moved by the *Wall Street Journal* piece, Bush named Kotlowitz one of his "Thousand Points of Light."[145] Wanting federal action to eradicate slums rather than a presidential "gold star," the author was incredulous. He claimed that Bush "missed the point . . . [and] just didn't get it."[146] Further crystallizing the interrelated issues of race and crime was Rodney King. In March 1991, the Los Angeles Police Department engaged in an eight-mile high-speed chase, culminating in the police arresting and bludgeoning the intoxicated motorist, Rodney King. King's beating by five to six officers with fifty-six baton blows and a series of kicks and punches was captured on a bystander's video recorder.[147] The episode, which later sparked the May 1992 Los Angeles riots, merely supplemented calls for the president to enunciate his domestic vision.

With liberals and conservatives galvanized to reduce violent crime, alleviate urban slums, and professionalize police departments, McCurdy acted. Reviving a dormant Police Corps bill, he used the unique moment to his advantage. Championed by a former Robert Kennedy aide, Adam Walinsky, and modeled on ROTC, the Police Corps became McCurdy's national service bill writ small and in reverse. In exchange for university tuition, corps members agreed to serve a four-year stint as a police officer on graduation. Theoretically, the corps would aid overworked police officers, raise force training and education levels, and reduce race-related incidents.[148] Supported by William F. Buckley, the archconservative Bob Dornan, Senator Arlen Specter, the *Village Voice*'s Pete Hamill, and the muckraking journalist Jack Newfield, McCurdy's proposal had obvious appeal.[149]

While battling for the Police Corps, McCurdy also flirted with a presidential run. Despite the president's "vision thing," most observers agreed with the Democratic insider Jim Ruvolo's assessment that "George Bush is . . . close to unbeatable."[150] As a result, Sam Nunn, Chuck Robb, Dick Gephardt, and Oklahoma senator David Boren all declined to challenge the president.[151] With party heavyweights sitting 1992 out, McCurdy seriously considered a campaign. Blocked from House leadership by his propensity to challenge liberal powerbrokers, and with Oklahoma's two senators, David Boren and Don Nickles, popular and relatively young, the White House, paradoxically, seemed the most likely path for advancement.

The impetus for McCurdy's campaign came from unlikely sources:

George Will and Ben Wattenberg.[152] In glowing nationally syndicated columns, the conservative and neoconservative journalists compared the Oklahoman to John Kennedy, which prompted his House colleagues Tim Roemer, Jim Cooper, and Dick Swett to urge him to run.[153] With the DLC unofficially committed to Clinton, McCurdy relied on House moderates to help him test the waters.

One September 1991 campaign swing ended in California, where McCurdy addressed the DNC.[154] Delivered before an audience, and possessing all the trappings of a presidential debate, McCurdy's talk was a long-delayed *j'accuse:* "It is time we spoke the obvious. We have lost Middle America . . . and we wonder why. We have taxed, neglected them, and embarrassed them. Now it is their turn."[155] Turning his attention to the New Politics liberals who had controlled the party since the early 1970s, he challenged them to accept the DLC's modifications: "Those of you who arrived here in foreign cars, wear foreign watches and drink wine must accept the reality of a changing world. . . . There is nothing for nothing any longer."[156]

The speech might have fallen flat in the auditorium, but McCurdy caught yet another conservative commentator's attention. A few nights later on the *Johnny Carson Show,* John McLaughlin named McCurdy the likely Democratic nominee.[157] Armed with low-level national buzz and proposed state legislation enabling him to run for Congress and the White House, McCurdy edged toward an official announcement.[158] Following a long weekend of campaigning in New Hampshire, McCurdy asked his wife: "What do you think?" Expressing surprise at the possibility of her husband's candidacy, Pam McCurdy lapsed into silence. When he implored, "What do you *really* think?" her reply, "I have a migraine," convinced him that the time away from his three young children and the strains placed on his family were simply too much.[159]

Once the congressman announced his noncandidacy, Bill Clinton immediately solicited McCurdy's endorsement. Before approving Clinton's candidacy, McCurdy had one misgiving: "rumors" about the governor's marital infidelities. After promising, "Dave, there is nothing to it . . . you don't need to worry about it . . . there is nothing to it," Clinton earned the congressman's endorsement. His fears allayed, McCurdy not only became the first non-Arkansan to endorse Clinton; he also served as a foreign policy adviser and was key in defusing the governor's early "draft dodging" controversy.[160]

Campaigning in twenty-five states for the Democratic ticket, McCurdy found that his close ties to the military establishment and neoconservative intellectuals proved significant. Arguing that Clinton-Gore "may not be the dream ticket but it's as close as they're going to get," he helped secure Admiral William Crowe's endorsement.[161] This surprise move by President Bush's former chair of the Joint Chiefs of Staff presaged a neoconservative surge to the Arkansas governor. Unhappy with Bush's realism, and believing that "it's not healthy for the political system for someone to do as mediocre a job as Bush and be rewarded," Joshua Muravchik, and McCurdy, convinced a legion of neocons to endorse the governor.[162]

Seconding Clinton's nomination at the Democratic convention, McCurdy delivered a prime-time, nationally televised speech.[163] Claiming, "People like Bill Clinton's folks and mine have always been the heart and soul of the Democratic Party," he staked the Democrats' claim to Middle America.[164] Running as a DLC New Democrat, Clinton made national service a centerpiece of his domestic agenda. Though James Carville griped that the issue did not "poll well," Marshall sensed otherwise. To his mind, the "no more somethin' for nothing" New Democrat mantra struck an emotional chord. Once elected, Clinton maintained a "fever" for national service.[165] From penning a *New York Times* op-ed on the subject to naming Al From assistant transition director, Clinton kept the issue a top priority.[166]

Through the 1993 National and Community Service Trust Act, the AmeriCorps program established a legislative foothold for national service. Traditional political metrics, however, failed to measure the success of the New Democratic ethos. Sadly, national service—the brainchild and issue of apostate Democrats—became captive to a "brain dead Congress." Weeks before Clinton's inauguration, McCurdy had warned the president-elect against just that eventuality. While dining at Pamela Harriman's Washington, DC, home, McCurdy used the occasion to offer Clinton some last-minute advice: "You ran against a brain dead Congress. Don't hook up life support to them now." He then begged the Washington newcomer to maintain his distance from the old liberalism that he had implicitly, if haltingly, run against.[167]

Focused on passing his agenda, Clinton was puzzled. Since the current Democratic Congress "determine[d] the future of [his] legislative programs," he hitched his political fate to congressional liberals.[168] And, though national service passed, the president, by allying himself with Tom Foley, Ted Kennedy, et al., committed a strategic mistake. Programmatically, AmeriCorps was successful. The legislation made higher education more affordable, supported nonprofits, and gave community service the presidential imprimatur.

The program's moral critique of entitlement liberalism had definitively softened, however. Nevertheless, a Democratic president had made and then passed a high-priority piece of domestic legislation that called on recipients to give before they got. Making sure "there [was] nothing for nothing any longer" would be a long, multipronged slog, but it was one that Clinton ultimately won.

Conclusion

In 1992, Bill Clinton handily defeated George H. W. Bush and took the White House. At the outset of his presidency, it was New Politics liberals, not conservatives, who very nearly wrecked the administration. No longer insurgents, by 1993 they were the Democratic Party establishment. Chairing powerful congressional committees, and staffing the White House and federal bureaucracies, they largely controlled Clinton's agenda. The former DLC chair might have campaigned as a New Democrat, but the lines between centrist and New Politics liberalism remained hazy and difficult to discern. As a result, the president stumbled.

Allowing diversity politics to dominate the cabinet selection process, and then haphazardly wading into the gays-in-the-military issue, Clinton bumbled from one controversy to the next. By 1994, these New Politics issues overshadowed his administration's centrist (and successful) domestic policies: debt reduction, government reorganization, and free trade. A partial product of the New Politics movement himself, Clinton simultaneously inhabited both liberal worlds. Born and raised in rural Arkansas, he received an elite education at Georgetown, Yale, and Oxford. After working in the 1972 McGovern campaign, he possessed nearly all the classic New Politics traits: privilege, education, and losing.

Serving as governor of Arkansas is where Clinton diverged from his generation. There, voters taught their young governor irrefutable and hard-won lessons. An unpopular motor vehicle tax enacted during his first term led to defeat in 1980. In 1982, the political wunderkind staged a comeback. Thereafter, he governed as a moderate and helped transform his state. Unlike during his time as governor, as president Clinton headed a national party controlled by the New Politics. Temporarily eschewing lessons of the past, the president pushed New Politics social issues and enabled Newt Gingrich to take the Congress and endanger the entire New Democrat experiment.

Through triangulation, personnel changes, and policy shifts, Clinton righted his presidency. And, though it hardly presents an untarnished example of centrist liberalism, the administration's fiscal responsibility, foreign policy activism, and domestic achievements are telling. In contrast to Clinton's enduring popularity, New Politics liberals have continually failed to win voters' approval. In the political vacuum resulting from liberalism's collapse, conservatives came to dominate the American political landscape.

This conservative hegemony shapes the terms of contemporary policy debates—so much so that many pundits and thinkers now assume an inherent conservative bent in America's political culture. Capitalizing on the Left's frustrations with this perceived reality, Tom Frank's 2004 *What's the Matter with Kansas* became a best seller. Faulting the "false consciousness" of the Middle American voter, Frank claims that conservatives "trick" voters into conservatism.[1] Rejecting Frank's wishful thinking, the journalist and historian Jon Meacham simply accepts the reality that "we live in a center right nation."[2] Unfortunately, Frank and Meacham look at the American scene from a conventional, West European Left-Right continuum. From that perspective, downscale voters' antipathy to universal health care or social welfare spending does make Americans appear stupid or irredeemably conservative.

America, however, is not Western Europe. The political environments giving rise to Western Europe's social democracies simply do not exist in America. For generations, academics have wrestled with the age-old dilemma, "Why is there no socialism in the United States?" While parliamentary systems surely enable niche parties to advance an agenda and an immigrant workforce hindered the American labor movement's development, the cause is more basic: the United States is not Western Europe.

An authentically American Left must necessarily govern in accordance with an unfashionable paradigm: American exceptionalism. Though critics find the concept responsible for "Americans' . . . tendency to preach at other nationals rather than listen to them" and their "human rights narcissism," most overthink a relatively pedestrian and sound idea. *Exceptionalism* is not a Limbaughesque, a priori verification of America's supreme awesomeness; the term simply means "outside the norm." And, according to most indices, the United States most certainly stands outside most West European standards. From leading developed countries in homicide rates and poverty to boasting the "only major anti-statist libertarian party in the industrialized world," the United States largely remains the redheaded stepchild of the Western world.[3]

If Democrats are to build a viable welfare state, they must come to terms with American exceptionalism's root cause: eighteenth-century liberalism. The Rosetta stone of America's antistatist political culture, Lockean liberalism and its enduring power explain much about the past and the present. Unfortunately, many contemporary historians discount classical liberalism's influence because of its association with "consensus history."

Emerging in the early post–World War II era, consensus history downplayed conflict and proclaimed an unspoken liberal accord. In the rearview mirror, all consensus historians appear similar. This is not the case. Daniel Boorstin's celebration of the nation's placid past somehow glossed over a bloody civil war, while Louis Hartz's "born free" claim assumed a rigid homogeneity stretching throughout the American past. In contrast to these uncritical celebrations, Richard Hofstadter "perceived the consensus from a radical perspective . . . and deplored it."[4] Moreover, he confined his consensus history to political elites. While many of Hofstadter's formulations are outdated, specialists should reconsider his central message: a common (liberal) climate of opinion dominates American political life.[5]

Hofstadter's consensus history is not a conservative school of thought dedicated to trumpeting American values. Indeed, Hofstadter yearned for social democracy. Unlike many academics, he saw his country as it was, not as he wished it to be, a lesson contemporary academics and intellectuals would be well served by heeding.

Unlike Hofstadter and other consensus historians, currently specialists realize that a multiplicity of ideological conflicts and sources shaped the American past. From republicanism to free labor and the organizational synthesis and beyond, classical liberalism was but one among many ideas in circulation. Not all ideas exchanged and circulated equally.

By the mid-nineteenth century, liberal, capitalist values held sway.[6] Populists, anarchosyndicalists, and Eugene Debs might have battled industrial capitalism and the supremacy of bourgeois competitive norms, but all ultimately failed to unseat a dominant political culture. Specialists should debate when the "economic virtues of capitalist culture" became the "necessary qualities of man" in American life.[7] Arguing against the hegemony of classically liberal norms, however, defies logic. If the study of elections, grassroots activists, politicians, and their rhetoric tells us anything, we know that twentieth-century Americans largely and enthusiastically embraced the "self-interested pursuit of happiness."[8] This is the bedrock of modern America's political culture.

Accepting classical liberalism's hegemony remains the key to any reform movement's success. Whether consciously or not, Franklin Roosevelt founded Social Security on a liberal premise. Insisting that citizens pay into a social welfare system before receiving benefits is the root of that program's political durability. In the same way, LBJ's Medicare program remains true to the liberal ideal. Only after a lifetime of labor can an elderly American receive a government-administered health-care benefit. In this way, both Medicare and Social Security remain sacrosanct. Jon Meacham is wrong; we do not live in a center-right country. Most Americans are not conservative or liberal; they are Lockean. And contemporary liberals ignore that reality at their peril.

Liberals are bound for additional wilderness years if they fail to heed that central lesson.

Acknowledgments

Writing and researching are lonely enterprises. No book, however, is the product of a lone author. In the seven years I labored to complete *Losing the Center,* scores of people contributed mightily to the project. I would like to take this opportunity to repay their kindness and hard work with my appreciation. Lord knows that a few words on the page are not equal to their contribution, but it is a start.

As much as academics like to pretend that we are interested in things beyond the grubby world of finance, it takes significant sums of money to research, write, and publish a book. In that vein, I certainly must thank Ohio University's Contemporary History Institute for funding portions of my dissertation-cum-book. In addition to my graduate institution, the John Kennedy, Lyndon Johnson, and Gerald Ford presidential libraries provided me with generous grants.

Surely, the unsung heroes of the historical profession are the archivists. This book required me to consult five presidential libraries and scores of manuscript collections located at universities and state historical societies across the nation. I simply lack the room and memory to thank all the archivists by name. Every serious researcher would simply be lost without the folks who quite literally hold the keys to the history kingdom.

Not every helpmate comes bearing a document collection. Friends and colleagues are also an indispensable part of completing any manuscript. At Ohio University I had the pleasure of befriending and working alongside a cast of very talented young historians. I simply must thank James Waite and Jon Peterson for reading early drafts of this project. In addition, Robert Davis, J. D. Wyneken, Tom Bruscino, Rick Dodgson, Shae Davidson, Hallvard Notaker, Mathieu Moss, Jamie Fries, Julian Nemeth, Ray Haberski, and Brent, Renee, and Lobo Geary provided friendship, beer, and intellectual stimulation throughout my time in Athens, Ohio.

Speaking of graduate school, I was blessed to have world-class mentors. Jim Giglio at Missouri State University worked tirelessly to help me get into the Ph.D. program at Ohio University. Without Jim's aid and belief in me, I simply could not have achieved my dreams. From there, Ohio University's Kevin Mattson served as a model of an engaged historian. In addition to Mattson, Chester Pach revealed himself to be a master teacher and scholar.

Above all, I must thank my dissertation adviser, mentor, and friend Alonzo Hamby. Lon, as many in the profession realize, is a rare bird: a grandee in his field yet a down-to-earth and all-around great human being. I am lucky to call Lon and his wife, Joyce, good friends. Lon was the perfect dissertation adviser—he offered sound advice and a keen eye for writing while also giving me the room to make my own decisions (and share of mistakes).

Since graduate school, I was lucky enough to land a tenure-track gig at Gannon University. While here, Mark Jubulis, Tim Downs, John Young, Linda Fleming, Bobbi Jo Fye, John Vohlidka, Geoff Grundy, Suzanne Richard, Ian Van Dyke, Bob Sparks, and Mary Beth Earl have provided significant support, without which I could not have finished this book. In addition to Gannon's faculty, staff, and administration, I must extend a hearty thanks to my students, who make teaching a joy rather than work.

My best friends from high school, Karl Greiner and Mike Moore, provided me with room, board, and friendship on too many occasions to count. Meghan Cressman read drafts of later chapters while her husband Tye Cressman poured drinks. In addition to longtime friends, my sister and her husband and two beautiful kids, Kim, Mike, Kaylee, and Brett Gibson, were a great diversion from the rigors of research, writing, and travel.

The folks at the University Press of Kentucky are simply superb. Stephen Wrinn offered encouragement and sound advice every step of the way. Meanwhile, Allison Webster was quick to respond to every email and picayune request.

No words can fully express the debt I owe to Momma. My mom is an American original—a steel magnolia come to life. Her southern accent and sweet nature belie a truly strong and tough woman. Momma worked two jobs to ensure that my sister and I had a good life and every opportunity. This book is not at all possible without Shirley Bloodworth's strength, compassion, and life-giving love.

Sadly my two best friends did not live to see this book. My grandparents, William and Maxine McGill, were more Mississippi than Faulkner and a glass of sweet iced tea. Ma gave me a love for storytelling and reading—

even if her yarns were a bit dark. Meanwhile, Ga-Ga taught me everything else. My grandfather surely had some faults, but he remains the finest human being I have ever known. His admonition that I should "be a good boy and do right" remains my personal touchstone.

Like Ma, I married up. My wife, Andrea, is my best friend, a great traveling companion, and the love of my life. No spouse could possibly be more supportive. Whether I am in Jerusalem or Bug Tussle, Oklahoma, Andrea puts up with my nerdy obsession for political history. She is pretty, sweet, smart, and funny and everything one could hope for in a companion. Along with Finny, Lucy, and Memphis, Andrea makes my life worth living.

Notes

Introduction

1. Maureen Dowd, "The House Republican Leader; Vengeful Glee (and Sweetness) at Gingrich's Victory Party," *New York Times,* November 9, 1994; Peter Applebome, "The South; The Rising GOP Tide Overwhelms the Democratic Levees in the South," *New York Times,* November 11, 1994.

2. Kevin Merida, "Last Rites for Liberalism?" *Washington Post,* December 28, 1994, 1A.

3. Dowd, "The House Republican Leader"; Applebome, "The South."

4. Merida, "Last Rites for Liberalism?"

5. U.S. President, "January 23, 1996, Address Before a Joint Session of the Congress on the State of the Union," in *Public Papers of the Presidents of the United States—William J. Clinton, 1996 Book I—January to June 30, 1996: Containing the Public Messages, Speeches, and Statements of the President, 1993–2001* (Washington, DC: U.S. Government Printing Office, 1996), 79.

6. Sam Verhovek, "The Contender: Phil Gramm's Offbeat Charm as a Persistent Conservative," *New York Times,* December 27, 1995.

7. Gary Gerstle, "The Protean Character of American Liberalism," *American Historical Review* 99, no. 4 (October 1994): 1043–73.

8. See Arthur Schlesinger Jr., *The Vital Center: The Politics of Freedom* (Boston: Houghton Mifflin, 1949).

9. Arthur Schlesinger Jr., *A Life in the 20th Century: Innocent Beginnings, 1917–1950* (New York: Houghton Mifflin, 2000), and "The Legacy of Andrew Jackson," *American Mercury,* February 1947, 172; Ours Is an Age without Heroes, file "The Decline of Greatness," box W-34, AMS Papers, John F. Kennedy Papers, John F. Kennedy Presidential Library and Museum; Nothing Is More Common These Days Than Lamentation over the Plight of the Liberals (August 4, 1957), p. 7, file "Where Does a Liberal Go from Here," box W-34, AMS Papers, John F. Kennedy Papers; James Nuechterlein, "Arthur M. Schlesinger, Jr. and the Discontents of Postwar American Liberalism," *Review of Politics* 39, no. 1 (January 1977): 4; Stephen P. Depoe, *Arthur M. Schlesinger, Jr., and the Ideological History of American Liberalism* (Tuscaloosa: University of Alabama Press, 1994), 5.

10. Arthur Schlesinger Jr., "Not Right, Not Left, but a Vital Center," *Sunday New York Times Magazine,* April 4, 1948.

11. Memorandum for the President: Walter Lippmann and Paris (February 1, 1961), file "Schlesinger 3/61–4/61," box 65, President's Office Files Staff Memos,

John F. Kennedy Papers; Letter from Schlesinger to JFK ("Marian and I could not have had a better time at luncheon"; November 14, 1960), p. 3, file "Schlesinger 3/61–4/61," box 65, President's Office Files Staff Memos, John F. Kennedy Papers; "The Presidency in the 1960s," file "State of the Union Message Memoranda," box 63, Ted Sorensen Papers, John F. Kennedy Presidential Library and Museum; Remarks of Senator John F. Kennedy—Hillsborough High School (May 17, 1960), file "President's Responsibility in Foreign Affairs," box 1031, Pre-Presidential Papers, John F. Kennedy Library; Letter from Niebuhr to Schlesinger (September 9, 1960), folder 2, file "R. Niebuhr, 1955–61," box P20, AMS Papers, John F. Kennedy Papers.

12. Dominic Sandbrook, *Eugene McCarthy: The Rise and Fall of Postwar American Liberalism* (New York: Knopf, 2004), 221.

13. Ibid., 222–23.

14. Bruce Miroff, *The Liberals' Moment: The McGovern Insurgency and the Identity Crisis of the Democratic Party* (Lawrence: University Press of Kansas, 2007), 3.

15. Ibid., 300–301.

16. Ibid., 3.

17. Steve Gillon, *The Democrats' Dilemma: Walter F. Mondale and the Liberal Legacy* (New York: Columbia University Press, 1992), xxiv.

18. Ibid., 395, 401–2.

19. "Remarks by Ben Wattenberg" (March 31, 1981), folder "Speeches: Kirkpatrick; February 2, 1981," box 18, Peter Rosenblatt Papers, LBJ Presidential Library.

20. Peter Bourne, *Jimmy Carter: A Comprehensive Biography from Plains to Post-Presidency* (New York: Scribner, 1997), 441.

21. Ibid., 442.

22. U.S. President, "Energy and National Goals" (July 15, 1979), in *Public Papers of the Presidents of the United States—Jimmy Carter: Containing the Public Messages, Speeches, and Statements of the President, 1977–1981* (Washington, DC: U.S. Government Printing Office, 1979), 1235–37.

23. James Giglio, *Call Me Tom: The Life of Thomas F. Eagleton* (Columbia: University of Missouri Press, 2011), 152–53.

24. Richard Scammon and Ben Wattenberg, *The Real Majority* (1970; New York: Primus/Donald I. Fine, 1992), 35–44.

25. Elizabeth Drew, "Letter from Washington," *New Yorker,* December 12, 1988, 123.

26. Ibid., 124.

27. Matthew Kelly, "Dukakis Responds Again to Rape Query," *Seattle Times,* November 2, 1988, 10A.

28. Christopher Lasch, *The New Radicalism in America, 1889–1963* (New York: Knopf, 1965), xviii.

29. Alonzo Hamby, *Liberalism and Its Challengers: From FDR to Bush* (New York: Oxford University Press, 1992); Richard Hofstadter, *The American Political Tradition and the Men Who Made It* (New York: Knopf, 1948).

1. Latte Liberals

1. Sandbrook, *Eugene McCarthy,* 84–85.

2. Ibid., 173.

3. Press Release: The Steering Committee of Concerned Wisconsin Democrats (November 20, 1967), folder 1, box 6, Eugene McCarthy Papers, University of Minnesota Special Collections.

4. Donald Peterson Oral History, p. 4, file 27, box 246, Eugene McCarthy Papers.

5. Robert David Johnson, *The Peace Progressives and American Foreign Relations* (Cambridge, MA: Harvard University Press, 1995), 3.

6. Ibid., 4.

7. Robert Griffith, "Old Progressives and the Cold War," *Journal of American History* 66 (September 1979): 339.

8. Ibid.

9. Ibid.

10. Margo Jefferson, "The American Way of Class, a Game of Self-Delusion," *New York Times,* March 31, 1993, 2E; Steve Lohr, "Forget Peoria; It's Now: 'Will It Play in Tulsa?'" *New York Times,* June 1, 1992, 1A.

11. Richard Leopold, "The Mississippi Valley and American Foreign Policy," *Mississippi Valley Historical Review* 4 (1951): 625–42.

12. Sam Lubell, "Who Votes Isolationist and Why," *Harper's,* April 1951, 30.

13. Ray Allen Billington, "The Origins of Middle Western Isolationism," *Political Science Quarterly* 60 (March 1945): 53.

14. Donald Peterson Oral History, file 27, box 246, Eugene McCarthy Papers; John Patrick Hunter, "McCarthy Man Don Peterson: 'Pizza and Politics,'" *Capital Times* (Madison, WI), March 25, 1968, 35.

15. Donald Peterson Oral History, file 27, box 246, Eugene McCarthy Papers.

16. Candidate Stand on Issue, Newspaper Clipping, folder 1, box 5, Donald O. Peterson Papers, Wisconsin State Historical Society.

17. "Peterson Storm Center of Democratic Convention," *Eau Claire (WI) Leader,* August 31, 1968, 1A.

18. Letter from Donald Peterson to Employer (n.d.), folder 1, box 5, Donald O. Peterson Papers.

19. Letter from Donald Peterson to Robert Bernstein (n.d.), folder "Loose Papers," box 7, Donald O. Peterson Papers.

20. Letter from Peterson to George McGovern (September 3, 1962), folder 25, box 4, Donald O. Peterson Papers.

21. Letter from Donald Peterson to Robert Bernstein (n.d.), folder "Loose Papers," box 7, Donald O. Peterson Papers.

22. Donald Peterson Oral History, file 27, box 246, Eugene McCarthy Papers.

23. "Johnny Appleseeds," *New Republic,* October 28, 1967, 9; Letter from Allard Lowenstein to Donald Peterson (October 20, 1967), folder 376, box 4340, Allard Lowenstein Papers, Southern Folk Life Collection, University of North Carolina, Chapel Hill.

24. "Johnny Appleseeds," 9; Letter from Allard Lowenstein to Donald Peterson (October 20, 1967), folder 376, box 4340, Allard Lowenstein Papers, Southern Folk Life Collection, University of North Carolina, Chapel Hill.

25. Press Release: Concerned Wisconsin Democrats. What Is It? folder 1, box 6, Donald O. Peterson Papers.

26. R. W. Apple Jr., "The 'Ethnics' Vote in the States That Really Count," *New York Times,* October 10, 1976, 175.

27. Russell Brines, "Dulles Faces Questioning at Capitol," *Washington Post,* February 27, 1955, 4A; "Toughness on Aid," *Washington Post,* May 14, 1952, 12.

28. "Zablocki Sees Viet-Nam Gains," *Washington Post,* October 15, 1963, 1A; "List of 175 Supporters of Civil Rights," *New York Times,* January 22, 1960, 11; "Minority Groups Combat Wallace," *New York Times,* April 3, 1964, 67.

29. "The Real Clem Zablocki," *Washington Post,* December 24, 1983, 1A.

30. James Selk, "McCarthy Bid in State," *Wisconsin State Journal* (Madison), November 22, 1967, 4.

31. Donald Peterson Oral History, file 27, box 246, Eugene McCarthy Papers.

32. Press Release: The Steering Committee of Concerned Wisconsin Democrats (November 20, 1967), folder 1, box 6, Eugene McCarthy Papers.

33. News Release from Donald Peterson (January 24, 1968), file 49, box 287, Eugene McCarthy Papers.

34. Letter from Arnold Serwer to the *New York Times* (February 13, 1968), folder 1, box 1, McCarthy for President Papers, Wisconsin State Historical Society.

35. Telegram to Eugene McCarty (March 10, 1968), folder 49, box 287, Eugene McCarthy Papers.

36. Letter from Blair to Peterson (April 8, 1968), file 49, box 287, Eugene McCarthy Papers.

37. Letter from McGovern to Peterson (March 25, 1968), file 25, box 4, Eugene McCarthy Papers.

38. "A Double Standard for McCarthyites," *Minneapolis Tribune,* July 16, 1968, 4A.

39. John Patrick Hunter, "McCarthy Leaders Seek 'Pure' Slate," *Capital Times* (Madison, WI), April 19, 1968, 14; "Delegate Choice Hit by McCarthy Official," folder 19, box 287, Eugene McCarthy Papers.

40. "Dems Agree on Plan to Select Delegates," *Eau Claire (WI) Leader,* March 4, 1968, page obscured.

41. Letter from Peterson to Wyngaard (May 13, 1968), file 17, box 1, Donald O. Peterson Papers.

42. Donald Peterson Oral History, p. 4, file 27, box 246, Eugene McCarthy Papers.

43. Ibid.

44. Letter from Frank Nickolay to Roy Traynor (May 13, 1968), Donald O. Peterson Papers on Microfilm, Wisconsin State Historical Society; Letter from Peterson to John Nixon (May 15, 1968), file 19, box 287, Eugene McCarthy Papers; John Patrick Hunter, "McCarthy Will Veto Many State Dem Delegates in Meeting with Peterson," *Capital Times* (Madison, WI), May 24, 1968, 9A.

45. Peterson Says He Will Retaliate, folder 19, box 287, Eugene McCarthy Papers.

46. Letter from Frank Nickolay to Roy Traynor (May 13, 1968), Donald O. Peterson Papers on Microfilm.

47. "State Dem Platform under Fire," *Eau Claire (WI) Leader,* July 26, 1968, 2A; "War Foes Gain Victory," *Eau Claire (WI) Leader,* July 20, 1968, 1A.

48. "Dem Group Opposes McCarthy Delegates," *Eau Clair (WI) Daily Telegram,* August 5, 1968, 3A.

49. Area Delegates Win Credentials Unit OK, folder 19, box 287, Eugene McCarthy Papers.

50. "McCarthy Backers Pick City Professor," *Eau Claire (WI) Leader,* July 2, 1968, 3A.

51. Wisconsin Delegation's Biographies (June 25, 1968), folder 27, box 246, Eugene McCarthy Papers.

52. Eugene Harrington, "State Caucus Hears Maddox, Wife Gets the Only Applause," *Milwaukee Journal,* August 27, 1968, 14A.

53. "Wisconsin Greets Delegation Head," *New York Times,* September 1, 1968, 38A.

54. Ibid.

55. George Marder, "Dems Face Six Fights on the Floor," *Capital Times* (Madison, WI), August 26, 1968, 2A.

56. Ibid.

57. Miles McMillin, "Gene's Badgers Still Hopeful Despite Early Floor Setback," *Capital Times* (Madison, WI), August 27, 1968, 1A; Erwin Knoll, "Badger Delegates Trigger Delay in Vietnam Debate," *Capital Times* (Madison, WI), August 28, 1968, 1A.

58. Ibid.

59. Ibid., 4A.

60. "Badger Delegates Angered over 'Role' of Johnson," *Capital Times* (Madison, WI), August 26, 1968, 2A.

61. Knoll, "Badger Delegates Trigger Delay."

62. "State Delegates Bitter over Platform Defeat," *Milwaukee Journal,* August 29, 1968, 13A.

63. McMillin, "Gene's Badgers Still Hopeful," 4A.

64. Ibid.

65. "Hundreds Join Wisconsin's Protest Walk," *Milwaukee Journal,* August 30, 1968, 4A.

66. Donald Peterson, "I'm So Naïve I Thought I Could Walk the Streets," *Capital Times* (Madison, WI), August 30, 1968, 4A.

67. "Peterson Makes Hit with TV," *Milwaukee Journal,* August 29, 1968, 9A.

68. "State Delegates Urged to Support Nominee," *Milwaukee Journal,* August 29, 1968, 4A.

69. Eugene Harrington, "Bitter, Frustrated State Group in Heart of Convention Storm," *Milwaukee Journal,* August 29, 1968, 14A.

70. "District Chairman Raps State Showing," *Eau Claire (WI) Leader,* August 31, 1968, 3A.

71. "Humphrey Wins on First Ballot," *Eau Claire (WI) Leader,* August 29, 1968, 1A.

72. McMillin, "Gene's Badgers Still Hopeful," 4A.

73. Racine Friends of Don Peterson Letter (October 29, 1969), file "'70 Campaign," box 2, Donald O. Peterson Papers.

74. Erwin Knoll, "Mourners Walk Chicago Streets," *Capital Times* (Madison, WI), August 29, 1968, 1A.

75. "Badger Delegates Fight to Bitter End," *Capital Times* (Madison, WI), August 30, 1968, 1A.

76. "District Chairman Raps State Showing"; Letter from Roy Waehler to Peterson (n.d.), folder 3, box 5, Donald O. Peterson Papers.

77. Letter from A. W. Stanton to Peterson (September 3, 1968), folder 3, box 5, Donald O. Peterson Papers.

78. Letter from Glorianne Leck to Peterson (August 30, 1968), folder 2, box 5, Donald O. Peterson Papers.

79. Letter from Dick Schaap to Peterson (August 31, 1968), folder 1, box 6, Donald O. Peterson Papers.

80. Miles McMillin, "Peterson Says He Won't Leave Party," *Capital Times* (Madison, WI), August 29, 1968, 1A; "Dem Party Bolters Start 2 New Groups," *Capital Times* (Madison, WI), August 31, 1968, 1A.

81. The Chicago Convention: Politics of Confrontation, folder 1, box 6, Donald O. Peterson Papers; "Peterson Unveils Dissident Demo Coalition for Liberals," *Wisconsin State Journal* (Madison), September 5, 1968, 15A.

82. National Conference for New Politics, folder "New Politics," box 7, Donald O. Peterson Papers.

83. "New Coalition of Democrats Formed in Rhode Island," *Providence Journal,* September 9, 1968, 1A; Letter from TW to LS (October 11, 1969), folder 2, box 1, Donald O. Peterson Papers; Dissident Democrats Move Out of Chicago, folder 1, box 6, Donald O. Peterson Papers.

84. Robert Walters, "The New Democratic Coalition Eyes Nixon, Wallace Fans Too," *Washington (DC) Evening Star,* October 7, 1968, 4A.

85. Ibid.

86. New Democratic Coalition National Dinner, folder 1, box 1, Donald O. Peterson Papers.

87. Peterson Speech to Wisconsin Public Welfare Association (June 11, 1970), folder "Speeches," box 3, Donald O. Peterson Papers.

88. New Democratic Coalition Pamphlet: Policy Statement of the NDC, folder 34, box 3, Donald O. Peterson Papers.

89. "'New Coalition' Democrats from 40 States Plan Future," *Chicago Sun-Times,* October 6, 1968, 5A.

90. Ibid., 5A.

91. Statement of Peterson of New Democratic Coalition, folder "Speeches," box 3, Donald O. Peterson Papers.

92. New Democratic Coalition Pamphlet, p. 6, folder "NDC Pamphlet," box 2, Donald O. Peterson Papers.

93. Al Eisele, "McCarthy Disappoints NDC," *St. Paul Pioneer Press,* February 4, 1969, 8A.

94. Loudon Wainwright, "Confessions of a Fair Country Ballplayer," *Life Magazine,* October 1968, 70.

95. Ibid.

96. "Democrats Seek Unity Here," *Stevens Point (WI) Daily Journal,* June 13, 1969, 1A.

97. "State Dems Reject Endorsement Bid," *Stevens Point (WI) Daily Journal,* June 13, 1969, 3A.

98. "New Coalition 'Runs' State Dems' Session," *Eau Claire (WI) Daily Telegram,* June 16, 1969, 1A; Gordon Randolph, "Vote on Troops Won by Liberal Democrats," *Milwaukee Journal,* June 15, 1969, 10A.

99. "New Coalition 'Runs' State Dems' Session," 1A.

100. Ibid.

101. Letter from Zablocki to James Hannah (June 16, 1969), Clement Zablocki Papers, Marquette University Library Special Collections.

102. Letter from Zablocki to William Gerrard (June 20, 1972), Clement Zablocki Papers.

103. John Patrick Hunter, "'New' Democrats Take Over," *Capital Times* (Madison, WI), June 28, 1971.

104. State Democrats Censure LBJ for Vietnam Deceptions, folder 19, box 1, Donald O. Peterson Papers.

105. Liberals Dominate Democrats, folder 1, box 1, Donald O. Peterson Papers.

106. Letter from DF to Peterson (July 14, 1969), folder "'70 Campaign," box 2, Donald O. Peterson Papers.

107. Though Zablocki supported President Reagan's anticommunism in the Caribbean and El Salvador, he refused to fund an insurgency. John W. Kole, "Peterson Warns Democrats against Purging Liberals," *Milwaukee Journal,* October 6, 1971, page obscured; Letter from Leon Shull to Peterson (April 13, 1972), folder 2, box 1, Donald O. Peterson Papers; ADA Voting Record of Clement Zablocki, folder 2, box 1, Donald O. Peterson Papers.

108. Dave Schreiner, "Nation in State of Flux: Peterson," *Sheboygan (WI) Press,* October 29, 1969, 6A.

109. "Democrats Seek Unity Here," 1A.

110. McCarthy Salts Old Dem Wounds, folder 38, box 3, Donald O. Peterson Papers; "Democrats Seek Unity Here," 1A.

111. Letter from John Kenneth Galbraith to Leon Shull (August 13, 1970), folder 38, box 3, Donald O. Peterson Papers.

112. Biography of Patrick J. Lucey, folder 2, box 1, Pat Lucey Papers, Wisconsin State Historical Society.

113. "Peterson Attractive Governor Candidate," *Waukesha (WI) Freeman,* April 27, 1970, 5A.

114. Letter from Gordon Loehr to Peterson (March 22, 1970), folder 2, box 9, Donald O. Peterson Papers.

115. Dave Wagner, "Peterson Begins 'Grass Roots' Campaign," *Capital Times* (Madison, WI), June 15, 1970, 37A.

116. Anthropological Evaluation of the Don Peterson Campaign, by Joyce O'Brien, folder 43, box 4, Donald O. Peterson Papers.

117. Straight Shooting . . . Don Peterson Style, folder "Schedules," box 3, Donald O. Peterson Papers.

118. "Peterson Raps Party Attacks and Rhetoric," *Eau Claire (WI) Daily Telegram,* May 25, 1970, page obscured.

119. "Group to Aid Moderate Republicans; Peterson Asks Consumer Protection," *Fond du Lac (WI) Commonwealth Reporter,* July 13, 1970, page obscured.

120. "Hemline Controversy Hits Politics," *Eau Claire (WI) Daily Telegram,* August 10, 1970, 3A; "Peterson Urges Probe of Midiskirt Market," *Sheboygan (WI) Press,* August 11, 1970, 4A; "Skirting the Issue," *Green Bay Press Gazette,* August 10, 1970, 2A.

121. "Mini-Skirt Becomes Political Issue," *Green Bay Press Gazette,* August 14, 1970, 6A.

122. Fred Graham, "F.B.I. Hunts 4 Young Men Charged in Madison Blast," *New York Times*, September 3, 1970, 1A.

123. "Madison, Wis., Is Tense After Blast," *New York Times*, August 30, 1970, 40A.

124. Ibid.

125. Madison Bombing, folder "Writings—*New York Times*," box 2, John Patrick Hunter Papers, Wisconsin State Historical Society.

126. Gordon Randolph, "Bombing Sparks Shift in Political Attitudes," *Milwaukee Journal*, September 6, 1970, page obscured.

127. Kenneth Roesslein, "Lucey Turns Campus Issue into Small Political Coup," *Milwaukee Sentinel*, September 4, 1970, 1A.

128. "Peterson Attacks Use of Troops on Campus," *Milwaukee Journal*, July 24, 1970.

129. "Peterson Suggests Switch to 'Neighbor' Police Forces," *Eau Claire (WI) Leader-Telegram*, August 28, 1970, 1A.

130. "Zablocki Rebuked on Governor Race," *Milwaukee Sentinel*, July 29, 1970, 7A.

131. Letter from Pat Lucey to Sister Delores, folder 1, box 5, Pat Lucey Papers.

132. "Zablocki Rebuked on Governor Race," 7A.

133. Lucey for Governor Press Release: Former Ambassador to Poland to Tour Southside for Lucey (August 10, 1970), folder 2, box 10, Pat Lucey Papers.

134. "Lucey Victor in Wisconsin Democrat Bid," *Chicago Tribune*, September 9, 1970, 8.

135. Memo: An Analysis of the Election Returns, folder "Maps and Such," box 5, Richard Wagner Papers, Wisconsin State Historical Society.

2. Revolt of the Joe Six-Packs

1. Austin Wehrwein, "Humphrey Talks in Kennedy Area," *New York Times*, March 7, 1960, 18.

2. Barbara Mikulski, "Who Speaks for the Ethnics?" in *The Eloquence of Protest: Voices of the 70's*, ed. Harrison Salisbury (Boston: Houghton Mifflin, 1972), 65; Jack Rosenthal, "Angry Ethnic Voices Decry 'Racist and Dullard' Image," *New York Times*, June 17, 1970, 49.

3. See Michael Novak, *The Rise of the Unmeltable Ethnics: Politics and Culture in the Seventies* (New York: Macmillan, 1973).

4. Rosenthal, "Angry Ethnic Voices," 49.

5. Richard Perlstein, *Nixonland: The Rise of a President and the Fracturing of America* (New York: Scribner, 2008), 351; Scammon and Wattenberg, *The Real Majority*, 174.

6. Richard Hamilton, "Liberal Intelligentsia and White Backlash," *Dissent*, Fall 1972, 225.

7. Michael Harrington, "Old Working Class, New Working Class," *Dissent*, Winter 1972, 147.

8. Robert Martinson, "Crime and the Election," *Dissent*, Fall 1972, 559.

9. Michael Flamm, *Law and Order: Street Crime, Civil Unrest, and the Crisis of Liberalism in the 1960s* (New York: Columbia University Press, 2005), 5.

10. Ross Douthat and Reihan Salam, *Grand New Party: How Republicans Can Win the Working Class and Save the American Dream* (New York: Doubleday, 2008), 47.

11. Martinson, "Crime and the Election," 559; Flamm, *Law and Order*, 125.

12. Flamm, *Law and Order*, 125.

13. Sandbrook, *Eugene McCarthy*, xi.

14. E. W. Kenworthy, "Law Issue Pushed in Minneapolis Race," *New York Times*, May 18, 1969, 57A.

15. Jacob Lentz, *Electing Jesse Ventura: A Third Party Success Story* (Boulder, CO: Lynne Rienner, 2002), 8.

16. "Minnesota Poll: 88% 'Strongly' Believe in God," *Minneapolis Tribune*, April 27, 1969, B4.

17. Jeffrey Manuel and Andrew Urban, "'You Can't Legislate the Heart': Minneapolis Mayor Charles Stenvig and the Politics of Law and Order," *American Studies* 49, nos. 3/4 (Fall/Winter 2008): 209.

18. "Guardsmen Sent into Minneapolis," *New York Times*, July 22, 1967, 11A.

19. Donald Janson, "Guard on Patrol in Minneapolis," *New York Times*, July 23, 1967, 21A.

20. W. Harry Davis, *Overcoming: The Autobiography of Harry Davis* (Minneapolis: Afton Historical Society Press, 2002), 159.

21. Dick Cunningham, "Police Aide Says '66 Race Strife Was Different," *Minneapolis Tribune*, July 21, 1967, 1A.

22. "Fire Set, Rocks Thrown in City Mob Outbreaks," *Minneapolis Tribune*, July 20, 1967, 1A.

23. "Fires, Fights Continue on North Side," *Minneapolis Tribune*, July 21, 1967, 1A.

24. Ibid.

25. Kenworthy, "Law Issue Pushed in Minneapolis Race," 57A.

26. "A Year Later, Stenvig's Luster Lingers," *Minneapolis Tribune*, July 18, 1970, 4A.

27. Kenworthy, "Law Issue Pushed in Minneapolis Race."

28. Finlay Lewis, "Cohen: 'I'm the One Who Knows What's Going On,'" *Minneapolis Tribune*, April 30, 1969, 19.

29. Davis, *Overcoming*, 165.

30. Voter's Guide, "10 Candidates Enter Primary Election Hoping to Succeed Mayor Naftalin," *Minneapolis Tribune*, April 23, 1969, 6A.

31. Fred Powledge, "The Flight from City Hall," *Harper's*, November 1969, 73; "Stenvig to Run as Independent Mayor Candidate," *Minneapolis Tribune*, January 9, 1969, 10A; "Stenvig: Conciliation Is Key to Preventing Mob Violence in City," *Minneapolis Star*, May 9, 1969, 18A; Peter Vanerpoel, "Broad Unease Elected Stenvig," *Minneapolis Tribune*, June 16, 1969.

32. "'Marxist' Groucho Expresses Some Revolutionary Opinions," *Minneapolis Tribune*, April 9, 1969, 1A.

33. "The March of the 'U' Students," *Minneapolis Tribune*, April 5, 1969, 4A; "Minnesota Trial of 3 Students On," *New York Times*, October 26, 1969, 59; Powledge, "The Flight from City Hall," 74.

34. "Cornell Signs Pact as Armed Blacks Stand," *Minneapolis Tribune*, April 21, 1969, 1A.

35. "Blacks Seize Building, Fight at Cornell U," *Minneapolis Tribune*, April 20, 1969, 1A.

36. Kenworthy, "Law Issue Pushed in Minneapolis Race," 57A.

37. Finlay Lewis, "At Home Stenvig's for Discipline, Religion," *Minneapolis Tribune*, June 11, 1969, 19A.

38. World of People, folder 1, box 1, Charles Stenvig Newspaper Clippings, Minneapolis Public Library Special Collections.

39. Lewis, "At Home Stenvig's for Discipline, Religion," 19A.

40. Finlay Lewis, "Stenvig: People Tired of Politicians, Hoodlums," *Minneapolis Tribune*, April 30, 1969, 19.

41. Ibid.

42. Al Woodruff, "Cohen Charges Stenvig with 'Double Standard,'" *Minneapolis Star*, May 13, 1969, 1A.

43. "Stenvig Denies Permit Lacking for '67 March," *Minneapolis Star*, May 14, 1969, 1B.

44. Bob Lundegaard, "Stenvig Tops Mayor Race; Cohen Ousts Hegstrom," *Minneapolis Tribune*, April 30, 1969, 1A; Maurice Goldbloom, "Is There a Backlash Vote?" *Commentary*, August 1969, 20.

45. Kenworthy, "Law Issue Pushed in Minneapolis Race," 57A; Goldbloom, "Is There a Backlash Vote?" 20.

46. Stenvig: I've 50–50 Chance, folder 1, box 1, Charles Stenvig Newspaper Clippings; Campaigning Stenvig Declares Thank You, folder 1, box 1, Charles Stenvig Newspaper Clippings.

47. Stenvig: I've 50–50 Chance, folder 1, box 1, Charles Stenvig Newspaper Clippings.

48. Ibid.

49. Bernie Shellum, "DFL Ponders Write-in Notion," *Minneapolis Tribune*, May 1, 1969, 9A.

50. "Minnesota Poll: Race Problems Cause Worry," *Minneapolis Tribune*, June 15, 1969, 6B.

51. Cohen Likens Stenvig to George Wallace, folder 1, box 1, Charles Stenvig Newspaper Clippings.

52. Candidates for Mayor: Stenvig Expects Backing from N.E. Voters, folder 1, box 1, Charles Stenvig Newspaper Clippings.

53. Ibid.

54. Manuel and Urban, "You Can't Legislate the Heart," 211; John Shaver, "Pair Will Always Be Welcome," *Minneapolis Tribune*, January 2, 1966, 9B.

55. Finlay Lewis, "'Politician' or 'Guy Next Door,'" *Minneapolis Tribune*, January 25, 1970, 12A, and "Stenvig: People Tired of Politicians, Hoodlums," 1A.

56. Stenvig Puts Emphasis on Law and Order as Mayoral Drive Starts, folder 1, box 1, Charles Stenvig Newspaper Clippings.

57. Ibid.

58. "A Year Later, Stenvig's Luster Lingers," 4A.

59. Stenvig Assumes Role of Underdog, folder 1, box 1, Charles Stenvig Newspaper Clippings.

60. Finlay Lewis, "Stenvig Says Business Leaders Are 'Scared,'" *Minneapolis Tribune*, June 4, 1969, 1A, 6A.

61. Leonard B. Peterson, "Letters to the Editor: Why Stenvig Will Win," *Minneapolis Tribune,* June 9, 1969, 5A.

62. "A Year Later, Stenvig's Luster Lingers," 4A.

63. Stenvig Appears Choice of State's Largest Union, folder 1, box 1, Charles Stenvig Newspaper Clippings.

64. City Police Supervisors' Unit Backs Stenvig, folder 1, box 1, Charles Stenvig Newspaper Clippings.

65. Finlay Lewis, "Nixon Letter Endorses Cohen; Stenvig Hears Group's Complaint," *Minneapolis Tribune,* June 3, 1969, 18.

66. "Law-and-Order Appeal: 'Dedicated Manpower' Fought Stenvig Battle," *Minneapolis Star,* June 11, 1969, 2B.

67. "A Year Later, Stenvig's Luster Lingers," 4A; Bernie Shellum, "The How and Why of the Minneapolis Vote," *Minneapolis Tribune,* June 12, 1969, 10A.

68. Finlay Lewis, "Detective's 61.8% of Vote Beats Cohen," *Minneapolis Tribune,* June 11, 1969, 1A.

69. "Minnesota Poll: 88% 'Strongly' Believe in God."

70. Joe Reigert, "Stenvig Mandate: Cut Crime, Stop Militants?" *Minneapolis Tribune,* June 12, 1969, 6A.

71. Ibid.

72. "Council Will Have to Run City, Hennepin GOP Chairman Says," *Minneapolis Star,* June 11, 1969, 8B.

73. Ron Way, "Mayor-Elect to Hold Conference with Naftalin," *Minneapolis Tribune,* June 11, 1969, 7A.

74. Jim Shoop, "Stenvig Picks Olson as Changeover Aide," *Minneapolis Star,* June 17, 1969, 4A.

75. Jim Shoop, "Stenvig Demands Respect," *Minneapolis Star,* June 20, 1969, 1A.

76. "Hard-Line Mayor Picks Ex-Convicts," *New York Times,* July 6, 1969, 28A.

77. Finlay Lewis, "Mayor Plays Drums during Festive Day," *Minneapolis Tribune,* July 8, 1969, 1A.

78. Text of Stenvig's Inaugural Speech, folder 1, box 1, Charles Stenvig Newspaper Clippings.

79. Stenvig Gets VIP Treatment in D.C., folder 1, box 1, Charles Stenvig Newspaper Clippings.

80. Police Pay-Aid Bid Defeated, folder 1, box 1, Charles Stenvig Newspaper Clippings.

81. Finlay Lewis, "LeVander Spurns Stenvig Call for Special Session," *Minneapolis Tribune,* December 17, 1969, 1A.

82. Finlay Lewis, "Stenvig Seeks Backing in Quest for Special Legislative Session," *Minneapolis Tribune,* December 18, 1969, 1A.

83. Finlay Lewis, "GOP Alderman Assails Stenvig," *Minneapolis Tribune,* January 9, 1970, 1A.

84. Ibid.

85. Stenvig Seeks End to Meeting Format, folder 1, box 1, Charles Stenvig Newspaper Clippings.

86. More Laud Than Assail Mayor, folder 1, box 1, Charles Stenvig Newspaper Clippings.

87. Lewis, "'Politician' or 'Guy Next Door,'" 12A.

88. Stenvig Story Inspires Movie Idea; Lee Marvin May Star, folder 1, box 1, Charles Stenvig Newspaper Clippings.

89. Mayoral Proclamations, Charles Stenvig Papers, folder "Mayoral Proclamations," box 1, Hennepin County Library, Minneapolis.

90. Seth King, "Stenvig Kept Policeman's Image during Moratorium Day Protest," *New York Times,* October 27, 1969, 2A.

91. "Stenvig Vetoes Peace Action Day Resolution," *Minneapolis Tribune,* September 21, 1971, 6C.

92. "Davis Chides Stenvig on U.N. Backing," *Minneapolis Tribune,* June 1, 1971, 8A.

93. "The First Year for Mayor Stenvig," *Minneapolis Tribune,* July 18, 1970, 4A.

94. Michael Fedo, "Minneapolis Mayor Called Tough Candidate," *Christian Science Monitor,* February 3, 1971, 3.

95. Davis, *Overcoming,* 149.

96. Ibid., 212.

97. Ibid., 205.

98. Ibid., 211.

99. Lewis, "'Politician' or 'Guy Next Door,'" 12A.

100. Dennis Cassano, "Labor Leaders Back Stenvig Election," *Minneapolis Tribune,* January 19, 1971, 1A.

101. "Labor Council Backs Stenvig for Reelection," *Minneapolis Tribune,* February 25, 1971, 6D.

102. Davis, *Overcoming,* 216.

103. Lewis, "'Politician' or 'Guy Next Door,'" 12A.

104. Dennis Cassano, "Davis to Seek Mayor's Job," *Minneapolis Tribune,* January 14, 1971, 1B.

105. Dennis Cassano, "Stenvig, Davis Win Primary for Mayor," *Minneapolis Tribune,* April 28, 1971, 1A.

106. Dennis Cassano, "GOP Candidate Is Financial Underdog in Mayoral Primary," *Minneapolis Tribune,* April 21, 1971, 13A.

107. Ibid.

108. Cassano, "Stenvig, Davis Win Primary for Mayor," 1A.

109. Ibid.

110. Dennis Cassano, "Davis Wonders If Campaign Is Worthwhile," *Minneapolis Tribune,* May 19, 1971, 1B.

111. Ibid.

112. Davis, *Overcoming,* 219.

113. Dennis Cassano, "City Voters to Judge Stenvig," *Minneapolis Tribune,* April 25, 1971, 8A.

114. Dennis Cassano, "Davis Claims Stenvig Condones Police Brutality," *Minneapolis Tribune,* May 6, 1971, 1B.

115. Greg Pinney, "Davis Brands Stenvig as Racist," *Minneapolis Tribune,* May 11, 1971, 1B.

116. Shellum, "The How and Why of the Minneapolis Vote," 13A.

117. Greg Pinney, "Mrs. Borea, Olson Win Posts on School Board," *Minneapolis Tribune,* June 9, 1971, 1B.

118. Davis, *Overcoming*, 206–7.

119. Eric Vanderpoel, "Stenvig Postpones Orient Tour until after Fall Election," *Minneapolis Tribune*, March 3, 1973, 1A.

120. Stenvig Will Debate Ethics of Orient Trip, folder 1, box 1, Charles Stenvig Newspaper Clippings.

121. Nick Coleman, "Labor Leaders Tell Why They Oppose Mayor," *Minneapolis Tribune*, July 5, 1973, 1A.

122. Ibid., 11A.

123. Ibid.

124. Nick Coleman, "Mayor," *Minneapolis Tribune*, November 7, 1974, 1A; Sam Newlund, "Hard-Line Busing Foes Lose School Election," *Minneapolis Tribune*, November 7, 1974, 4A; M. Howard Gelfand, "Mayor Stenvig May Have Lost Election because of Changing Political Climate," *Minneapolis Tribune*, November 7, 1973, 1B.

125. Nick Coleman, "Stenvig Quits as City Mayor 2 Days Early," *Minneapolis Tribune*, January 1, 1974, 1A.

126. Charles Stenvig, Another Recent GOP Convert Tests the Political Waters, folder 1, box 1, Charles Stenvig Newspaper Clippings.

127. Nick Coleman, "Stenvig Joins Republican Party in Minnesota," *Minneapolis Tribune*, February 13, 1974, 1A.

128. Nick Coleman, "DFL 'Machine' Spoils Stenvig's Comeback Hopes," *Minneapolis Tribune*, November 7, 1974, 8A.

129. Robert Guenther, "Stenvig Job-Offer Swirl Had DFL Dabbler at Center," *Minneapolis Star*, April 5, 1977, 1A.

130. Dennis Cassano and M. Howard Gelfand, "Stenvig May Quit for Right Offer," *Minneapolis Tribune*, March 3, 1976, 1A.

3. Too Big to Fail

1. "Jailed Farmer Tells of Fight for Grain," *New York Times*, May 19, 1982, 20A.

2. "U.S. Aides Warn Potential Buyers of Beans Repossessed by Farmers," *New York Times*, February 18, 1981, 26A.

3. "Farmers Protest Jailing in Soybean 'Liberation,'" *New York Times*, May 1, 1982, 12.

4. Andrew Malcolm, "New Midwest Protests Erupt over Problems on the Farm," *New York Times*, January 20, 1985, 16.

5. Ibid.

6. David Hackett Fischer, *Albion's Seed: Four British Folkways in America* (New York: Oxford University Press, 1989), 606.

7. David Hackett Fischer claims they settled the Old West, West Virginia, Kentucky and parts of Indiana and Illinois, and the central South, Tennessee, Missouri, Alabama, Mississippi, and Texas.

8. Fischer, *Albion's Seed*, 613–15. See also Walter Russell Mead, "The Jacksonian Tradition," *National Interest*, no. 58 (Winter 1999/2000): 5–29, available at http://denbeste.nu/external/Mead01.html.

9. Michael Kazin, *The Populist Persuasion* (Ithaca, NY: Cornell University Press, 1995), 2.

10. Mean, "The Jacksonian Tradition."

11. Alan Matusow, *The Unraveling of America: A History of Liberalism in the 1960s* (New York: Harper & Row, 1984), xiii.

12. Lane Kenworthy, Sondra Barringer, Daniel Duerr, and Garrett Andrew Schneider, "The Democrats and Working-Class Whites" (University of Arizona, 2007), available at http://www.u.arizona.edu/~lkenwor/thedemocratsandworking-classwhites.pdf.

13. "Is There Anything New about Neo-Populism?" *Bulletin of the American Academy of Arts and Sciences* 26, no. 6 (March 1973): 13.

14. Civic Club Happenings, folder 4, box 208, Fred R. Harris Collection, Congressional Archives, Carl Albert Congressional Research and Studies Center.

15. Harris Called "Bright, New Star" in Senate, folder 10, box 212, Fred R. Harris Collection.

16. Ibid.

17. Michael McGerr, *A Fierce Discontent: The Rise and Fall of the Progressive Movement in America, 1870–1920* (New York: Free Press, 2003), 159.

18. Ellis Hawley, *The Great War and the Search for a Modern Order: A History of the American People and Their Institutions, 1917–1933* (New York: St. Martin's, 1979), 120.

19. Ellis Hawley, *The New Deal and the Problem of Monopoly: A Study in Economic Ambivalence* (Princeton, NJ: Princeton University Press, 1966), 12.

20. Ibid., 472.

21. Matusow, *The Unraveling of America*, 33.

22. Anne Hodges Morgan, *Robert S. Kerr: The Senate Years* (Norman: University of Oklahoma Press, 1977), 3.

23. Donald Janson, "Wilkinson Wins Oklahoma Race," *New York Times*, May 6, 1964, 21A.

24. "Wilkinson Eyes Shift in Career," *New York Times*, January 4, 1964, 17A.

25. "Wilkinson Resigns as Johnson Adviser," *New York Times*, January 30, 1964, 14A.

26. Austin Wehrwein, "Wilkinson Stand: He Is 'Oklahoman,'" *New York Times*, February 9, 1964, 56A.

27. "Oklahoma Vote Won by Johnson," *New York Times*, November 4, 1964, 20A.

28. Fred R. Harris, the Man, His Record, folder 4, box 208, Fred R. Harris Collection; "One Hundred Hours of Presiding over the Senate," *Congressional Record* (August 24, 1965), 39th Cong., 1st sess., 111, pt. 16:21538; *Congressional Record—Senate* (March 2, 1968), folder 10, box 212, Fred R. Harris Collection.

29. US Senator Fred R. Harris (March 1967), folder 12, box 285, Fred R. Harris Collection; 10 Outstanding Young Men of 1965, folder 10, box 212, Fred R. Harris Collection.

30. News Release (January 15, 1969), folder 4, box 208, Fred R. Harris Collection.

31. They Communicate in Comanche, folder 9, box 286, Fred R. Harris Collection.

32. LaDonna Harris . . . Radical Indian, folder 9, box 286, Fred R. Harris Collection.

33. Senator Harris's LaDonna, folder 9, box 286, Fred R. Harris Collection.

34. University of South Dakota Compilation of Roll Call Votes, 1968, folder 28, box 160, Fred R. Harris Collection.

35. "Harris to Support Request for More Vietnam Troops," *The Oklahoman* (Oklahoma City), July 16, 1967, 10; Allan Cromley, "Sooners Stay Close to LBJ," *The Oklahoman* (Oklahoma City), December 31, 1967, 8.

36. Otis Sullivan, "Critics of LBJ Haven't Turned against Harris," *The Oklahoman* (Oklahoma City), September 17, 1966, 35.

37. U.S. Congress, "Vietnam—Speech of Senator Harris Before the State Convention of the Oklahoma Bankers Association," *Congressional Record—Senate* (May 7, 1965), 89th Cong., 1st sess., 111:11461; "Congress Leaders Support Johnson," *New York Times*, May 4, 1965, 21A; Richard Lowitt, *Fred Harris: His Journey from Liberalism to Populism* (Lanham, MD: Rowman & Littlefield, 2002), 9.

38. "Harris Cites New Problems," *The Oklahoman* (Oklahoma City), January 6, 1967, 3.

39. Alan Cromley, "Harris Appeals to Highbrows," *The Oklahoman* (Oklahoma City), June 25, 1967, 18.

40. Fred Harris, *Potomac Fever* (New York: Norton, 1977), 108.

41. *Congressional Record—Senate* (March 2, 1968), folder 10, box 212, Fred R. Harris Collection.

42. Rowland Evans and Robert Novak, "Harris Meets Deep Hatred," *The Oklahoman* (Oklahoma City), November 18, 1967, 10.

43. Harris Tours Atlanta Slums, folder 6, box 224, Fred R. Harris Collection.

44. In the Summer of 1967, folder 6, box 224, Fred R. Harris Collection.

45. Fred Harris: Young Senator in a Hurry, folder 33, box 160, Fred R. Harris Collection.

46. Lowitt, *Fred Harris*, 96.

47. Allan Cromley, "'New Populism': Harris Slogan for Democrats," *The Oklahoman* (Oklahoma City), December 31, 1969, 3.

48. "Harris to Support Request for More Vietnam Troops," 10.

49. "Harris Urges Protest Day," *The Oklahoman* (Oklahoma City), October 4, 1969, 1.

50. Letter from Beulah Attebery to Fred Harris (n.d.), folder 1, box 167, Fred R. Harris Collection; Allan Cromley, "Albert Assails Vietnam Views of Senator Harris," *The Oklahoman* (Oklahoma City), October 10, 1969, 1, and "Harris Steers Clear of New Peace Rallies," *The Oklahoman* (Oklahoma City), November 6, 1969, 1.

51. "Fred Hails Protests; Spiro Raps 'Snobs,'" *Oklahoma Journal* (Oklahoma City), October 20, 1969; "Agnew Says Democrats Embrace Radicalism," folder 26, box 215, Fred R. Harris Collection.

52. Press Release: Use My Exact Press Which You Should Get from Jim (October 15, 1970), folder 16, box 215, Fred R. Harris Collection; Dellums for Congress: Thank You Letter to Harris (n.d.), folder 26, box 215, Fred R. Harris Collection; Senator Harris Backs Negro Candidate: Paper Explains Agnew Blast, folder 26, box 215, Fred R. Harris Collection; Letter from Joseph Hull to Fred Harris (October 21, 1970), box 215, folder 26, Fred R. Harris Collection.

53. "Present Voters Harder to Fool," *The Oklahoman* (Oklahoma City), January 26, 1970, 10.

54. Jim Jackson, "State Harrises Give Variety of Opinions," *The Oklahoman* (Oklahoma City), May 26, 1970, 52.

55. Hot under the Blue Collar, folder 10, box 220, Fred R. Harris Collection.

56. Walter Rugaber, "Hecklers Disrupt Talks by Wallace," *New York Times*, October 2, 1968, 28.

57. C. Vann Woodward, "The Ghost of Populism Walks Again," *Sunday New York Times Magazine*, June 4, 1972, 22.

58. Harris: Would Face Wallace in Florida, folder 9, box 286, Fred R. Harris Collection; Fred Harris, *The New Populism* (New York: Saturday Review Press, 1972), 10.

59. News Release: Harris President '72 (September 22, 1971), folder 15, box 249, Fred R. Harris Collection; Uses Dad as Example: Harris Sees Coalition Electing Him in '72, folder 5, box 288, Fred R. Harris Collection.

60. Richard Goldstein, "Earl L. Butz, Secretary Felled by Racial Remark, Is Dead at 98," *New York Times*, February 4, 2008.

61. William Blair, "Senate Will Vote on Butz Today; His Confirmation Is Held Likely," *New York Times*, December 2, 1971, 39.

62. James Risser and George Anthan, "Why They Love Earl Butz," *New York Times*, June 13, 1976, 195.

63. Timothy Noah, "Earl Butz, History's Victim," *Slate*, February 4, 2008, at http://www.slate.com/articles/news_and_politics/chatterbox/2008/02/earl_butz_historys_victim.html.

64. Fred Harris Speech to National Farmers Organization (n.d.), folder 18, box 271, Fred R. Harris Collection.

65. Immediate Release: Senate Resolution 463 (November 17, 1970), folder 42, box 215, Fred R. Harris Collection.

66. "The Farm Revolution—II," *New York Times*, December 28, 1971, 28.

67. B. Drummond Ayres Jr., "Rise of Corporate Farming a Worry to Rural America," *New York Times*, December 5, 1971, 1.

68. Letter from Mrs. Carl Avery to Fred Harris (n.d.), folder 22, box 224, Fred R. Harris Collection.

69. "Harris Attacks Big Farmers' Trust 'Break,'" *The Oklahoman* (Oklahoma City), December 15, 1972, 111.

70. U.S. Senate Memorandum, Family Farm Act, folder 57, box 242, Fred R. Harris Collection.

71. Allan Cromley, "Harris Building Absence Record," *The Oklahoman* (Oklahoma City), October 3, 1971, 12.

72. Shed Fred: GOP Urges, folder 1, box 248, Fred R. Harris Collection.

73. "Harris, Lindsey Have Common Woe," *The Oklahoman* (Oklahoma City), July 30, 1971, 12.

74. Allan Cromley, "Status in State No Bar to Bid, Harris Says," *The Oklahoman* (Oklahoma City), August 18, 1971, 40.

75. Statement of US Senator Fred R. Harris at Press Conference: Harris President 72 News (September 24, 1971), folder 21, box 241, Fred R. Harris Collection.

76. Rowland Evans and Robert Novak, "Fred Lightens Load for Race," *The Oklahoman* (Oklahoma City), July 12, 1971, 10.

77. Harris Campaign Off to Unorthodox Start, by Loye Miller, folder 22, box

288, Fred R. Harris Collection; Harris President '72 News: Sam Brown (October 24, 1971), folder 13, box 289, Fred R. Harris Collection.

78. John Reilly, "Harris: Radical Approach to Big Business," *The Hurricane* (Miami, FL), October 1, 1971, 5.

79. Harris President '72 News (September 22, 1971), folder 15, box 249, Fred R. Harris Collection.

80. Gene Smith, "Auto Maker Plans to Offer Dividend Investing Plan," *New York Times*, May 20, 1972, 39.

81. Statement of Senator Fred R. Harris (February 3, 1972), folder 45, box 271, Fred R. Harris Collection.

82. From the Desk of Senator Fred R. Harris (January 21, 1972), folder 2, box 271, Fred R. Harris Collection; Remarks of US Senator Fred R. Harris, to Midwest Electric Consumer's Association (n.d.), folder 17, box 271, Fred R. Harris Collection.

83. Michael O'Brien, *Philip Hart: The Conscience of the Senate* (East Lansing: Michigan State University Press, 1995), 1.

84. Hart Bill Aims at Monopolies, folder 4, box 262, Fred R. Harris Collection.

85. 200 Visit Headquarters, folder 35, box 288, Fred R. Harris Collection.

86. Sen. Fred Harris: The Candidate, by Garry Wills, folder 18, box 289, Fred R. Harris Collection.

87. John R. Barry, "'Modern Florida' to Harris' Liking," *Jacksonville Journal*, August 26, 1971, 29.

88. So This Is Washington, by Ethel Payne, folder 25, box 288, Fred R. Harris Collection.

89. Harris Scouts Race Support for Primaries, folder 35, box 288, Fred R. Harris Collection.

90. Allan Cromley, "Harris Tackles Prisoner Issue," *The Oklahoman* (Oklahoma City), September 9, 1971, 1.

91. Statement of US Senator Fred R. Harris (n.d.), folder 23, box 249, Fred R. Harris Collection; Money Still Talks: NYT Article by Tom Wicker, folder 5, box 288, Fred R. Harris Collection.

92. Fred Harris, "The Easy Chair: The Frog Hair Problem," *Harpers*, May 1972, 15.

93. Ibid., 16.

94. David Broder, "Populism's Popularity," *Washington Post*, March 28, 1972, 19A.

95. Ibid.; The Platform Committee Decision (June 26, 1972), folder 43, box 271, Fred R. Harris Collection.

96. Allan Cromley, "Sen. Harris, Wearing Mustache, Longer Hair, Lists Future Plans," *The Oklahoman* (Oklahoma City), January 15, 1972, 17.

97. Harris Wants to Be Another Ralph Nader, folder 36, box 288, Fred R. Harris Collection.

98. Harris Hits Finance Committee as Roadblock to Tax Reform, folder 13, box 271, Fred R. Harris Collection.

99. Tax Action Campaign Fund-Raising Letter, folder 5, box 287, Fred R. Harris Collection.

100. David Broder, "Getting Returns from Tax Gripes," *Washington Post*, April 8, 1973.

101. Has the Fight Gone Out of the U.S. Tax Revolt? by Clayton Fritchey, folder 12, box 305, Fred R. Harris Collection.

102. Ibid.

103. Major Lenders to Date on Tax Action Day, folder 3, box 287, Fred R. Harris Collection.

104. William Raspberry, "Fred Harris: Crusading for Tax Reform," *Washington Post,* January 31, 1973, 19A.

105. A Taxing Bluegrass Affair, folder 12, box 305, Fred R. Harris Collection.

106. Janet Battalie, "West Virginia," *New York Times,* November 5, 2000, 47.

4. Good Intentions, Bad Results

1. Paul Coppock, "The Men Who Balanced the Powers That Be," *Memphis Commercial Appeal,* July 29, 1979, G7; Bernard Grofman, "Criteria for Districting: A Social Science Perspective," *UCLA Law Review* 33 (October 1985): 1; Stephen Ansolabehere and James Snyder, *The End of Inequality: One Person, One Vote and the Transformation of American Politics* (New York: Norton, 2008), 2.

2. David Brady and Douglas Edmonds, "One Man, One Vote—So What?" *Trans-Action* 4 (1967): 41.

3. Ansolabehere and Snyder, *The End of Inequality,* 3.

4. Brady and Edmonds, "One Man, One Vote," 43.

5. Ansolabehere and Snyder, *The End of Inequality,* 3.

6. Bruce Cain, Karin MacDonal, and Michael McDonald, "From Equality to Fairness: The Path of Political Reform since *Baker v. Carr*" (paper prepared for the Brookings Institution/Institute of Governmental Studies Conference "Competition, Partisanship, and Congressional Redistricting," Washington, DC, April 16, 2004), 4.

7. Ansolabehere and Snyder, *The End of Inequality,* 10–12.

8. Brady and Edmonds, "One Man, One Vote," 43.

9. David Lublin, "Racial Redistricting and African American Representation: A Critique of 'Do Majority Minority Districts Maximize Substantive Black Representation in Congress'?" *American Political Science Review* 93, no. 1 (March 1999): 186; Kevin Hill, "Does the Creation of Majority Black Districts Aid Republicans? An Analysis of the 1992 Congressional Elections in Eight Southern States," *Journal of Politics* 57, no. 2 (May 1995): 384.

10. Nick Kotz, *Judgment Days: Lyndon Johnson, Martin Luther King, Jr., and the Laws That Changed America* (New York: Houghton Mifflin, 2005), 154.

11. Kevin Hill and Nicol Rae, "What Happened to the Democrats in the South? US House Elections, 1992–96," *Party Politics* 6, no. 5 (2000): 6–7.

12. David Lublin and Stephen Voss, "The Missing Middle: Why Median-Voter Theory Can't Save Democrats from Singing the Boll-Weevil Blues," *Journal of Politics* 65, no. 1 (February 2003): 227; Bernard Grofman, Robert Griffin, and Amihai Glazer, "The Effect of Black Population on Electing Democrats and Liberals to the House of Representatives," *Legislative Studies Quarterly* 17, no. 3 (August 1992): 374–75, and "Racial Redistricting and Realignment in Southern State Legislatures," *American Journal of Political Science* 44, no. 4 (October 2000): 805; Charles Bullock, "Redistricting and Changes in the Partisan and Racial Composition of Southern Legislatures," *State and Local Government Review* 19 (Spring 1987): 66.

13. Sharon Wright, *Race, Power, and Political Emergence in Memphis* (New York: Garland, 2000), 89.

14. "The Memphis Strike," *New York Times,* April 9, 1968, 46.

15. Fred Graham, "High Court Say Memphis Schools Must Integrate," *New York Times,* March 10, 1970, 1; "Memphis Residents Are Split by the 'Magic Circle,'" *New York Times,* September 8, 1970, 33; Evan Jenkins, "School Conflict in the South Is Intensifying," *New York Times,* August 19, 1973, 48; "Memphis Schools Facing Loss of Pupils in Bus Order," *New York Times,* August 24, 1973, 40.

16. George Vecsey, "2 Memphis Boys Hopeful on Inquiry," *New York Times,* October 23, 1971, 25.

17. "9 Lawmen Charged in Death of Black Memphis Youth," *New York Times,* December 10, 1971, 31; "Memphis Store Is Fire-Bombed during Negro Youth's Funeral," *New York Times,* October 20, 1971, 38.

18. Recognition Banquet Honoring the N. J. Ford Family, Sponsored by Greater Prospect Baptist Church, folder "Personal," box 55, Harold Ford Sr. Papers, University of Memphis, Mississippi Valley Special Collections.

19. Bill Terry, "Nun, Mortician Vie in Tenn. Hill Race," *Washington Post,* August 1, 1974, 12A; John Lewis, "New Ford in Congress," *Chicago Defender,* December 28, 1974, 12B.

20. Harold Ford's Nomination to the Jaycees, folder "Memphis Jaycees Man of the Year," box 45, Harold Ford Sr. Papers.

21. "An Unexpected Race," *Memphis Commercial Appeal,* October 23, 1970, folder "Harold Ford Sr.," Harold Ford Sr. Newspaper Clippings, Memphis City Library's Newspaper Clippings Collection, Memphis and Shelby County Room.

22. Null Adams, "Harold Ford Had to Beat Same Man Twice," *Memphis Press-Scimitar,* November 25, 1970, folder "Harold Ford Sr.," Harold Ford Sr. Newspaper Clippings.

23. Ibid.

24. Harold Ford: Majority Leader, folder 18, box 6, Harold Ford Sr. Papers; Lewis, "New Ford in Congress," 12B.

25. Constituent Letter to Kuykendall: Busing (December 20, 1971), folder "Department of HEW," box 6, Dan Kuykendall Papers, University of Memphis, Mississippi Valley Special Collections; House Joint Resolution 981, 92nd Cong., 1st Sess., folder 93, box "Bills Introduced in 92nd Congress," Dan Kuykendall Papers.

26. *Memphis Commercial Appeal* News Story, June 16, 1966, Dan Kuykendall Clippings File, Memphis City Library's Newspaper Clippings Collection.

27. "Kuykendall Urges All-Out Bombing of Vietnam," *Memphis Press-Scimitar,* April 25, 1967, Dan Kuykendall Clippings File; "Kuykendall Proposes 'Rice War' to Starve Vietnamese Reds into Peace Talks," *Memphis Commercial Appeal,* January 23, 1967, Dan Kuykendall Clippings File; "Kuykendall Lashes Rescue Try Critics," *Memphis Press-Scimitar,* November 25, 1970, Dan Kuykendall Clippings File.

28. Kuykendall Admits "Closed Mind" on Question of Impeachment, Dan Kuykendall Clippings File; Brown Allen Flynn, "Nixon Quizzes Kuykendall: Do They Want to Pick Carcass?" *Memphis Press-Scimitar,* August 1974, 1; Thomas Bevier, "A Strange, Historic Day Has Overcast Sky, Leaden Hearts," *Memphis Commercial Appeal,* August 9, 1974, 1.

29. Michael Barone, Grant Ujifusa, and Douglas Matthews, *The Almanac of American Politics: 1972* (Boston: Gambit, 1972), 774.

30. Kay Pittman Black, "Election Suit Challenges District Lines," *Memphis Press-Scimitar,* July 3, 1974, 1, and "Briefs Charge Election Board 'Deliberately' Moved Boundaries to Aid Kuykendall," *Memphis Press-Scimitar,* July 25, 1974, 8.

31. Black, "Briefs Charge Election Board 'Deliberately' Moved Boundaries," 8; "Kuykendall to Push for Redistricting," *Memphis Press-Scimitar,* October 23, 1972, 17; "A Black Runs in Tennessee," *New York Times,* April 18, 1972, 41.

32. Wayne Trotter, "The 'Get Dan Kuykendall' Bill May Not," *Memphis Commercial Appeal,* March 16, 1974, 1; William Bennett, "Senate Override of Dunn Veto Imperils Kuykendall Bastion," *Memphis Commercial Appeal,* March 14, 1974, 1; Black, "Briefs Charge Election Board 'Deliberately' Moved Boundaries," 8.

33. "Judges Refuse Primaries Halt," *Memphis Commercial Appeal,* July 27, 1974, 23; "Rep. Ford Opens Race against Kuykendall," *Memphis Press-Scimitar,* April 22, 1973, Harold Ford Clippings File, Memphis Room, Memphis Public Library.

34. Terry, "Nun, Mortician Vie in Tenn. Hill Race," 12A.

35. V. O. Key Jr., *Southern Politicians in State and Nation* (New York: Random House, 1949), 59–61.

36. "E. H. Crump Is Dead: Political Boss Was 80," *New York Times,* October 17, 1954, 1; William D. Miller, *Mr. Crump of Memphis* (Baton Rouge: Louisiana University Press, 1964), 101; G. Wayne Dowdy, *Mayor Crump Don't Like It: Machine Politics in Memphis* (Oxford: University of Mississippi Press, 2006).

37. The Following Community Leaders Are among Those Who Support Harold Ford for Congress, folder "Press Clippings," box 29, Harold Ford Sr. Papers; Art Gilliam, "A Different Ford," folder "Press Clippings," box 29, Harold Ford Sr. Papers.

38. Beth Tamke, "Ford, Kuykendall Trade Barbs at Lunch," *Memphis Commercial Appeal,* October 6, 1974, 3.

39. Haynes Johnson, "Nixon's the One Hurting the GOP," *Washington Post,* October 27, 1974, 1C.

40. Ibid.

41. Oral History Interview: Harold Ford (August 19, 1974), p. 39, University of North Carolina Libraries, Southern Historical Collection at the Louis Round Wilson Special Collections Library, Chapel Hill, NC.

42. Alex Poinsett Article on Ford Family (n.d.), folder "Press Clippings," box 29, Harold Ford Sr. Papers.

43. Joseph Weiler, "Vote Count Proved an Upset," *Memphis Commercial Appeal,* November 7, 1974, 1.

44. "Ford in Congress," *Dawn Magazine,* December 14, 1974, 12; Alex Poinsett Article on Ford Family (n.d.), folder "Press Clippings," box 29, Harold Ford Sr. Papers; Lynn Lewis, "Harold Ford Stuns Kuykendall; Robin Beard Beats Schaeffer," *Memphis Press-Scimitar,* November 6, 1974, 1.

45. Jim Will and Tim Wyngaard, "Kuykendall Says He Will Not Run in '76," *Memphis Press-Scimitar,* November 7, 1974, page obscured.

46. Alex Poinsett Article on Ford Family (n.d.), folder "Press Clippings," box 29, Harold Ford Sr. Papers.

47. Ibid.

48. Weiler, "Vote Count Proved an Upset," 1.

49. "Ford's Win Sparks Scenes Reminiscent of '60s—without Anger," *Memphis Commercial Appeal*, November 6, 1974, Harold Ford Press Clippings, Memphis Room, Memphis Public Library.

50. "Minorities in Big Win," *Chicago Defender*, November 7, 1974, 4; Thomas Bevier, "Harold Ford: An Inevitable Change," *Memphis Commercial Appeal*, November 13, 1974, 7A.

51. Jack Bass and Walter DeVries, *The Transformation of Southern Politics: Social Change and Political Consequence since 1945* (Athens: University of Georgia Press, 1995), 298.

52. Tim Wyngaard, "A Commentary: A Look at His First Year," *Memphis Press-Scimitar*, folder "Harold Ford Sr.," Harold Ford Sr. Newspaper Clippings.

53. Tim Wyngaard, "Harold Ford Assesses Impact on Washington," *Memphis Press-Scimitar*, folder "Harold Ford Sr.," Harold Ford Sr. Newspaper Clippings; Letter from Barry Sussman on New Member Survey (n.d.), folder "Voting Record," box 27, Harold Ford Sr. Papers.

54. Memo from Norman Mineta to 94th Freshmen Class Democrats, folder "Freshmen Class," box 30, Harold Ford Sr. Papers.

55. Tim Wyngaard, "Freshman Congressman Ford Has Climbed Ladder Quickly," *Memphis Press-Scimitar*, folder "Harold Ford Sr.," Harold Ford Sr. Newspaper Clippings.

56. News Release: Congressman Harold Ford, folder "Ways and Means Election," box 43, Harold Ford Sr. Papers.

57. Ford's Citizen Advisory Committee, folder "Citizen Advisory Committee," box 29, Harold Ford Sr. Papers; Michael Lollar's Article: Ford Turns Down Banker's Gift, folder "Press Clippings," box 29, Harold Ford Sr. Papers; "Ford's Ethical Stand," *Memphis Commercial Appeal*, January 8, 1975, 6.

58. Representative Ford Seeks Reduction in Government Owned Limousines, folder "Harold Ford Sr.," Harold Ford Sr. Newspaper Clippings.

59. Morris Cunningham and A. B. Albritton, "Harold Ford Keeps Promises, Rates High," *Memphis Commercial Appeal*, January 5, 1976, 17.

60. Letter from Harold Ford to Ray Blanton (February 7, 1975), folder "Memphis—February 1975," box 24, Harold Ford Sr. Papers.

61. Henry Mitchell, "A Symbolic Gathering of Political Power," *Washington Post*, January 5, 1977, 2B; Michael Lollar, "District Realignment by Panel Strengthens Hold of Beard, Ford," *Memphis Commercial Appeal*, March 26, 1976, 1A; Joseph Weller, "Harold Ford, Bear Triumph," *Memphis Commercial Appeal*, November 3, 1976, 1A.

62. A. B. Albritton, "Harold, among Others, Is Pleased with Ford," *Memphis Commercial Appeal*, January 22, 1978, 1; Terry Keeter, "Ford War Chest Gets Ammunition," *Memphis Commercial Appeal*, August 31, 1979, folder "Harold Ford Sr.," Harold Ford Sr. Newspaper Clippings; Clark Porteous, "All Areas of Memphis Politics Represented at Fund-Raiser," *Memphis Press-Scimitar*, November 11, 1977, folder "Press Clippings," box 29, Harold Ford Sr. Papers.

63. Clark Porteous, "Politics Today: 800 Attend Ford Holiday Party," *Memphis Press-Scimitar*, December 21, 1979, 11.

64. Otis Sanford, "Baldwin Testifies He Handed Campaign Donation to Ford," *Memphis Commercial Appeal,* September 21, 1979, 15.

65. Anne McDonald, "Extortion Trial Witness Tells of Giving Money to Ford," *Memphis Press-Scimitar,* September 20, 1979, 1.

66. Ibid.

67. Peggy Burch, "Insurer Claims Emmitt Ford Had 34 Policies on His Wife," *Memphis Press-Scimitar,* November 11, 1978, 1; Leroy Williams, "Emmitt Ford, Wife Convicted of Conspiracy, Mail Fraud," *Memphis Commercial Appeal,* November 8, 1980, 1; Otis Sanford, "Fraud Charges Levied against Emmitt Ford," *Memphis Commercial Appeal,* March 28, 1980, 1.

68. David Rapp, "Rep. Ford, Wife Are Convicted," *Memphis Press-Scimitar,* November 7, 1980, 1.

69. Otis Sanford, "Fine, Prison Term Given Emmitt Ford," *Memphis Commercial Appeal,* January 15, 1981, 1.

70. Ibid.; Ruth Ingram, "Ford Backed Campaign for Brother's Release," *Memphis Press-Scimitar,* August 11, 1982, 1.

71. "Wellford Picked for Judgeship," *Memphis Press-Scimitar,* November 24, 1970, folder "Harold Ford Sr.," Harold Ford Sr. Newspaper Clippings; "Swearing Set for Jan. 13 for Wellford," *Memphis Press-Scimitar,* December 19, 1970, folder "Harold Ford Sr.," Harold Ford Sr. Newspaper Clippings; Charles Thornton, "Civil Rights Group Fights Nomination of Wellford," *Memphis Press-Scimitar,* August 8, 1976, folder "Harold Ford Sr.," Harold Ford Sr. Newspaper Clippings; Louis Graham, "Events Clear Judicial Path for Wellford," *Memphis Commercial Appeal,* August 4, 1982, 1.

72. "Rough Sailing Predicted for Wellford's Bid," *Memphis Press-Scimitar,* September 2, 1976, folder "Harry Wellford Press Clippings," Harold Ford Sr. Newspaper Clippings.

73. "Wellford Supported for Appeals Court," *Memphis Commercial Appeal,* May 25, 1982, folder "Harry Wellford," Harold Ford Sr. Newspaper Clippings.

74. Louis Graham, "Wellford Cuts Year Off Ford Sentence," *Memphis Commercial Appeal,* August 4, 1982, 1.

75. "Wellford's Decision," *Memphis Commercial Appeal,* August 4, 1982, 6.

76. Graham, "Events Clear Judicial Path for Wellford," 1; "Wellford Clears All Hurdles," *Memphis Press-Scimitar,* August 21, 1982, folder "Harry Wellford," Harold Ford Sr. Newspaper Clippings.

77. Graham, "Wellford Cuts Year Off Ford Sentence," 4.

78. Louis Graham, "Ford Accused of Pressuring U.S. Official," *Memphis Commercial Appeal,* September 14, 1982, 11.

79. Ibid.; Louis Graham, "Disbar Ewing for Comment, Ford Will Ask," *Memphis Commercial Appeal,* September 18, 1982, Harold Ford Sr. Newspaper Clippings.

80. Wendell Potter, "GOP Targets Harold Ford as 'Vulnerable' in 1978," *Memphis Press-Scimitar,* Harold Ford Sr. Newspaper Clippings.

81. Johnson, "Nixon's the One Hurting the GOP."

82. "Mayor's Victory Bruises Memphis' Ford Family," *Washington Post,* October 8, 1983, 2A.

83. Thomas Jordan and Terry Keeter, "Ford's Strength Is Doubted but Unchallenged," *Memphis Commercial Appeal,* February 8, 1984, 1B; "Mayor's Victory Bruises Memphis' Ford Family," 2A.

84. Jordan and Keeter, "Ford's Strength Is Doubted," 1B.

85. Thomas Lippman, "Wallace Easily Sweeps Back to Power," *Washington Post*, November 3, 1982, 27A.

86. Roy Reed, "Wallace Redux," *New York Times*, November 6, 1982, 27; Lippman, "Wallace Easily Sweeps Back to Power," 27A.

87. Adam Clymer, "Mississippi Loss: 2 Warnings for G.O.P.," *New York Times*, Voting Rights Act Materials I, OA 5102, Ed Meese Papers, Ronald Reagan Presidential Foundation and Library.

88. Richard Cohen, "Will the VRA Become a Victim of Its Own Success," *National Journal*, August 1, 1981, 1366.

89. Ibid.

90. "South Is a Glum Belt for G.O.P.," *New York Times*, November 7, 1982, 197.

91. Howard Ball, "Racial Vote Dilution," *Publius*, Fall 1986, 30; Bernard Grofman and Lisa Handley, "The Impact of the VRA on Black Representation in Southern State Legislatures," *Legislative Studies Quarterly* 16, no. 1 (February 1991): 112.

92. Abigail Thernstrom, *Voting Rights—and Wrongs: The Elusive Quest for Racially Fair Elections* (Washington, DC: American Enterprise Institute Press, 2009), 4.

93. Ibid., 6.

94. Ibid., 7.

95. Stephen Lawson, *In Pursuit of Power* (New York: Columbia University Press, 1985), 160–61.

96. Ibid., 160–61.

97. Ibid., 281.

98. Ibid., 265.

99. "110 Years of Voting Rights Legislation," *Congressional Quarterly Weekly Report*, April 11, 1981, 635.

100. Robert Pear, "Congress Begins Fight over Extension of VRA," *New York Times*, April 8, 1981, 10A.

101. Bert Robinson, "Edwards' Long Fight against Bias," *San Jose Mercury News*, June 6, 1991, 8A.

102. Abigail Thernstrom, *Whose Votes Count? Affirmative Action and Minority Voting Rights* (Cambridge, MA: Harvard University Press, 1989), 80–81.

103. Ibid.

104. Robert Pear, "Campaign to Extend VRA Gains Support," *New York Times*, July 2, 1981, 17D.

105. Steven Roberts, "One Congressman Finds Pragmatism," *New York Times*, July 19, 1981, 15; David Michael Hudson, *Along Racial Lines: Consequences of the 1965 VRA* (New York: Peter Lang, 1998), 41.

106. Robert Pear, "Conversations: Don Edwards; A Champion of Civil Liberties Lays Down His Lance," *New York Times*, April 3, 1994.

107. Ibid.

108. Ibid.

109. Roberts, "One Congressman Finds Pragmatism," 15.

110. Pear, "Campaign to Extend VRA Gains Support."

111. Lee Lescase and Spencer Rich, "Reagan Favors VRA Extension," *Washington Post*, August 6, 1981, Voting Rights Act Materials I, OA 5102, Ed Meese Papers.

112. The Baron Report, no. 125: Voting Rights and Political Risks (May 25, 1981), p. 1, Voting Rights Act Materials I, OA 5101, Ed Meese Papers; Reagan Wants All States under VRA, Voting Rights Act Materials I, OA 5102, Ed Meese Papers; Reagan Dodges Voting Rights Issues, by Lou Cannon, Voting Rights Act Materials I, OA 5102, Ed Meese Papers.

113. The Baron Report, no. 125: Voting Rights and Political Risks (May 25, 1981), p. 1, Voting Rights Act Materials I, OA 5101, Ed Meese Papers; Clymer, "Mississippi Loss."

114. William French Smith, "VRA: Extend It as Is," *Washington Post*, March 29, 1982, Michael Uhlmann Files, Voting Rights Act Materials, OA 9439, Ed Meese Papers; Memo from Michael Uhlmann to Ed Meese (October 16, 1981), pp. 1–2, Voting Rights Act Materials I, OA 5102, Ed Meese Papers.

115. Steven Roberts, "President Backs Bipartisan Plan on Voting Law," *New York Times*, May 4, 1982, 1A.

116. David Lublin, *The Paradox of Representation* (Princeton, NJ: Princeton University Press, 1999), 3.

117. Seth McKee, *Republican Ascendancy in Southern U.S. House Elections* (Boulder, CO: Westview, 2009), 72–73.

118. Merle Black, "The Transformation of the Southern Democratic Party," *Journal of Politics* 66, no. 4 (November 2004): 1006.

119. R. W. Apple, "Delivering the South," *New York Times*, November 30, 1986, 274.

120. Robin Toner, "Southern Democrats' Decline Is Eroding the Political Center," *New York Times*, November 15, 2004, 1A.

121. Black quoted in ibid., 18A.

122. Robert Pear, "Redistricting Expected to Bring Surge in Minority Lawmakers," *New York Times*, August 3, 1992, 14A.

123. Bobby Lovett, *The Civil Rights Movement in Tennessee: A Narrative History* (Knoxville: University of Tennessee Press, 2005), 310–11.

124. Edward Walsh, "House Republicans Bask in the Glow of Population Shift to Sun Belt," *Washington Post*, July 5, 1981, 8A.

125. Gregg Gordon, "Black Votes Push Ford to Landslide," *Memphis Commercial Appeal*, November 7, 1984, 1.

126. Terry Keeter, "9th District Considered Ford Area," *Memphis Commercial Appeal*, August 8, 1986, 6A.

127. "Rep. Ford Indicted; Says He Will Fight Charges," *Jet* 72, no. 7 (May 11, 1987): 4.

128. Richard Powelson, "25–0 Vote Puts Ford over Subcommittee," *Memphis Press-Scimitar*, September 23, 1981, folder "Harold Ford Sr.," Harold Ford Sr. Newspaper Clippings.

129. Jimmie Covington, "Ford Family Gained Clout in Early 1970s," *Memphis Commercial Appeal*, April 25, 1987, 2C; James Brosnan, "No Apologies," *Memphis Commercial Appeal*, April 21, 1996, 5B; Clifford Krauss, "The Class of '74," *New York Times*, April 18, 1992, 1A.

130. Lewis Nolan, "Tangled Finances Shroud Ford Empire," *Memphis Commercial Appeal*, November 1, 1983, 1.

131. Howard Kurtz, "Tennessee Rep. Ford Indicted on Tax, Bank Fraud Charges," *Washington Post*, April 25, 1987, 10A.

132. Ibid.

133. Lela Garlington, "Company Shuttled Loans of Rep. Ford, Says Barr," *Memphis Commercial Appeal*, August 3, 1986, 1B.

134. John Branston, "Jury in Rep. Ford's Retrial Define What Is a Loan or Bribe," *Washington Post*, March 7, 1993, 20A.

135. Garlington, "Company Shuttled Loans," 1B.

136. Ibid.; Kurtz, "Tennessee Rep. Ford Indicted," 10A.

137. Branston, "Jury in Rep. Ford's Retrial," 20A.

138. Garlington, "Company Shuttled Loans," 1B; Kurtz, "Tennessee Rep. Ford Indicted," 10A.

139. Lela Garlington, "Ford Indicted on Fraud Counts," *Memphis Commercial Appeal*, April 25, 1987, 1A.

140. William Raspberry, "Harold Ford's Side," *Washington Post*, June 3, 1987, 19A; Michael Barone and Grant Ujifusa, *The Almanac of American Politics: 1994* (Boston: Gambit, 1994), 1197.

141. Garlington, "Ford Indicted on Fraud Counts," 1A.

142. Ibid.

143. Michael Barone and Grant Ujifusa, *The Almanac of American Politics: 1992* (Boston: Gambit, 1992), 1168.

144. Branston, "Jury in Rep. Ford's Retrial," 20A.

145. Kenneth Cooper, "Justice Dept. Backs Ford Request to Dismiss Nearly All-White Jury," *Washington Post*, February 20, 1993, 3A.

146. Ronald Smothers, "Lawmaker's Trial Is Entwined with Racial Issues," *New York Times*, February 28, 1993, 22.

147. "Supreme Court Clears Way for Rep. Ford Retrial," *Washington Post*, October 6, 1992, 10A; Barone and Ujifusa, *The Almanac of American Politics: 1994*, 1197; Michael Isikoff, "Lobbying by Rep. Ford, Black Caucus Preceded U.S. Reversal on Trial Jury," *Washington Post*, February 26, 1993, 4A.

148. Isikoff, "Lobbying by Rep. Ford, Black Caucus," 4A.

149. John Branston, "Jurors about to Get Rep. Ford Case," *Washington Post*, April 7, 1993, 4A.

150. Peter Applebome, "Representative Is Acquitted in Fraud and Bribery Case," *New York Times*, April 10, 1993, 6.

151. John Beifuss, "Supporters See Ford as Imperiled Symbol of Black Success," *Memphis Commercial Appeal*, March 3, 1993, 15.

152. Ibid.

153. "A Fiery Ex-Congresswoman Hopes to Make a Comeback," *New York Times*, April 11, 2004, N26.

5. Liberal Interventionism

1. "McGovern Cites Genocide, Asks Cambodia Military Intervention," *Toledo Blade*, August 22, 1978, 1A.

2. "McGovern Suggests Cambodia Invasion," *Miami News*, August 22, 1978, 2A.

3. Samantha Power, *A Problem from Hell: America and the Age of Genocide* (New York: Harper, 2002), 134.

4. Ibid., 136.

5. "No to Senator McGovern," *Montreal Gazette,* August 24, 1978, 8.

6. Ibid.

7. Lloyd Ambrosius, *Wilson Statecraft: Theory and Practice of Liberal Internationalism during World War I* (Wilmington, DE: Scholarly Resource, 1991), 1.

8. Alonzo Hamby, *Man of the People: A Life of Harry S. Truman* (New York: Oxford University Press, 1995), 560.

9. Malcolm Magee, *What the World Should Be: Woodrow Wilson and the Crafting of a Faith-Based Foreign Policy* (Waco, TX: Baylor University Press, 2008), 2.

10. James Skillen, "Three Zionisms in the Shaping of American Foreign Policy," in *God and Global Order: The Power of Religion in American Foreign Policy,* ed. Jonathan Chaplin and Robert Joustra (Waco, TX: Baylor University Press, 2010), 89–91.

11. Anders Stephanson, *Manifest Destiny: American Expansionism and the Empire of Right* (New York: Hill & Wang, 1995), 3–4, 6–7; Ernest Lee Tuveson, *Redeemer Nation: The Idea of America's Millennial Role* (Chicago: University of Chicago Press, 1968), viii–ix.

12. Bradford Perkins, "Interests, Values, and the Prism: The Sources of American Foreign Policy," *Journal of the Early Republic* 14, no. 4 (Winter 1994): 466; George Herring, *From Colony to Superpower: U.S. Foreign Relations since 1776* (New York: Oxford University Press, 2008), 2–3.

13. David Hendrickson, *Union, Nation, or Empire: The American Debate over International Relations* (Lawrence: University Press of Kansas, 2009), xiv–xv; James Field, *America and the Mediterranean World, 1776–1882* (Princeton, NJ: Princeton University Press, 1969), 25–26; Herring, *From Colony to Superpower,* 4–5.

14. Elizabeth Edwards Spalding, *The First Cold Warrior: Harry Truman, Containment, and the Remaking of Liberal Internationalism* (Lexington: University Press of Kentucky, 2006), 13.

15. Ibid.

16. Ibid., 9–13.

17. Walter McDougall, "Back to Bedrock," *Foreign Affairs,* March/April 1997, 136.

18. This is a primary thrust of Robert Kaufman's recent biography: *Henry Jackson: A Life in Politics* (Seattle: University of Washington Press, 2000). See also Thomas Gaskin, "Henry M. Jackson: Snohomish County Prosecutor, 1939–1940," *Pacific Northwest Quarterly* 81, no. 3 (July 1990): 89.

19. Ambrosius, *Wilson Statecraft,* 1.

20. Jerry Cornfield, "Everett Lives in Scoop Jackson's Shadow," *Everett (WA) Herald,* September 11, 2010.

21. Gaskin, "Henry M. Jackson," 89; "The Scoop on Scoop," *Newsweek,* February 16, 1976, 31.

22. Letter to Mr. Keiron Reardon, *Monroe Monitor,* April 21, 1941, folder 27, box 4, Henry Jackson Papers, University of Washington Special Collections.

23. Letter from Jackson to Harry Wackter (June 9, 1941), folder 26, box 56, Henry Jackson Papers.

24. Letter from Cooper to Jackson (February 9, 1941), folder 27, box 4, Henry Jackson Papers; Letter from Jackson to Judge Denney (March 1, 1941), folder 28, box 56, Henry Jackson Papers; Letter from Jackson to Keiron Reardon (April 21, 1941), folder 27, box 4, Henry Jackson Papers; Letter from Jackson to Squeak and Gundy (January 25, 1941), folder 28, box 56, Henry Jackson Papers.

25. Kaufman, *Henry Jackson,* 39.

26. Henry Jackson Speech to the University of Alaska (n.d.), p. 14, folder 19, box 48, Henry Jackson Papers.

27. Townsend Hoopes and Douglass Brinkley, *FDR and the Creation of the U.N.* (New Haven: Yale University Press, 1997), 205–6; Stephen Schlesinger, *Act of Creation: The Founding of the United Nations* (Boulder, CO: Westview, 2003).

28. Letter from HJ to Constituent, Shirley Wiseman (March 2, 1948), accession no. 3560-2, folder 1, box 53, Henry Jackson Papers; Letter from HJ to Marion Corbett (June 20, 1947), accession no. 3560-2, folder 5, box 53, Henry Jackson Papers.

29. Henry Jackson Congressional Speech (June 7, 1949), folder 32, box 43, Henry Jackson Papers.

30. Henry Jackson Statement concerning a Resolution Favoring the Development of UN into World Federation (n.d.), folder 32, box 43, Henry Jackson Papers.

31. Walter McDougall, *Promised Land, Crusader State: The American Encounter with the World since 1776* (New York: Houghton Mifflin, 1997), 173.

32. Henry Jackson Address on America's Town Meeting of the Air (October 19, 1949), folder 31, box 48, Henry Jackson Papers.

33. Merril Bush, "World Organization or Atomic Destruction," in *United Nations or World Government,* ed. Julia Johnsen (New York: H. W. Wilson, 1947), 55–60; Joseph Preston Baratta, *The Politics of World Federation* (Westport, CT: Praeger, 2004); Grenville Clark and Louis Sohn, *World Peace through World Law: Two Alternative Plans* (Cambridge, MA: Harvard University Press, 1966).

34. George Axlesson, "Boyd Orr Gets Nobel Award for World Peace for 1949," *New York Times,* October 13, 1949, 1.

35. Henry Jackson Statement concerning a Resolution Favoring the Development of UN into World Federation (n.d.), folder 32, box 43, Henry Jackson Papers.

36. United World Federalist, Incorporated (March 1, 1950), folder 12, box 41, Henry Jackson Papers; An Act Making Application to the Congress . . . Preamble, folder 12, box 41, Henry Jackson Papers.

37. Alan Cranston, *The Killing of the Peace* (New York: Viking, 1945); LeRoy Ashby and Rod Gramer, *Fighting the Odds: The Life of Senator Frank Church* (Pullman: Washington State University Press, 1994).

38. An Act Making Application to the Congress . . . Preamble, folder 12, box 41, Henry Jackson Papers; "8,000 at Rally Here for World Unity," *New York Times,* June 10, 1949, 3.

39. "Undermining the Republic," *Seattle Post-Intelligencer,* February 7, 1950, 14A.

40. "8,000 at Rally Here for World Unity," 3.

41. Kaufman, *Henry Jackson,* 56–57; Hamby, *Man of the People.*

42. Congressional Resolution 219 (June 6, 1950), folder 33, box 43, Henry Jackson Papers.

43. Ibid., p. 2.

44. Hamby, *Man of the People;* Anne Pierce, *Woodrow Wilson and Harry Truman: Mission and Power in American Foreign Policy* (Westport, CT: Praeger, 2003).

45. Henry Jackson Statement over Mutual Broadcast System (June 26, 1950), folder 22, box 56, Henry Jackson Papers.

46. Henry Jackson Speech (September 1, 1951), p. 8, folder 3, box 67, Henry

Jackson Papers; Jackson Says Russ Might Have Launch World War Three (n.d.), folder 2, box 66, Henry Jackson Papers.

47. Congressional Resolution 219 (June 6, 1950), p. 2, folder 33, box 43, Henry Jackson Papers.

48. Michael Thompson, "An Exception to Exceptionalism: A Reflection on Reinhold Niebuhr's Vision of 'Prophetic' Christianity and the Problem of Religion and U.S. Foreign Policy," *American Quarterly* 59, no. 3 (September 2007): 846.

49. Mark Edwards, "'God Has Chosen Us': Re-Membering Christian Realism, Rescuing Christendom, and the Contest of Responsibilities during the Cold War," *Diplomatic History* 33, no. 1 (January 2009): 67.

50. Thompson, "An Exception to Exceptionalism," 845–46.

51. Ibid., 838.

52. Henry Jackson, "Russia Strong because Its People Poor," *Seattle Post-Intelligencer,* September 23, 1956, 24A, 1A, "Red Nation's No Paradise for Workers," *Seattle Post-Intelligencer,* September 24, 1956, 1A, and "Tourists Always Being Watched by Secret Police," *Seattle Post-Intelligencer,* September 25, 1956, 1A.

53. Henry Jackson's Review of Oscar Morgenstern's, *The Question of National Defense* (November 8, 1959), folder 8, box 232, Henry Jackson Papers. See also John Gaddis, *The United States and the Origins of the Cold War, 1941–47* (New York: Columbia University Press, 1972), and *Strategies of Containment: A Critical Appraisal of Postwar American National Security Policy* (New York: Oxford University Press, 1982); Walter Hixson, *George F. Kennan: Cold War Iconoclast* (New York: Columbia University Press, 1989); and Dean Acheson, *Present at the Creation: My Years in the State Department* (New York: Norton, 1969).

54. "Russia Hasn't Changed, Says Sen. Jackson," *Seattle Times,* May 31, 1969, 13A.

55. Henry Jackson Address: National Security: Basic Tasks (October 12, 1967), p. 2, folder 12, box 232, Henry Jackson Papers.

56. "Russia Hasn't Changed, Says Sen. Jackson," 13A.

57. Raymond Garthoff, *Détente and Confrontation: American-Soviet Relations from Nixon to Reagan* (Washington, DC: Brookings Institution, 1985).

58. Henry Jackson, "First, Human Détente," *New York Times,* September 9, 1973, 219.

59. Kenneth Cmiel, "The Emergence of Human Rights Politics in the United States," *Journal of American History* 86 (December 1999): 1234–36.

60. Nancy Cassels, "Bentinck: Humanitarian and Imperialist—the Abolition of the Suttee," *Journal of British Studies* 5, no. 1 (November 1965): 77–87; Peter Marsh, "Lord Salisbury and the Ottoman Massacres," *Journal of British Studies* 11, no. 2 (May 1972): 63–83; Gary Bass, *Freedom's Battle: The Origins of Humanitarian Intervention* (New York: Knopf, 2008), 7; Geoffrey Robertson, *Crimes against Humanity: The Struggle for Global Justice* (New York: New Press, 2000), 12–13.

61. Douglas Maynard, "Reform and the Origin of the International Organization Movement," *Proceedings of the American Philosophical Society* 107, no. 3 (June 1963): 220.

62. Karen Halttunen, "Humanitarianism and the Pornography of Pain," *American Historical Review* 100, no. 2 (April 1995): 303; Kevin Rozario, "'Delicious Horrors': Mass Culture, the Red Cross and the Appeal of Modern American Humanitarianism," *American Quarterly* 55, no. 3 (September 2003): 417–55.

63. Bass, *Freedom's Battle*, 8, 22–23.

64. Benedict Anderson, *Imagined Communities: Reflections on the Origin and Spread of Nationalism* (London: Verso, 1983).

65. *The Armenian Massacres, 1894–1896: U.S. Media Testimony*, ed. Arman Kirakossian (Detroit: Wayne State University Press, 2004), 41.

66. Caroline Moorhead, *Dunant's Dream* (New York: Carroll & Graf, 1999), 99–101; Peter Balakian, *Burning Tigris* (New York: Harper Perennial, 2004), 70.

67. Balakian, *Burning Tigris*, 64.

68. Message of POTUS Communicated to Congress "Relations of the United States to Spain by Reason of Warfare in the Island of Cuba" (April 11, 1898), p. 11, Library of Congress.

69. Henry Jackson Speech to B'nai B'rith (April 8, 1957), folder 25, box 235, Henry Jackson Papers.

70. Recent History—One of an Explosion of Jewish Consciousness (n.d.), p. 3, folder 3, box 10, Henry Jackson Papers.

71. "U.S. Is Protesting Soviet Exit Taxes," *New York Times*, September 9, 1972, 8.

72. Address by Senator Henry Jackson: Blue Key Dinner (November 16, 1973), p. 1, folder 92, box 10, Henry Jackson Papers.

73. Garthoff, *Détente and Confrontation*, 25–28.

74. National Security Advisor Mem-Con: Kissinger, Jackson (September 20, 1974), folder "Ford," box 5, Gerald Ford Papers, Gerald R. Ford Presidential Library and Museum; Henry Jackson: We Must Not Mismanage SALT II (n.d.), p. 1, folder 31, box 10, Henry Jackson Papers; Henry Jackson: Détente and Human Rights, Commencement Address at Yeshiva University (n.d.), p. 1, folder 33, box 10, Henry Jackson Papers.

75. Andrew Preston, *The Sword of the Spirit, Shield of Faith: Religion in American War and Diplomacy* (New York: Knopf, 2012), 130.

76. "Scoop Jackson: Running Hard Uphill," *Time*, February 17, 1975, 11; Walter Gordon, "Jackson's Image Problem," *New Leader*, May 12, 1975, 6.

77. Nicholas Bethell, "Solzhenitsyn Can Still Write—He Just Can't Publish," *Sunday New York Times Magazine*, April 12, 1970, 40; Bernard Gwertzman, "Solzhenitsyn Shuns Nobel Trip," *New York Times*, November 28, 1970, 1.

78. Harrison Salisbury: The Transformation of Solzhenitsyn (n.d.), folder 38, box 1, Henry Jackson Papers.

79. Harrison Salisbury, "The Only Living Soviet Classic," *New York Times*, October 9, 1970, 16.

80. Bethell, "Solzhenitsyn Can Still Write," 40.

81. Ibid., 41; George Saunders, *Samizdat: Voices of the Soviet Opposition* (New York: Monad, 1974).

82. Anthony Astrachan: Solzhenitsyn Work Bares Stalin Terror (n.d.), folder 30, box 37, Henry Jackson Papers.

83. Robert Kaiser, "Book Defies Current Rulers," *Washington Post*, December 29, 1973, 1.

84. Robert Kaiser, "Arrest Shows Soviet System Still the Same," *Washington Post*, February 13, 1974, 30A.

85. Hedrick Smith, "7 Russians Make Forcible Arrest of Solzhenitsyn," *New York Times*, February 13, 1974, 12.

86. "Solzhenitsyn in Exile," *Christian Science Monitor* (n.d.), folder 1, box 38, Henry Jackson Papers.

87. "Jackson Ired at Silence on Solzhenitsyn," *Seattle Post-Intelligencer,* February 16, 1974, 1A.

88. Letter from John Ashbrook to Gerald Ford (n.d.), File "Solzhenitsyn," box 62, Gerald Ford Papers; Memo from John Marsh to Ford (n.d.), file "Solzhenitsyn," box 62, Gerald Ford Papers.

89. *No Left Turns: A Handbook for Conservatives Based on the Writings of John M. Ashbrook,* ed. Randy McNutt (Fairfield, OH: Hamilton Hobby, 1986), 56; Ernest Furgurson, *Hard Right: The Rise of Jesse Helms* (New York: Norton, 1986), 204.

90. Bernard Gwertzman, "U.S. Devises Plan for Rise in Flow of Soviet Jews," *New York Times,* September 8, 1974, 1.

91. White House Press Conference (August 15, 1974), p. 1, folder 6, box 11, Henry Jackson Papers; "Kissinger and Senators Seek Accord on Soviet Jews," *New York Times,* August 14, 1974, 4.

92. Letter from Kissinger to Henry Jackson (October 18, 1974), folder 32, box 11, Henry Jackson Papers.

93. Joseph Albright, "The Pact of Two Henrys," *New York Times,* January 5, 1975, 19.

94. Memo from Goldwin to Rumsfeld (January 14, 1975), folder "Jewish," box 3, White House Subject Files, Gerald Ford Papers.

95. Irving Spiegel, "Candidates Support Campaign for Jews in Soviet," *New York Times,* March 29, 1971, 24. See also Jules Witcover, *Marathon: The Pursuit of the Presidency, 1972–1976* (New York: Viking, 1977).

96. News Release: Ad Hoc Committee for Intellectual Freedom (n.d.), p. 1, folder 1, box 38, Henry Jackson Papers; Princeton Committee for Solzhenitsyn and Freedom in the Soviet Union (n.d.), folder 1, box 38, Henry Jackson Papers.

97. News Release: Ad Hoc Committee for Intellectual Freedom (n.d.), p. 2, folder 1, box 38, Henry Jackson Papers.

98. Henry Jackson Speech: A Human Dimension of Détente (n.d.), folder 75, box 11, Henry Jackson Papers.

99. News from the AFL-CIO: March 15, 1974, folder 1, box 38, Henry Jackson Papers.

100. Letter from Solzhenitsyn to Henry Jackson (April 7, 1974), folder 11, box 4, Henry Jackson Papers; Nan Robertson, "Solzhenitsyn Speaks Out on Paris TV," *New York Times,* April 13, 1975, 10.

101. White House Letter to George Meany (June 27, 1975), file "Solzhenitsyn," box 2998, White House Central File, Gerald Ford Papers; Ron Nessen Press Conference (July 7, 1975), p. 10, file "July 7, 1975," box 10, Ron Nessen Files, Gerald Ford Papers.

102. James Naughton, "Ford Now Trying to Arrange Solzhenitsyn Meeting," *New York Times,* July 18, 1975, 4; George Will Article: Solzhenitsyn and the President (n.d.), folder "Solzhenitsyn," box 10, Richard Cheney Files, Gerald Ford Papers.

103. Bernard Gwertzman, "Détente Scored by Solzhenitsyn," *New York Times,* July 1, 1975, 6.

104. Speech by Aleksandr Solzhenitsyn (June 30, 1975), p. 17, file 3, box 42, Henry Jackson Papers.

105. Hilton Kramer, "Solzhenitsyn in City, Warns of Soviet Danger," *New York Times*, July 10, 1975, 63; William Shannon, "The Russian Visitor," *New York Times*, July 16, 1975, 33.

106. Kramer, "Solzhenitsyn in City," 63.

107. George Will Article: Solzhenitsyn and the President (n.d.), folder "Solzhenitsyn," box 10, Richard Cheney Files, Gerald Ford Papers.

108. Memo from Cheney to Rumsfeld (July 8, 1975), p. 1, file "Solzhenitsyn," box 10, Richard Cheney Files, Gerald Ford Papers; Clare Boothe Luce Editorial in *American Views: Prescription for America: A New Policy of Containment* (n.d.), file "Clare Boothe Luce," box 9, Richard Cheney Files, Gerald Ford Papers; Russell Baker, "Don't Invite Proust," *New York Times*, August 31, 1975, 170.

109. Announcement of Solzhenitsyn Senate Reception (n.d.), folder 106, box 42, Henry Jackson Papers.

110. Naughton, "Ford Now Trying to Arrange Solzhenitsyn Meeting," 4; Kaufman, *Henry Jackson*, 292.

111. Henry Jackson, "Congress Welcomes Alexander Solzhenitsyn," *East Europe* 24, nos. 4–5 (August–September 1975): 2.

112. Henry Jackson Speech to Convention of Pennsylvania State American Legion (July 16, 1975), p. 4, folder 111, box 11, Henry Jackson Papers.

113. Associated Press: President Ford Is Willing to Meet with Solzhenitsyn (n.d.), file "Solzhenitsyn," box 10, Richard Cheney Files, Henry Jackson Papers.

114. Naughton, "Ford Now Trying to Arrange Solzhenitsyn Meeting," 4.

115. Douglass Kneeland, "The Jackson Campaign: An Exercise in How to Undo It," *New York Times*, May 9, 1976, 136.

116. R. W. Apple, "How Carter Saw It All: Very Clearly," *New York Times*, June 13, 1976, 153.

117. Douglass Kneeland, "Jackson Is Edging toward the Left," *New York Times*, March 26, 1976, 1.

6. The Middle East of Domestic Politics

1. William Griffin, "'Welfare Queen' Is under New Probe," *Chicago Tribune*, April 10, 1975, 8A, and "Medical 'Practice' Just That for Welfare Queen," *Chicago Tribune*, July 14, 1975, 3.

2. "Follow-Up on the News," *New York Times*, January 9, 1977, 39.

3. Griffin, "'Welfare Queen' Is under New Probe," 8A.

4. William Safire, "Reagan's Anecdotage," *New York Times*, March 8, 1982, 19A.

5. In 1977, welfare was a five-part, $30 billion system in a federal budget of $411 billion. It consisted of Aid to Families with Dependent Children (AFDC), $6.2 billion and 11 million recipients; Supplemental Security Income (SSI), $5.3 billion and 4.4 million recipients; Food Stamps, $5.6 billion and 17.2 million recipients; the Earned Income Tax Credit, $3.1 billion and 20 million recipients; and General Assistance, $1.2 billion and 1 million recipients. Forty percent of all recipients received benefits from three of the five programs, and 20 percent received all five, yet, despite $30 billion in spending, 25 million Americans or 11.6 percent were technically in poverty. The most controversial of all the programs was AFDC, which dispensed

cash and other welfare benefits to the nonworking poor. U.S. Bureau of Census, *Statistical Abstract of the United States: 1977*, 98th ed. (Washington, DC: U.S. Government Printing Office, 1977), 247; "Facts We Dare Not Forget," *Dissent*, Spring 1981, 165.

6. Letter from Mrs. Clarence Howe to Rep. Al Ullman (n.d.), folder 15, box 172, Albert Conrad Ullman Papers, University of Oregon Libraries: Special Collections; Letter from M. Gregg Smith to Rep. Al Ullman (n.d.), folder 15, box 172, Albert Conrad Ullman Papers.

7. Anthony Campagna, *Economic Policy in the Carter Administration* (Westport, CT: Greenwood, 1995), 4.

8. "The Changing Economy: Inflation, Stagflation, and Deregulation, Alfred Kahn and Paul Volcker," *FMC Program Segments, 1960–2000*, http://www.pbs.org/fmc/segments/progseg14.htm.

9. Martin Waldron, "Costs of Welfare Soar," *New York Times*, April 25, 1976, sec. 11NJ, p. 26.

10. Gareth Davies, *From Opportunity to Entitlement: The Transformation and Decline of Great Society Liberalism* (Lawrence: University Press of Kansas, 1996), 8.

11. Ibid.

12. Ibid., 58.

13. Ibid., 3.

14. Charles Mohr, "Carter and His Audiences," *New York Times*, June 2, 1976, 20A.

15. R. W. Apple, "Humphrey May Attempt to Stop Carter," *New York Times*, April 29, 1976, 1A.

16. Ibid.

17. Joseph Califano, *Governing America: An Insider's Report from the White House and the Cabinet* (New York: Simon & Schuster, 1981), 276.

18. William Leuchtenburg, *In the Shadow of FDR: From Harry Truman to George W. Bush* (Ithaca, NY: Cornell University Press, 2001), 3.

19. "Post-War Economic Program," *New York Times*, January 8, 1945, 16.

20. "Wallace Explains Full Employment," *New York Times*, September 6, 1945, 40.

21. Hamby, *Man of the People*, 366–67.

22. Leon Keyserling, "Must We Have Another Depression?" *New York Times*, June 8, 1947, 7.

23. Edward Cowan, "Difficulty of Defining Full Employment," *New York Times*, October 2, 1977, E4; Edwin Dale, "Unemployment: The Legacy of the Recession," *New York Times*, April 11, 1976, 105.

24. A. H. Raskin, "Nationwide Rallies for 'Decent' Jobs at 'Decent' Wages," *New York Times*, August 31, 1977, 66; Leon Keyserling, *Toward Full Employment within Three Years* (Washington, DC: Conference on Economic Progress, 1976), 1.

25. Califano, *Governing America*, 276.

26. U.S. President, "Report to the American People" (President's Address to the Nation), in *Public Papers of the President of the United States—Jimmy Carter: Containing the Public Messages, Speeches, and Statements of the President, 1977–1981* (Washington, DC: U.S. Government Printing Office, 1978), 142.

27. Califano, *Governing America*, 321.

28. Stephen Skowronek, *The Politics Presidents Make: Leadership from John Adams to George Bush* (Cambridge, MA: Belknap Press of the Harvard University Press, 1993), 381.

29. Adam Clymer, "Daniel Patrick Moynihan Is Dead; Senator from Academia Was 76," *New York Times*, March 27, 2003, 1A.

30. "Moynihan Memos: The Political Danger of Thinking," *New York Times*, March 15, 1970, 172.

31. Henry Raymont, "Moynihan Charges 'Sloppy Work' Hurt Poverty Program," *New York Times*, December 19, 1968, 1; Daniel Patrick Moynihan, *Maximum Feasible Misunderstanding: Community Action in the War on Poverty* (New York: Free Press, 1970).

32. "Moynihan Memos," 172.

33. Edward Burks, "Moynihan Aims for Top Panel: Senate Finance," *New York Times*, January 23, 1977, 19, and "Moynihan: How He Won His Senate Spurs," *New York Times*, April 5, 1977, 70.

34. Ben Heineman Biography (n.d.), p. 1, folder "Ben Heineman," WHCF—Name File, Jimmy Carter Library and Museum.

35. Henry Aaron, *Politics and Professors: The Great Society in Perspective* (Washington: Brookings Institution, 1978), n.p. (foreword).

36. Ibid., 159.

37. Ben Heineman, *Memorandum for the President: A Strategic Approach to Domestic Affairs in the 1980s* (New York: Random House, 1980), 284.

38. Califano, *Governing America*, 323.

39. Memo from Hamilton Jordan to President Carter on Welfare Reform, p. 2, folder "Welfare Reform," box "Chief of Staff: Hamilton Jordan," WHCF—Subject File, Jimmy Carter Library; Linda Demkovich, "Carter Gets Some Outside Advice for His Welfare Reform Package," *National Journal*, April 30, 1977, 673.

40. James Patterson, "Jimmy Carter and Welfare Reform," in *The Carter Presidency: Policy Choices in the Post–New Deal Era*, ed. Gary Fink (Lawrence: University Press of Kansas, 1998), 124.

41. Ibid., 125.

42. Ibid.

43. Memo from President Carter to Joseph Califano (February 3, 1977), folder "Welfare Reform Memo, 2/77," box 317 DPS Eizenstat, Stu Eizenstat Files, Jimmy Carter Library and Museum.

44. Memo from Joseph Califano to Jimmy Carter (February 5, 1977), folder "Welfare Reform, 2/77," box 17 DPS Eizenstat, Stu Eizenstat Files.

45. Demkovich, "Carter Gets Some Outside Advice," 673.

46. Ibid.

47. Frank Moore, Liaison to Congress, Interview by Colin Campbell, p. 12, folder 80 310, box 1, Colin Campbell Collection, Georgetown University Special Collections; Joe Onek, Associate Director: Domestic Policy Staff, Health Issues, Interview by Colin Campbell, p. 8, folder 185, box 1, Colin Campbell Collection.

48. Van Doorn, Assistant Director for Economic Policy, Office of Management and Budget, Interview by Colin Campbell, p. 9, folder 21, box 1, Colin Campbell Collection.

49. Benjamin Huberman, Assistant Director, Office Science and Technology Poli-

cy, White House, Interview by Colin Campbell, p. 13, folder 54, box 1, Colin Campbell Collection.

50. Jimmy Carter, *Keeping Faith: Memoirs of a President* (New York: Bantam, 1983), 201; Grayson Mitchell, "Carter Would Scrap Present Aid System," *Los Angeles Times,* May 3, 1977, 1A.

51. Mitchell, "Carter Would Scrap Present Aid System," 1A.

52. Califano, *Governing America,* 344.

53. Ibid.

54. Memo from Stu Eizenstat, Carp, Raines, and Spring to the President (June 1, 1977), p. 1, file "WE (10) 6/1/77–7/31/77," box 13, WHCF—Welfare Reform, Jimmy Carter Library and Museum.

55. Gordon Weil, *The Welfare Debate of 1978* (White Plains, NY: Institute for Socioeconomic Studies, 1978), 87. The employment programs would cost $8.8 billion, cash assistance $20.2 billion, the expansion of EITC $1.5 billion, and the emergency assistance program $600 million.

56. Carter's Welfare Plan Cost Projection Is $10 Billion Short, Budget Office Says, file 4, box 184, Albert Conrad Ullman Papers.

57. David Rosenbaum, "Obituary: Tom Joe, 64, Policy Maker on Poverty," *New York Times,* October 5, 1999.

58. Memo from Tom Joe to Stu Eizenstat (July 27, 1977), p. 2, folder "Welfare Reform (3)," box 318 DPS-Eizenstat, Stu Eizenstat Files, Jimmy Carter Library and Museum.

59. Ibid., 6.

60. Ibid., 11.

61. Memo from Stu Eizenstat to the President (July 27, 1977), p. 1, folder "Welfare Reform (1)," box 319 DPS-Eizenstat, Stu Eizenstat's Office Files.

62. Memo from Stu Eizenstat to the President (July 31, 1977), p. 1, folder "7/31/77," box "Handwriting File 7/28/77–8/1/77," WHCF—Presidential Handwriting File, Jimmy Carter Library and Museum; U.S. President, "Report to the American People" (President's Address to the Nation), in *Public Papers of the President of the United States—Jimmy Carter* (1978), 1198; Press Conference no. 13 (August 6, 1977), p. 2, folder "Welfare Reform (1)," box 92 CEA, WHCF—Council of Economic Advisors, Jimmy Carter Library and Museum.

63. Newsletter, HEW News: Welfare Reform (August 6, 1977), p. 1, folder "Welfare Reform 8/77," box 319 DPS, WHCF-DPS, Jimmy Carter Library.

64. Weil, *The Welfare Debate of 1978,* 26.

65. Califano, *Governing America,* 354.

66. "Welfare Plan a 'Tax Relief for Millions,'" *St. Louis Post-Dispatch,* August 8, 1977, 1A; David Rosenbaum, "Carter Aides Predict a Savings of Billions in New Welfare Plan," *New York Times,* June 1, 1977, 1A.

67. David Witman, "Liberal Rhetoric and the Welfare Underclass," *Society* 21, no. 1 (November/December 1983): 66.

68. Ibid.

69. Frank Moore, Liaison to Congress, Interview by Colin Campbell, p. 12, folder 80 301, box 1, Colin Campbell Collection.

70. Letter from President Carter to Robert Byrd (March 22, 1978), folder "Presidentials Only," box "Name File (Robert Byrd)," WHCF—Name File.

71. Letter from President Carter to Robert Byrd (August 2, 1977), folder "July 77–September 77," box "Name File (Robert Byrd)," WHCF—Name File.

72. Memo, Senator Byrd's Grandchildren (October 14, 1977), folder "October 1977–December 1977," box "Name File (Robert Byrd)," WHCF—Name File.

73. David Rosenbaum, "Senators Fighting Carter on Welfare Reform," *New York Times*, October 3, 1977.

74. Robert Mann, *Legacy to Power: Senator Russell Long of Louisiana* (New York: Paragon, 1992), 341.

75. Ibid., 342.

76. Stuart Eizenstat, "The Carter Presidency," in *The Presidency and Domestic Policies of Jimmy Carter*, ed. Herbert Rosenbaum and Alexeji Ugrinsky (Westport, CT: Greenwood, 1994), 187.

77. Memo from Bert Carp to Dick Warden (July 25, 1977), folder "Russell Long: 1/20/1977–9/30/1977," WHCF—Name File.

78. Mann, *Legacy to Power*, 359.

79. Stephen Green and Margot Hornblower, "Mills Admits Being Present during Tidal Basin Scuffle," *Washington Post*, October 11, 1974, 1A; "Ullman Shuns Vice Presidency," *East Oregonian* (Pendleton), June 19, 1976, 4A.

80. Bill Keller, "Ullman Dislikes Full Employment Bill," *The Oregonian* (Portland), June 4, 1976, 5A; Memo from Al Ullman to Joseph Califano (April 1, 1977), p. 3, file 4, box 184, Albert Conrad Ullman Papers.

81. *Television News Index and Abstracts, 1977* (Nashville, TN: Vanderbilt Television News Archives, 1978), 1831.

82. Kathryn Waters Gest, "Carter, Congress, and Welfare: A Long Road," *Congressional Quarterly Weekly Report*, August 13, 1977, 3.

83. Desmond King, "Sectionalism and Policy Formulation in the United States: President Carter's Welfare Initiative," *British Journal of Political Science* 26, no. 3 (July 1996): 355.

84. Memo from Stu Eizenstat to the President: My Meeting with Moynihan (May 12, 1979), p. 1, folder "1/20/77–1/20/81," box 12, WHCF—Name File.

85. Ibid.

86. Memo from Stu Eizenstat to the President: Moynihan and Welfare Reform (October 11, 1977), p. 2, folder "Welfare Reform 8/77 (2)," box 318 DPS-Eizenstat, Stu Eizenstat's Office Files.

87. Ibid., p. 1.

88. Moynihan Testimony to Welfare Reform Subcommittee, folder "Welfare Reform 8/77 (2)," box 318 DPS-Eizenstat, Stu Eizenstat's Office Files.

89. Memo from Stu Eizenstat to the President: Moynihan and Welfare Reform (October 11, 1977), p. 2, folder "Welfare Reform 8/77 (2)," box 318 DPS-Eizenstat, Stu Eizenstat's Office Files.

90. Memo from Joseph Califano to the President: Meeting with Welfare Reform Committee (November 30, 1977), p. 3, folder "12/1/77," box "Office of Staff Secretary—Handwriting File 11/29/77–12/1/77," WHCF—Presidential Handwriting File.

91. Ibid., p. 7.

92. Notes of Meeting (September 22, 1977), p. 1, folder "EPG Steering Group," box "EPG Meeting," WHCF—Council of Economic Advisors, Jimmy Carter Library and Museum.

93. Walter Pincus, "Advice Is Welcome," *New York Times*, May 26, 1977, 7A.

94. Patterson, "Jimmy Carter and Welfare Reform," 129.

95. Weil, *The Welfare Debate of 1978*, 13.

96. Memo from Vice President Mondale to the President (November 23, 1977), p. 3, folder "11/28/77–12/1/77," box "Office of Staff Secretary—Handwriting File 11/29/77–12/1/77," WHCF—Presidential Handwriting File.

97. Letter from President Carter to Congressman James Corman (January 25, 1978), p. 1, folder "Welfare Reform (1) 8/77," box 318, WHCF-DPS Eizenstat, Jimmy Carter Library.

98. "Ullman to Introduce Welfare Plan Substitute," *The Oregonian* (Portland), February 2, 1978, A8; "Ullman, President at Odds over Welfare Reform Plans," *East Oregonian* (Pendleton), February 2, 1978, 17.

99. Jimmy Carter, "Carter at the Center," *The Center Magazine*, January/February 1977, 50.

100. Leslie Lenkowsky, *Politics, Economics and Welfare Reform* (Lanham, MD: University Press of America, 1986), 58.

7. "America Ain't What's Wrong with the World"

The quotation that serves as the title of this chapter is taken from Ben Wattenberg, *Fighting Words: A Tale of How Liberals Created Neo-Conservatism* (New York: Thomas Dunne, 2008), 42.

1. Joseph Loftus, "Rift in Liberal Forces Becomes More Marked," *New York Times*, January 4, 1947, 7E.

2. Steve Gillon, *Politics and Vision: The ADA and American Liberalism, 1947–1985* (New York: Oxford University Press, 1987), 25.

3. Ibid., 24.

4. Schlesinger, "Not Right, Not Left, But a Vital Center."

5. Ibid.

6. Ibid.

7. Alonzo Hamby, "The Vital Center, the Fair Deal, and the Quest for a Liberal Political Economy," *American Historical Review* 77, no. 3 (June 1972): 655.

8. Alonzo Hamby, *Beyond the New Deal: Harry S. Truman and American Liberalism* (New York: Columbia University Press, 1973), 279.

9. Gillon, *Politics and Vision*, 26; Hamby, *Beyond the New Deal*, 225.

10. James Ring Adams, "Battle Royal among the Socialists," *Wall Street Journal*, December 8, 1972, unlabeled folder, box 26, Peter Rosenblatt Papers.

11. Memo: Short Type-Written Note (n.d.), folder "Eshkol Toast," box 7, Office Folders of Ben Wattenberg, Ben Wattenberg Papers, LBJ Presidential Library.

12. Ben Wattenberg Interview I, p. 1–2, Oral Histories of the Johnson Administration, LBJ Presidential Library.

13. Ben Wattenberg in collaboration with Richard Scammon, *This U.S.A.: An Unexpected Family Portrait of 194,067,296 Americans Drawn from the Census* (Garden City, NY: Doubleday, 1965), 305.

14. Ben Wattenberg Interview I, p. 27, Oral Histories of the Johnson Administration, LBJ Presidential Library.

15. The New Class and Its Morals (n.d.), folder "YSR," box 26, Socialist Party U.S.A. Papers, Duke University, Special Collections Library.

16. Scammon and Wattenberg, *The Real Majority*, 225.

17. Ibid., 39.

18. Richard Scammon and Ben Wattenberg, "Strategy for Democrats," *New Republic*, August 15, 1970, 21.

19. See Ben Wattenberg, *Fighting Words: A Tale of How Liberals Created Neo-Conservatism* (New York: Thomas Dunne, 2008).

20. Ibid., 51.

21. Press Release: A Word Edgewise (September 17, 1974), folder "Ben Wattenberg," box 30, Peter Rosenblatt Papers; The Lessons of 1968, by George McGovern (n.d.), p. 1, folder "McGovern Commission," box 14, Peter Rosenblatt Papers.

22. The Machiavellianism of Reform (n.d.), folder "Ben Wattenberg," box 30, Peter Rosenblatt Papers; Penn Kemble and Josh Muravchik, "The New Politics and the Democrats," *Commentary*, December 1972, 79.

23. William Greider, "Democrats Widen Delegations," *Washington Post*, November 20, 1969, 6A.

24. Ibid.

25. Kemble and Muravchik, "The New Politics and the Democrats," 79.

26. Toward Fairness and Unity for '76, p. 2, folder "CDM 1975," box 26, Socialist Party U.S.A. Papers.

27. Penn Kemble, "Who Needs the Liberals," *Commentary*, October 1970, 64.

28. "War Foes Here Attacked by Construction Workers," *New York Times*, May 8, 1970, 1A.

29. Ibid.

30. Ibid.

31. William Chapman, "'Ethnic' Voter Biases Are Redefined," *Washington Post*, September 10, 1972, 29A.

32. Lanny Davis: Why Lowenstein Lost: Ethnics, Crooks, and Carpetbaggers (n.d.), p. 1, folder "ADA," box 2, Peter Rosenblatt Papers.

33. William Shannon, "The Legends of George McGovern," *Sunday New York Times Magazine*, July 3, 1972, 10.

34. Miles Stanley's Four Days in Miami, folder "Labor/McGovern Reforms," box 14, Peter Rosenblatt Papers.

35. Miscellaneous McGovern Articles, folder "Labor/McGovern Reforms," box 14, Peter Rosenblatt Papers; Haynes Johnson, "A Portrait of the New Delegate," *Washington Post*, July 8, 1972, 1A.

36. Miscellaneous McGovern Articles, folder "Labor/McGovern Reforms," box 14, Peter Rosenblatt Papers.

37. Michael Jensen, "Young Millionaires Are Big McGovern Contributors," *New York Times*, August 23, 1972, 29C; Maureen Orth, "Sore Losers: Mayor Daley, Meet Captain Crunch," *Village Voice*, July 20, 1972, 18; "The Battle for the Democratic Party," *Time*, July 17, 1972, 12.

38. George Meany Speech (December 17, 1972), folder "People and Campaigns: George Meany," box 29, Peter Rosenblatt Papers; Open Letter from Sidney Hook (September 20, 1972), Addendum to Socialist Party Papers on Microfilm: Series A, no. 12 B, reel 2, Duke University Microfilm Collections.

39. Mike Royko: Jesse Jackson the Delegate, folder "Labor/McGovern Reforms," box 14, Peter Rosenblatt Papers.

40. A Hard Look at Singer '59, folder "Labor/McGovern Reforms," box 14, Peter Rosenblatt Papers; Jack Newfield, "Of Reform Hacks and Guideline Junkies," *Village Voice*, July 20, 1972, 11.

41. Newfield, "Of Reform Hacks and Guideline Junkies," 11.

42. "Delegate Breslin: The Gang That Couldn't Vote Straight," *Village Voice*, July 20, 1972, folder "DNC," box 14, Peter Rosenblatt Papers.

43. Democrat Planning Group Report #1 (January 16, 1973), folder "Organizing Council," box 58, Peter Rosenblatt Papers; Letter from Ben Wattenberg to Herman Wouk (October 28, 1972), folder "Potential Sponsors," box 38, Peter Rosenblatt Papers.

44. Robert Sam Anson, *McGovern: A Biography* (New York: Holt, Rinehart & Winston, 1972), 60.

45. Ibid., 151, 158.

46. George McGovern, *An American Journey: The Presidential Campaign Speeches of George McGovern* (New York: Random House, 1974), 20.

47. Clark Hoyt and James McCartney, "Old Guard Demos Join to Regain Party," *Miami Herald*, July 13, 1972, 27A; Democrat Planning Group Report #1 (January 16, 1973), folder "Organizing Council," box 58, Peter Rosenblatt Papers.

48. Bill Kovach, "McGovern Will Open Urban Ethnic Office in an Effort to Widen Base," *New York Times*, August 13, 1972, 46A.

49. Press Release by John Roche: Class Struggle and McGovern, August 13, 1972, folder "People and Campaigns: McGovern," box 29, Peter Rosenblatt Papers; Louis Harris, "The Harris Survey: Unionists Lean to President 49 to 40 Pct.," *Washington Post*, September 4, 1972, 2A.

50. Press Release by John Roche: Class Struggle and McGovern (August 13, 1972), folder "People and Campaigns: McGovern," box 29, Peter Rosenblatt Papers.

51. Josh Muravchik, *Heaven on Earth: The Rise and Fall of Socialism* (San Francisco: Encounter, 2003), 252.

52. George Meany Speech (December 17, 1972), folder "People and Campaigns: George Meany," box 29, Peter Rosenblatt Papers; Open Letter from Sidney Hook (September 20, 1972), Addendum to Socialist Party Papers on Microfilm: Series A, no. 12 B.

53. "Meany Says Voters Rejected 'Neo-Isolationism' of McGovern," *New York Times*, November 9, 1972, folder "Media: Miscellaneous," box 17, Peter Rosenblatt Papers.

54. Morton Kondracke, "81 Old-Line Liberals Form Democratic Coalition," *Chicago Sun-Times*, December 7, 1972, 1A; Memo from Penn Kemble to Ben Wattenberg (n.d.), folder "Ben Wattenberg," box 30, Peter Rosenblatt Papers; New Members, 1973, folder "Newsletter," box 1, Peter Rosenblatt Papers.

55. Philip Shabecoff, "Labor Struggles to Unify Ranks and Regain Influence in Democratic Party," *New York Times*, November 13, 1972, folder "Media: Miscellaneous," box 17, Peter Rosenblatt Papers.

56. Geri Joseph, "Democratic Coalition Rejects New Left," *Minneapolis Tribune* (n.d.), folder "CDM: 1972–1973," box 63, Peter Rosenblatt Papers.

57. CDM: Founding Statement: Come Home Democrats (n.d.), folder "CDM," box 17, Peter Rosenblatt Papers.

58. Victor Riesel, "Tale of Two Parties," *Northern Virginia Sun* (Arlington), May 29, 1973, folder "Media: Miscellaneous," box 17, Peter Rosenblatt Papers.

59. David Broder, "New Democratic Coalition Plans Reforming Reforms," *Washington Post*, folder "CDM: 1972–1973," box 63, Peter Rosenblatt Papers.

60. Memo from Richard Schifter to Hubert Humphrey: A New ADA (July 27, 1972), folder "Organization: ADA," box 2, Peter Rosenblatt Papers.

61. Democrat Planning Group Report #1, January 16, 1973, folder "Organizing Council," box 58, Peter Rosenblatt Papers.

62. Democrats: A Blow for Moderation (December 11, 1972), folder "Media: Miscellaneous," box 17, Peter Rosenblatt Papers.

63. Report #3: The Commission on Delegate Selection (January 18, 1973), folder "Organizing Council," box 58, Peter Rosenblatt Papers; David Broder, "Democrats Begin Long Task of Pulling Party Together," *Washington Post*, folder "CDM 1972–1973," box 63, Peter Rosenblatt Papers.

64. David Broder, "New Democratic Coalition Plans Reforming Reforms," *Washington Post*, folder "CDM 1972–1973," box 63, Peter Rosenblatt Papers.

65. Penn Kemble's Testimony Before the Delegate Selection Commission of the Democratic Party (August 11, 1973), folder "CDM: Task Force," box 40, Peter Rosenblatt Papers.

66. James Sterba, "Democrats Vote to Limit '74 Meeting," *New York Times*, July 23, 1973, 21.

67. Lanny Davis, *The Emerging Democratic Majority: Lessons and Legacies from the New Politics* (New York: Stein & Day, 1974), 20.

68. SP Plans Major Conference—Building the Democratic Left, by Penn Kemble, Addendum to Socialist Party Papers on Microfilm: Series A, no. 12 B, reel 2.

69. Letter from Michael Harrington to Bayard Rustin (October 14, 1972), folder "Harrington Resignation," box 45, Socialist Party U.S.A. Papers; Michael Harrington, "A Call to American Socialists," *The Nation*, November 13, 1972, page obscured.

70. Synopsis of the November Election (August 23, 1972), unlabeled folder, box 26, Peter Rosenblatt Papers.

71. Harold Meyerson, "Michael Harrington, an American Socialist," *In These Times*, August 30–September 5, 1989, 22; Adams, "Battle Royal among the Socialists."

72. The New Class and Its Morals (November 1971), p. 3, folder "YSR," box 26, Socialist Party U.S.A. Papers.

73. Anthony Astrachan, "Democrats Discuss Appeal to Party's Left," *Washington Post*, February 20, 1973, 2A.

74. Adams, "Battle Royal among the Socialists."

75. Letter from Michael Harrington to Comrades (June 21, 1973), unlabeled folder, box 26, Peter Rosenblatt Papers.

76. Meyerson, "Michael Harrington, an American Socialist," 22.

77. For the Record: The Report of Social Democrats, U.S.A. on the Resignation of Michael Harrington and His Attempt to Split the American Socialist Movement (n.d.), p. 13, folder "Harrington," box 45, Socialist Party U.S.A. Papers.

78. Adams, "Battle Royal among the Socialists."

79. The Politics of Michael Harrington (n.d.), p. 6, folder 2 "Ron Radosh," box 3, Socialist Party U.S.A. Papers.

80. Peter Kihss, "Socialists Plan Founding Parley," *New York Times*, September

10, 1973, folder "Harrington," box 47, Socialist Party U.S.A. Papers; Adams, "Battle Royal among the Socialists."

81. Penn Kemble and Josh Muravchik, "Quarrels over Quotas: 'Balancing' the Democrats," *New Leader,* January 20, 1975, 4.

82. Memo from Peter Rosenblatt to Members (November 28, 1975), p. 2, folder "New D.C. Chapter," box 65, Peter Rosenblatt Papers.

83. Rowland Evans and Robert Novak, "Democrats: A Moderate Majority," *Washington Post,* October 6, 1974, folder "CDM 1972–1973," box 63, Peter Rosenblatt Papers.

84. David Broder, "'Regulars' Regain Party Command," *Washington Post,* June 30, 1974, 1A.

85. Woodcock Frets over Democrats' Selection System (n.d.), folder "Political Observer: July," box 1, Peter Rosenblatt Papers.

86. R. W. Apple, "Liberal Democrats Target of Chanting Busing Foes," *New York Times,* November 23, 1975, 52A.

87. Ben Wattenberg's Speech in Louisville (November 21, 1975), folder "Ben Wattenberg," box 30, Peter Rosenblatt Papers.

88. Memo from Ben Wattenberg to CDM Board of Directors (July 31, 1976), folder "New D.C. Chapter," box 65, Peter Rosenblatt Papers.

89. Ben Wattenberg: The Democratic Party; What Policy Role with an Incumbent President (January 24, 1977), folder "Democratic Party," box 33, Peter Rosenblatt Papers.

90. CDM: Foreign Policy (n.d.), p. 73, unlabeled folder, box 17, Peter Rosenblatt Papers; Letter from Eugene Rostow to Henry Kissinger (September 4, 1974), folder "U.S. Foreign Policy," box 34, Peter Rosenblatt Papers; Letter from Eugene Rostow to Hubert Humphrey (April 12, 1976), folder "Miscellaneous," box 52, Peter Rosenblatt Papers.

91. CDM: Foreign Policy (n.d.), p. 77, unlabeled folder, box 17, Peter Rosenblatt Papers; Mike Zagarell, "Top Dems Outdo President, Seek More Military Spending," *Daily World,* April 12, 1975, 10A.

92. Bernard Gwertzman, "Ford Denies Moscow Dominates Eastern Europe: Carter Rebuts Him," *New York Times,* October 7, 1976, 1A.

93. Ben Wattenberg, "Mao's Funeral," *Harper's,* February 1977, 33.

94. Ibid.

95. Political Observer: Monthly News Bulletin of CDM (Summer 1977), p. 1, folder "CDM Press," box 1, Ben Wattenberg Papers.

96. Remarks by Ben Wattenberg (n.d.), p. 1, folder "Statements," box 2, Ben Wattenberg Papers.

97. Ibid.

98. Letter from Paul Seabury to Daniel Patrick Moynihan (n.d.), p. 3, folder "CDM Future," box 40, Peter Rosenblatt Papers.

99. Speech by Ben Wattenberg: The Democratic Party; What Policy Role with an Incumbent President (January 24, 1977), folder "Democratic Party," box 33, Peter Rosenblatt Papers.

100. Paul Warnke, "Apes on a Treadmill," *Foreign Policy* 18 (Spring 1975): 12–29.

101. Memorandum: Re Paul Warnke (n.d.), p. 2, folder "CDM Press," box 1, Ben Wattenberg Papers.

102. Warnke Affair, p. 2, folder "Newsletter Summer," box 32, Peter Rosenblatt Papers.

103. Political Observer, p. 1, folder "CDM Press," box 1, Ben Wattenberg Papers.

104. Letter from the CDM to Daniel Patrick Moynihan (March 28, 1977), p. 1, folder "CDM Future," box 40, Peter Rosenblatt Papers.

105. Jerry Sanders, *Peddlers of a Crisis: The Committee on the Present Danger and the Politics of Containment* (Boston: South End, 1983), 23–46.

106. William Beecher, "Hawk or Dove? In Capital, Carter Has Many Guessing," *Boston Evening Globe*, August 19, 1977, 23A.

107. Rowland Evans and Robert Novak, "A Touchy Carter: Shades of Former Presidents?" *Washington Post*, August 13, 1977, 15A.

108. Ibid.

109. Speech by Wattenberg to Democratic National Party Conference (December 9, 1978), folder "Wattenberg Articles," box 5, Peter Rosenblatt Papers; Unilateral Restraint: The Experiment That Failed, folder "Unilateral Restraint," box 23, Peter Rosenblatt Papers.

110. Handwritten Notes (n.d.), folder "Human Rights," box 34, Peter Rosenblatt Papers; Beyond the Cold War; Beyond Détente: Toward a Foreign Policy of Human Rights, pp. 5, 17, folder "Statements," box 2, Ben Wattenberg Papers.

111. Confidential Memo from Josh Muravchik to CDM Exec Committee (April 17, 1978), folder "Executive Committee," box 18, Peter Rosenblatt Papers; Letter from Joshua Muravchik to Congressman John Breckinridge (March 22, 1978), unlabeled folder, box 1, Ben Wattenberg Papers.

112. Memo from Josh Muravchik to Congressman Jim O'Hara (April 10, 1978), folder "CDM Press," box 1, Ben Wattenberg Papers.

113. Letter from Penn Kemble to Harrisson Dogle (May 16, 1978), folder "1978 Elections," box 33, Peter Rosenblatt Papers.

114. The Alex Seith Door-to-Door Report (April 1978), folder "1978 Elections," box 33, Peter Rosenblatt Papers; M. Stanton Evans, "Here's a Democrat Worth Supporting," *Human Events*, June 3, 1978, folder "1978 Elections," box 33, Peter Rosenblatt Papers.

115. Gary Adkins, "The State of the State," *Illinois Issues*, December 2, 1978, 1.

116. Ben Wattenberg, "It's Time to Stop America's Retreat," *Sunday New York Times Magazine*, p. 1, folder "Wattenberg Article," box 18, Peter Rosenblatt Papers.

117. Ibid.

118. CDM Executive Committee Meeting: October 19, 1979, folder "Ex-Comm 10/19/1979," box 18, Peter Rosenblatt Papers.

119. Draft (n.d.), p. 1, folder "Press Conference Statement," box 18, Peter Rosenblatt Papers.

120. Ibid., 3.

121. Ibid., 2.

122. Press Conference Statement (n.d.), p. 1, folder "Press Conference Statement," box 18, Peter Rosenblatt Papers; Memo to Sonny Dogole, Scoop, et al. (n.d.), folder "Conference on Terrorism," box 1, Ben Wattenberg Papers.

123. The Taking of American Hostages: Wattenberg Statement (n.d.), folder "Statements," box 2, Ben Wattenberg Papers.

124. Kaufman, *Henry Jackson*, 397.

125. Jeanne Kirkpatrick Notes (n.d.), folder "Press Conference Statement," box 18, Peter Rosenblatt Papers.

126. *Political Observer: News Bulletin on Policy, Politics, and People,* p. 1, folder "Statements," box 2, Ben Wattenberg Papers.

127. Wattenberg, *Fighting Words,* 166; Kaufman, *Henry Jackson,* 397.

128. Kaufman, *Henry Jackson,* 398.

129. Letter from Wattenberg to CDM Members (September 19, 1980), folder "CDM Minutes of Meeting," box 1, Ben Wattenberg Papers.

130. Remarks by Ben Wattenberg (March 31, 1981), folder "Speeches: Kirkpatrick; February 2, 1981," box 18, Peter Rosenblatt Papers.

131. Wattenberg, *Fighting Words,* 43.

8. "Everybody Is People"

1. Karen Foerstel and Herbert N. Foerstel, *Climbing the Hill: Gender Conflict in Congress* (New York: Praeger, 1996), 109.

2. Congresswoman Bella Abzug, Nude Bathing, file 2, box 23, Bella Abzug Papers, Columbia University, Special Collections.

3. "Bella on Bella," *Moment* 1, no. 7 (August 20, 1975): 1, file 22, box 64, Bella Abzug Papers.

4. Ibid.

5. Ibid., 2.

6. Kathy Roders, "Bella Abzug: A Leader of Vision and Voice," *Columbia Law Review* 98, no. 5 (June 1998): 1145.

7. Ibid.

8. "Bella on Bella."

9. About Bella Abzug: Background, file 6, box 910, Bella Abzug Papers; Womanpower! A New American Doctrine, p. 1, file 1, box 23, Bella Abzug Papers.

10. About Bella Abzug: Background, p. 3, file 6, box 910, Bella Abzug Papers.

11. Oral History: Abzug, tape 5 (March 26, 1971), p. 1, file "Oral History," box 63A, Bella Abzug Papers.

12. League of Women Voters Questionnaire, July 22, 1970, file 11, box 64, and Personal Biography: Citizens Look at Congress, by Ralph Nader, p. 4, folder 1, box 63, Bella Abzug Papers.

13. "Bella on Bella."

14. About Bella Abzug: Background, file 6, box 910, Bella Abzug Papers; "Womanpower! A New American Doctrine," p. 1, file 1, box 23, Bella Abzug Papers.

15. Myra MacPherson, "Abzug: Maturity Is the Key," *New York Times,* February 12, 1971, 1C.

16. "For Martin Abzug, Women's Lib Is an Old Story," *New York Times,* September 21, 1970, 38.

17. Letter from Mim Kelber to Anita Sumner (September 16, 1974), folder 1, box 23, Bella Abzug Papers.

18. Lawrence Van Gelder, "The Hat Shows Signs of Life," *New York Times,* October 20, 1975, 38.

19. Myra MacPherson, "'Everybody Is People,'" *Washington Post,* May 3, 1972, 3B.

20. Personal Biography: Citizens Look at Congress, by Ralph Nader, p. 4, folder 1, box 63, Bella Abzug Papers.

21. "Group Joins in Fight for Execution Stay," *New York Times*, July 20, 1950, 23.

22. John Popham, "4th McGee Appeal to High Court Due," *New York Times*, May 7, 1951, 16; MacPherson, "Abzug: Maturity Is the Key," 1C.

23. MacPherson, "Abzug: Maturity Is the Key," 1C.

24. Amy Swerdlow, *Women Strike for Peace: Traditional Motherhood and Radical Politics in the 1960s* (Chicago: University of Chicago Press, 1993), 145.

25. Personal Biography: Citizens Look at Congress, by Ralph Nader, p. 4, folder 1, box 63, Bella Abzug Papers.

26. Ibid., 143, 54.

27. Swerdlow, *Women Strike for Peace*, 1.

28. Richard Hunt, "2 Fight DeSapio in 'Village Test,'" *New York Times*, August 7, 1961, 18; "Against the Tiger: Carmine Gerard DeSapio," *New York Times*, May 8, 1964, 19.

29. Douglas Dales, "Democrats Urge Party Reforms," *New York Times*, July 13, 1959, 49; James S. Ottenberg, "Electing Reform Democrats" (Letter to the Editor), *New York Times*, December 7, 1961, 42.

30. Peter Rosenblatt, "The New Politics: Cautionary Tale," *Washington Post*, September 3, 1972, 2C; Edith Evans Asbury, "Koch Is a Guest at Italian Party," *New York Times*, May 9, 1965, 60.

31. "Mayor Proposes Party Reforms," *New York Times*, July 19, 1961, 18.

32. Jack Newfield, "Reformers vs. Farbstein: Sharp Contest Develops," *Village Voice*, January 27, 1966, 9; "Haddad to Seek Farbstein's Seat," *New York Times*, February 11, 1964, 25.

33. "Reform Club Urges Shift in Asia Policy," *New York Times*, February 21, 1967, 17; "Reformer Group Rejects Johnson," *New York Times*, May 19, 1967, 19; Robert Tomasson, "Democratic Club Faces War Test," *New York Times*, November 29, 1967, 9; M. S. Handler, "Bingham Is Opposed by Alexander Sachs in the 23rd District," *New York Times*, November 1, 1968, 52; Bella Abzug Testimony Before the 1968 Platform Committee of the DNC, p. 3, file 15, box 64, Bella Abzug Papers; David Boldt, "Women Protesters March on Capitol," *Washington Post*, March 27, 1969, 18A.

34. Lacey Fosburgh, "Women's Unit Bids Congress Shun War to Aid Human Needs," *New York Times*, June 17, 1969, 37.

35. Ibid.

36. Ibid.

37. Arnold Kaufman, October 5, 1968, Speech to New Democratic Coalition, p. 1, file 15, box 64, Bella Abzug Papers.

38. Ibid., 3.

39. Linda Charlton, "Women March Down Fifth in Equality Drive," *New York Times*, August 27, 1970, 1A.

40. Margaret Crimmins, "Lower Manhattan's Bella Abzug Rasps It Like It Is," *New York Times*, July 5, 1970, 101.

41. Woman Activist, N.D.C. Founder to Oppose Farbstein, Friday, March 13, p. 2, file 1, box 64, Bella Abzug Papers.

42. Grace Lichtenstein, "Farbstein Faces a Strong Challenge by Bella Abzug," *New York Times*, June 9, 1970, 30; J. Milton, February 1971 Oral History, tape 12, side B, p. 29, file "Oral History," box 63A, Bella Abzug Papers.

43. William Barry Furlong, "This Morning: Cosell Tries Again on TV," *New York Times*, October 13, 1975, 1B.

44. Letter from Abzug to Arthur Farash (March 9, 1972), file "November 1971," box 2, Bella Abzug Papers; Abzug Radio Spot, pp. 1–2, file 19 "1970 Race," box 64, Bella Abzug Papers.

45. Crimmins, "Lower Manhattan's Bella Abzug," 101.

46. "Miss Streisand Sings Bella Abzug's Praises," *New York Times*, June 15, 1970, 45; Rita Reif, "Barbara Streisand's 5-Story Compromise," *New York Times*, June 5, 1970, 47.

47. Richard Madden, "Badillo Wins House Race; Rooney, Scheurer Victors," *New York Times*, June 24, 1970, 1.

48. Chalmers Roberts, "Peace and 3rd-Party Candidates Fared Badly with Voters," *Washington Post*, November 5, 1970, 1A.

49. Personal Biography: Citizens Look at Congress, by Ralph Nader, p. 6, folder 1, box 63, Bella Abzug Papers; Brooks Jackson, AP Story on Abzug, p. 1, file 1 "Correspondence, 1971," box 1, Bella Abzug Papers.

50. J. Milton, February 1971 Oral History, tape 1, pp. 1, 3, file "Oral History," box 63A, Bella Abzug Papers; About Bella Abzug: Voted Third Most Influential, file 6, box 910, Bella Abzug Papers.

51. Comments from Congresswoman Bella Abzug . . . Workday, p. 1, folder 2, box 23, Bella Abzug Papers.

52. "Ex–Abzug Aide Finds Quieter Job," *Washington Post*, August 30, 1974, 20A; Mary McGrory, "The Capital Letter: Bella Sandpapers the House into Shape," *Washington Post*, April 14, 1975, 7; Special Order Tributes to Abzug, *Congressional Record* (September 30, 1976), 122, no. 150, p. 4, box 64, file "Congressional Record," Bella Abzug Papers.

53. J. Milton, February 1971 Oral History, tape 1, pp. 23, 5, 6, 11, file "Oral History," box 63A, Bella Abzug Papers; Tony Hiss, "Dilemma in the New 20th Congressional District—Bella Should Be There and So Should Ryan," *Sunday New York Times Magazine*, June 18, 1972, 12.

54. J. Milton, February 1971 Oral History, tape 1, p. 24, file "Oral History," box 63A, Bella Abzug Papers; Richard Lyons, "Liberal Democrats Get Key House Unit Posts," *Washington Post*, January 28, 1971, 2A; McGrory, "The Capital Letter: Bella Sandpapers the House into Shape," 7.

55. "Rep. Abzug Asks for Probe of Viet Oil," *New York Times*, March 16, 1971, 8A; Dear Friend, August 6, 1971, Letter Regarding Abzug Legislation, file "Aug 1971," box 1, Bella Abzug Papers.

56. J. Milton, February 1971 Oral History, tape 1, p. 25, file "Oral History," box 63A, Bella Abzug Papers.

57. Letter from Ken Simmons to Abzug (October 20, 1971), file 2, box 23, Bella Abzug Papers.

58. National Constituents for Bella Abzug, p. 2, file 6, box 65, Bella Abzug Papers.

59. Richard Madden, "Ms. Abzug Finds Mr.'s Rule House," *New York Times*, October 11, 1971, 37.

60. Abzug Speech to National Press Club Luncheon (July 21, 1971), p. 1, file "National Press Club," box 759, Bella Abzug Papers.

61. Tim O'Brien, "Women Organize for More Power," *Washington Post*, July 11, 1971, 1.

62. Laurie Johnston, "Women's Caucus Has New Rallying Cry: 'Make Policy, Not Coffee,'" *New York Times*, February 6, 1972, 60; Speech by Abzug to WEDS Conference, Nashville, TN (February 12, 1972), p. 3, file "WED Conference," box 759, Bella Abzug Papers.

63. Speech by Abzug to WEDS Conference, Nashville, TN (February 12, 1972), p. 4, file "WED Conference," box 759, Bella Abzug Papers.

64. Personal Biography: Citizens Look at Congress, by Ralph Nader, p. 21, folder 1, box 63, Bella Abzug Papers.

65. Nan Robertson, "Democrats Feel Impact of Women's New Power," *New York Times*, July 15, 1972, 1A.

66. Billy Graham, "Jesus and the Liberated Woman," *Ladies' Home Journal*, December 1970, file "Sexism and Religion," box 22, NOW-NYC Papers, Tamiment Library and Robert F. Wagner Labor Archives; Mass: Feminist Conscious Raising, file "Sexism and Religion," box 22, NOW-NYC Papers.

67. "Women Urged Not to Contribute Free Help to Male Candidates," *Washington Post*, June 30, 1974, 3A.

68. Oral History: Abzug, tape 16, side A, p. 6, file "Oral History," box 63A, Bella Abzug Papers.

69. Letter from Betty Friedan to Professor Herbert Richardson (August 22, 1967), file 8, box 4, NOW-NYC Papers.

70. Statement of Jean Faust of NOW, February 13, 1969, Hearing New York State Legislative Committee, p. 1, file 1, box 4, NOW-NYC Papers.

71. "Threat to Abortion Law," *New York Times*, May 1, 1972, folder 2 "Abortion," box 65, Bella Abzug Papers.

72. Statement of Jean Faust of NOW, February 13, 1969, Hearing New York State Legislative Committee, p. 1, file 1, box 4, NOW-NYC Papers.

73. 92nd Congress, 1st Session, A Bill to Enforce the Constitutional Right of Woman . . . , p. 1, file "Reproduction: Abortion," box 22, NOW-NYC Papers; Letter from Professor Cyril Means to Harriet Pilpel (January 21, 1972), file "Reproduction: Abortion," box 22, NOW-NYC Papers.

74. Karlyn Barker, "1,000 Vote Drive for Abortion," *Washington Post*, February 14, 1972, 12A; "Pro-Abortion Group Walks to Capitol," *Washington Post*, May 7, 1972, 6C; Memo from Marilyn to Bella, 5/7/74, Meeting with Carol Forman/Arvonne Fraser on Abortion in National Health Insurance, file 1, box 69, Bella Abzug Papers.

75. Judy Klemesrud, "The Lesbian Issue and Women's Lib," *New York Times*, December 18, 1970, 60.

76. MacPherson, "Abzug: Maturity Is the Key," 1C.

77. Austin Scott, "NOW Faces Major Crisis," *Washington Post*, November 30, 1975, 3.

78. Ibid.

79. Ibid.

80. Congressional Record: Martha Griffiths (March 26, 1970), p. 1, file 3, box 13, NOW-NYC Papers.

81. Letter from Nixon to Hugh Scott (Minority Leader) (May 18, 1972), file 1 "ERA," box 40, Bella Abzug Papers.

82. Linda Charlton, "Sisterhood, Powerful but Not Omnipotent," file "ERA," box 13, NOW-NYC Papers.

83. Personal Biography: Citizens Look at Congress, by Ralph Nader, p. 22, folder 1, box 63, Bella Abzug Papers; Voting Record: How Major Public Interest Groups Rated the Voting Record of Congresswoman Bella Abzug, p. 9, file 6 "Legislative Record," "Women's Rights" box 910, Bella Abzug Papers.

84. Oral History: Abzug, tape 5 (March 26, 1971), p. 14, file "Oral History," box 63A, Bella Abzug Papers.

85. Bella Abzug, "Should NYC Become a State? . . . Yes," file "August '71," box 1, Bella Abzug Papers.

86. Ibid.

87. Abzug and Statehood Committee, *Congressional Record* (August 4, 1971), 117, no. 125, pt. 2, file 5, box 65, Bella Abzug Papers.

88. Francis Clines, "Look What They Did to Bell Abzug!" *New York Times,* March 12, 1972, 3E.

89. Oral History: Abzug, tape 38, side A, p. 2, file "Oral History," box 63A, Bella Abzug Papers; Letter from Abzug to Constituents (March 30, 1972), p. 2, file 21, box 64, Bella Abzug Papers; Flora Lewis, "A Future in Congress for Bella Abzug?" *New York Times,* March 8, 1972, 20A.

90. Hiss, "Dilemma in the New 20th Congressional District," 12.

91. Ibid.

92. Paul Hodge, "Rep. Ryan: An Early Foe of the War," *Washington Post,* file 21 "1972," box 64, Bella Abzug Papers.

93. Debate: Abzug v. Ryan, pp. 1–2, file 21, box 64, Bella Abzug Papers; "Abzug-Ryan Debate: Issue Is Advocacy of Change," *New York Times,* June 12, 1972, 37.

94. Linda Charlton, "An Alleged G.O.P. Partisan Temporarily Pulls Mrs. Abzug's Hat Out of the Ring," *New York Times,* June 6, 1972, 27.

95. Ibid.

96. Hiss, "Dilemma in the New 20th Congressional District," 12.

97. MacPherson, "'Everybody Is People,'" 1B; Hiss, "Dilemma in the New 20th Congressional District," 12.

98. Pro–Mrs. Ryan Union Endorsers, file 5, box 65, Bella Abzug Papers; Hiss, "Dilemma in the New 20th Congressional District," 12.

99. Lou Cannon, "Rep. Abzug, Lowenstein Are Beaten," *Washington Post,* June 21, 1972, 1A.

100. Pete Hamill, "The Quality of Mercy," *New York Post,* September 22, 1972, file 21, box 64, Bella Abzug Papers.

101. Richard Madden, "Bella Abzug Wins Easily; Reid Leads as Democrat," *New York Times,* November 8, 1972, 97.

102. "Rep. Abzug Reports Her Telephones Tapped," *Washington Post,* October 11, 1972, 3B.

103. Investigations, Inc. October 9, 1972, Summary of Investigation, pp. 1–3, file "October 9, 1972," box 3, Bella Abzug Papers.

104. Ibid.; Letter from Abzug to Carl Albert (October 9, 1972), file "October 9, 1972," box 3, Bella Abzug Papers.

105. Martin Tolchin, "Mrs. Abzug's Image Shifts, But Is She Same Old Bella?" *New York Times*, November 29, 1973, 45.

106. McGrory, "The Capital Letter: Bella Sandpapers the House into Shape," 7.

107. Congresswoman Abzug's Record: Protection of Individual Rights and an End to Government Secrecy, p. 2, file 2, box 727, Bella Abzug Papers.

108. Marjorie Hyer, "Rep. Abzug Scores Nixon at Protest," *Washington Post*, January 17, 1973, 7B; Oral History: Abzug, tape 16, side A, p. 4, file "Oral History," box 63A, Bella Abzug Papers; Testimony of Abzug Before Senate Rules Committee, Nov. 14, 1973, on Confirmation of Gerald Ford as VP, p. 6, file 2, box 517, Bella Abzug Papers.

109. Jules Witcover, "Women Candidates Capitalizing on Clean Political Image," *Washington Post*, June 16, 1974, L1.

110. Ibid.

111. McGrory, "The Capital Letter: Bella Sandpapers the House into Shape," 7.

112. Ronald Smothers, "House Majority Leader Backs Abzug Candidacy," *New York Times*, August 10, 1976, 15; McGrory, "The Capital Letter: Bella Sandpapers the House into Shape," 7; Letter from Abzug to President Ford, "Human Suffering and Chaos in South Vietnam" (April 3, 1975), pp. 1–2, file 2, box 40, Bella Abzug Papers; Letter from Vernon Loen to Abzug, December 30, 1975, Diplomatic Recognition, file 3, box 40, Bella Abzug Papers.

113. Congresswoman Abzug's Record: Protection of Individual Rights and an End to Government Secrecy, p. 1, file 2, box 727, Bella Abzug Papers; "C.I.A. Opened Bella Abzug's Mail, Kept 20-Year File," *New York Times*, March 6, 1975, 77.

114. Jack Anderson and Les Whitten, "Abzug May Air Assassination Data," *Washington Post*, November 8, 1975, B26.

115. What Abzug Has Produced for NY State, p. 1, file 2, box 727, Bella Abzug Papers.

116. Personal Biography: Citizens Look at Congress, by Ralph Nader, p. 21, folder 1, box 63, Bella Abzug Papers.

117. Ibid.

118. Congresswoman Abzug's Record: Women's Rights, p. 1, file 2, box 727, Bella Abzug Papers.

119. "Bella Abzug Eyes Buckley Senate Seat," *Washington Post*, February 6, 1975, 9A.

120. Furlong, "This Morning: Cosell Tries Again on TV," 1B; Mary Breasted, "Mrs. Abzug's Pace Is Hectic in Westchester," *New York Times*, August 24, 1976, 33.

121. Letter from Abzug to Friends (August 20, 1975), p. 1, file 22, box 64, Bella Abzug Papers.

122. Frank Lynn, "The Two Images of Bella Abzug," *New York Times*, August 31, 1976, 18.

123. Mary Breasted, "Women's Caucus Ends on Cheering Note," *New York Times*, March 17, 1975, 20.

124. Thomas Ronan, "Abzug Supporters Adopt Revised Buckley Slogan," *New York Times*, September 20, 1975, 10; "Campaign Tied by Mrs. Abzug to Women's Equality," *New York Times*, August 27, 1976, 18.

125. Breasted, "Mrs. Abzug's Pace Is Hectic in Westchester," 33.

126. Smothers, "House Majority Leader Backs Abzug Candidacy," 15.

127. Dee Wedemeyer, "Bella Abzug Right at Home in Social Whirl," *New York Times*, July 22, 1976, 39.

128. Ibid.

129. Ibid.

130. Tom Wicker, "Abzug vs. Moynihan: Sound and Fury," *New York Times*, September 12, 1976, 175.

131. "Moynihan Accuses Rep. Abzug of 'Rule-or-Ruin' Stand," *New York Times*, August 30, 1976, 29; Wicker, "Abzug vs. Moynihan," 175.

132. Damon Stetson, "Shanker Assails Mrs. Abzug; She Denies His 'Scab' Charge," *New York Times*, September 3, 1976, B17.

133. Henry Stern, "Pat Moynihan Remembered," *New York Civic*, October 1, 2003, 1.

134. Frank Lynn, "Moynihan Edges Out Mrs. Abzug; Buckley Also Victor in Primary; Badillo, Mrs. Chisholm Winners," *New York Times*, September 15, 1976, 1A.

9. Leave Us Alone

1. Gladwin Hill, "Stakes Are High in the 'Sagebrush Rebellion,'" *New York Times*, September 2, 1979, 5E.

2. R. McGregor Cawley, *Federal Land, Western Anger: The Sagebrush Rebellion and Environmental Politics* (Lawrence: University Press of Kansas, 1993), 66; "'Sagebrush Rebels' Are Reveling in Reagan," *New York Times*, November 24, 1980, D9.

3. Joseph M. Chomski, *The Sagebrush Rebellion: A Concise Analysis of the History, the Law, and Politics of Public Land in the United States*, prepared for the State of Alaska, Legislative Affairs Agency (Juneau, AK: The Agency, 1980), 39.

4. Rachel Carson, *Silent Spring*, 25th anniversary ed. (Boston: Houghton Mifflin, 1987), 15.

5. Martin Melosi, "Lyndon Johnson and Environmental Policy," in *The Johnson Years*, vol. 2, *Vietnam, the Environment, and Science*, ed. Robert Divine (Lawrence: University Press of Kansas, 1987), 113.

6. National Parks Service, Public Use Statistics Office, https://irma.nps.gov/Stats/SSRSReports/Park Specific Reports/Annual Park Visitation (All Years)?Park=ZION.

7. William Graf, *Wilderness Preservation and the Sagebrush Rebellions* (Savage, MD: Rowan & Littlefield, 1990), 200.

8. Ibid., 9.

9. Donald Worster, *An Unsettled Country: Changing Landscapes of the American West* (Albuquerque: University of New Mexico Press, 1994), 10–13, and *A River Running West: The Life of John Wesley Powell* (Oxford: Oxford University Press, 2001), 50.

10. Jack Ward Thomas, "America's First Forrester," *Range*, Winter 2003, 12; Graf, *Wilderness Preservation*, 188–93.

11. Donald Worster, *The Wealth of Nature: Environmental History and the Ecological Imagination* (New York: Oxford University Press, 1993), 201.

12. Ibid., 261.

13. Hill, "Stakes Are High in Sagebrush Rebellion," E5.

14. "'Sagebrush Rebels' Are Reveling in Reagan," D9.

15. The West is generally considered to be composed of thirteen states: Alaska, Hawaii, Washington, Oregon, Idaho, Montana, Wyoming, Colorado, New Mexico, Arizona, Utah, Nevada, and California.

16. Clive Thomas, "The West and Its Brand of Politics," in *Politics and Public Policy in the Contemporary American West,* ed. Clive Thomas (Albuquerque: University of New Mexico Press, 1991), 7.

17. Richard Foster, "The Federal Government and the West," in ibid., 85.

18. Lou Cannon, "Sagebrush Rebellion Challenges U.S. Grip on Western Land," *Washington Post,* April, 9, 1979, page missing.

19. "Nevada Trying to Reclaim Land Held by Government since 1864," *New York Times,* June 10, 1979, 50.

20. Foster, "The Federal Government and the West," 79.

21. James Bailey, "The Politics of Dunes, Redwoods, and Dams: Arizona's 'Brothers Udall' and America's National Parklands, 1961–1969" (Ph.D. diss.), 18–20, folder 8, box 90, Morris K. Udall Papers, University of Arizona Special Collections Library.

22. Morris K. Udall Interview with James McNulty (March 29, 1989), pp. 1–3, folder 18, box 1, Morris K. Udall Papers.

23. Donald Carson and James Johnson, *Mo: The Life and Times of Morris K. Udall* (Tucson: University of Arizona Press, 2001), 2–4.

24. Sean Griffin, "From the Lip: Mo Known for Zinging Politics, Self with Wit," *Phoenix Gazette,* April 20, 1991, S2.

25. Bailey, "The Politics of Dunes, Redwoods, and Dams," 23.

26. Clay Thompson, "Always a Leader, Always a Prankster," *Phoenix Gazette,* April 20, 1991, S2.

27. Bailey, "The Politics of Dunes, Redwoods, and Dams," 21; Interview of Morris K. Udall, by Randy Udall (April 28, 1971), p. 1, folder 10, box 7, Morris K. Udall Papers.

28. Bailey, "The Politics of Dunes, Redwoods, and Dams," 22.

29. Ibid., 23.

30. Sean Griffin, "Udall Unbowed in Public Despite Private Pain," *Phoenix Gazette,* September 7, 1988, 2.

31. Thompson, "Always a Leader," S2.

32. Carson and Johnson, *Mo,* 15.

33. Interview of Morris K. Udall, by Randy Udall (April 28, 1971), p. 2, folder 10, box 7, Morris K. Udall Papers.

34. Thompson, "Always a Leader," S2.

35. Official Ballot: Student Ticket/Future Farmer Ticket, folder 1, box 1, Morris K. Udall Papers; 20th Annual Commencement Week: St. Johns High School 1940, p. 2, folder 1, box 1, Morris K. Udall Papers.

36. Thompson, "Always a Leader," S2.

37. Assorted Columns from *The Wildcat* (n.d.), folder 3, box 1, Morris K. Udall Papers.

38. Morris K. Udall Interview with James McNulty (March 29, 1989), p. 24, folder 18, box 1, Morris K. Udall Papers.

39. Letter from Sergeant Herbert Davis to Morris Udall (July 22, 1944), folder 5, box 1, Morris K. Udall Papers.

40. Griffin, "Udall Unbowed in Public Despite Private Pain," 2.

41. "U's Best Squad Ends Season with Banquet," *The Wildcat*, folder 3, box 1, Morris K. Udall Papers; Claie Jordan, "Physical Disability No Handicap in Udall's Bright Success Story," *Denver Post*, folder 5, box 3, Morris K. Udall Papers; Interview of Morris K. Udall, by Randy Udall (April 28, 1971), p. 29, folder 10, box 7, Morris K. Udall Papers.

42. Interview of Morris K. Udall, by Randy Udall (April 28, 1971), p. 29, folder 10, box 7, Morris K. Udall Papers.

43. Molly Ivins, "Liberal from Goldwater Country," *Sunday New York Times Magazine*, February 1, 1976, 4.

44. Interview of Morris K. Udall, by Randy Udall (April 28, 1971), p. 32, folder 10, box 7, Morris K. Udall Papers.

45. Bailey, "The Politics of Dunes, Redwoods, and Dams," 28.

46. Ibid., 33.

47. Robert Dolezal, "Quarter of a Century, Mo Udall: 25 Years of Politicking," *Tucson Weekly*, September 30–October 6, 1987, 4.

48. Bailey, "The Politics of Dunes, Redwoods, and Dams," 32.

49. "Goldwater Welcomes Fight against 'Left Wingers,'" *Tucson Daily Citizen*, September 8, 1954, 1A.

50. Jim Hart, "Udall Loses to 'Machine,'" *Tucson Daily Citizen*, September 8, 1954, 1A.

51. Morris K. Udall Interview with James McNulty (March 29, 1989), p. 33, folder 18, box 1, Morris K. Udall Papers.

52. Carson and Johnson, *Mo*, 56.

53. Morris K. Udall, *Arizona Law of Evidence* (St. Paul: West, 1960); Edward Cleary, review of *Arizona Law of Evidence*, by Morris K. Udall, *Arizona Law Review*, p. 104, folder 1, box 3, Morris K. Udall Papers.

54. Dolezal, "Quarter of a Century," 4.

55. Don Carson, "Congressional Candidates Hurl Hot Words at Press Club Bout," *Arizona Daily Star*, March 22, 1961, 3; "Udall's Brother Faces Close Test," *New York Times*, April 30, 1961, 51.

56. Carson and Johnson, *Mo*, 63–65.

57. Morris Udall, *Education of a Congressman: The Newsletters of Morris K. Udall*, ed. Robert Peabody (New York: Bobbs-Merrill, 1972), 14–16.

58. "Veteran Solon Wins Battle over Mecham," *Arizona Daily Star*, November 7, 1962, 1A; "Mo Udall Shows Greater District Pull Than Stew," *Arizona Daily Star*, November 7, 1962, 3B.

59. Carson and Johnson, *Mo*, 57–69.

60. "Rep. Udall's Wife Seeks a Divorce," *Arizona Daily Star*, November 20, 1965, 8A; Ivins, "Liberal from Goldwater Country," 4.

61. Wilderness Society, *Wilderness America: A Vision for the Future of the Nation's Wildlands* (Layton, UT: Wilderness Society, 1989), 1; "Good Year for Conservation," *New York Times*, August 23, 1964, 10E; *America's National Park System: The Critical Documents*, ed. Lary Dilsaver (Lanham, MD: Rowan & Littlefield, 1994), 237–44.

62. Arnold Hano, "The Battle of the Grand Canyon," *Sunday New York Times Magazine*, December 12, 1965, 56.

63. "Pious Irrigation Scheme," *New York Times,* October 4, 1903, 13.

64. Earl Zarbin, "CAP Was Agricultural Dream of 1890s," *Arizona Republic,* February 6, 1977, 1A.

65. Gladwin Hill, "Western State: California and Arizona Battle for Colorado River Water," *New York Times,* June 6, 1948, E6; Carson and Johnson, *Mo,* 118–19.

66. Russell Porter, "Arizona Is Victor in Claim to Water of the Colorado," *New York Times,* May 9, 1960, 1A; William Blair, "Arizona Upheld over California on Water Rights," *New York Times,* January 4, 1963, 1A.

67. Letter from Stewart Udall to Carl Hayden: Personal and Confidential (June 12, 1963), folder "May–July 1963," box 476, Morris K. Udall Papers; Memo from Hayden to Arizona Congressional Delegation (May 10, 1963), folder "May–July 1963," box 476, Morris K. Udall Papers; "Udall, Where Are You?" *Arizona Republic,* August 14, 1963, 6; Bailey, "The Politics of Dunes, Redwoods, and Dams," 203; Letter from Morris Udall to William Mathews (August 20, 1963), folder "August–October 1963," box 476, Morris K. Udall Papers.

68. Bailey, "The Politics of Dunes, Redwoods, and Dams," 203.

69. In Carson and Johnson, *Mo,* 123, the environmental historian Roderick Nash is quoted as calling the public reaction to the Grand Canyon dams "one of the largest outpourings of public sentiment in American Conservation History."

70. Bailey, "The Politics of Dunes, Redwoods, and Dams," 218; "I.R.S. Threatens the Sierra Club," *New York Times,* June 12, 1966, 50; "Sierra Club Gains in Fight on Taxes," *New York Times,* August 7, 1966, 50.

71. John Finney, "Rep. Udall Splits with Administration over War," *New York Times,* October 23, 1967, 34.

72. Bailey, "The Politics of Dunes, Redwoods, and Dams," 225; William Blair, "Senate Approves Arizona Project," *New York Times,* August 8, 1967, 14.

73. "C.A.P. to Produce 4,000 Arizona Jobs: Lawmakers Hail Long-Sought Bill," *Tucson Daily-Citizen,* September 30, 1968, 1A.

74. Larry King, "The Road to Power in Congress: The Education of Mo Udall—and What It Cost," *Harper's Magazine,* June 1971, 40.

75. Ella Royston Udall—a Biography: Series of *Arizona Republic* Articles, folder 9, box 1, Morris K. Udall Papers.

76. Ben Cole, "The Capital Focus: Mo Next House Speaker?" *Arizona Republic,* May 21, 1967, 3.

77. "Mr. Udall Speaks Up," *New York Times,* December 27, 1968, 32A; John Finney, "Congress: The Democrats Grapple with the Generation Gap," *New York Times,* December 29, 1968, 2E; Carson and Johnson, *Mo,* 107–9.

78. Memo, Morris Udall to Self: Some Thought on How to Win While Losing (n.d.), p. 1, file 1, box 78, Morris K. Udall Papers.

79. King, "The Road to Power in Congress," 40; Memo from Morris Udall to Carl Albert: Regarding Leadership Challenge (n.d.), folder 1, box 78, Morris K. Udall Papers.

80. Myra MacPherson, "Humble Giant: Udall Gracefully Weathers Victories, Defeats with Touch of Down-Home Wit," *Arizona Republic,* January 12, 1986, 11A; Dennis Farney, "Faded Fiefdoms," *Wall Street Journal,* May 3, 1979, folder 4, box 3, Morris K. Udall Papers; Memo, Morris Udall to Self: Some Thought on How

to Win While Losing (n.d.), p. 1, file 1, box 78, Morris K. Udall Papers; Sean Griffin, "O'Neill's Book Relates Udall's Biggest Mistake," *Phoenix Gazette*, folder 2, box 2, Morris K. Udall Papers.

81. "Mo Udall Is Honored a 'Man of the Year,'" *St. Louis Post-Dispatch*, January 15, 1969, folder 17, box 7, Morris K. Udall Papers.

82. Loye Miller, "Amateur Toreador Campaigns against Popular Morris Udall," *Miami Herald*, May 31, 1970, folder 9, box 2, Morris K. Udall Papers.

83. Statement by Udall on Abortion, folder 2, box 42, Morris K. Udall Papers; Statement by Udall on School Desegregation and Busing (n.d.), folder 2, box 42, Morris K. Udall Papers; Statement by Udall on Sexual Preference (n.d.), file 3, box 42, Morris K. Udall Papers.

84. Yanek Mieczkowski, *Gerald Ford and the Challenges of the 1970s* (Lexington: University Press of Kentucky, 2005), 200–201.

85. Ibid., 206.

86. Ibid., 99; Article by Morris Udall, "After the Boom: Growth in the Public Interest," p. 39, folder 14, box 91, Morris K. Udall Papers; Speech by Udall to Consumers Federation of America (January 31, 1975), 1, folder 27, box 39, Morris K. Udall Papers; Congressman's Report, by Morris Udall: Enter, an Age of Scarcity (February 14, 1974), folder 4, box 39, Morris K. Udall Papers.

87. Memo from Roger to Udall: Electro Sport Cart (n.d.), folder 15, box 657, Morris K. Udall Papers; Letter from Morris Udall to Dale Worthem: I Like Your Idea for Adoption of the Squirrel (October 31, 1974), folder 1, box 657, Morris K. Udall Papers.

88. Congressman's Report, "A Time Bomb Called Population" (August 10, 1964), p. 4, folder 1, box 79, Morris K. Udall Papers; Article, Morris Udall: A Reader's Digest Reprint; "Standing Room Only on Spaceship Earth," p. 10, folder 40, box 90, Morris K. Udall Papers.

89. Morris Udall, "Spaceship Earth—Standing Room Only: A Bold Plan to Save Us from Ourselves," *Arizona Magazine*, July 27, 1969, 10; Morris Udall, "The Democratic Party: Where Do We Go from Here?" *New Republic*, November 24, 1973, 18; Article by Morris Udall, "After the Boom: Growth in the Public Interest," p. 39, folder 14, box 91, Morris K. Udall Papers.

90. Carson and Johnson, *Mo*, 146–47.

91. Ibid., 152.

92. Memo from Udall to Files: Udall's Definition of Liberalism (September 9, 1976), folder 12, box 7, Morris K. Udall Papers.

93. Letter from Maurice Lazarus to Junius Hoffman, "Dear Junie, It's just as well that you did not beat your way over to Phoenix" (April 29, 1975), folder 1, box 37, Morris K. Udall Papers; Carson and Johnson, *Mo*, 155.

94. Barry Farrell, "Morris Udall: Playing by Winners' Rules," *The Progressive*, December 1975, 28; Letter from Archibald Cox to Udall, "Dear Mo, A visit to Maine explains the long delay" (February 28, 1977), folder 2, box 8, Morris K. Udall Papers; Letter from Robert Redford to Udall, "I appreciated the conversation by phone the other day" (June 25, 1975), folder 1, box 37, Morris K. Udall Papers; Letter from Linda Ronstadt to Udall, "I hear that you're going to be here for a concert" (November 18, 1975), folder 1, box 37, Morris K. Udall Papers; Letter from Arthur Schlesinger to Udall, "As I said the other day before the BBC Broadcast"

(July 15, 1976), folder 2, box 78, Morris K. Udall Papers; Letter from Jimmy Breslin to Udall, "Walk right out and put the first shot into the hole and let it go from there" (March 1976), folder 1, box 37, Morris K. Udall Papers; Stan to Mo: Mo! From Doonesbury to the *New York Times* (February 2, 1977), folder 4, box 3, Morris K. Udall Papers.

95. Ken Burton, "Udall Breaks Arms in Fall from Roof," *Arizona Daily Star,* November 15, 1976, folder 4, box 3, Morris K. Udall Papers.

96. Carson and Johnson, *Mo,* 242–43.

97. Speech, Congressional Record of the 95th Congress (January 4, 1977), p. 1, folder 7, box 353, Morris K. Udall Papers.

98. Ibid., 2.

99. Carson and Johnson, *Mo,* 195.

100. Office Memo from Udall to MKU Files: Meeting with the President (January 1, 1978), folder 6, box 682, Morris K. Udall Papers.

101. "Morris Udall's Congressman Report," *Preserving Our Heritage,* December 7, 1961, 1, folder 31, box 98, Morris K. Udall Papers.

102. Stacy Fritz, "The Role of National Missile Defense in the Environmental History of Alaska" (paper presented at the Phi Alpha Theta Conference, Northern Studies Program, University of Alaska—Fairbanks, April 2000), 1.

103. "Kennedy Starts Tour of Alaska," *New York Times,* September 4, 1960, 1; "Democrats Feel Sure of Alaska," *New York Times,* September 18, 1960, 56.

104. Fritz, "The Role of National Missile Defense," 1; "Kennedy Starts Tour of Alaska," 1.

105. Fritz, "The Role of National Missile Defense," 1.

106. Ibid.

107. William Blair, "Dam on the Yukon Stymied by Udall," *New York Times,* June 25, 1967, 13; and "Alaskans Hopeful on Yukon Power," *New York Times,* June 18, 1961, 57.

108. Blair, "Dam on the Yukon Stymied by Udall," 13.

109. "U.S. Plan for New Aleutian Blasts Meeting Growing Opposition," *New York Times,* April 30, 1970, 16.

110. Wallace Turner, "Alaskans Accept Cannikin but They Still Don't Like It," *New York Times,* November 2, 1971, 26; David Rosenbaum, "Fame Travels with Senator Gravel, the Man Who Read Pentagon Papers," *New York Times,* October 26, 1971, 29.

111. "Blast at Amchitka Set Off 22 Quakes," *New York Times,* August 31, 1972, 30; Mathew Walk, "Bomb Site Cleanup Is Put at Billions," *New York Times,* July 2, 1988, 8.

112. Charles Mohr, "Congress Is Pondering the Future of Wild Alaska," *New York Times,* March 26, 1978, 18E.

113. Speech by Morris Udall, Loving Critic Takes Aim at the Conservation Movement (n.d.), folder 18, box 91, Morris K. Udall Papers.

114. D-2 Survey Summary, Conclusions and Discussion (n.d.), p. 6, folder 3, box 327, Morris K. Udall Papers.

115. Bill Kovach, "Bill on Future of Federal Lands in Alaska Generates Bitter and Emotional Controversy," *New York Times,* June 19, 1978, 4B.

116. Memo from Karen to Udall (July 28, 1977), folder 13, box 328, Morris K. Udall Papers.

117. Memo from Udall to Staff: Echardt Amendment (n.d.), folder 2, box 336, Morris K. Udall Papers.

118. "Wilderness Plan Disputed in Alaska City," *New York Times*, August 22, 1977, 16; Ed Hein, "Timber Industry Would Be Affected Forest Service Reports on Udall Bill," *Anchorage Times*, July 14, 1977, 1A.

119. Memo from Karen to Udall: Alaska—Major Issues (August 4, 1977), p. 2, folder 14, box 328, Morris K. Udall Papers.

120. Report, State D-2 Steering Council Report on Alaska (March 7, 1978), p. 11, folder 3, box 327, Morris K. Udall Papers.

121. "Hickel Bid Marks Alaska's Primary," *New York Times*, August 26, 1974, 23.

122. Kovach, "Bill on Future of Federal Lands in Alaska," 4B; Report, State D-2 Steering Council Report on Alaska (March 7, 1978), p. 11, folder 3, box 327, Morris K. Udall Papers.

123. Kay Brown, "Akron Congressman 'Can't Even Believe' Alaska's D-2 Debate," *Alaska Advocate*, August 18, 1977, 6.

124. Hearings, Alaska National Interest Lands Hearing: Testimony of Gary Friedman (April 22, 1977), folder 6, box 328, Morris K. Udall Papers; Hearings, Alaska National Interest Lands Hearing: Cammie Israil (n.d.), folder 6, box 328, Morris K. Udall Papers.

125. Carson and Johnson, *Mo*, 196.

126. Seth King, "Alaska Officials Irked by Order Barring U.S. Land Development," *New York Times*, November 18, 1978, 14.

127. Cawley, *Federal Land, Western Anger*, 85.

128. Seth King, "Carter Designates U.S. Land in Alaska for National Parks," *New York Times*, December 2, 1978, 1.

129. Carson and Johnson, *Mo*, 199.

130. "Around the Nation," *New York Times*, September 8, 1979, 10.

131. Warren Weaver, "G.O.P. Policy Panel in Platform, Says 'Carter Must Go!'" *New York Times*, July 11, 1980, 1A.

132. Philip Shabecoff, "Senate Starts Debating Legislation on Future Use of Land in Alaska," *New York Times*, July 22, 1980, 12A.

133. Memo from Karen to Udall: Alaska—Major Issues (August 4, 1977), p. 1, folder 14, box 328, Morris K. Udall Papers.

134. Howell Raines, "State's Rights Move in West Influencing Reagan's Drive," *New York Times*, July 5, 1980, 7.

135. "'Sagebrush Rebels' Are Reveling in Reagan," 9D.

136. Carson and Johnson, *Mo*, 200.

137. Seth King, "Carter Signs a Bill to Protect 104 Million Acres in Alaska," *New York Times*, December 3, 1980, 20A.

10. "Zero, None, Zip, Nada"

1. Jane Perlez, "Ferraro Says She Senses Surprise Vote by Women," *New York Times*, November 4, 1984, 39.

2. "Zero, None, Zip, Nada," *New York Times*, November 15, 1984, 30A.

3. David Rosenbaum, "How the Candidates Divided the Voting," *New York Times*, November 8, 1984, A1, A19; Perlez, "Ferraro Says She Senses Surprise Vote," 39.

4. Bella Abzug and Mim Kelber, "Despite the Reagan Sweep, a Gender Gap Remains," *New York Times*, November 23, 1984, 35A.

5. Jane Perlez, "Women, Power, and Politics," *Sunday New York Times Magazine*, June 24, 1984, 22.

6. Brad Lemley, "Eleanor Smeal in Overdrive," *Washington Post Magazine*, November 24, 1985, 12.

7. Eleanor Smeal, *Why and How Women Will Elect the Next President* (New York: Harper & Row, 1984), 10–13.

8. Ibid., 12.

9. Ibid., 11–12.

10. Carol Mueller, "The Gender Gap and Women's Political Influence," *Annals of the American Academy of Political and Social Science* 515 (May 1991): 24.

11. "Men and Women: Is Realignment Under Way?" *Public Opinion*, April/May 1982, 21–22.

12. Ibid., 27.

13. Janet Smith, "Vice President? Rep. Lindy Boggs Says She's Ready," *Daily Iberian* (New Iberia, LA), February 5, 1984, sec. 5, p. 7.

14. Ibid.; Shirley Haupt, "Boggs Seeks Veep Slot," *West Bank Guide* (Gretna, LA), February 8, 1984, 5A.

15. Bella Abzug and Mim Kelber, "Women vs. Reagan," *New York Times*, February 12, 1984, 19E.

16. Mueller, "The Gender Gap and Women's Political Influence," 36.

17. "Men and Women," 27.

18. Karen Kaufmann and John Petrocik, "The Changing Politics of American Men: Understanding the Sources of the Gender Gap," *American Journal of Political Science* 43, no. 3 (July 1999): 866; Louis Bolce, "The Role of Gender in Recent Presidential Elections: Reagan and the Reverse Gender Gap," *Presidential Studies Quarterly* 15 (1985): 384.

19. Mueller, "The Gender Gap and Women's Political Influence," 35.

20. Franco Mattier, "The Gender Gap in Presidential Evaluations: Assessments of Clinton's Performance in 1996," *Polity* 33, no. 2 (Winter 2000): 201–2.

21. Kaufmann and Petrocik, "The Changing Politics of American Men," 884.

22. Draft: Catholic/Ethnic Strategy, p. 8, folder "Ethnics 3 of 4," F003 Elizabeth Dole Files, Ronald Reagan Presidential Foundation and Library; Memo from Elizabeth Dole to Edwin Meese, James Baker, Michael Deaver, and William Clark—Proposed Action Plan for Ethnics (November 2, 1982), p. 1, folder "Ethnics 1 of 4," F003 Elizabeth Dole Files.

23. Catholic Portfolio, p. 1, folder "Ethnics 1 of 4," F003 Elizabeth Dole Files.

24. Gillon, *The Democrats' Dilemma*, 355.

25. Katherine Reinhard, "Campaigns Hard-Nosed in the 5th," *Allentown (PA) Morning Call*, November 4, 1984, B1.

26. Steven Roberts, "Mondale Attracts Pittsburgh's Poles," *New York Times*, April 8, 1984, 38.

27. Ethnic Blue Collar Strategy (January 6, 1983), p. 3, folder "Ethnics 1 of 4," F003 Elizabeth Dole Files.

28. Sara Solovitch, "A Lehigh Valley Race That Has Drawn National Interest," *Philadelphia Inquirer*, October 24, 1984, B1.

29. Ibid.; Reinhard, "Campaigns Hard-Nosed in the 5th," B1.

30. Memo from Gary Bauer to Edwin Harper, June 18, 1982, Abortion Impact on Our Coalition, pp. 1, 2, file "Abortion," OA 7112, William Barr Files, Ronald Reagan Presidential Foundation and Library.

31. Draft: Catholic/Ethnic Strategy, pp. 15, 16, folder "Ethnics 3 of 4," F003 Elizabeth Dole Files.

32. Elizabeth Dole to Edwin Meese, James Baker, Michael Deaver, and William Clark—Proposed Action Plan for Ethnics (November 2, 1982), p. 2, folder "Ethnics 1 of 4," F003 Elizabeth Dole Files.

33. Draft: Catholic/Ethnic Strategy, pp. 15, 16, folder "Ethnics 3 of 4," F003 Elizabeth Dole Files.

34. Margo Hornblower, "Catholic Church Turns Activist," *Washington Post*, November 12, 1984, 1A; Marjorie Hyer, "Bernardin Views Prolife as 'Seamless Garment,'" *Washington Post*, December 10, 1983, 6B.

35. D. J. R. Bruckner, "Chicago's Activist Cardinal," *Sunday New York Times Magazine*, May 1, 1983, 42; James Franklin, "In Search of Moral in the Nuclear Age: The US Bishops Take Their Stand," *Boston Globe*, May 8, 1983, page unknown.

36. Bruckner, "Chicago's Activist Cardinal," 42.

37. Hyer, "Bernardin Views Prolife as 'Seamless Garment,'" 6B.

38. Ibid.

39. "Who Will Be the 4 New Cardinals," *Miami Herald*, October 7, 1983, 1B.

40. Hornblower, "Catholic Church Turns Activist," 1A; James Franklin, "New Analysis: Bishop O'Connor and Arms Policy," *Washington Post*, February 1, 1984, page unknown; Marjorie Hyer, "Bishops Praise Draft of Economics Pastoral," *Washington Post*, November 15, 1984, 9A.

41. Gillon, *The Democrats' Dilemma*, 367.

42. Mary McGrory, "The Bishops May Have Deferred More to Rome Than to Reagan," *Washington Post*, April 7, 1983, 3A.

43. David Farrell, "Politics and Abortion," *Boston Globe*, February 13, 1984, page unknown.

44. Sam Roberts, "Cuomo to Challenge Archbishop over Criticism of Abortion Stand," *New York Times*, August 3, 1984, 1A; "A Faith to Trust," *New York Times*, September 15, 1984, 22; "Excerpts from Kennedy's Remarks on Religion," *New York Times*, September 11, 1984, 26A.

45. Robert Shaw, "Abortion an Issue in VP Campaigns," *Philadelphia Inquirer*, September 12, 1984, 8A; "The Religion Issue, with Gusto," *New York Times*, September 16, 1984, 1E; Patricia O'Brien, "Aides Fear Abortion Issue Could Cost Ferraro Votes," *Philadelphia Inquirer*, September 14, 1984, 1A.

46. O'Brien, "Aides Fear Abortion Issue Could Cost Ferraro Votes," 1A.

47. Benjamin Taylor, "Ferraro States Views in Pro-Life Country," *Boston Globe*, September 13, 1984, page unknown.

48. "Excerpts from Interview with Ferraro on Campaign Plane," *New York Times*, August 14, 1984, 21A.

49. Taylor, "Ferraro States Views in Pro-Life Country."

50. Rick Atkinson and Kathy Sawyer, "Ferraro Defends Her Abortion Stand, but Is Criticized by Scranton Bishop," *Washington Post*, September 13, 1984, 3A; Jane Perlez, "Ferraro Says Religion Won't Influence Policy," *New York Times*, September 13, 1984, 16B.

51. Michael Ruane, "Outside the Civic Center, the Debate Was over Abortion," *Philadelphia Inquirer*, October 12, 1984, 24A.

52. Lindy Boggs, *Washington through a Purple Veil: Memoirs of a Southern Woman* (New York: Harcourt, 1994), vii.

53. Steve Smith, "Lindy Boggs Wears Politics Well," *Dallas Times Herald*, February 16, 1984, Living Section, 1.

54. Interview with Lindy Boggs (January 31, 1974), p. 1, Interview A-0082, Southern Oral History Program Collection, University Library, University of North Carolina, Chapel Hill, http://docsouth.unc.edu/sohp/A-0082/A-0082.html; Twin Circle Article, p. 1, folder 6, box 3082, Lindy Boggs Papers, Tulane University Special Collections.

55. Boggs, *Washington through a Purple Veil*, 65.

56. Jack Davis, "Your Next Congressman . . . Lindy Boggs," *Figaro* (New Orleans), January 20, 1973, 4; Lindy Boggs Written Replies to Queries, folder 16, box 3082, Lindy Boggs Papers.

57. Carolanne Griffith Roberts, "Strong Women of Capitol Hill," *Southern Living*, May 1996, 149.

58. Davis, "Your Next Congressman . . . Lindy Boggs," 5.

59. See "Women in Congress," http://womenincongress.house.gov/.

60. Smith, "Lindy Boggs Wears Politics Well," 3.

61. Handwritten Answers to Queries, folder 16, box 3082, Lindy Boggs Papers.

62. Betty Guillaud, "Lagniappe: Lindy's the Lauded Leader of the Feminine Branch of Congress," *New Orleans Times-Picayune/States-Item*, August 3, 1983, sec. 5, p. 3.

63. Lindy Boggs: Is She Tough Enough, file 6, box 3082, Lindy Boggs Papers; In House, Newspaper Clipping, folder 6, box 3082, Lindy Boggs Papers; For Carter Ladies, a Georgia "Pig-Pickin," Newspaper Clipping, file 2, box 3082, Lindy Boggs Papers.

64. Speech to Leadership Conference for Democratic Women (September 27, 1983), file 29, box 3083, Lindy Boggs Papers.

65. Joyce Davis Robinson, "Battered Wives . . . They Just Want the Beatings to Stop," *New Orleans Times-Picayune*, March 30, 1978, sec. 1, p. 4.

66. Steven Roberts, "Now, a Select Committee for Families," *New York Times*, February 23, 1983, 18A.

67. "Domestic Violence Bill May Be Lost in Last-Minute Congressional Rush," *New Orleans Times Picayune*, September 27, 1980, sec. 2, p. 4; "'Battered' Bill Pushed by Boggs," *New Orleans Times-Picayune*, September 22, 1978, sec. 1, p. 13.

68. Tom Shales, "Violence at Home," *Washington Post*, September 26, 1978, 1C.

69. "*Bivens* Actions for Equal Protection Violations: *Davis v. Passman*," *Harvard Law Review* 92, no. 3 (January 1979): 746; "Passman Settles Sex Bias Lawsuit," *Washington Post*, August 25, 1979, 9A.

70. "Employment Discrimination in Congress," *Washington Post,* May 24, 1988, 22A; Kenneth Weiss, "Lindy Backs Justice Position," *New Orleans Times-Picayune,* April 2, 1977, sec. 1, p. 15; John MacKenzie, "Job Bias Said to Apply to Congress," *Washington Post,* January 4, 1977, 1A.

71. Weiss, "Lindy Backs Justice Position," 15; "Passman Settles Sex Bias Lawsuit," 9A; "Home Violence Bill Introduced," *New Orleans Times-Picayune,* June 21, 1977, sec. 1, p. 10.

72. "Family Violence Bill Approved by House," *New Orleans Times-Picayune,* October 2, 1980, sec. 6, p. 18.

73. Boggs's original bill was subsumed into the 1994 Violence against Women Act. "Domestic Violence Bill May Be Lost in Last-Minute Congressional Rush," 4.

74. Lindy Boggs Has Earned Her Place in the Line-Up with Style, by Joan McKinney, Subseries 34, Scrapbook Volume 10, Lindy Boggs Papers.

75. Spencer Rich, "New House Panel to Study Children," *Washington Post,* December 9, 1982, 9E.

76. Dorothy Gilliam, "The DC," *Washington Post,* April 30, 1983, 1B; Roberts, "Now, a Select Committee for Families," 18A.

77. "Panel of House Issues Study on Child Support," *New York Times,* June 12, 1983, 30.

78. Worth Cooley, "Making Sure Dad Pays for His Kids," *Washington Post,* September 5, 1982, 1C.

79. Steven Roberts, "Political Survival: It's Women and Children First," *New York Times,* December 6, 1983, 8B.

80. Steven Roberts, "Congress Stages a Pre-Emptive Strike on the Gender Gap," *New York Times,* May 6, 1984, 227.

81. Robert Hershey, "Women's Pay Fight Shifts to 'Comparable Worth,'" *New York Times,* November 1, 1983, 15A.

82. David Vise, "Costs vs. Benefits in Ferraro's Pension Bill," *Washington Post,* August 19, 1984, 3G.

83. Jane Perlez, "Senate Approves Pension Measure to Benefit Women," *New York Times,* August 7, 1984, 1A.

84. Equality for Women's Pensions, p. 1, Women's Issues, folder 14, Wendy Borcheredt Papers, Ronald Reagan Presidential Foundation and Library; Francis Clines, "Reagan Gives Plan on Pension Equity," *New York Times,* September 30, 1983, 15A.

85. Judy Mann, "A Chance to Improve Women's Economic State," *Washington Post,* April 8, 1981, 1C.

86. Ibid.; "Women's Greatest Political Opportunity . . . Rests with the Republican Party," *Washington Post,* August 27, 1983, 6A.

87. Maria Riccardi, "Lindy Boggs: All That Charm—Plus Savvy," *Cleveland Plain Dealer,* April 1, 1984, 2C.

88. Smith, "Lindy Boggs Wears Politics Well," 3.

89. "Rep. Lindy Boggs: Savvy, Persuasive, and Charming," *Ann Arbor News,* Subseries 34, Scrapbook Volume 10, Lindy Boggs Papers.

90. Riccardi, "Lindy Boggs: All That Charm," 2C.

91. Donald Critchlow, *Phyllis Schlafly and Grassroots Conservatism: A Woman's Crusade* (Princeton, NJ: Princeton University Press, 2005), 215.

92. Ibid.

93. Ibid., 218.

94. Carol Felsenthal, "How Feminists Failed," *Chicago Magazine*, June 1982, 140.

95. Ibid.

96. Critchlow, *Phyllis Schlafly and Grassroots Conservatism*, 247–48.

97. Mary Frances Berry, *Why ERA Failed: Politics, Women's Rights, and the Amending Process of the Constitution* (Bloomington: Indiana University Press, 1988), 80–81.

98. Steven Roberts, "6 Republican Women and a Special Constituency," *New York Times*, August 3, 1983, 14A.

99. Judith Nies, "Women's New Issue," *New York Times*, June 9, 1983, 23A.

100. Abzug and Kelber, "Women vs. Reagan," 19E.

101. Francis Clines, "'Vengeance Vote' Worries White House," *New York Times*, June 12, 1983, 5E.

102. Sydney Schanberg, "The G.O.P. vs. Women," *New York Times*, April 5, 1983, 27A.

103. Nadine Cohodas, "New Unity Evident: Women Shift Focus on Hill to Economic Equity Issues," *Congressional Quarterly Weekly Report*, April 23, 1983, 782.

104. Felicity Barringer, "Director of Gender Task Force Resigns Justice Job," *Washington Post*, August 23, 1983, 1A.

105. Barbara Honegger, "Reagan Has Not Fulfilled His Promise," *Washington Post*, August 21, 1983, 8C.

106. Barringer, "Director of Gender Task Force Resigns Justice Job," 1A; David Gates, "The Munchkin's Musical," *Newsweek*, May 13, 1985, 13.

107. Memo from Uhlmann to Craig Fuller (September 1, 1983), p. 1, and Women's Issues: Memo to Fuller re Memo to President (September 1, 1983), OA 9442, Michael Uhlmann Papers, Ronald Reagan Presidential Foundation and Library.

108. Memo from Wendy Borcheredt to Elizabeth Dole (June 14, 1982), file "Women," OA 7114, Wendy Borcheredt Papers.

109. Steven Weisman, "President Seeks to Gain Support from Minorities," *New York Times*, January 16, 1983, 2A.

110. Draft SOTU Language Re: Women, p. 1, file "Women—State of the Union," folder 14, Elizabeth Dole Files.

111. Phil Gailey, "Transit Post Nominee," *New York Times*, January 6, 1983, 25A.

112. Marjorie Hunter, "Reagan's Choice for Health Chief," *New York Times*, January 13, 1983, 22D.

113. Steven Weisman, "Reagan's Joke Sours His Apology to Women," *New York Times*, August 4, 1983, 13A.

114. Schanberg, "The G.O.P. vs. Women," 27A.

115. William Farrell, "U.S. Amendment on Equal Rights Beaten in the House," *New York Times*, November 16, 1983, 1A.

116. Ibid.

117. Abzug and Kelber, "Women vs. Reagan," 19E; Patricia Schroeder, "Patricia Schroeder: O'Neill Was Justified in Bringing ERA Up for a Vote in the House," *Boston Globe*, November 25, 1983, page unknown; "Hyde Sees Rights Measure's De-

feat as an '84 Issue," *New York Times*, November 21, 1983, 13A; Nies, "Women's New Issue," 23A.

118. Letter from Terrell Bell to Donald Regan (June 20, 1985), p. 1, John Roberts File 1, box 27, John Roberts Papers, Ronald Reagan Presidential Foundation and Library.

119. Statement of William Bradford Reynolds Before the House Judiciary Committee concerning the Civil Rights Act of 1984, p. 4, Title IX Legislation (2), OA 11841, Ed Meese Papers.

120. Donna de Varona, "Women's Fight for Sports Equality Begins Again," *New York Times*, March 18, 1984, 2S; Judy Mann, "Title IX," *Washington Post*, August 15, 1984, 1C.

121. Mann, "Title IX," 1C.

122. De Varona, "Women's Fight for Sports Equality Begins Again," 2S.

123. William Raspberry, "The Grove City Dilemma," *New York Times*, December 2, 1983, 15A.

124. "Failed Repair for Civil Rights," *New York Times*, October 5, 1984, 30A.

125. Robert Pear, "Justice Dept. Open to New Rights Bill," *New York Times*, March 3, 1984, 11.

126. Ruth Marcus, "Grove City Decision Has Stifled Hundreds of Bias Complaints," *Washington Post*, March 7, 1988, 8A.

127. Ibid.

128. Mark Asher and Sandra Bailey, "Driesell Call Issue: Information vs. Pressure," *Washington Post*, March 25, 1983, 1D.

129. Alison Muscatine, "Furor on Campus," *Washington Post*, April 3, 1982, 1B.

130. Ibid.

131. Ibid.; Judy Mann, "Setback," *Washington Post*, May 25, 1984, 1B.

132. Felicity Barringer, "Reagan's Record on Women Gives Ammunition to Friends, Foes," *Washington Post*, October 10, 1983, 4A.

133. "House Approves Civil Rights Bill," *New York Times*, June 27, 1984, 24A.

134. Memo from Mike Horowitz to Dave Stockman, Joe Wright, M. B. Oglesby, and Chris Demuth (May 4, 1984), p. 1, Title IX Legislation, OA 11841, Ed Meese Papers; Briefing Memorandum on S. 2568: The Civil Rights Act of 1984, p. 1, Title IX Legislation, OA 11841, Ed Meese Papers.

135. Pear, "Justice Dept. Open to New Rights Bill," 11.

136. Testimony of Charles Fried on S. 2568 Before the Subcommittee on the Constitution, p. 8, folder "Faith Ryan Whittlesey," box 14, Title IX, Ronald Reagan Presidential Foundation and Library; Statement of Wm. Bradford Reynold concerning S. 2568—"Civil Rights Act of 1984" (June 5, 1984), p. 8, Ronald Reagan Presidential Foundation and Library; Grove City Case File 1, OA 12739, Christina Bach Files, Ronald Reagan Presidential Foundation and Library.

137. Robert Pear, "Bill to Expand Coverage Stirs a Dispute," *New York Times*, May 6, 1984, 1A.

138. Martin Tolchin, "Civil Rights Plan Shelved as Senate Moves on Spending," *New York Times*, October 3, 1984, 1A; "House Approves Civil Rights Bill," 24A.

139. Olympians on Hill with Rights Torch, Title IX Legislation File 1, OA 11841, Ed Meese Papers.

140. Tolchin, "Civil Rights Plan Shelved," 1A, 20A.

141. Martin Tolchin, "Senate Crushes a Move to Block Civil Rights Bill," *New York Times*, September 30, 1984, 1A; "Failed Repair for Civil Rights," 30A.

142. Confidential: Lindy Boggs Vice President USA '84, file 1, box 2130, Lindy Boggs Papers.

143. Joan McKinney, "Mrs. Boggs Ready for Vice President If Democrats Are," *Sunday Baton Rouge Advocate*, July 3, 1983, 3B; Haupt, "Boggs Seeks Veep Slot," 5A.

144. Here's What People Are Saying about a Woman Veep, box 2155, folder "Political, DNC, 1984," Lindy Boggs Papers.

145. Lindy Boggs Has Earned Her Place in the Line-Up with Style, by Joan McKinney, Subseries 34, Scrapbook Volume 10, Lindy Boggs Papers.

146. Raymond Strothers, "Forget It—a Woman Can't Be Elected Vice President," *Washington Post*, July 9, 1984, 1B.

147. Ibid.

148. Edwards: Fritz Needs Woman Veep, Newspaper Clipping, file 1, box 2184, Lindy Boggs Papers.

149. James Reston, "Mondale and Who Else?" *New York Times*, June 24, 1984, 23E.

150. Smith, "Lindy Boggs Wears Politics Well," 1, 3; Confidential: Lindy Boggs Vice President USA '84, p. 2, file 1, box 2130, Lindy Boggs Papers.

151. Confidential: Lindy Boggs Vice President USA '84, p. 2, file 1, box 2130, Lindy Boggs Papers.

152. Bob Talbet, "Democratic Dealings in the *Detroit Free Press*," file "VP, Press Clips, 1984," box 2155, Lindy Boggs Papers.

153. Lindy Boggs Has Earned Her Place in the Line-Up with Style, by Joan McKinney, Subseries 34, Scrapbook Volume 10, Lindy Boggs Papers.

154. Letter from LB to Katie Indiglia (May 18, 1984), file 1, box 2184, Lindy Boggs Papers; Letter from Peggy to LB (April 4, 1984), file 1, box 2184, Lindy Boggs Papers; George Hager, "Washington Report: Campaign War Chests," *New Orleans Times-Picayune*, April 22, 1984, sec. 1, p. 20.

155. Letter from Boggs to Debbie Bridges (April 3, 1973), file 14, box 3082, Lindy Boggs Papers.

156. Caryle Murphy, "26,000 March to Hill to Protest Legalizing Abortion," *Washington Post*, January 23, 1983, 13A.

157. Colman McCarthy, "Abortion Crossfire," *Washington Post*, July 15, 1984, 2K.

158. "Opponents of Abortion Back Boggs for Veep," *New Orleans Times-Picayune*, July 18, 1984, 4A.

159. Ibid.

160. William Raspberry, "Smothering a Civil Rights Bill," *Washington Post*, April 5, 1985, 17A.

161. Linda Greenhouse, "Abortion Issue Weaves an Intricate Web," *New York Times*, April 22, 1986, 20A.

162. Ibid.

163. Marcus, "Grove City Decision," 8A.

164. Joanne Sills, "Temple Settles Sex-Bias Suit with Women Athletes," *Philadelphia Daily News*, June 14, 1988, 3.

165. Jim Smith, "Owl Men Said to Get Special Treatment," *Philadelphia Daily News*, April 5, 1988, 15.

166. Marian Uhlman, "Title IX Reeling, Its Backers Say," *Philadelphia Inquirer*, June 17, 1987, 1E.

167. "Grove City Bill," in *Congress and the Nation*, vol. 7, *1985–88* (Washington, DC: Congressional Quarterly Press, 1990), 763–64.

168. Letter from Reagan to Jim Wright (March 1, 1988), p. 1, Grove City Bill, OA 18654, Political Affairs White House Office of Records, Ronald Reagan Presidential Foundation and Library.

169. Newsstory: Religious Leaders Assail Moral Majority's "Scare Tactics" over Civil Rights, Grove City Press Coverage File 1, 16534, David McIntosh Papers, Ronald Reagan Presidential Foundation and Library.

170. Senate vote 72–24; House vote 292–133. "Grove City Bill," 763–64.

171. Greenhouse, "Abortion Issue Weaves an Intricate Web," 20A.

172. Mitchell Killian and Clyde Wilcox, "Do Abortion Attitudes Lead to Party Switching?" *Political Research Quarterly* 61, no. 4 (December 2008): 571.

173. Alan Abramowitz, "It's Abortion, Stupid: Policy Voting in the 1992 Presidential Election," *Journal of Politics* 57, no. 1 (February 1995): 179.

174. Ibid.

11. "There Is Nothing for Nothing Any Longer"

1. Marshall Frady, *Jesse: The Life and Pilgrimage of Jesse Jackson* (New York: Simon & Schuster, 2006), 415.

2. Christopher Madison, "Radical Moderate," *National Journal*, May 23, 1992, 1231.

3. Dudley Clendinen, "Politics Gets Personal in Louisiana's 8th Congressional District," *New York Times*, October 31, 1986, 20.

4. Diane Granat, "Secret Meetings Restore Vigor: Democratic Caucus Renewed as Forum for Policy Questions," *Congressional Quarterly Weekly Report*, October 15, 1983, 2115–19; Richard Cohen, "Gillis Long Presses House Democrats to Establish a New Party Identity," *National Journal: Congressional Report*, December 4, 1982, 2075–76; Richard Pearson, "Rep. Gillis Long, 61, Influential Democrat," *Washington Post*, January 22, 1985, D4; Clendinen, "Politics Gets Personal," 20; Kenneth Baer, *Reinventing Democrats* (Lawrence: University Press of Kansas, 2000), 60–63, 66; Phil Gailey, "Dissidents Defy Top Democrats; Council Formed," *New York Times*, March 1, 1985, 1A, and "Democratic Group Seeks Mainstream," *New York Times*, May 19, 1985, 29; Peter Rosenblatt, "Centrism Is Crucial," *New York Times*, November 19, 1984, 23A.

5. Baer, *Reinventing Democrats*, 36–39; Tom Sherwood and James Dickinson, "Robb Trying to Form New Party Policy Group," *Washington Post*, February 16, 1985, 9A.

6. Cohen, "Gillis Long Presses House Democrats," 2075–76; Granat, "Secret Meetings Restore Vigor," 2215; Breakfast Seminar on Monetary Policy (September 15, 1982), pp. 5, 6, folder 9, box 15, Papers of the House Democratic Caucus, Library of Congress.

7. Amity Shlaes, *The Forgotten Man: A New History of the Great Depression* (New York: Harper, 2007), 10–11.

8. Cohen, "Gillis Long Presses House Democrats," 2076; "Democratic Candidates to Address House Caucus," *Washington Post*, June 12, 1983, 10A.

9. Breakfast Seminar on Monetary Policy (September 15, 1982), pp. 5, 6, folder 9, box 15, Papers of the House Democratic Caucus.

10. Ibid.; Malvina Stephenson, "Four State Congressmen Prepare Demo Blueprint," folder 22, box 45, Dave McCurdy Collection, Congressional Archives, Carl Albert Congressional Research and Studies Center.

11. Funeral Service Announcement of Thomas McCurdy' Death, file 9, box 44, Dave McCurdy Collection.

12. Biographical Sketch of Pam McCurdy, file 4, box 51, Dave McCurdy Collection.

13. Chips Fall for Democrats in '92 Race, by George Will, folder 1, box 48, Dave McCurdy Collection; Greg Hardin, "McCurdy's in Washington: Congressman Finds Life's Hard in the Capital City," *Sunday Lawton (OK) Constitution*, April 26, 1981, 1B.

14. Sarah Button, "Squeezed on the Hill," *Money Magazine*, May 1983, 106.

15. The Non-Candidate, p. 2, folder 2, box 48, Dave McCurdy Collection.

16. Man for the Job, folder 7, box 23, Dave McCurdy Collection; Race to Watch: OK 4, folder 89, box 22, Dave McCurdy Collection.

17. Race to Watch: OK 4, folder 89, box 22, Dave McCurdy Collection.

18. Dave McCurdy, Politics in America, 1994, p. 1247, folder 22, box 49, Dave McCurdy Collection; Rutledge Thumps Party's Kooks, folder 8, box 48, Dave McCurdy Collection.

19. Steve Patterson, "McCurdy Claims 4th District Post in Close Election," *Lawton (OK) Constitution*, November 5, 1980, 1A; Tim Ford, "Republican Wants to Curb Democrats: Rutledge Eyes End of 'Obstructionists,'" *Lawton (OK) Morning Press*, May 28, 1982, 5A; Rutledge Campaign Firm Find Support in Fourth District (June 9, 1982), folder 8, box 45, Dave McCurdy Collection.

20. Judy Fossett, "Dave McCurdy a 'Quick Study' in Fast-Paced Congress," *(Sunday) Oklahoman* (Oklahoma City), January 24, 1982, 4A.

21. Hardin, "McCurdy's in Washington," 1B; Donna Evers, "McCurdy to Fight for Caddo County," *Lawton (OK) Constitution*, July 2, 1981, 1.

22. Mark Galvin, "Approval of Holy City Bill Predicted," *Sunday Lawton (OK) Constitution*, March 29, 1981, folder 7, box 45, Dave McCurdy Collection; "McCurdy Attends Meeting," *Cache Times Weekly*, April 2, 1981, folder 7, box 45, Dave McCurdy Collection.

23. Smith vs. McCurdy: Jerry Smith Campaign Literature, folder 30, box 45, Dave McCurdy Collection.

24. Evers, "McCurdy to Fight for Caddo County," 1, 2A; Madison, "Radical Moderate," 1233.

25. Madison, "Radical Moderate," 1233.

26. The Non-Candidate, p. 2, folder 2, box 48, Dave McCurdy Collection.

27. McCurdy Critical of Reagan on Defense, folder 26, box 45, Dave McCurdy Collection.

28. Madison, "Radical Moderate," 1233; McCurdy Critical of Reagan on Defense, folder 26, box 45, Dave McCurdy Collection.

29. Bill Peterson, "House Democrats Launch Effort to Sell Alternatives to the Public," *Washington Post*, July 20, 1983, 3A.

30. National House Democratic Caucus, *Renewing America's Promise: A Democratic Blueprint for Our Nation's Future* (Washington, DC: National House Democratic Caucus, 1984); James Dickenson and Bill Peterson, "The Future of the Democratic Party," *Washington Post,* November 24, 1983, 7A; Margaret Shapiro, "Democrats Draw Up a Future 'Blueprint' for 1984 Campaign," *Washington Post,* January 8, 1984, 11A; Saul Friedman, "House Democrats Make the Deficit Their Main Target," *Philadelphia Inquirer,* January 8, 1984, 5A; Stephenson, "Four State Congressmen Prepare Demo Blueprint."

31. Baer, *Reinventing Democrats,* 47–49.

32. Tom Wicker, "Mr. Mondale's Backbone," *New York Times,* February 17, 1984, 31A.

33. Gillon, *The Democrats' Dilemma,* 334–40.

34. Elizabeth Drew, *Campaign Journal: The Political Events of 1983–1984* (New York: Macmillan, 1985), 521.

35. Gillon, *The Democrats' Dilemma,* 35.

36. Ibid., 354.

37. Ibid., 354–55; Dom Bonafede, "In Choosing a Running Mate, Mondale May Have Uncovered a Hornet's Nest," *National Journal,* July 14, 1984, 1349–50; William Geist, "About New York: 'Pardon Our Pride Queens Says Proudly,'" *New York Times,* August 4, 1984, 27.

38. Gillon, *The Democrats' Dilemma,* 363.

39. "Democrats Once Again Decide That the Party . . . Should Go Another Round on Its Rules," *National Journal,* July 28, 1984, 1439.

40. Tom Sherwood, "Robb Says Party Must Learn to Say 'No' to Special Interests," *Washington Post,* July 19, 1984, 15A; Gary Percefull, "McCurdy Home, Still Likes John Glenn," *Tulsa World,* July 22, 1984, 2A; McCurdy Cast Hart Vote because of Convictions, folder 26, box 45, Dave McCurdy Collection.

41. Percefull, "McCurdy Home, Still Likes John Glenn," 2A; McCurdy Cast Hart Vote because of Convictions, folder 26, box 45, Dave McCurdy Collection; Handwritten Notes on Geraldine Ferraro, folder 26, box 45, Dave McCurdy Collection.

42. Oklahoma Democrats Say Changes Needed in Party's Liberal Image, folder 30, box 45, Dave McCurdy Collection.

43. Gailey, "Democratic Group Seeks Mainstream," 29; Baer, *Reinventing Democrats,* 66.

44. Jon Hale, "The Making of New Democrats," *Political Science Quarterly* 110, no. 2 (Summer 1995): 214.

45. Fred Barnes, "Flying Nunn: The Democrats Top Hawk," *New Republic,* April 28, 1986, 18; Gailey, "Democratic Group Seeks Mainstream," 29.

46. Gailey, "Dissidents Defy Top Democrats," 1A.

47. Hale, "The Making of New Democrats," 216; Baer, *Reinventing Democrats,* 66, 67.

48. Hedrick Smith, "Democrats Try to Turn Swods into Swords," *New York Times,* June 7, 1985, 14A; Wayne Biddle, "Push in House Military Panel to Depose Price Is Reported," *New York Times,* January 3, 1985, 19A.

49. Madison, "Radical Moderate," 1231.

50. Rosenblatt, "Centrism Is Crucial," 23A; Hale, "The Making of New Democrats," 215–16; Baer, *Reinventing Democrats,* 60–63; Richard Cohen, "Democratic

Leadership Council Sees Party Void and Is Ready to Fill It," *National Journal,* February 1, 1986, 269.

51. Cohen, "Democratic Leadership Council Sees Party Void," 269.

52. Hale, "The Making of New Democrats," 216–17; Baer, *Reinventing Democrats,* 60–63.

53. Gailey, "Democratic Group Seeks Mainstream," 29.

54. Baer, *Reinventing Democrats,* 104–5.

55. Ibid., 107.

56. "Mr. Gephardt's Bleak Promises," May 17, 1987, *New York Times,* 231.

57. Dave McCurdy, "Dukakis, Jackson: Too Far Left," *New York Times,* May 3, 1988, folder 3, box 44, Dave McCurdy Collection.

58. Maureen Dowd, "Bush Paints Rival as Elitist, with 'Harvard Yard' Views," *New York Times,* June 10, 1988, 6B.

59. Scott Shepard, "Nunn Out On a Limb," *Atlanta Journal and Constitution,* folder 23, box 12, Dave McCurdy Collection.

60. E. J. Dionne, "Seeking Reasons besides Dukakis, Democrats Mull Last Fall's Defeat," *New York Times,* February 19, 1989, 30.

61. Ibid.

62. McCurdy, "Dukakis, Jackson: Too Far Left," A35.

63. Baer, *Reinventing Democrats,* 127–29; E. J. Dionne, "Washington Talk: The New Think Tank on the Block," *New York Times,* June 28, 1989, 20A.

64. Dan Balz, "Moderate, Conservative Democrats Buck 'Constraints' from Think Tank," *Washington Post,* June 30, 1989, Progressive Policy Institute Archives, Washington, DC; Dionne, "Washington Talk," 20A.

65. Charles Babcock, "Democratic Conference Bankrolled—100 Lobbyists Underwrite Annual Session of Moderates, Conservatives," *Washington Post,* March 9, 1989, 11A.

66. *DLC Newsgram* 3, no. 1 (April 1989): 1, Dave McCurdy Collection, folder 7, box 47.

67. Ibid.; William Galston and Elaine Kamarck, "The Democrats' Delusion: The Party Is Fooling Itself to Death," *Washington Post,* September 24, 1989, 1B, folder 26, box 14, Dave McCurdy Collection; Thomas Edsall, "Jackson, Robb Tussle over Democratic Strategy," *Washington Post,* March 11, 1989, 4A; John Harwood, "Democratic Leaders Take Issue with Jackson on Party's Course," *St. Petersburg Times,* March 11, 1989, 3A.

68. Michael Frisby, "In the Postelection Doldrums, Storm Swirls around Jackson," *Boston Globe,* March 13, 1989, 3; "Democrats Debate 'White Male' Vote," *Chicago Tribune,* March 11, 1989, 3A.

69. Susan Feeney, "Demos Tangle over New Course," *New Orleans Times-Picayune,* March 11, 1989, 11A.

70. *DLC Newsgram* 3, no. 1 (April 1989): 1, Dave McCurdy Collection, folder 7, box 47.

71. Frisby, "In the Postelection Doldrums," 3A; Douglas Turner, "Jackson Asks for Children's March on D.C.," *Buffalo News,* March 12, 1989, 16A.

72. Dirk Johnson, "Daley Wins Primary in Chicago; Mayoral Vote Is Racially Divided," *New York Times,* March 1, 1989, 1A.

73. Curtis Wilkie, "Jesse Jackson's Magic Deserts Him in Chicago," *Boston*

Globe, April 9, 1989, Focus Section, 74; Andrew Rosenthal, "Letter by Jackson Hints at Shift," *New York Times*, March 7, 1989, 21A.

74. Edsall, "Jackson, Robb Tussle," 4A.

75. Ibid.; *DLC Newsgram* 3, no. 1 (April 1989): 1, Dave McCurdy Collection, folder 7, box 47; Michael Frisby, "Dilemma for Democrats: Woo the Poor or the Middle Class?" *Boston Globe*, March 14, 1989, 5A; "Democrats Debate 'White Male' Vote," 3A.

76. *DLC Newsgram* 3, no. 1 (April 1989): 1, Dave McCurdy Collection, folder 7, box 47; Larry Eichel, "Robb Spars with Jackson over Party's Direction," *St. Paul Pioneer Press*, March 11, 1989, 16A.

77. Larry Eichel, "Democrats Divided over Who to Woo," *Philadelphia Inquirer*, March 11, 1989, 2A; E. J. Dionne, "Party Told to Win Middle Class Vote," *New York Times*, March 12, 1989, 32; "Democrats Debate Best Way to Rebuild Party— Jackson, Centrists Clash over Direction Leaders Should Take," *Atlanta Journal and Constitution*, March 12, 1989, 10A.

78. Will Marshall and Al From, "Ideas, Not Litmus Tests, Can Lift the Democrats," *Los Angeles Times*, November 30, 1988, Progressive Policy Institute Archives, Washington, DC.

79. Ron Goldwyn, "Democrats Try a New Idea Here," *Philadelphia Daily News*, March 9, 1989, 13; Peter Hardin, "National Service Idea Backed," *Richmond Times-Dispatch*, March 11, 1989, 15.

80. Handwritten Notes regarding Steve Gunderson, folder 48, box 7, Dave McCurdy Collection; Seymour Martin Lipset, *Political Renewal on the Left: A Comparative Perspective* (Washington, DC: Progressive Policy Institute Press, January 1990), 21–24.

81. *Manpower Effectiveness of the All-Volunteer Force: Report to Congress* (Washington, DC: U.S. General Accounting Office, 1981), 1; Bernard Rostker, *I Want You! The Evolution of the All-Volunteer Force* (Santa Monica, CA: Rand, 2006), 292.

82. Charles Moskos, "National Service and Its Enemies," p. 14, folder 42, box 12, Dave McCurdy Collection; Richard Halloran, "To Serve One's Country: An Ideal Persists," *New York Times*, November 22, 1987, 5E, and "Reviving the Draft: Partisan Debate," *New York Times*, December 29, 1986, 10B; George Wilson, "Army's Recruiting Falters as Manpower Pool Shrinks," *Washington Post*, February 4, 1989, 5A.

83. William Farrell, "The Man Who Put Neo in Neoliberal," *New York Times*, November 1, 1984, 12B.

84. Dave McCurdy, "It's Time for a National Service Corps," *USA Today: The Magazine of the American Scene*, July 1992, 14.

85. Davies, *From Opportunity to Entitlement*.

86. Phil Gailey, "Reviving a Love of Duty," *St. Petersburg Times*, March 20, 1988, folder 23, box 12, Dave McCurdy Collection.

87. David Broder, "Young America's Civic Failings," folder 21, box 12, Dave McCurdy Collection.

88. Michael Walzer, "The Communitarian Critique of Liberalism," *Political Theory* 18, no. 1 (February 1990): 14; James Q. Wilson, "The Rediscovery of Character," *Public Interest*, Fall 1985, 3–5.

89. David Broder, "Citizen Corps," *Washington Post,* May 11, 1988, folder 21, box 12, Dave McCurdy Collection.

90. Baer, *Reinventing Democrats,* 112.

91. Jill Zuckman, "President's 'Points of Light' Still Only a Dim Twinkle," *Congressional Quarterly Weekly Report,* January 27, 1990, 240.

92. Moskos, "National Service and Its Enemies," 2–3.

93. A Quid Pro Quo for Youth, folder 23, box 12, Dave McCurdy Collection; Baer, *Reinventing Democrats,* 112–13.

94. Citizenship and National Service, by Dave McCurdy, pp. 60–61, folder 42, box 12, Dave McCurdy Collection.

95. Washington Student Aid Dilemma, folder 17, box 12, Dave McCurdy Collection; Barbara Vobejda, "Competition for College Feeds Elitism," *Washington Post,* May 4, 1989, 1A, 14A; Citizenship and National Service, by Dave McCurdy, box 12, folder 42, p. 61, Dave McCurdy Collection.

96. Citizenship and National Service, by Dave McCurdy, box 12, folder 42, p. 61, Dave McCurdy Collection.

97. Charles Moskos, "Letter to the Editor," *Oklahoma Observer* (Oklahoma City), July 11, 1990, folder 25, box 12, Dave McCurdy Collection; Citizenship and National Service, by Dave McCurdy, p. 61, folder 42, box 12, Dave McCurdy Collection.

98. Phil Kuntz, "Nunn, McCurdy Plan Ignites National Service Debate," *Congressional Quarterly Weekly Report,* March 25, 1989, folder 7, box 47, Dave McCurdy Collection; Citizenship and National Service, by Dave McCurdy, p. 61, folder 42, box 12, Dave McCurdy Collection.

99. Proposals Linking School Aid to Service Criticized, Newspaper Clipping (March 8, 1989), folder 21, box 12, Dave McCurdy Collection; Citizenship and National Service, by Dave McCurdy, p. 61, folder 42, box 12, Dave McCurdy Collection.

100. "Universal National Service," *Newsweek,* May 14, 1979, p. 101, folder 22, box 12, Dave McCurdy Collection; "National Servitude," *Washington Times,* April 3, 1989, folder 22, box 12, Dave McCurdy Collection.

101. Zuckman, "President's 'Points of Light,'" 240.

102. The National Interest: Wandering in the Desert, by Joe Klein (December 3, 1990), folder 26, box 14, Dave McCurdy Collection.

103. Report: President Bush's "Points of Light": National Service or Volunteerism (June 27, 1989), folder 4, box 13, Dave McCurdy Collection; Remarks by the President to Youth Engaged in Service Group (June 21, 1989), p. 2, folder 41, box 13, Dave McCurdy Collection; Shepard, "Nunn Out On a Limb."

104. Remarks by the President to Youth Engaged in Service Group (June 21, 1989), p. 2, folder 41, box 13, Dave McCurdy Collection; Shepard, "Nunn Out On a Limb."

105. Memo from Will Marshall to Nunn, Robb, and McCurdy (April 11, 1989), p. 2, folder 36, box 13, Dave McCurdy Collection; Ed Kelley, "McCurdy's Volunteer-Voucher Plan Stumbles in Committee," *The Oklahoman* (Oklahoma City), April 21, 1989, 15.

106. Lawmakers Still Hope to Link National Service to College Aid, by Steve Huettel, folder 23, box 12, Dave McCurdy Collection.

107. Memo from Will Marshall to Nunn, Robb, and McCurdy (April 11, 1989), p. 2, folder 36, box 13, Dave McCurdy Collection; "Investing in Idealism," *New York Times*, November 30, 1990, 32A.

108. Bill Alexander, "My Fellow Democrats: Answer Gingrich or Lose," *New York Times*, April 25, 1989, 29A.

109. E. J. Dionne, "Fierce G.O.P. Partisan: Harvey Lee Atwater," *New York Times*, November 18, 1988, D19.

110. Ibid.

111. Steve Gillon, *The Pact: Bill Clinton, Newt Gingrich, and the Rivalry That Defined a Generation* (New York: Oxford University Press, 2008), 52–53.

112. Ibid., 61.

113. John Farrell, *Tip O'Neill and the Democratic Century* (Boston: Little, Brown, 2001), 631.

114. Ibid., 632.

115. "O'Neill Assails a Republican and Is Rebuked by the Chair," *New York Times*, May 16, 1984, 16A.

116. Steven Roberts, "New Conflict a Threat to Old Ways," *New York Times*, May 19, 1984, 7; Robin Toner, "Tired of Cooling Their Heels, Republicans Turn Up the Heat," *New York Times*, January 16, 1989, 13A.

117. Farrell, *Tip O'Neill and the Democratic Century*, 636.

118. Gillon, *The Pact*, 60.

119. Robin Toner, "Climax to a Storm," *New York Times*, June 1, 1989, 1A.

120. Michael Dreskes, "Political Memo; For GOP Arsenal, 133 Words to Fire," *New York Times*, September 9, 1990.

121. Alexander, "My Fellow Democrats: Answer Gingrich or Lose," 29A; Toner, "Tired of Cooling Their Heels," 13A.

122. L. D. Barney, "Democrat Group's Goal: 'Declare What We Stand For,'" *Tulsa Tribune*, March 23, 1990, 4A.

123. The New Orleans Declaration—a Democratic Agenda for the 1990s, *Congressional Record—House* (June 26, 1990), pp. 4208–10, folder 51, box 7, Dave McCurdy Collection.

124. Paul Taylor and Maralee Schwartz, "Jackson's Unity Address Baffles, Irks Some Moderate Democrats," *Washington Post*, March 25, 1990, 10A.

125. "Democratic Council Meets, Debates Philosophy, Policy," *Daily Press* (Newport News, VA), March 25, 1990, 3A.

126. Speech: The Road Ahead, by Bill Clinton, March 24, 1990, folder 14, box 14, Dave McCurdy Collection.

127. From Interview with John Mahalchek, GNS, folder 51, box 7, Dave McCurdy Collection; Susan Glasser, "Moderate Democrats Form Caucus to Use Gingrich's TV Tactics," *Roll Call*, June 1990, folder 38, box 11, Dave McCurdy Collection.

128. Glasser, "Moderate Democrats Form Caucus"; Mainstream Forum, folder 38, box 11, Dave McCurdy Collection.

129. Jim Drinkard, "Dems' Show—Boring on Purpose," folder 38, box 11, Dave McCurdy Collection; Mainstream Forum, folder 38, box 11, Dave McCurdy Collection; "Democrats Use Cable to Promote Mainstream," *Stevens Point (WI) Journal*, July 9, 1990, folder 51, box 7, Dave McCurdy Collection.

130. Chris Casteel, "McCurdy Battles for Moderate Congress," *Sunday Oklahoman* (Oklahoma City), May 27, 1990, 16A.

131. Ibid.

132. Mike Brothers, "Democratic Energy Spreads at Poshard Gathering in Marion," July 27, 1992, folder 29, box 48, Dave McCurdy Collection.

133. E. J. Dionne, "Loss of Faith in Egalitarianism Alters U.S. Social Vision," *Washington Post*, April 30, 1990, 1A. See also Lipset, *Political Renewal on the Left.*

134. Elaine Kamarck, "America's Political Leaders Have Lost Their Way—the Collapse of Communism Leaves Everyone Looking for a New Way to Understand the World," *Buffalo News*, June 24, 1990, 11H.

135. Richard Viguerie and Steve Allen, "Bush Loses the Right Wing," *New York Times*, December 18, 1990, 25A.

136. Irving Kristol, "The G.O.P. Message: A State of Disunion," *New York Times*, January 27, 1991, 17E.

137. Ibid.

138. Thomas Friedman, "Selling Sacrifice: Gulf Rationale Still Eludes Bush," *New York Times*, November 16, 1990, 12A.

139. Ibid.

140. E. J. Dionne, "Pressing the Case for National Service," *Washington Post*, March 12, 1991, folder 36, box 47, Dave McCurdy Collection; Fred Hechinger, "About Education," *New York Times*, July 4, 1990, 60; Memo from Joel Berg to Julie and Jenny Alden, Support for National Service, folder 25, box 13, Dave McCurdy Collection.

141. Will Marshall and Joel Berg, "Open Forum," folder 1, box 14, Dave McCurdy Collection.

142. Pete Hamill, "How to Halt City's Slide into Savagery," *New York Post*, March 22, 1990, 4.

143. Will Marshall and Joel Berg, "Open Forum," folder 1, box 14, Dave McCurdy Collection.

144. Urban Trauma, folder 1, box 14, Dave McCurdy Collection.

145. George Bush, "Remarks at the Wall Street Journal Anniversary Dinner in New York, New York" (June 22, 1989), http://www.presidency.ucsb.edu/ws/index.php?pid=17201; http://www.chicagoreader.com/chicago/a-voice-for-the-left-behindwar-is-heckcomrades-vs-com-ed/Content?oid=877281.

146. Michael Miner, "A Voice for the Left-Behind," *Chicago Reader*, March 21, 1991, http://www.chicagoreader.com/chicago/a-voice-for-the-left-behindwar-is-heckcomrades-vs-com-ed/Content?oid=877281.

147. Seth Mydans, "Pressure Grows over Police Beating," *New York Times*, March 20, 1991, 18A; Robert Reinhold, "Violence and Racism Are Routine in Los Angeles Police, Study Says," *New York Times*, July 10, 1991, 1A. In May 1992, a jury exonerated the officers of all major charges, sparking a deadly spree of violence and riots that rocked Los Angeles and drew further attention to the issues of race, crime, and poverty. Adam Walinsky, Crusader Lobbyist, Sees Dream of an ROTC-Style Police Corps Nearing Reality, folder 2, box 14, Dave McCurdy Collection.

148. Adam Walinsky, Crusader Lobbyist, Sees Dream of an ROTC-Style Police Corps Nearing Reality, folder 2, box 14, Dave McCurdy Collection.

149. Hamill, "How to Halt City's Slide," 4; Jack Newfield, "A Police Corps Could

Be City's Lifeboat," *Daily News*, February 5, 1990, 12; Gene Taylor, From Congress, folder 3, box 14, Dave McCurdy Collection; William F. Buckley, "L.A. Midwife to a Civvy Policy Corps?" folder 3, box 14, Dave McCurdy Collection.

150. Robin Toner, "Bush's War Success Confers an Aura of Invincibility in '92," *New York Times*, February 27, 1991, 1A.

151. Wayne Woodlief, "Gulf War Seen Shooting Down Nunn's Run for President in '92," *Boston Herald*, March 5, 1991, folder 36, box 47, Dave McCurdy Collection.

152. Ben Wattenberg, "Now, Back to the Democrats," *New York Post*, March 12, 1991, 25; George Will, "Democrat in Waiting," folder 1, box 48, Dave McCurdy Collection.

153. Dave McCurdy, interview with author, Washington, DC, November 12, 2010.

154. Michael Kerrigan, "McCurdy Before Committee," *Tulsa World*, September 18, 1991, 3A.

155. McCurdy Speech to the DNC (September 21, 1991), folder 1, box 48, Dave McCurdy Collection.

156. Ibid.

157. Alan Cromley, "Jay Leno Helps Spread McCurdy's Name across U.S.," *The Oklahoman* (Oklahoma City), September 24, 1991, 3.

158. McCurdy Able to Run for 2 Houses in '92, folder 9, box 48, Dave McCurdy Collection.

159. Dave McCurdy, interview with author, Washington, DC, November 12, 2010.

160. Ibid.; Malvina Stephenson, "Dave McCurdy in Eye of Clinton Draft Storm," *Tulsa World*, September 22, 1992, 11A.

161. Fred Barnes, "They're Back! Neocons for Clinton," *New Republic*, August 3, 1992, 14.

162. Ibid.

163. McCurdy Discovers Speech Well-Coached Operation, folder 54, box 7, Dave McCurdy Collection.

164. Remarks by U.S. Rep. Dave McCurdy to DNC (July 15, 1992), p. 1, folder 54, box 7, Dave McCurdy Collection.

165. Gerald Seib, "Clinton Is Fervent about Tying College Loans to National Service, but Cold Realities Set In," *Wall Street Journal*, November 30, 1992, 14A.

166. Bill Clinton, "National Service—Now," *New York Times*, February 28, 1993, folder 42, box 13, Dave McCurdy Collection; Chris Black, "National Service Could Be Clinton's 'Signature' Issue," *Boston Globe*, November 30, 1992, folder 13, box 13, Dave McCurdy Collection.

167. Dave McCurdy, interview with author, Washington, DC, November 12, 2010.

168. Ibid.

Conclusion

1. Thomas Frank, *What's The Matter with Kansas: How Conservatives Won the Heart of America* (New York: Holt, 2004).

2. Jon Meacham, "The Trouble with Barack," *Daily Beast,* January 21, 2010, http://www.thedailybeast.com/newsweek/2010/01/21/the-trouble-with-barack.html.

3. The United States leads the developed world in homicide rates; American businesses' risk management policy is an outlier in the Western world; Seymour Martin Lipset claims that the Republican Party is the "only major anti-statist libertarian party in the industrialized world." See Seymour Martin Lipset, "Steady Work: An Academic Memoir," *Annual Review of Sociology* 22 (1996): 25. See also Shelia Jasanoff, "American Exceptionalism and the Political Acknowledgment of Risk," *Daedalus* 119, no. 4 (Fall 1990): 61–81; Eric Monkkonen, "Homicide: Explaining America's Exceptionalism," *American Historical Review* 111, no. 1 (February 2006): 76–94; and Harold Hongju Koh, "On American Exceptionalism," *Stanford Law Review* 55, no. 5 (May 2003): 1480, 1482.

4. Daniel Joseph Singal, "Beyond Consensus: Richard Hofstadter and American Historiography," *American Historical Review* 89, no. 4 (October 1984): 977.

5. Hofstadter, *The American Political Tradition,* vii.

6. Gordon Wood, "Ideology and the Origins of Liberal America," in "The Constitution of the United States," special issue, *William and Mary Quarterly,* 3rd ser., 44, no. 3 (July 1987): 640.

7. Richard Hofstadter, *Age of Reform: From Bryan to F.D.R.* (New York: Knopf, 1955), viii.

8. Wood, "Ideology and the Origins of Liberal America," 635.

Bibliography

Manuscript Collections

Congressional Archives, Carl Albert Congressional Research and Studies Center, University of Oklahoma, Norman, OK
Fred R. Harris Collection
Dave McCurdy Collection

Jimmy Carter Library and Museum, Atlanta, GA
Jimmy Carter Presidential Papers
Stu Eizenstat Files
Stu Eizenstat's Office Files
WHCF—Name File
WHCF-Presidential Handwriting File

Columbia University, Special Collections, New York, NY
Bella Abzug Papers

Duke University, Special Collections Library, Durham, NC
Socialist Party U.S.A. Papers

Duke University Microfilm Collections, Durham, NC
Addendum to Socialist Party Papers on Microfilm

Gerald R. Ford Presidential Library and Museum, Ann Arbor, MI
Dick Cheney Papers
Gerald Ford Papers
Ron Nessen Papers

Georgetown University Special Collections, Washington, DC
Colin Campbell Collection

Hennepin County Library, Minneapolis, MN
Charles Stenvig Papers

LBJ Presidential Library, Austin, TX
Oral Histories of the Johnson Administration
Peter Rosenblatt Papers
Ben Wattenberg Papers

John F. Kennedy Presidential Library and Museum, Boston, MA
John F. Kennedy Papers
Arthur Schlesinger Jr. Papers

Library of Congress, Washington, DC
Papers of the House Democratic Caucus

Marquette University Library Special Collections, Milwaukee, WI
Clement Zablocki Papers

Memphis City Library's Newspaper Clippings Collection, Memphis and Shelby County Room, Memphis, TN
Harold Ford Sr. Newspaper Clippings
Dan Kuykendall Clippings File

Minneapolis Public Library Special Collections, Minneapolis, MN
Charles Stenvig Newspaper Clippings

Ronald Reagan Presidential Foundation and Library, Simi Valley, CA
Wendy Borcheredt Papers
F003 Elizabeth Dole Files
Ed Meese Papers

Tamiment Library and Robert F. Wagner Labor Archives, New York University, New York, NY
NOW-NYC Papers

Tulane University Special Collections, New Orleans, LA
Lindy Boggs Papers

University of Arizona Special Collections Library, Tucson, AZ
Morris Udall Papers

University of Memphis, Mississippi Valley Special Collections, Memphis, TN
Harold Ford Sr. Papers
Dan Kuykendall Papers

University of Minnesota Special Collections, Minneapolis, MN
Eugene McCarthy Papers

University of North Carolina, Folk Life Collection, Chapel Hill, NC
Allard Lowenstein Papers

University of Oregon Libraries: Special Collections, Eugene, OR
Albert Conrad Ullman Papers

University of Washington Special Collections, Seattle, WA
Henry Jackson Papers

Wisconsin State Historical Society, Madison, WI
John Patrick Hunter Papers
Pat Lucey Papers
Donald O. Peterson Papers
Donald O. Peterson Papers on Microfilm

Government Documents

U.S. President. *Public Papers of the Presidents of the United States—John F. Kennedy: Containing the Public Messages, Speeches, and Statements of the President, 1961–1963.* Washington, DC: U.S. Government Printing Office, 1962–64.

———. *Public Papers of the Presidents of the United States—Gerald Ford: Containing the Public Messages, Speeches, and Statements of the President, 1975.* Washington, DC: U.S. Government Printing Office, 1977.

———. *Public Papers of the Presidents of the United States—Jimmy Carter: Containing the Public Messages, Speeches, and Statements of the President, 1977.* Washington, DC: U.S. Government Printing Office, 1977.

———. *Public Papers of the Presidents of the United States—Jimmy Carter: Containing the Public Messages, Speeches, and Statements of the President, 1977–1981.* Washington, DC: U.S. Government Printing Office, 1978.

———. *Public Papers of the Presidents of the United States—Jimmy Carter: Containing the Public Messages, Speeches, and Statements of the President, 1977–1981.* Washington, DC: U.S. Government Printing Office, 1979.

———. *Public Papers of the Presidents of the United States—William J. Clinton, 1996 Book I—January to June 30, 1996: Containing the Public Messages, Speeches, and Statements of the President, 1993–2001.* Washington, DC: U.S. Government Printing Office, 1996.

U.S. Congress. "One Hundred Hours of Presiding over the Senate." *Congressional Record* (August 24, 1965), 39th Cong., 1st sess., 111, pt. 16:21538. Box 31, folder 45, General Series, Carl Albert Congressional Research and Studies Center.

———. "Special Message to Congress on Law Enforcement and the Administration of Justice." March 8, 1965. The American Presidency Project, http://www.presidency.ucsb.edu/ws/index.php?pid=26800.

———. "Vietnam—Speech of Senator Harris Before the State Convention of the Oklahoma Bankers Association." *Congressional Record—Senate* (May 25, 1965), 89th Cong., 1st sess., 111:11461.

U.S. Bureau of the Census. *Statistical Abstract of the United States: 1977.* 98th ed. Washington, DC: U.S. Government Printing Office, 1977.

Books

Aaron, Henry. *Why Is Welfare So Hard to Reform? A Staff Paper by Henry Aaron.* Washington, DC: Brookings Institution, 1973.
———. *Politics and Professors: The Great Society in Perspective.* Washington, DC: Brookings Institution, 1978.
Acheson, Dean. *Present at the Creation: My Years in the State Department.* New York: Norton, 1969.
Ambrosius, Lloyd. *Wilson Statecraft: Theory and Practice of Liberal Internationalism during World War I.* Wilmington, DE: Scholarly Resource, 1991.
Anderson, Benedict. *Imagined Communities: Reflections on the Origin and Spread of Nationalism.* London: Verso, 1983.
Ansolabehere, Stephen, and James Snyder. *The End of Inequality: One Person, One Vote and the Transformation of American Politics.* New York: Norton, 2008.
Anson, Robert. *McGovern: A Biography.* New York: Holt, Rinehart, & Winston, 1972.
Ashbrook, John. *No Left Turns: A Handbook for Conservatives Based on the Writings of John M. Ashbrook.* Edited by Randy McNutt. Fairfield, OH: Hamilton Hobby, 1986.
Ashby, LeRoy, and Rod Gramer. *Fighting the Odds: The Life of Senator Frank Church.* Pullman: Washington State University Press, 1994.
Baer, Kenneth. *Reinventing Democrats: The Politics of Liberalism from Reagan to Clinton.* Lawrence: University Press of Kansas, 2000.
Baratta, Joseph. *The Politics of World Federation.* Westport, CT: Praeger, 2004.
Bass, Jack, and Walter DeVries. *The Transformation of Southern Politics: Social Change and Political Consequence since 1945.* Athens: University of Georgia Press, 1995.
Berry, Mary Frances. *Why ERA Failed: Politics, Women's Rights, and the Amending Process of the Constitution.* Bloomington: Indiana University Press, 1988.
Black, Earl, and Merle Black. *The Vital South: How Presidents Are Elected.* Cambridge, MA: Harvard University Press, 1992.
Boggs, Lindy. *Washington through a Purple Veil: Memoirs of a Southern Woman.* New York: Harcourt, 1994.
Bourne, Peter. *Jimmy Carter: A Comprehensive Biography from Plains to Post-Presidency.* New York: Scribner, 1997.
Brinkley, Douglass. *The Boys of Pointe Du Hoc: Ronald Reagan, D-Day, and the U.S. Army 2nd Ranger Battalion.* New York: Harper Collins, 2005.
Califano, Joseph. *Governing America: An Insider's Report from the White House and the Cabinet.* New York: Simon & Schuster, 1981.
Campagna, Anthony. *Economic Policy in the Carter Administration.* Westport, CT: Greenwood, 1995.
Carroll, Peter. *It Seemed Like Nothing Happened: The Tragedy and Promise of America in the 1970s.* New York: Holt, Rinehart, & Winston, 1982.
Carson, Donald, and James Johnson. *Mo: The Life and Times of Morris K. Udall.* Tucson: University of Arizona Press, 2001.

Carson, Rachel. *Silent Spring*. 25th anniversary ed. Boston: Houghton Mifflin, 1987.

Carter, Jimmy. *Keeping Faith: Memoirs of a President*. New York: Bantam, 1983.

Cawley, R. McGreggor. *Federal Land, Western Anger: The Sagebrush Rebellion and Environmental Politics*. Lawrence: University Press of Kansas, 1993.

Chaplin, Jonathan, and Robert Joustra. *God and Global Order: The Power of Religion in American Foreign Policy*. Waco, TX: Baylor University Press, 2010.

Chomski, Joseph. *The Sagebrush Rebellion: A Concise Analysis of the History, the Law, and Politics of Public Land in the United States*. Prepared for the State of Alaska, Legislative Affairs Agency. Juneau, AK: The Agency, 1980.

Clark, Grenville, and Louis Sohn. *World Peace through World Law: Two Alternative Plans*. Cambridge, MA: Harvard University Press, 1966.

Cranston, Alan. *The Killing of the Peace*. New York: Viking, 1945.

Critchlow, Donald. *Phyllis Schlafly and Grassroots Conservatism: A Woman's Crusade*. Princeton, NJ: Princeton University Press, 2005.

Davies, Gareth. *From Opportunity to Entitlement: The Transformation and Decline of Great Society Liberalism*. Lawrence: University Press of Kansas, 1996.

Davis, Harry. *Overcoming: The Autobiography of Harry Davis*. Minneapolis: Afton Historical Society Press, 2002.

Davis, Lanny. *The Emerging Democratic Majority: Lessons and Legacies from the New Politics*. New York: Stein & Day, 1974.

Depoe, Stephen. *Arthur M. Schlesinger, Jr., and the Ideological History of American Liberalism*. Tuscaloosa: University of Alabama Press, 1994.

Dilsaver, Lary. *America's National Park System: The Critical Documents*. Edited by Lary Dilsaver. Lanham, MD: Rowan & Littlefield, 1994.

Douthat, Ross, and Reihan Salam. *Grand New Party: How Republicans Can Win the Working Class and Save the American Dream*. New York: Doubleday, 2008.

Dowdy, G. Wayne. *Mayor Crump Don't Like It: Machine Politics in Memphis*. Oxford: University of Mississippi Press, 2006.

Drew, Elizabeth. *Campaign Journal: The Political Events of 1983–1984*. New York: Macmillan, 1985.

Eizenstat, Stuart. "President Carter, the Democratic Party and the Making of Domestic Policy." In *The Presidency and Domestic Policies of Jimmy Carter*, ed. Herbert Rosenbaum and Alexeji Ugrinsky, 3–16. Westport, CT: Greenwood, 1994.

Farber, David. *Taken Hostage: The Iran Hostage Crisis and America's First Encounter with Radical Islam*. Princeton, NJ: Princeton University Press, 2005.

Farrell, John. *Tip O'Neill and the Democratic Century*. Boston: Little, Brown, 2001.

Field, James. *America and the Mediterranean World, 1776–1882*. Princeton, NJ: Princeton University Press, 1969.

Fischer, David Hackett. *Albion's Seed: Four British Folkways in America*. New York: Oxford University Press, 1989.

Flamm, Michael. *Law and Order: Street Crime, Civil Unrest, and the Crisis of Liberalism in the 1960s*. New York: Columbia University Press, 2005.

Foerstel, Karen, and Herbert Foerstel. *Climbing the Hill: Gender Conflict in Congress*. New York: Praeger, 1996.

Frady, Marshall. *Jesse: The Life and Pilgrimage of Jesse Jackson*. New York: Simon & Schuster, 2006.

Frank, Thomas. *What's The Matter with Kansas? How Conservatives Won the Heart of America.* New York: Metropolitan, 2004.

Frum, David. *How We Got Here: The 70's: The Decade That Brought You Modern Life (For Better or Worse).* New York: Basic, 2000.

Furgurson, Ernest. *Hard Right: The Rise of Jesse Helms.* New York: Norton, 1986.

Gaddis, John. *The United States and the Origins of the Cold War, 1941–47.* New York: Columbia University Press, 1972.

———. *Strategies of Containment: A Critical Appraisal of Postwar American National Security Policy.* New York: Oxford University Press, 1982.

Garthoff, Raymond. *Détente and Confrontation: American-Soviet Relations from Nixon to Reagan.* Washington, DC: Brookings Institution, 1985.

Genovese, Eugene. *The Southern Tradition: The Achievement and Limitations of an American Conservatism.* Cambridge, MA: Harvard University Press, 1994.

Giglio, James. *The Presidency of John F. Kennedy.* Lawrence: University Press of Kansas, 2006.

———. *Call Me Tom: The Life of Thomas F. Eagleton.* Columbia: University of Missouri Press, 2011.

Gillon, Steve. *Politics and Vision: The ADA and American Liberalism, 1947–1985.* Oxford: Oxford University Press, 1987.

———. *The Pact: Bill Clinton, Newt Gingrich, and the Rivalry That Defined a Generation.* New York: Oxford University Press, 2008.

Graf, William. *Wilderness Preservation and the Sagebrush Rebellions.* Savage, MD: Rowan & Littlefield, 1990.

Hamby, Alonzo. *Beyond the New Deal: Harry S. Truman and American Liberalism.* New York: Columbia University Press, 1973.

———. *Liberalism and Its Challengers: From FDR to Bush.* New York: Oxford University Press, 1992.

———. *Man of the People: A Life of Harry S. Truman.* New York: Oxford University Press, 1995.

Hardemen, D. B., and Donald Bacon. *Rayburn: A Biography.* Austin: Texas Monthly Press, 1987.

Harris, Fred. *The New Populism.* New York: Saturday Review Press, 1972.

———. *Potomac Fever.* New York: Norton, 1977.

Hawley, Ellis. *The New Deal and the Problem of Monopoly: A Study in Economic Ambivalence.* Princeton, NJ: Princeton University Press, 1966.

———. *The Great War and the Search for a Modern Order: A History of the American People and Their Institutions, 1917–1933.* New York: St. Martin's, 1979.

Heineman, Ben. *Memorandum for the President: A Strategic Approach to Domestic Affairs in the 1980s.* New York: Random House, 1980.

Hendrickson, David. *Union, Nation, or Empire: The American Debate over International Relations.* Lawrence: University Press of Kansas, 2009.

Henggeler, Paul. *The Kennedy Persuasion: The Politics of Style since JFK.* Chicago: Ivan R. Dee, 1995.

Hettle, Walter. *The Peculiar Democracy: Southern Democrats in Peace and Civil War.* Athens: University of Georgia Press, 2001.

Hinton, Harold. "Crump of Tennessee: Portrait of a Boss." *New York Times,* September 29, 1946.

Hixson, Walter. *George F. Hixson: Cold War Iconoclast.* New York: Columbia University Press, 1989.

Hofstadter, Richard. *The American Political Tradition and the Men Who Made It.* New York: Knopf, 1948.

———. *Age of Reform: From Bryan to F.D.R.* New York: Knopf, 1955.

Hoopes, Townsend, and Douglass Brinkley. *FDR and the Creation of the U.N.* New Haven, CT: Yale University Press, 1997.

Hudson, David. *Along Racial Lines: Consequences of the 1965 VRA.* New York: Peter Lang, 1998.

Johnson, Robert David. *The Peace Progressives and American Foreign Relations.* Cambridge, MA: Harvard University Press, 1995.

Kaufman, Robert. *Henry Jackson: A Life in Politics.* Seattle: University of Washington Press, 2000.

Kazin, Michael. *The Populist Persuasion: An American History.* New York: Basic, 1995.

Key, V. O., Jr. *Southern Politicians in State and Nation.* New York: Random House, 1949.

Keyserling, Leon. *Toward Full Employment within Three Years.* Washington, DC: Conference on Economic Progress, 1976.

Kirakossian, Arman. *The Armenian Massacres, 1894–1896: U.S. Media Testimony.* Detroit: Wayne State University Press, 2004.

Kotz, Nick. *Judgment Days: Lyndon Johnson, Martin Luther King, Jr., and the Laws That Changed America.* New York: Houghton Mifflin, 2005.

Lasch, Christopher. *The New Radicalism in America, 1889–1963.* New York: Knopf, 1965.

Lawson, Stephen. *In Pursuit of Power.* New York: Columbia University Press, 1985.

Lentz, Jacob. *Electing Jesse Ventura: A Third Party Success Story.* Boulder, CO: Lynne Rienner, 2002.

Leuchtenburg, William. *In the Shadow of FDR: From Harry Truman to George W. Bush.* Ithaca, NY: Cornell University Press, 2001.

Lipset, Seymour Martin. *Political Renewal on the Left: A Comparative Perspective.* Washington, DC: Progressive Policy Institute Press, January 1990.

Lovett, Bobby. *The Civil Rights Movement in Tennessee: A Narrative History.* Knoxville: University of Tennessee Press, 2005.

Lowitt, Richard. *George W. Norris: The Persistence of a Progressive, 1861–1912.* Syracuse, NY: Syracuse University Press, 1971.

———. *Fred Harris: His Journey from Liberalism to Populism.* Lanham, MD: Rowman & Littlefield, 2002.

Lublin, David. *The Paradox of Representation.* Princeton, NJ: Princeton University Press, 1999.

Magee, Malcolm. *What the World Should Be: Woodrow Wilson and the Crafting of a Faith-Based Foreign Policy.* Waco, TX: Baylor University Press, 2008.

Mann, Robert. *Legacy to Power: Senator Russell Long of Louisiana.* New York: Paragon, 1992.

Matusow, Alan. *The Unraveling of America: A History of Liberalism in the 1960s.* New York: Harper & Row, 1984.

McCoy, Drew. *The Elusive Republic: Political Economy in Jeffersonian America.* Chapel Hill: University of North Carolina Press, 1980.

McDougall, Walter. *Promised Land, Crusader State: The American Encounter with the World since 1776.* New York: Houghton Mifflin, 1997.

McDowell, Gary. *Reason and Republicanism: Thomas Jefferson's Legacy of Liberty.* Edited by Gary McDowell and Sharon Noble. Lanham, MD: Rowan & Littlefield, 1997.

McGerr, Michael. *A Fierce Discontent: The Rise and Fall of the Progressive Movement in America, 1870–1920.* New York: Free Press, 2003.

McGovern, George. *An American Journey: The Presidential Campaign Speeches of George McGovern.* New York: Random House, 1974.

McKee, Seth. *Republican Ascendancy in Southern U.S. House Elections.* Boulder, CO: Westview, 2009.

Mieczkowski, Yanek. *Gerald Ford and the Challenges of the 1970s.* Lexington: University Press of Kentucky, 2005.

Miller, William. *Mr. Crump of Memphis.* Baton Rouge: Louisiana State University Press, 1964.

Miroff, Bruce. *The Liberals' Moment: The McGovern Insurgency and the Identity Crisis of the Democratic Party.* Lawrence: University Press of Kansas, 2007.

Moorhead, Caroline. *Dunant's Dream.* New York: Carroll & Graf, 1999.

Morgan, Ann Hodges. *Robert S. Kerr: The Senate Years.* Norman: University of Oklahoma Press, 1977.

Muravchik, Josh. *Heaven on Earth: The Rise and Fall of Socialism.* San Francisco: Encounter, 2003.

Novak, Michael. *The Rise of the Unmeltable Ethnics: Politics and Culture in the Seventies.* New York: Macmillan, 1973.

O'Brien, Michael. *Philip Hart: The Conscience of the Senate.* East Lansing: Michigan State University Press, 1995.

Patterson, James. "Jimmy Carter and Welfare Reform." In *The Carter Presidency: Policy Choices in the Post–New Deal Era,* ed. Gary Fink, 117–35. Lawrence: University Press of Kansas, 1998.

Perlstein, Richard. *Nixonland: The Rise of a President and the Fracturing of America.* New York: Scribner, 2008.

Peterson, Merrill. *The Jefferson Image in the American Mind.* New York: Oxford University Press, 1960.

Phillips, Kevin. *The Emerging Republican Majority.* New Rochelle, NY: Arlington House, 1969.

Pierce, Ann. *Woodrow Wilson and Harry Truman: Mission and Power in American Foreign Policy.* Westport, CT: Praeger, 2003.

Power, Samantha. *A Problem from Hell: America and the Age of Genocide.* New York: Harper, 2002.

Preston, Andrew. *The Sword of the Spirit, Shield of Faith: Religion in American War and Diplomacy.* New York: Knopf, 2012.

Rostker, Bernard. *I Want You! The Evolution of the All-Volunteer Force.* Santa Monica, CA: Rand, 2006.

Sandbrook, Dominic. *Eugene McCarthy: The Rise and Fall of Postwar American Liberalism.* New York: Knopf, 2004.

Saunders, George. *Samizdat: Voices of the Soviet Opposition.* New York: Monad, 1974.

Scammon, Richard, and Ben Wattenberg. *The Real Majority.* 1970; New York: Primus/Donald I. Fine, 1992.

Schlesinger, Arthur, Jr. *The Vital Center: The Politics of Freedom*. Cambridge, MA: Riverside, 1949.

———. *A Life in the 20th Century: Innocent Beginnings, 1917–1950*. New York: Houghton Mifflin, 2000.

———. *Journals, 1952–2000*. New York: Penguin, 2007.

Schlesinger, Stephen. *Act of Creation: The Founding of the United Nations*. Boulder, CO: Westview, 2003.

Schulman, Bruce. *The Seventies: The Great Shift in American Culture, Society, and Politics*. New York: Free Press, 2001.

Schwarz, Jordan. *The New Dealers: Power Politics in the Age of Roosevelt*. New York: Knopf, 1993.

Sehlinger, Peter, and Holman Hamilton. *Spokesman for Democracy: Claude G. Bowers, 1878–1958*. Indianapolis: Indiana Historical Society, 2000.

Sheldon, Garrett Ward. *The Political Philosophy of Thomas Jefferson*. Baltimore: Johns Hopkins University Press, 1991.

Shlaes, Amity. *The Forgotten Man: A New History of the Great Depression*. New York: Harper, 2007.

Smeal, Eleanor. *Why and How Women Will Elect the Next President*. New York: Harper & Row, 1984.

Spalding, Elizabeth Edwards. *The First Cold Warrior: Harry Truman, Containment, and the Remaking of Liberal Internationalism*. Lexington: University Press of Kentucky, 2006.

Steinberg, Alfred. *The Bosses*. New York: Macmillan, 1972.

Stephanson, Anders. *Manifest Destiny: American Expansionism and the Empire of Right*. New York: Hill & Wang, 1995.

Swerdlow, Amy. *Women Strike for Peace: Traditional Motherhood and Radical Politics in the 1960s*. Chicago: University of Chicago Press, 1993.

Tate, Adam. *Conservatism and Southern Intellectuals, 1789–1861: Liberty, Tradition, and the Good Society*. Columbia: University of Missouri Press, 2005.

Television News Index and Abstracts. Nashville: Vanderbilt Television News Archives, 1968–79.

Thernstrom, Abigail. *Whose Votes Count? Affirmative Action and Minority Voting Rights*. Cambridge, MA: Harvard University Press, 1989.

———. *Voting Rights—and Wrongs: The Elusive Quest for Racially Fair Elections*. Washington, DC: American Enterprise Institute Press, 2009.

Thomas, Clive. *Politics and Public Policy in the Contemporary American West*. Albuquerque: University of New Mexico Press, 1991.

Troy, Gil. *Morning in America: How Ronald Reagan Invented the 1980s*. Princeton, NJ: Princeton University Press, 2005.

Tuveson, Ernest Lee. *Redeemer Nation: The Idea of America's Millennial Role*. Chicago: University of Chicago Press, 1968.

Twelve Southerners. *I'll Take My Stand: The South and the Agrarian Tradition*. New York: Harper, 1930.

Udall, Morris. *Arizona Law of Evidence*. St. Paul: West, 1960.

———. *Education of a Congressman: The Newsletters of Morris K. Udall*. Edited by Robert Peabody. New York: Bobbs-Merrill, 1972.

Wattenberg, Ben. *Fighting Words: A Tale of How Liberals Created Neo-Conservatism*. New York: Thomas Dunne, 2008.

Wattenberg, Ben, in collaboration with Richard Scammon. *This U.S.A.: An Unexpected Family Portrait of 194,067,296 Americans Drawn from the Census.* Garden City, NY: Doubleday & Co., 1965.

Weil, Gordon. *The Welfare Debate of 1978.* White Plains, NY: Institute for Socioeconomic Studies, 1978.

Witcover, Jules. *Marathon: The Pursuit of the Presidency, 1972–1976.* New York: Viking, 1977.

Woodward, C. Vann. *Origins of the New South, 1877–1913.* Baton Rouge: Louisiana State University Press, 1951.

Worster, Donald. *The Wealth of Nature: Environmental History and the Ecological Imagination.* New York: Oxford University Press, 1993.

———. *An Unsettled Country: Changing Landscapes of the American West.* Albuquerque: University of New Mexico Press, 1994.

———. *A River Running West: The Life of John Wesley Powell.* Oxford: Oxford University Press, 2001.

Wright, Sharon. *Race, Power, and Political Emergence in Memphis.* New York: Garland, 2000.

Dissertations and Conference Proceedings

Bailey, James. "The Politics of Dunes, Redwoods, and Dams: Arizona's 'Brothers Udall' and America's National Parklands, 1961–1969." Ph.D. diss. Folder 8, box 90, Morris K. Udall Papers, University of Arizona Special Collections Library, Tucson, AZ.

Fritz, Stacy. "The Role of National Missile Defense in the Environmental History of Alaska." Paper presented at the Phi Alpha Theta Conference, Northern Studies Program, University of Alaska—Fairbanks, April 2000.

Wilderness Society. *Wilderness America: A Vision for the Future of the Nation's Wildlands.* Layton, UT: Wilderness Society, 1989.

Articles

Abramowitz, Alan. "It's Abortion, Stupid: Policy Voting in the 1992 Presidential Election." *Journal of Politics* 57, no. 1 (February 1995): 176–86.

Alt, James. "The Impact of the Voting Rights Act on Black and White Voter Registration in the South." In *Quiet Revolution in the South: The Impact of the Voting Rights Act, 1965–1990,* ed. Chandler Davidson and Bernard Grofman, 351–77. Princeton, NJ: Princeton University Press, 1994.

Barnes, Fred. "Flying Nunn: The Democrats Top Hawk." *New Republic,* April 28, 1986, 17–19.

———. "They're Back! Neocons for Clinton." *New Republic,* August 3, 1992, 12–14.

Billington, Ray Allen. "The Origins of Middle Western Isolationism." *Political Science Quarterly* 60 (March 1945): 44–64.

Black, Merle. "The Transformation of the Southern Democratic Party." *Journal of Politics* 66, no. 4 (November 2004): 1001–17.

Bolce, Louis. "The Role of Gender in Recent Presidential Elections: Reagan and the Reverse Gender Gap." *Presidential Studies Quarterly* 15 (1985): 372–85.

Brady, David, and Douglas Edmonds. "One Man, One Vote—So What?" *Trans-Action* 4 (1967): 41–46.

Brownlee, W. Elliot. "Introduction: Revisiting the 'Reagan Revolution.'" In *The Reagan Presidency: Pragmatic Conservatism and Its Legacies,* ed. W. Elliot Brownlee and Hugh Davis Graham, 1–16. Lawrence: University Press of Kansas, 2003.

Bullock, Charles. "Redistricting and Changes in the Partisan and Racial Composition of Southern Legislatures." *State and Local Government Review* 19 (Spring 1987): 62–67.

Bush, Merril. "World Organization or Atomic Destruction?" In *United Nations or World Government,* ed. Julia Johnsen, 55–60. New York: H. W. Wilson, 1947.

Button, Sarah. "Squeezed on the Hill." *Money Magazine,* May 1983, 99–108.

Cain, Bruce, Karin MacDonald, and Michael McDonald. "From Equality to Fairness: The Path of Political Reform since Baker v. Carr." Paper prepared for the Brookings Institution/Institute of Governmental Studies conference "Competition, Partisanship, and Congressional Redistricting," April 16, 2004, Brookings Institution, Washington, DC.

Carter, Jimmy. "Carter at the Center." *The Center Magazine,* January/February 1977, 49–62.

Cassels, Nancy. "Bentinck: Humanitarian and Imperialist—the Abolition of the Suttee." *Journal of British Studies* 5, no. 1 (November 1965): 77–87.

Cmiel, Kenneth. "The Emergence of Human Rights Politics in the United States." *Journal of American History* 86 (December 1999): 117–35.

Demkovich, Linda. "Carter Gets Some Outside Advice for His Welfare Reform Package." *National Journal,* April 30, 1977, 673–75.

Edwards, Mark. "'God Has Chosen Us': Re-Membering Christian Realism, Rescuing Christendom, and the Contest of Responsibilities during the Cold War." *Diplomatic History* 33, no. 1 (January 2009): 67–94.

"Facts We Dare Not Forget." *Dissent,* Spring 1981, 164–72.

Gaskin, Thomas. "Henry M. Jackson: Snohomish County Prosecutor, 1939–1940." *Pacific Northwest Quarterly* 81, no. 3 (July 1990): 87–95.

Gates, David. "The Munchkin's Musical." *Newsweek,* May 13, 1985, 13.

Gerstle, Gary. "The Protean Character of American Liberalism." *American Historical Review* 99, no. 4 (October 1994): 1043–73.

Goldbloom, Maurice. "Is There a Backlash Vote?" *Commentary,* August 1969, 18–26.

Griffith, Robert. "Old Progressives and the Cold War." *Journal of American History* 66 (September 1979): 334–47.

Grofman, Bernard. "Criteria for Districting: A Social Science Perspective." *UCLA Law Review* 33 (October 1985): 77–184.

———. "The Effect of Black Population on Electing Democrats and Liberals to the House of Representatives." *Legislative Studies Quarterly* 17, no. 3 (August 1992): 365–79.

Grofman, Bernard, and Lisa Handley. "The Impact of the VRA on Black Representation in Southern State Legislatures." *Legislative Studies Quarterly* 16, no. 1 (February 1991): 111–28.

Hale, Jon. "The Making of New Democrats." *Political Science Quarterly* 110, no. 2 (Summer 1995): 207–32.

Halttunen, Karen. "Humanitarianism and the Pornography of Pain." *American Historical Review* 100, no. 2 (April 1995): 303–34.

Hamby, Alonzo. "The Vital Center, the Fair Deal, and the Quest for a Liberal Political Economy." *American Historical Review* 77, no. 3 (June 1972): 653–78.

Hamilton, Richard. "The Liberal Intelligentsia and White Backlash." *Dissent*, Fall 1972, 227–38.

Harrington, Michael. "Old Working Class, New Working Class." *Dissent*, Winter 1972, 148–59.

Harris, Fred. "The Easy Chair: The Frog Hair Problem." *Harper's*, May 1972, 12–16.

Hill, Kevin. "Does the Creation of Majority Black Districts Aid Republicans? An Analysis of the 1992 Congressional Elections in Eight Southern States." *Journal of Politics* 57, no. 2 (May 1995): 384–401.

Hill, Kevin, and Nicol Rae. "What Happened to the Democrats in the South?: US House Elections, 1992–96." *Party Politics* 6, no. 5 (2000): 5–22.

"Is There Anything New about Neo-Populism?" *Bulletin of the American Academy of Arts and Sciences* 26, no. 6 (March 1973): 4–19.

Jackson, Henry. "Congress Welcomes Alexander Solzhenitsyn." *East Europe* 24, nos. 4–5 (August–September 1975): 2–3.

Jasanoff, Shelia. "American Exceptionalism and the Political Acknowledgment of Risk." *Daedalus* 119, no. 4 (Fall 1990): 61–81.

"Johnny Appleseeds." *New Republic*, October 28, 1967, 9–10.

Kaufmann, Karen, and John Petrocik. "The Changing Politics of American Men: Understanding the Sources of the Gender Gap." *American Journal of Political Science* 43, no. 3 (July 1999): 864–77.

Killian, Mitchell, and Clyde Wilcox. "Do Abortion Attitudes Lead to Party Switching?" *Political Research Quarterly* 61, no. 4 (December 2008): 561–73.

King, Desmond. "Sectionalism and Policy Formulation in the United States: President Carter's Welfare Initiative." *British Journal of Political Science* 26, no. 3 (July 1996): 337–67.

King, Larry. "The Road to Power in Congress: The Education of Mo Udall—and What It Cost." *Harper's*, June 1971, 40–63.

Koh, Harold Hongju. "On American Exceptionalism." *Stanford Law Review* 55, no. 5 (May 2003): 1480–1526.

Leopold, Richard. "The Mississippi Valley and American Foreign Policy." *Mississippi Valley Historical Review* 4 (1951): 625–42.

Lipset, Seymour Martin. "Steady Work: An Academic Memoir." *Annual Review of Sociology* 22 (1996): 1–27.

Lubell, Sam. "Who Votes Isolationist and Why." *Harper's*, April 1951, 29–36.

Lublin, David. "Racial Redistricting and African American Representation: A Critique of 'Do Majority Minority Districts Maximize Substantive Black Representation in Congress?'" *American Political Science Review* 93, no. 1 (March 1999): 183–86.

Lublin, David, and Stephen Voss. "The Missing Middle: Why Median-Voter Theory Can't Save Democrats from Singing the Boll-Weevil Blues." *Journal of Politics* 65, no. 1 (February 2003): 227–37.

Madison, Christopher. "Radical Moderate." *National Journal*, May 23, 1992, 1231–35.

Marsh, Peter. "Lord Salisbury and the Ottoman Massacres." *Journal of British Studies* 11, no. 2 (May 1972): 63–83.

Martinson, Robert. "Crime and the Election." *Dissent,* Fall 1972, 559–62.

Mattier, Franco. "The Gender Gap in Presidential Evaluations: Assessments of Clinton's Performance in 1996." *Polity* 33, no. 2 (Winter 2000): 199–228.

Maynard, Douglas. "Reform and the Origin of the International Organization Movement." *Proceedings of the American Philosophical Society* 107, no. 3 (June 1963): 220–31.

McDougall, Walter. "Back to Bedrock." *Foreign Affairs,* March/April 1997, 134–46.

McGovern, George. "The State of the Union." *Rolling Stone,* March 13, 1975, 24–27.

McMath, Robert. "Constructing Southern Lives: Jimmy Carter, Bill Clinton, and the Art of Political Biography." In *Is There a Southern Political Tradition?* ed. Charles Eagles, 175–98. Jackson: University Press of Mississippi, 1996.

Mead, Walter Russell. "The Jacksonian Tradition." *National Interest,* no. 58 (Winter 1999/2000): 5–29. Available at http://denbeste.nu/external/Mead01.html.

Melosi, Martin. "Lyndon Johnson and Environmental Policy." In *The Johnson Years,* vol. 2, *Vietnam, the Environment, and Science,* ed. Robert Divine, 113–49. Lawrence: University Press of Kansas, 1987.

Monkkonen, Eric. "Homicide: Explaining America's Exceptionalism." *American Historical Review* 111, no. 1 (February 2006): 76–94.

Mueller, Carol. "The Gender Gap and Women's Political Influence." *Annals of the American Academy of Political and Social Science* 515 (May 1991): 23–37.

Nuechterlein, James. "Arthur M. Schlesinger, Jr. and the Discontents of Postwar American Liberalism." *Review of Politics* 39, no. 1 (January 1977): 3–40.

Perkins, Bradford. "Interests, Values, and the Prism: The Sources of American Foreign Policy." *Journal of the Early Republic* 14, no. 4 (Winter 1994): 458–66.

Powledge, Fred. "The Flight from City Hall." *Harper's,* November 1969, 69–85.

Roberts, Carolanne Griffith. "Strong Women of Capitol Hill." *Southern Living,* May 1996, 148–50.

Rozario, Kevin. "'Delicious Horrors': Mass Culture, the Red Cross and the Appeal of Modern American Humanitarianism." *American Quarterly* 55, no. 3 (September 2003): 417–55.

Schlesinger, Arthur, Jr. "The Future of Liberalism." *The Reporter,* May 3, 1956, 8–11.

Singal, Daniel Joseph. "Beyond Consensus: Richard Hofstadter and American Historiography." *American Historical Review* 89, no. 4 (October 1984): 976–1004.

Thernstrom, Stephan. "The Myth of American Affluence." *Commentary,* October 1969, 74–78.

Thomas, Clive. "The West and Its Brand of Politics." In *Politics and Public Policy in the Contemporary American West,* ed. Clive Thomas, 1–20. Albuquerque: University of New Mexico Press, 1991.

Thomas, Jack. "America's First Forrester." *Range,* Winter 2003, 10–13.

Thompson, Michael. "An Exception to Exceptionalism: A Reflection on Reinhold Niebuhr's Vision of 'Prophetic' Christianity and the Problem of Religion and U.S. Foreign Policy." *American Quarterly* 59, no. 3 (September 2007): 833–55.

Wainwright, Loudon. "Confessions of a Fair Country Ballplayer." *Life Magazine,* October 1968, 67–74.

Walzer, Michael. "The Communitarian Critique of Liberalism." *Political Theory* 18, no. 1 (February 1990): 6–23.

Warnke, Paul. "Apes on a Treadmill." *Foreign Policy* 18 (Spring 1975): 12–29.

Waters, Kathryn. "Carter, Congress, and Welfare: A Long Road." *Congressional Quarterly* 35, no. 33 (August 13, 1977): 12–29.

Wattenberg, Ben. "Mao's Funeral." *Harper's*, February 1977, 32–33.

Wilson, James. "The Rediscovery of Character: Private Virtue and Public Policy." *Public Interest*, no. 81 (Fall 1985): 3–16.

Witman, David. "Liberal Rhetoric and the Welfare Underclass." *Society* 21, no. 1 (November/December 1983): 63–69.

Wood, Gordon. "Ideology and the Origins of Liberal America." In "The Constitution of the United States," special issue, *William and Mary Quarterly*, 3rd ser., 44, no. 3 (July 1987): 628–40.

Index

CPSIA information can be obtained at www.ICGtesting.com
Printed in the USA
BVOW041435050613

322339BV00003B/3/P

✓   2014/06/23